JEWS BY THE SEASIDE

JEWS BY THE SEASIDE

The Jewish Hotels and
Guest Houses of Bournemouth

PAM FOX

VALLENTINE MITCHELL
LONDON • CHICAGO

First published in 2022 by Vallentine Mitchell

Catalyst House,
720 Centennial Court,
Centennial Park, Elstree WD6 3SY, UK

814 N. Franklin Street,
Chicago, Illinois,
60610 USA

www.vmbooks.com

British Library Cataloguing in Publication Data:
An entry can be found on request

ISBN 978 1 912676 92 7 (Cloth)
ISBN 978 1 912676 93 4 (Paper)
ISBN 978 1 912676 94 1 (Ebook)

Library of Congress Cataloging in Publication Data:
An entry can be found on request

Contents

Acknowledgements

I could not have written this book without the help, encouragement and support of many people to whom I would like to express my sincere thanks.

First and foremost, I would like to thank everyone who shared with me their knowledge and memories of the Jewish hotels and guest houses of Bournemouth. While I was researching and writing the book, I spoke with literally hundreds of people from whom I learned a vast amount. Everyone I interviewed added value to the book and I feel greatly enriched as a result of talking to so many interesting and warm people. Especially significant was the input from Hettie Marks, Simon Keyne, David Marriott, Brian Lassman, Richard Inverne, Shirley Davidson, Joan Doubtfire, Paul and Jon Harris, Jonathan Perlmutter, Roger Vickers, David Abrahams, Frances Israel, Joanna Benarroch and Sheila Morris.

At the outset of the project, I identified a number of people who proved to be invaluable sources of information, including Marsha Lee, Elissa Bayer, Sheila Davies, Anne Filer, Larry and Mandy Kaye, Lennie Segal, Kenny Arfin, Sheila Samuels and Marian Stern, to name but a few. However, there were also people whom I discovered rather late in the day and I was very pleased that I did, including Jonathan Woolfson, Ben Grower and Howard Taylor.

There were several people to whom I spoke who had once or who still live in Bournemouth. This meant that they were not only able to speak authoritatively about the hotels and guest houses, but were also able to talk about the town in which they existed. I am very grateful for this perspective to Rhona Taylor, Esther Schneider, Miriam Marcus, Hazel Green, Janet Pins, Rochelle Selby, Barry Levinson, Janet Pins, Pat Cravitz, Anne Flor Szewczyk and Helena Greene. The 'Jewish Hotels and Guest Houses' tour that Judi Lyons very kindly gave me during a brief window of opportunity when we were able to meet up last summer was invaluable.

In my Introduction, I mentioned the extraordinary feedback I received as the result of posts placed on Facebook. These posts resulted in some very productive conversations, including those with Ruth Shire, Carol Reggel,

Marilyn Murray, Janeen Shaw, Adriano Brioschi, Paul Millington and Mark Murawski. The Facebook feedback also included many reminiscences that I was able to include in the book and which were greatly welcomed.

Some interviewees asked to remain anonymous. I would like to thank them; they know who they are! Some people contacted me and wanted to tell me 'just one story'. They were perfect. Thank you to Diana Langleben, Martin Slowe, John Colvin and Michael Zeffertt.

There are some individuals whom I must single out for particular thanks due to their outstanding input, namely Geoffrey Feld, Barbara Glyn, Edward Hayman and Judi Lyons (née Kay). Geoffrey, Barbara and Edward furnished me with an enormous amount of information about the 'Big Eight' hotels and without Judi's input my coverage of the smaller hotels and guest houses would have been very thin indeed. All four, like many others I spoke with, were very patient and unstinting with their time when I contacted them repeatedly to ask yet more questions. Readers will note how extensively these four people are quoted throughout the book.

A number of people contributed not only in providing memories and stories for the book, but also in a range of other ways, including David Latchman, who wrote the Foreword, Professor Geoffrey Alderman who read and made many helpful comments on an early version and Hannah Jacobs who did likewise. Several other people read the book in draft and helped to knock it into shape – Professor Michael Alpert, Professor Colin Shindler, Geoffrey Feld, Judi Lyons and my husband, Michael Hart.

Specialist information was kindly provided by Rabbi Jonathan Romain, Professor Geoffrey Alderman, Professor Michael Alpert and Professor Panikos Panayi. I cannot fail to mention David Jacobs who, as with previous projects, gave me access to his extensive archives. On the subject of archives, I would also like to extend my thanks to Michael Stead at Bournemouth Library. During lockdown, when I was unable to visit the library, Michael kindly responded to a whole gamut of information requests. Marsha Lee was extremely generous in sending me and giving me permission to use out-takes from the documentary film on the Green Park Hotel.

In writing a book largely based on people's memories it was essential to make connections with those who had stories to tell. Luckily, I encountered a number of people with extensive address books who were prepared to share them with me. Thank you to Judi Lyons, Geoffrey Feld, Rhona Taylor, Josephine Jackson, Beverley-Jane Stewart and Alex Weiss for all the contacts you provided. In this respect, I am very grateful to Fiona Hulbert, Alex Galbinski at the *Jewish News* and to the Association of Jewish Refugees (AJR) for publicising the research I was carrying out, which put me in touch with several people who made important contributions to the book including: Rita Eker, Andy and Joe Kalmus, Stuart March, Chris Woodward and Clive Gold.

This book is replete with photographs and other illustrative material and I am indebted to all those people who provided images. The book would not have been the same without the images provided by Alwyn Ladell from his superb Flickr photostream. I have never come across such an extensive and professionally organised collection of material. I must also single out for thanks Gaby and David Marriott and Simon Keyne for providing photographs.

In addition to the photographs and other images that I have gathered from various sources, this book has been greatly enhanced by the artistic talent of Beverley-Jane Stewart who, having read my book, speaking with me extensively and conducting her own research, created the truly wonderful picture for the front cover. As she did with her painting that became the front cover of my Golders Green book in 2016, this new picture captures beautifully the essence of the Jewish hotel scene in Bournemouth. Beverley-Jane has also contributed the lovely sketches that have been incorporated into the text. Beverley-Jane, I cannot thank you enough.

I would like to say a big thank you to Jenny Zeffertt who painstakingly compiled the index for this book.

Producing this book has been quite challenging because of the impact of the COVID-19 pandemic, but also because of the vast amount of material I have had to synthesise and the thousands of items of information I have had to check. Throughout the process, my husband Michael has, as always, consistently supported and encouraged me. I hope he is not too horrified that I am already thinking about the next book!

Glossary

Aliyah (plural *aliyot*): Literally 'going up' but used to refer to emigration to Israel.

Ark: A cupboard in which the scrolls of the Pentateuch are placed.

Ashkenazi: Literally 'German' but used to refer to Jews from central or Eastern Europe, their culture and the way in which they pronounce Hebrew.

Bar Mitzvah: Literally 'son of the commandment'. Refers to the ceremony marking the time at which boys become responsible for their actions in Jewish law, usually aged thirteen.

Bat Mitzvah: As above, for girls. These ceremonies do not take place in the more orthodox synagogues. Some orthodox synagogues have ceremonies for girls but they do not have the same status.

Beth Din: Literally 'house of judgement' but used to refer to a body that adjudicates on Jewish law. In Orthodox Judaism, a *Beth Din* consists of three observant Jewish men, at least one of whom is knowledgeable in Jewish Law, *halachah* (q.v.).

Bet Hamidrash: House of study.

B'nai Mitzvah: Plural of *Bar* or *Bat Mitzvah* (q.v.) or both.

Chabad: A denomination of Judaism founded in 1775 by Rabbi Schneur Zalman of Liadi, the name Chabad is an acronym formed from three Hebrew words – *Chochmah, Binah, Da'at* - wisdom, understanding, and knowledge – which represent the intellectual underpinnings of the movement. Chabad are sometimes referred to as the Lubavitch Movement.

Challah (plural *challot*): Plaited bread loaf, used to welcome *Shabbat* (q.v.) and festivals.

Chametz: Leavened products, which are forbidden at *Pesach* (q.v.)

Chanukkah: Literally 'dedication'. The eight-day, midwinter Festival of Lights commemorating the re-dedication of the Temple at the time of the Maccabees.

Charedi (plural *charedim*): A relatively recent umbrella term for describing Jews who are very observant in their Judaism. Its literal meaning is 'the fearful' or 'trembling in the face of God'.

Charoset: A sweet paste made of fruit and nuts eaten at *Pesach* (q.v.).

Chassid (plural *Chassidim*): Member of a sect originating in Eastern Europe.

Chazanut: Cantorial singing.

Chazzan: Cantor.

Cheder: Literally 'room' but used to refer to a part-time religion school for younger children attached to a synagogue.

Chevra (plural *chevrot*): A small congregation, frequently established by Jews of Eastern European origin.

Cholent: A stew prepared in advance of *Shabbat* (q.v.).

Chumash: First five books of the Bible.

Dayan (plural *dayanim*): Religious judge.

Droshe (Yiddish): Religious talk.

Erev Shabbat: Eve of the Sabbath.

Frum (Yiddish): Literally 'observant', but used to refer to orthodox Jews.

Gabbai: Warden of a Jewish congregation.

Glatt kosher: The technical definition of *glatt* kosher is meat from animals with defect-free lungs, but it is often applied to products that have been processed under the stricter standard of *kashrut* (q.v.) set by the Kedassia (q.v.) licensing body. See Chapter 7.

Haftarah: The reading from the Prophets that follows the Pentateuchal reading in Jewish services.

Halachah: Literally 'the way of going' but used to refer to Jewish law.

Heimische: Literally 'homely' but sometimes used as an alternative to *frum* (q.v.).

Hechsher: A seal given to butchers who carry out *shechita* (q.v.) practices correctly.

High Holydays: *Rosh Hashanah* (Jewish New Year) (q.v.) and *Yom Kippur* (Day of Atonement) (q.v.) sometimes referred to as the 'Days of Awe'.

Kaddish: An Aramaic prayer of praise to God that has come to be used as a prayer for the dead.

Kashrus Commission: Supervising authority attached to the United Synagogue now called Kosher London Beth Din (KLBD).

Kashrut (Ashkenazi *kashrus*): Jewish dietary laws.

Kiddush (plural *kiddushim*): The act of declaring a day as holy, sometimes accompanied with wine and food.

Kippah (plural *kippot*): Skull cap. Sometimes *cappel* or *yarmulke*.

Kneidlach (Yiddish): Dumplings.

Kol Nidre: The eve of *Yom Kippur* (q.v.).

Kosher: English version of Ashkenazi Hebrew word *kasher* meaning 'fit' but used to mean food adhering to Jewish dietary laws.

Kvelled: (Yiddish): Feeling proud of someone or something.

Kvetching (Yiddish): Complaining.

Latkes (Yiddish): Traditional Ashkenazi (q.v.) dish similar to hash browns.

Leyn (Yiddish): Chanting of the scroll portion.

Lokshen (Yiddish): Noodles eaten either as a savoury dish or as a dessert.

Machzorim: The special prayer books used for *Rosh Hashanah* (q.v.) and *Yom Kippur* (q.v.).

Mah Nishtanah: 'The Four Questions' that form part of the *seder* (q.v.) service, usually recited by the youngest child present.

Ma'ariv: Evening service.

Maftir: The last person called up to read the Torah on *Shabbat* (q.v.) and festival mornings. This person also reads the *haftarah* (q.v.) portion from a related section of the *Nevi'im* (prophetic books).

Mashgiach: Another Hebrew word for religious supervisor, See *shomer*.

Matzah (plural *matzot*): Unleavened flat bread that forms an integral part of *Pesach* (q.v.).

Mazeltov: Literally 'good constellation', but used to mean 'congratulations'.

Mechitza: A screen separating men and women in an orthodox synagogue.

Mincha: Afternoon service.

Mikveh (plural *mikvaot*): Ritual bath.

Minyan (plural *minyanim*): A group of people (in Jewish law ten men or more), who come together informally to pray. A *minyan* does not require a dedicated building or a religious leader. A Jewish boy of thirteen may form part of the quorum after his *Bar Mitzvah* (q.v.).

Mohel: A Jew trained to perform circumcisions.

Nusach: Form of text or prayers.

Pesach: Passover, the festival celebrating the freedom gained for Jews with the Exodus from Egypt.

Purim: Literally 'lots'. A minor festival remembering the events described in the book of Esther, telling how the Jews were saved from persecution.

Rabbi (plural *rabbanim*): Jewish spiritual leader.

Rosh Hashanah: Jewish New Year.

Schlep (Yiddish): Carry.

Schmooze (Yiddish): Flatter to make a social connection.

Seder (plural *sedarim*): Literally 'order'. The name of the service for the first night of Pesach (q.v.) taking place in Jewish homes using symbolic foods. Orthodox Jews outside Israel observe two nights.

Sedra: Portion of text from the Torah.

Sefer Torah (plural *Sifrei Torah*): Scrolls of the Pentateuch.

Sephardi: Literally 'Spanish' but used to describe Jews who originate from the countries around the Mediterranean and from Islamic countries, their culture and their pronunciation of Hebrew.

Shabbat (Ashkenazi *Shabbos*): Jewish sabbath.

Shammas: Salaried sexton employed by a synagogue.

Shacharit: Early morning service.

Shavuot (Ashkenazi *Shavuos*): Literally 'weeks'. Pilgrimage festival, occurring at a similar time to Pentecost. It celebrates the giving of God's Revelation to the children of Israel.

Sheitel: Wig.

Shechita: The way in which both meat and poultry must be killed under Jewish law, *halachah* (q.v.).

Sheva berachot: The seven special blessings recited after meals when a wedding couple are present, but also used to refer to orthodox wedding celebrations.

Shidduch (Aramaic, plural *shidduchim*): Marital match.

Shiur (plural *shiurim*): Study session on a Torah subject.

Shochet: Butcher certified by the Jewish religious authorities.

Shofar: A musical instrument made from a ram's horn blown on important Jewish public and religious occasions.

Shomer (plural *shomrim*): Religious supervisor.

Shtreimel (Yiddish, plural *streimlech*): Fur hats worn by *Chassidic* (q.v.) Jews from Galicia, Romania and Hungary. *Chassidic* Jews from Poland wear spodniks.

Shtetl (Yiddish, plural *shtetlekh*): A small Jewish town or village in Eastern Europe.

Shul (Yiddish): Universal term for a synagogue. Used by both Sephardi and Ashkenazi Jews (q.v.).

Siddur (plural *siddurim*): Prayer books.

Simcha (plural *s'machot*): Celebration e.g. a *Bar Mitzvah* (q.v.).

Simchat Torah: Literally 'rejoicing of the Torah'. The festival for celebrating the end of the cycle of scroll readings and the beginning of the new cycle occurring at the end of *Sukkot* (q.v.).

Sukkah: The booth in which some Jews eat and sleep during the festival of *Sukkot* (q.v.).

Sukkot: The seven-day Jewish harvest festival. *Sukkot* is also plural of *Sukkah*.

Tallit (plural *tallitot*): Prayer shawl.

Talmud Torah: School at which Jewish children are given an elementary education in Hebrew, the scriptures (especially the Pentateuch), and the Talmud (boys only) and *halachah* (q.v.).

Tisha B'Av (Ashkenazi *Tisho-ba-Ab*): An annual fast day in Judaism, on which a number of disasters in Jewish history occurred, primarily the destruction of both Solomon's Temple by the Neo-Babylonian Empire and the Second Temple by the Roman Empire in Jerusalem.

Treif (Yiddish): Literally 'forbidden' but meaning not in accord with Jewish dietary laws.

Yamim Tovim: The four festivals/holy days occurring in the autumn: *Rosh Hashanah, Yom Kippur, Sukkot* and *Simchat Torah* (q.v.).

Yeshivah (plural *yeshivot*): A place of study for young Jewish men.

Yiddishkeit: Literally 'Jewishness' but has come to mean the culture of Ashkenazi Jews (q.v.).

Yom Kippur: Day of Atonement, occurring ten days after *Rosh Hashanah* (q.v.) on which observant Jews fast.

Yom Tov: Literally 'good day', but meaning festival.

Foreword

It is said that anyone above a certain age can remember where they were when President Kennedy was assassinated. In my case, this is certainly true. I was a young boy staying with my parents at the Majestic Hotel in Bournemouth to celebrate the silver wedding of my father's sister and her husband. I was convinced that our waiter had carried out the assassination and had to be restrained from reporting him to the police or at the very least to the hotel management!

This was the only time that I stayed at the Majestic Hotel. As Pam Fox points out in this fascinating book about the Jewish hotels of Bournemouth, individual families were loyal to one particular hotel. In our case, this was the Cumberland Hotel. Every year we stayed there from before *Rosh Hashanah* until after *Sukkot* (a festival that occurs shortly after *Rosh Hashanah* and *Yom Kippur*) as well as for *Pesach*. Indeed, one of my earliest memories is standing on a chair, dressed up in a dinner suit complete with bowtie, and reciting the *Mah Nishtanah* to the guests assembled in the Cumberland Hotel dining room for *seder* night. I can still see the bright lights and the sea of faces staring at me, dressed up in dinner suits or long gowns.

At that time, the Cumberland Hotel was considered number two in the hierarchy of Bournemouth hotels. It was ranked above the Majestic and the Ambassador, but below the Green Park, which was the clear number one. My mother tried for many years to persuade my father to transfer our affections to the Green Park, but he felt it was too snobbish. Eventually, however, following a weekend staying at the Green Park for a friend's son's *Bar Mitzvah* [coming of age celebration], he relented. Subsequently, we stayed at the Green Park for many *yom tovim* despite being rather shocked when we arrived for our first *yom tov* at the Green Park to see a number of vans unloading packed dress racks and piles of shoeboxes!

After a number of years staying at the Green Park, we followed another trend described in this book and began to holiday in Israel rather than Bournemouth. Subsequently, however, when my father became unwell and unable to travel to Israel, we returned to Bournemouth. Things had changed. Both the Cumberland and the Green Park had closed down, so we stayed at the Normandie Hotel. By this time the hotel was ultra-orthodox but many of the guests were staying there because they were unable to travel to Israel. Nonetheless, it was an enjoyable experience. The food was still good and plentiful whilst the attraction of walking on the Bournemouth front remained unchanged.

For those interested in Anglo-Jewry, this extensively researched book is a mine of information and anecdote, but also places the Bournemouth kosher hotels in context as a sociological phenomenon in both the history of Britain's Jewish community and the evolution of Bournemouth as a premier holiday resort. For those like me who were part of this phenomenon without realising it, the book will bring back many warm memories. For those who did not have the pleasure of staying in one of these hotels, the book will perhaps explain why their fathers and grandfathers still follow the results of Bournemouth AFC many years after their last visit to Bournemouth.

Professor David S. Latchman
January 2021

Introduction

Writing This Book

This book has been a long time in the making. When I was carrying out interviews for my book on the history of the Jewish community of Golders Green back in 2015,[1] I spoke with many people who mentioned their holidays in Jewish hotels in Bournemouth. They described in glorious detail the lavish *Shabbat kiddushim* (meals and wine following services on the Jewish sabbath) they had enjoyed or told me that they had met their husband or wife there. Since they were clearly an historical phenomenon, I made a mental note to find time to explore the Jewish hotels. Several years later, when I was writing a subsequent book on the history of the iconic Rinkoff bakery,[2] I again encountered a number of people who had holidayed in Bournemouth, which reawakened my interest in researching and possibly writing about the hotels.

Shortly after the Rinkoff book had gone to press, I met up with my friend Dawn Waterman, who enquired what I was going to write about next. When I said that I didn't have any clear ideas, she suggested: 'You should write about Jewish hotels.' I replied: 'It's funny you should say that, it's something that I've had in mind for a couple of years!' I carried out some background research and quickly decided that this was a topic that both merited serious attention and promised to be a thoroughly enjoyable undertaking, so I embarked on my new project almost immediately.

Commencing on this book coincided with the onset of the COVID-19 pandemic, which proved to have both pros and cons. On the one hand, lockdown meant that I had more time to concentrate on my research, and immersing myself in the history of Jewish hotels was a welcome distraction from the devastation being wrought by the Coronavirus. I also found that other people thought likewise. Whereas in the past I have sometimes encountered difficulties in arranging interviews, it seemed that many people were only too happy to speak with me.

On the other hand, there were a few unexpected challenges, some of which proved to be unsurmountable. Carrying out interviews by telephone and by Zoom (which became a ubiquitous form of communication while I was writing this book) is not the same as speaking with people face to face. It was much more challenging to strike up a rapport with interviewees, and to encourage them to speak about their memories and tell me stories. I also found it problematic to record information fully and accurately while concentrating on listening to someone on the telephone or watching them on screen. When writing previous books largely based on oral history interviews, I have been meticulous about obtaining people's permission to quote them in my writings. I quickly came to the conclusion that with this project it was doubly imperative that I check with contributors what I thought that I had heard them say. Although I am realistic, and know that achieving 100 per cent accuracy cannot be guaranteed when writing history, the systematic checking that I carried out increased my confidence that the information included in my book was as accurate as reasonably possible. I would like to apologise for any errors that remain.

Another challenge was that of obtaining access to relevant sources of information. Over the ten years that I have been writing Jewish social history, more and more material has become available online and I have also built up my own library, archives and databases as well as an extensive network of contacts, all of which proved invaluable for this project. However, some of the sources I wanted to consult (for example, street directories, copies of local newspapers, or the historic records of the London Beth Din and the Kashrus Commission) were kept in places that were closed for much of 2020, or which I was not able to visit due to travel restrictions. I found ways of obtaining some of the material but not all of it. While this is disappointing, I am hoping that the lack of access to some sources of information is vastly outweighed by the richness of the material yielded by the large number of interviews I have carried out over the last nine months.

Structure of the Book and its Coverage

This book is organised into two main sections. The first five chapters chronicle the rise and decline of the hotels within the context of Anglo-Jewish history, the development of Bournemouth as a premier holiday resort and the evolution of the town's Jewish community. Chapter 1 describes the appearance of the very first Jewish boarding houses as they were first called. Chapter 2 shows how the boarding houses became larger and more comfortable and were re-designated as 'guest houses'. The chapter also describes how they proliferated and were joined by increasingly luxurious hotels, setting the stage for the heyday of the Jewish hotels. Chapters 3 and 4 deal respectively with the Big Eight hotels (the Green Park, the Cumberland, the Normandie, the Majestic, the Ambassador, East Cliff Court, the Langham and East Cliff Manor), and the smaller hotels and guest houses when they were at their most popular. Chapter 5 charts the gradual demise of the hotels and guest houses that had offered a winning formula over three decades and how they were replaced by other types of holiday. This chapter ends on a note of optimism that Jewish holidaymaking in Bournemouth may experience something of a revival in the coming years, albeit in a different form from the mid-twentieth century.

The second part of the book deals with various aspects of hotel life: the food, religious activities and practices, the entertainment and the relationship between the hotels and the local community, both Jewish and non-Jewish. Chapter 10 examines the historical significance and legacy of the hotels and guest houses, concluding that they played a key role in accelerating the acculturation of the offspring of Jewish immigrants, and performed an even more crucial part in fostering and helping to fashion a new Anglo-Jewish identity. It is also argued that the hotels left both short-term and longer-term legacies, including making a major contribution to Jewish continuity and to the sustainability of the Anglo-Jewish community, particularly the Bournemouth community. For a while at least, they also reinforced communal solidarity. While few Jews still aspire to partake of the lifestyle of the hotels that was once so popular, they continue to be regarded with considerable warmth and as a big Jewish success story. The long afterglow left by the hotels is particularly strong in Bournemouth.

However, perhaps one of the most delightful discoveries of this book that is discussed in Chapter 10, is the lasting impact that the hotels have had on the non-Jewish community. When the hotels were in their heyday, a large number of non-Jews came into contact with them in a variety of ways – as employees, as the suppliers of goods and services. As a result, they gained first-hand experience of mixing with Jews and became acquainted with the way they lived their lives and with their religion, customs and practices. This gave rise to an understanding and respect for Judaism that for many people was enduring.

The book contains two appendices aimed at enhancing readers' understanding and enjoyment of its content: brief biographies of the Big Eight hotels covered in Chapter 3, and details of the smaller establishments discussed in Chapter 4.

A Note on Sources and the Rationale for Writing the Book

Once I had decided to write this book, I was pleased to discover there was a wealth of material relating to the Jewish hotels and other holiday establishments that once existed in Bournemouth. These sources included articles and editorial features in national and local newspapers and periodicals; information available on specialist websites (for example, the one that has been established for East Cliff Court, encouraging people to come forward with their memories of the hotels and holidaying in Bournemouth generally); mentions in autobiographies and biographies and memoirs (for example, *The Vow: Rebuilding the Fachler Tribe After the Holocaust* by Yanky Fachler[3] and Morella Kayman's *A Life to Remember*).[4] Particularly helpful was Ronald Hayman's full-length book of his experience of growing up at East Cliff Court. In 2015, a documentary film was made about the Green Park Hotel. Directed by Jack Fishburn and Justin Hardy, based on a story provided by Marsha Lee, this film contains footage on the Jewish holiday trade in Bournemouth generally. I was also given access to the transcripts of talks given by people who formerly owned, were brought up in or managed the hotels. Particularly helpful were the series of interviews conducted with Bluma Feld by her grandson Richard Inverne. The insights that were provided by listening to Bluma Feld speak were quite outstanding.

Useful contextual material was provided by books and websites relating to the history of Bournemouth. In 2010, Bournemouth celebrated its 200th anniversary and a range of publications was produced to commemorate the event, including a series of papers entitled 'The Streets of Bournemouth' project, on the history of various aspects of life in the town. Particularly relevant to the subject of this book were 'The Streets of Bournemouth: Tourism and Town' and 'The Streets of Bournemouth, History and Heritage'.[5] Also useful were Jackie Edwards' *A Bed by the Sea: A History of Bournemouth's Hotels*,[6] M. A. Edgington's publications on Bournemouth in both the First and Second World Wars[7] and Vincent May and Jan Marsh's book on the history of Bournemouth.[8]

Several of my previous books, especially my history of the Jewish community of Golders Green, contained information on the development of Anglo-Jewry, which I was able to use as a backdrop to the story of the Jewish hotels. Plentiful information was also available on the evolution of the Bournemouth Jewish community, including the book celebrating the hundredth anniversary of Bournemouth Hebrew Congregation.[9]

At the end of November 2020, when I was nearing the completion of my book, I came across a Facebook group named Memories of Old Poole and Bournemouth, which appeared to be very active. As an experiment, I decided to try submitting a post asking for information for my book. The response was staggering. I received over 700 responses, which included some names and dates that had eluded me despite painstaking research, as well as numerous anecdotes and memories. As a result, I either extended or rewrote a number of sections of the book and added several paragraphs to the concluding chapter. A large proportion of the people who responded to my post were non-Jewish, and I discovered that seeing Jewish history through the eyes of non-Jews can add an interesting and invaluable dimension to a Jewish history publication. I will certainly be building this learning into future research and writing projects.

However, the two main sources I used in the writing of this book were oral history interviews and the archives of the *Jewish Chronicle*. Since 2010, I have been developing a specialism in using memories and anecdotes. Telling the story of the Jewish hotels of Bournemouth really lent itself to an oral history approach as there are still many people who either themselves stayed in, worked in or ran the hotels, or who knew people closely acquainted with them. Over a nine-month period, I conducted over one hundred interviews with a wide range of people, which produced not only wonderful memories and anecdotes to bring my text alive, but also factual information about the hotels. Most of these interviews I organised myself but several interviewees also kindly referred me to other people able to assist me. Letters appealing for stories and anecdotes relating to the hotels placed in the *Jewish News* and the bulletin produced by the Association of Jewish Refugees (AJR) were very productive.

The material provided by my interviews was quite outstanding in terms of both its quality and quantity. However, as I have discovered previously, despite careful questioning and sensitive probing, people talk about the things on which they have most knowledge, and what interests them rather than with a view to furnishing a coherent historical account. I have sought to fill obvious gaps and imbalances in information (the most obvious of which is the wealth of information available on the Big Eight hotels compared to the smaller guest houses) in a variety of ways, such as carrying out further rounds of interviews with people able to provide missing information or returning to interviewees to request additional material, judicious editing and drawing on information from other sources.

The other potential drawback of oral history material is that people's memories are not infallible and people remember things in quite different ways. I have therefore endeavoured to ensure that the content of this book is as accurate as possible by checking and rechecking information and by using triangulation processes. This is where my second main source of information came into its own. At the start of my research, I entered the word 'Bournemouth' into the search engine for the archives of the *Jewish Chronicle* and was astounded when this resulted in nearly 29,000 hits! I tried ways of narrowing down my search, and experimented with looking at a sample of the references. I soon realised that being selective meant that I was missing important information. So, over a period of three months, I looked at all of the references to Bournemouth.

The investment of my time produced dividends. The pages of the *Jewish Chronicle* are filled with advertisements charting the rise and the decline of the hotels, provided information on the entertainment organised for their guests, showed how the services and facilities available at the hotels changed in response to changing lifestyles and rising expectations and much, much more. The material available in the advertisements was supplemented my numerous editorials, articles, letters and weekly digests of events. Never have I been so grateful to the *Jewish Chronicle* for digitizing its archives!

Some of the people I interviewed drew my attention to the odd scandal and some contentious issues relating to the Jewish hotels of Bournemouth. As with previous books, I have mentioned some of these, having of course checked their veracity. The view I take is that including them adds interest rather than detracts from the overwhelmingly positive picture of the hotels. I believe that not to allude to them would detract from the credibility of the narrative. On the other hand, I have taken great care not to over-focus on the scandals and contentious issues – they are often referred to in footnotes – to avoid giving an erroneous impression of the hotels that could detract from my overriding objective of celebrating their history and leaving readers with a feeling of warmth about this feature of Anglo-Jewish history. I was also acutely aware of the need to avoid offending people by handling information insensitively.

Although, as I discovered, there is copious material relating to the Bournemouth hotels, this has never been brought together to produce a dedicated, full-length publication. I made it my pleasurable task to address this notable gap in Anglo-Jewish history. It remains a mystery to me why such a legendary phenomenon has been neglected until now.

Use of Hebrew and Explanations of Jewish Customs and Practices

In this book, Hebrew words are transliterated from the Sephardi pronunciation, unless the Ashkenazi pronunciation was used by the person being quoted (for example, if he/she said *Shabbos* rather than *Shabbat*), or for which the pronunciation is so common that almost everybody uses it for the word in question, such as *kosher* rather than the Sephardi *kasher*. Likewise, Ashkenazi names of congregations are retained. There are several reasons that justify the use of Sephardi pronunciation as the basis for transliteration. Here are just three of them:

> Many Jewish schools, excepting some of the most orthodox ones, teach the Israeli pronunciation, which is Sephardi. It is standard in classes on spoken Hebrew, as well as in secular scholarship and at British and American universities.

> Furthermore, not only Sephardi and progressive synagogues (Liberal and Reform) but also Masorti ones and even some constituents of the United Synagogue, at least in part, use the Sephardi pronunciation, especially for the reading of the Torah.

> Possibly a greater justification for transliterating Hebrew according to the Sephardi pronunciation is that it is almost always the same irrespective of the speaker. This is not the case for the Ashkenazi pronunciation of Hebrew, which varies depending on the tradition of a community and the origin of the speaker.

Throughout the book, there are references to Jewish customs and practices that will be familiar to most Jewish readers. However, to assist non-Jewish readers, who may be less conversant with Jewish laws and ways of life, I have provided explanations. Where it is possible to give brief explanations, I have included information within the text, but where the explanations are long and would therefore be intrusive, I have provided relevant information in endnotes. As appropriate, I have also referred readers to the detailed glossary included at the beginning of this book, which provides information on both Hebrew and Yiddish words used in the text.

Read and Enjoy!

Writing this book has given me intense pleasure. Not only have I once again had the privilege of speaking with a large number of interesting, helpful and informative people, many of whom share my enthusiasm for Jewish social history, but I have also learned a lot. Who would have thought that so many things can go wrong in the running of a hotel? I was aware of the centrality of food to the Jewish way of life, but the Jewish hotels of Bournemouth took the importance of food to a whole new level. However, most rewarding of all was becoming acquainted with the array of fascinating characters who ran, staffed and stayed in the hotels. In particular, I was very taken with the so-called 'Grandes Dames of Bournemouth', the forceful women who were the driving force behind many of both the large luxury hotels, the 'Big Eight', and the less prominent holiday accommodation. Who could fail to be impressed by the high standards of personal service which they aspired to provide their guests? While memories of the Big Eight remain strong in the minds of many former guests, I was equally captivated by the operation of the smaller guest houses, which I discovered were run by some very interesting people and each had their individual character and clientele. I hope that readers will find other aspects of this book equally enthralling.

Pam Fox
January 2021

Notes

1. Pam Fox, *The Jewish Community of Golders Green: A Social History* (Stroud: The History Press, 2016).
2. Pam Fox, *History in the Baking, The Rinkoff Story* (London: Rinkoff, 2019).
3. Yanky Fachler, *The Vow, Rebuilding the Fachler Tribe After the Holocaust* (Victoria, Canada: Trafford Publishing, 2003).
4. Morella Kayman, *A Life to Remember* (London: John Blake Publishing Ltd, 2014).
5. See https://www.streets-of-bournemouth.org.uk/.
6. Jackie Edwards, *A Bed by the Sea: A History of Bournemouth's Hotels* (Christchurch: Natula Publications, 2010).
7. M. A. Edgington, *Bournemouth and the First World War, The evergreen valley, 1914–1919* (Bournemouth: Bournemouth Local Studies Publications, 2013) and M.A. Edgington, *Bournemouth and the Second World War, 1939–1945* (Bournemouth: Bournemouth Local Studies Publications, 2013).
8. Vincent May and Jan Marsh (eds), *1820–2010, From Smugglers to Surfers* (Wimborne Minster: Dovecote Press, 2010).
9. Ivor Weintroub, David Weitzman and Stephen H. White, *Bournemouth Hebrew Congregation Centenary 1905-2005: A celebration in writing and pictures of the Congregation's first 100 wonderful years* (Cheltenham: Zethics, 2005).

PART ONE

The Rise and Decline of Jewish Hotels and Guest Houses in Bournemouth

1

The Early History of Jewish Holiday Accommodation in Bournemouth

Anglo-Jewish History

Since the Readmission of the Jews to England in 1656, approximately two-thirds of the Anglo-Jewish community has always lived in London. The first recognisable Jewish community grew up around Old Jewry, off Cheapside in the City of London. As with most immigrant groups, the settlement of the first Jews influenced the location of those arriving after them. During the eighteenth century, a few wealthy families, mainly Sephardim (Jews of Spanish and Portuguese origin), bought country houses in Middlesex where they sometimes held religious meetings. However, they retained their membership of synagogues located in the City of London, and the vast majority of Sephardim continued to live in close proximity to their places of worship.

By comparison, the smaller Ashkenazi population (Jews of Central and Eastern European origin[1]) began to disperse and live adjacent to the synagogues the community had opened in the East End of London. By the early 1700s, twenty-five per cent of the population of the area around Aldgate was Jewish.[2] The wealthiest Ashkenazi Jews purchased large homes and country estates in areas such as Highgate, Totteridge and Morden.[3] Adopting the lifestyle of affluent non-Jews, they mainly used these country residences at weekends while they were still working. Once they had retired, they moved to more rural settings further outside London.[4]

By the turn of the nineteenth century, there were well-established communities in many of Britain's larger towns and seaports. While there remained significant variations in wealth, the community as a whole became more prosperous and more integrated into British society. During the nineteenth century, a range of Jewish communal bodies was founded, which together provided the infrastructure of British Jewish life.

Commencing in the late nineteenth century, there was a great tide of immigration of Jews fleeing persecution in Eastern Europe, which caused the London community to burst out of its long-established location between Aldgate and Commercial Street, flowing past Brick Lane into Mile End, through Hanbury Street to the fringes of Bethnal Green and across Whitechapel Road and Commercial Road as far as Cable Street.[5] The main streets in which the community coalesced were Wentworth Street, Middlesex Street, Butler Street, Thrawl Street, Fashion Street, Flower Street, Dean Street and the surrounding streets in Spitalfields formerly occupied by Huguenot weavers.

As boatloads of new immigrants arrived, conditions in Whitechapel and Spitalfields became increasingly overcrowded and the area began to resemble a ghetto, albeit a voluntary one. Whole families often lived in one room, and sometimes they also worked there.[6] By the latter part of the nineteenth century, a Jewish population of 125,000 lived in an area of less than five square kilometres.[7] This area became known as the 'Jewish East End', typified by the small houses of worship (*chevrot*), the sweated trades and vibrant street markets. Yiddish newspapers and literature abounded, youth clubs thrived and the Yiddish theatre flourished. The Jewish community of London was now socially, culturally and spatially differentiated from the rest of the population of the capital city.

During the twentieth century, the pattern of Jewish settlement in London and elsewhere was transformed. While moving to outlying areas had previously been confined to the wealthiest Jews, suburban living became the lifestyle for the majority of the Jewish community. This transformation began much earlier in London, and was far more geographically spread than for Jewish communities in other parts of the country. However, the small numbers who could afford to do so continued to make their homes in large properties further away from the main conurbations, including those located in the increasingly fashionable coastal resorts such as Bournemouth.

By the early years of the twentieth century, there was a generation of Jews who had been born in Britain, many of whom had been educated in state schools where they had associated with non-Jews. As a result, wider social aspirations penetrated their world. As they moved to the suburbs in increasing numbers, they quickly adopted the mores of those alongside whom they were now living, leaving behind them the conspicuous foreignness of their parents. One of the symbols of bourgeois respectability to which the new generation aspired was that of taking holidays and many now had the means to do so.

By the eve of the First World War, the financial status of the Jewish community as a whole was beginning to improve and some Jews still living in the first areas of settlement, especially the East End, were also beginning to take breaks from the toil of their daily lives. A number of boarding houses began to open up, catering for Jews with more limited incomes, mainly in places reasonably close to areas of Jewish settlement, such as Westcliff-on-Sea on the Essex coast.

The History of Bournemouth

English society had been quick to follow the continental belief in the health-giving qualities of sea bathing and, by the end of the eighteenth century, spending time at the seaside was increasingly popular among the upper and middle classes. However, it was not until the coming of the railways, providing cheaper and faster access to the coastline, that resorts began to expand, including Brighton, Eastbourne and Bognor Regis. Over time, railways changed the class structure of the English sea resort.

Bournemouth lagged behind the development of the first wave of English seaside resorts. Until the early nineteenth century, the area where Bournemouth now stands was wild heathland, on which cattle grazed. It was located between the long-established settlements of Christchurch to the east and Poole to the west. The heathland led down to a wide bay with a rugged shoreline known for smuggling.[8] In 1810, Lewis Tregonwell, who is regarded as the first inhabitant and founder of Bournemouth, visited the beach with his wife. She fell in love with the area and persuaded her husband to build a summer house named Exeter House (known locally as 'the Mansion')[9] on recently enclosed land for the enjoyment of themselves and their friends and relatives, who also decided to build houses. A small colony developed, and Tregonwell later bought more land in the area. He and other new landowners planted pines on the heath. However, until the 1830s, there was little further settlement and fortuitously, some parts of the common land were placed in trust for the benefit of local people.

1. A portrait of Lewis Tregonwell, regarded as the founder of Bournemouth. Photograph of original oil painting courtesy of the Heritage Collection, Bournemouth Library.

In 1836, Sir George Tapps-Gervis, the principal local landowner and MP for Christchurch, decided to create an exclusive 'Marine Village' around the mouth of the Bourne stream, hence the name of Bournemouth.[10] He appointed a young architect from Christchurch named Benjamin Ferrey to design it. The planning of Bournemouth was Ferrey's first commission, only part of which came to fruition. Detached villas were built for elite families to hire during the summer and the Bath Hotel (later the Royal Bath and East Cliff Hotel) and a smaller guesthouse, the Belle Vue (later the Belle Vue and Pier Hotel) were also erected overlooking the sea, both opening in 1838. This speculative development in virgin territory was unprecedented. Most of the earlier British seaside resorts had developed around existing settlements, such as harbours, ports and fishing villages.

By 1840, Bournemouth had become a small village, at which the stagecoach travelling from Southampton to Weymouth began to call. In the same year, a guidebook for the embryonic resort was published by John Sydenham of Poole, an indication that the village was beginning to be established and to promote itself. However, just as the guidebook appeared, the development slowed to a trickle and it was to be another decade before any noteworthy growth occurred.

The new phase of expansion was the result of two significant developments, the first of which happened in 1841 when Dr Augustus Granville, the leading authority on English spas, was invited to stay at the new Marine Village.[11] He subsequently wrote a book in which he extolled the virtues of Bournemouth, especially the benefits of the aroma from the town's pine trees. Due to its year-round mild climate, the town was particularity recommended for people with chest and lung complaints. Dr Granville's comments were used to promote the town and a number of sanatoriums opened in the area, notably the National Sanatorium (later the Royal National Sanatorium[12]) and Stourfield Park Sanatorium in nearby Pokesdown, where special arrangements were later made for Jewish patients.[13] The second development was the coming to the area of prominent people. In 1874, Queen Victoria heard of the recuperative attributes of Bournemouth and persuaded her favourite prime minister, Benjamin Disraeli, to stay at the Royal Bath Hotel for three months to recover from gout and a bronchial ailment.

As a result of these occurrences, there was a major increase in both the number of visitors and residents of Bournemouth. In 1851, the population of Bournemouth stood at 598; by 1861 it had risen to 1,707. The infrastructure to support these demographic changes began to be put in place. Bournemouth's famous pier started life as a short wooden jetty built in 1855. In 1856, the Bournemouth police force was founded, and in the same year local government began when the Bournemouth Improvement Act established a body of 'improvement commissioners' with responsibility for cleaning and lighting streets in the area and powers to provide sewers and drains. The commissioners worked hard to ensure that people would enjoy an attractive and healthy town. In 1864, gas street lighting was installed, and two years later the town gained a piped water supply.

During the early 1870s a volunteer fire brigade was formed, the Winter Gardens and Pleasure Gardens were laid out and work commenced on building the Bournemouth Arcade. This stimulated further development. Villas owned by the wealthy sprang up in all directions, and Bournemouth changed in character from an exclusive marine settlement and a health resort for upper-class 'invalids' to become a substantial seaside town. In *Tess of the D'Urbervilles*, Thomas Hardy described Bournemouth (which he called 'Sandbourne') as 'a Mediterranean lounging place on the English Channel'. By this time, villages adjacent to Bournemouth were also growing rapidly, especially Boscombe where the retired diplomat Sir Henry Drummond Wolff, a man of Jewish descent, built large villas and hotels and developed Boscombe Chine as a pleasure ground.[14] In 1876, Boscombe and Springbourne were incorporated into Bournemouth.

2. *The Sands, Bournemouth*, an engraving by Philip Brannon, 1850, showing the beginnings of development, including the first jetty. Image courtesy of the Heritage Collection, Bournemouth Library.

By 1881, the population of Bournemouth had reached 16,859 and, over the next decade, Bournemouth and neighbouring settlements continued to expand. In 1884, Westbourne became part of Bournemouth and the following year, the Mont Dore Hotel was opened. It was designed as a health resort, where guests drank spring water from the Auvergne in France and were afforded 'every conceivable luxury', including Turkish baths.[15] Boscombe pier was built in 1889.

However, this growth was slow compared to the development that followed. In 1870, the railway had reached the environs of Bournemouth, making it far easier for people to visit the resort. However, it still took a day for people to travel from London to Holmsley station in the New Forest and then transfer to a stage coach to journey a further twelve miles to Bournemouth. It was not until 1888 that the town had a direct link to London, provided by the London & South Western Railway that operated from London's Waterloo station.[16] Over the next ten years, Bournemouth experienced a rate of growth almost unmatched in Britain as road after road of residential and commercial properties spread inland, overseen by a municipal borough established in 1890 to replace the improvement commissioners. Bournemouth was now accessible to a greater range of visitors and was also becoming more attractive as a place to retire, creating a demand for cultural and leisure facilities. The Bournemouth Symphony Orchestra was founded in 1893, the first library was opened in 1895 and the *Bournemouth Echo* commenced publication in 1900.[17]

The settlement initially known as Southbourne-on-Sea was originally intended to be a rival resort to Bournemouth. A winter garden was opened in 1884, construction began on a pier in 1881[18] and an undercliff promenade was built in 1883. However, Southbourne was soon swallowed up by the growing conurbation and became part of Bournemouth in 1901. In 1881, Pokesdown was still a small village with a population of 838. By 1900, it was home to 5,500 people and a year later it was also made part of Bournemouth, bringing the town's population to 59,000.

The houses and hotels built in Bournemouth in the latter part of the nineteenth century and the early part of the twentieth century were mainly erected on the steep slopes of the Bourne valley and on the cliff tops (the East Cliff and West Cliff) on which roads were constructed running parallel to the sea-level promenades, East Overcliff Drive and West Overcliff Drive. The 1901 Census tells us that by the opening years of the twentieth century, there were at least 170 hotels and boarding houses in Bournemouth, catering for visitors as well as those working in the area.

Boscombe railway station opened in 1897 and, by the turn of the twentieth century, the first electric trams had started ferrying people around the Bournemouth.

Many of Britain's coastal resorts came of age towards the end of the Victorian era. Although the main features associated with a holiday at the seaside were in place by the first decade of the twentieth century and the population of Bournemouth was growing exponentially, it was still predominantly visited by convalescents and people suffering from various illnesses. However, this situation was changing rapidly. When the novelist D. H. Lawrence stayed in Bournemouth shortly before the First World War to recover from double pneumonia, he wrote to a friend saying that he had changed his view of the place, it was no longer like a huge hospital and had become a 'jolly and pretty town'.[19] It was now increasingly recognised that Bournemouth had a style and elegance that set it apart from other British seaside resorts. A symbol of the change was the re-designation of what was previously known as Invalids' Walk because of the parade of bath chairs that were pushed along it, to the Pine Walk.

The First Jews and Jewish-Run Accommodation

Jews began to arrive in Bournemouth in the late 1860s. In 1872, a Mr I. Touline advertised in the *Jewish Chronicle* for a clerk who could also teach his three children Hebrew in the evenings.[20] In the same year, it was reported in a local newspaper that a Jewish photographer, 'Mr Isaac Levy of Bournemouth', had been involved in an altercation with a non-Jewish photographer.[21] Five years later, a Jewish couple living in Bournemouth were advertising in the *Jewish Chronicle*, seeking employment opportunities for their offspring.[22]

Some of the Jews settling in and around Bournemouth purchased substantial properties. In 1879, the Sephardi businessman, philanthropist and communal leader, Joseph Sebag (later Sir Joseph Sebag-Montefiore) was living in Lisle House in Bournemouth (later the Jewish-owned East Cliff Court Hotel),[23] and in 1880, the *Jewish Chronicle* advertised the sale of a very large house close to Boscombe ('The Knole') that was 'fit for the reception of the family of a nobleman or gentleman of position'. The property stood in five acres of grounds, 'laid out by Milner', and 'abounding with the choicest of specimens of trees and shrubs, velvet lawns and lovely terraced Italian garden'.[24] This advertisement suggests that the property had either previously been owned by a Jew or that it was recognised that properties of this description were attractive to wealthy Jews. In 1890, Walter Myers, a retired jeweller from Birmingham, was living in Bourne Hall.[25]

During the latter years of the nineteenth century, the content of the columns of the *Jewish Chronicle* indicate that an increasing number of Jews were staying in Bournemouth for health reasons, such as a Mr Guedalla, who adjourned to Bournemouth to 'recover from the effects of vexation'.[26] The convalescents often recovered, but sadly there were also a number of death announcements, the earliest of which was the passing of Rebecca Issenberg in January 1876.[27] It was reported that there were some Jews who wished to visit Bournemouth 'for the season', but who were finding it difficult to do so because there were no supplies of kosher meat (meat that has been slaughtered and prepared according to Jewish dietary laws, see Chapter 7).[28] By 1886, it appears that this situation was beginning to be addressed. In that year, Mrs J. S. Coles was advertising that she could accommodate a family in 'well-furnished apartments' over Passover (Hebrew *Pesach*, the festival celebrating the freedom gained for Jews with their exodus from Egypt) and could provide 'Jewish cooking'.[29] The advertisement that Mrs Coles placed the following year stated that she had lived for several years with an orthodox (strictly observant of Jewish laws) Jewish family and could be well recommended.[30]

By the 1880s, a number of non-Jewish-owned boarding houses (the term then used for guest houses), providing both accommodation and food, began advertising in the *Jewish Chronicle*, including the Clifton Hall Boarding Establishment run by Mrs Harrison, which was located on the West Cliff, close to the pier and the Pleasure Gardens.[31] Also being advertised at this time was Devon Towers, again located on the West Cliff. This establishment might have been operating for some time because its proprietor, W. Shirley Day, describes it as 'well-known'.[32] In 1890, the Hotel Mont Dore, advertised in the *Jewish Chronicle*. Those Jews with health conditions might have been attracted by the general luxury of the hotel and its spa baths, but it does not appear to have been offering any special facilities for Jewish guests.[33]

In the final years of the nineteenth century, Jews were beginning to take holidays in Bournemouth in increasing numbers as well as visiting the town for health reasons. They stayed mainly in boarding houses located on the West Cliff, such as the Birtley Boarding Establishment, which was close to the railway station,[34] Holly Hurst Family Boarding House run by Mr and Mrs Cooper[35] and a 'Private Hotel and Boarding House' owned by the Whyte family, who had previously run a boarding house in Southgate in London. The Whytes were obviously catering for more discerning and wealthier clients since the advertisement stressed that the accommodation had recently been renovated and its facilities included lawn tennis, billiards and *en suite* apartments.[36] At Glenroy Hall, the proprietors offered 'spacious dining', a smoking room and a gravel tennis court.[37]

While some Jews may have been comfortable staying in establishments run by non-Jews, there was clearly an emerging demand for accommodation where Jewish observance was paramount. In 1892, Rev. Dr and Mrs Chotzner took out an advertisement to explain that they had acquired a property in Bournemouth named 'Ulundi', at 125 West Hill Road on the West Cliff.[38] They had discovered that Ulundi was too large for their needs, and they were pleased to be able to 'welcome guests to reside with them'.[39] Born in Cracow, Rev. Dr Chotzner was the first minister of the Belfast Jewish community. He wrote books about Jewish humour on which he spoke at meetings of the Jewish Historical Society of England (JHSE). Ulundi can be regarded as the first Jewish boarding house in Bournemouth.

"ULUNDI."
WEST CLIFF, BOURNEMOUTH.

THE Rev. Dr. and Mrs. CHOTZNER have taken the above charming residence, situated one minute from the sea, South. The house being too large for their requirements, they will be pleased to receive a few visitors to Board and Reside with them.

Communications to be sent to the above address.

---

3. Advertisement for the first Jewish-owned and run boarding house in Bournemouth, appearing in the *Jewish Chronicle* on 16 December 1892.

4. 'Ulundi' (later the Seaways Hotel and subsequently the Hedley Hotel), 125 West Hill Road, West Cliff, Bournemouth, *c.* 1900. It was the first Jewish-owned and run boarding house in the town. Image in the Flickr collection of Alwyn Ladell, https://www.flickr.com/photos/alwyn_ladell/30846209118.

By this time, the number of Jewish families living in Bournemouth was increasing. In July 1894, a meeting of Jewish residents, then consisting of 'eight families and several young men',[40] was held at the home of Mr Levene to discuss a proposal to establish a congregation. It was suggested that having a congregation with whom they could worship would be appreciated by visitors to the area. Mr Levene was elected as the *gabbai* (warden) of the embryonic community.[41] The following month, a letter appealing for funds to finance the building of a synagogue in Bournemouth, to be known as the Bournemouth Hebrew Congregation, appeared in the *Jewish Chronicle*. The letter went on to say that Bournemouth was a health resort that was 'strongly recommended by the faculty' and was visited by 'Jewish invalids, especially in winter', who were in need of a place to pray and a supply of kosher meat.[42]

This letter suggests that, notwithstanding the recent growth in boarding houses, Jewish visitors to Bournemouth were still predominantly convalescents. Advertisements placed in the *Jewish Chronicle* at this time indicate that Jews were continuing to holiday in far greater numbers in places such as Ramsgate, Margate, Eastbourne, Brighton, St Leonards-on-Sea and Southport. Writing in the *Jewish Chronicle* in September 1894, Rev. Isaac Philips of Portsmouth Synagogue, predicted that if a synagogue were to be erected in Bournemouth, 'robust' Jews as well as 'invalids' would flock to the town and that new boarding houses would be opened 'for their convenience'.[43] He was to be proved correct.

The shape of things to come was signalled when in October 1894, the 'Misses Twyman' (Shirley and Fanny), who had been running a Jewish boarding house in Ramsgate, announced that during the following month they would be opening a boarding house in Bournemouth at Merivale Hall.[44] Previously a substantial private house, Merivale Hall offered 'commodious bedrooms', 'a handsome drawing room' and 'stabling'. It was the precursor to the Jewish hotels that grew up in Bournemouth in the early part of the twentieth century. It stood in its own grounds on the 'favourite East Cliff' rather than on the West Cliff, and was much larger than the Jewish establishments that had been catering for visitors to date and which were still largely run by non-Jews. Editions of *Bright's Illustrated Guide to Bournemouth* for the late nineteenth century show that a pattern of smaller Jewish establishments being located on the West Cliff and the larger ones on the East Cliff mirrored the trend for non-Jewish holiday establishments.

Merivale Hall was to operate until well into the 1930s, with only one change of proprietor during a forty-five-year period.[45] An early (unnamed) guest at Merivale Hall was so delighted by his stay that he wrote to the *Jewish Chronicle*:

To-day being *Tisho-ba-Ab*[46] and many of the visitors to Merivale Hall
fasting, I consider that it would not be inappropriate to devote a few
moments in asking you to kindly give a small space in your widely
circulated paper in the interests of the Jewish visitor. For several years
I have visited Bournemouth twice annually, and I need not say how
exceedingly awkward I have been situated on account of being
compelled to stay at a non-Jewish house. It is almost an impossibility,
under those circumstances, not to contravene Jewish dietary laws, but
now, thanks to the enterprising and energetic hostesses of Merivale
Hall, a Jewish Boarding Establishment has been provided which does
credit not only to them and to Bournemouth, but to the Jewish
community of the British Empire. I have visited most of the English
watering-places, and have not the least hesitation in describing this
as the most lovely [sic] of 'home from homes' that I have met. The
surroundings are more charming than many Continental hotels, and
one wonders almost that visitors should travel to the South of France
or Switzerland when as beautiful a picture and as well-appointed
kosher house can be found at Bournemouth. If, Mr. Editor, these few
lines will only result in more Jewish visitors enjoying kosher food than
hitherto, then indeed, you will be well repaid for your generosity in
giving up your valuable space.[47]

5. Merivale Hall Hotel, the first Jewish-owned and run hotel in Bournemouth, *c.* 1908. Image
in the Flickr collection of Alwyn Ladell, https://www.flickr.com/photos/alwyn_ladell/
6105845782.

Following this review, the Misses Twyman began marketing Merivale Hall as 'the only Jewish boarding house in Bournemouth'. In 1898, they acquired adjacent premises to accommodate guests when Merivale Hall was fully booked, to be run under their 'own personal supervision'.[48] Merivale Hall had set a trend, and over the next few years, a number of new establishments began to advertise the availability of 'strictly Jewish boarding', including Eldon House in West Hill Road on the West Cliff run by Mrs M. Lotheim[49] and the Ravenscourt 'Private Jewish apartments' in Ophir Road close to the central station.[50]

During the late nineteenth century and early years of the twentieth century, there was a noticeable increase in the quantity, size and quality of Jewish holiday accommodation. Having run Eldon House, Mrs Lotheim took on the much larger Iris Hall in West Cliff Gardens,[51] and Eva Hyam, who announced that 'owing to an increase in demand', she would be moving from her current premises to open the recently renovated Sea View Hall in Durley Gardens on the West Cliff.[52] Both establishments were to remain in business for many years. Sea View Hall, which became known for its popular annual balls, claimed to be the 'largest Jewish boarding establishment in Great Britain'. It had a croquet lawn as well as tennis courts and was the first Jewish holiday establishment to advertise the availability of a garage for 'motor vehicles'.[53]

Merivale Hall's fame continued to spread and its visitors now included the Chief Rabbi, Hermann Adler and his wife, and well-known people from Germany and other countries.[54] In 1905, Miss Shirley Twyman became the first of many hundreds of matches to be made in Bournemouth's Jewish hotels when she married Jack Goodman of New York.[55] Her sister, Fanny Twyman, continued to run Merivale Hall for several years, maintaining its atmosphere of 'gentility', offering 'perfection' in comfort, cooking and 'service to patrons from London, the provinces and the colonies'.[56]

The increase in the number of Jewish visitors to Bournemouth at the beginning of the twentieth century was illustrated by the fact that copies of the *Jewish Chronicle* were now available for sale at the W. H. Smith stall in the central railway station.[57] The Bournemouth Hebrew Congregation (BHC) was also reporting that its services were regularly attended by over twenty people staying at the 'several Jewish boarding houses' that were providing 'everything required by families'.[58] Under the leadership of its first president Samuel Moses Silverman, a 'house furnisher', BHC had appointed its own *chazan* (cantor), *shochet* (butcher certified by the Jewish religious authorities) and teacher. The congregation was holding services at the

Bellevue Assembly Rooms opposite Bournemouth pier.[59] In 1906, the growing community acquired land in Boscombe from Bournemouth Corporation to use as a burial ground.[60]

Emulating wealthy non-Jews of a generation or so earlier, upwardly mobile Jews were now seeking more lavish accommodation and service. As a result, the recently opened and more substantial Jewish boarding houses began to compete with each other, taking out ever-larger advertisements in the *Jewish Chronicle*, which extolled their respective attractions in providing for the comfort of their guests.

However, there were also a number of smaller establishments offering accommodation for one or two visitors, including the guest house run by Mrs Klein, the wife of Rev. L. Klein, the first minister at BHC.[61] These smaller establishments, located mainly on the West Cliff, nevertheless claimed that they were able to offer 'lofty' and well-furnished rooms, perhaps aiming to attract those Jews of lesser means still living in cramped and airless accommodation in urban environments. Mrs Lotheim, who by this time had acquired Oswestria is Boscombe, was letting 'sunny rooms facing the sea'.[62] Clearly, the aim was to provide a holiday experience that was as different as possible from people's everyday lives. While resorts such as Westcliff-on-Sea, Cliftonville and Blackpool remained the main holiday destination for less well-off families, some Jews of moderate means were now making their way to Bournemouth.

In the years leading up to the First World War, there was a proliferation of small, strictly orthodox boarding houses, but there were also a number of new, larger establishments, such as Holmdale, close to the town centre, run by Mrs Philips.[63] Interestingly, prior to the war, several new establishments were opened by experienced proprietors who had moved to Bournemouth from other, longer-standing resorts. Bournemouth's potential as a resort for Jewish visitors was clearly becoming more evident. Mrs Benjamin and Mrs Follick moved from Margate to open Swanmore, a few minutes' walk from the purpose-built synagogue that in 1911 had opened in Wootton Gardens, off the Old Christchurch Road.[64] Closeness to the synagogue was to become a selling point for Jewish holiday accommodation. Mrs Schlom, who had moved to the town from Folkestone and had opened 'superior furnished apartments' in Old Christchurch Road, was therefore well placed.[65] As we will see in the next chapter, Mrs Schlom's arrival in Bournemouth was noteworthy.

Before moving on to examine how the Jewish boarding houses and small hotels fared during the First World War, it is worth discussing briefly their proprietors. In Eastern Europe, inn-keeping was one of the restricted range of occupations that Jews were able to pursue. They often ran small inns and taverns located on the main routes connecting the larger towns. As well as providing accommodation, these premises often became the nexus of Jewish secular networks, social, psychological, financial and informational. According to the writer Yohanan Petrovsky-Shtern, in these inns, Jews discussed business, looked for and found jobs, engaged in matchmaking, played billiards and cards, sang songs and listened to music.[66] They also ate, drank and smoked. They thus foreshadowed the main elements of life in the more sophisticated Jewish hotels that were to open in Bournemouth in the mid-twentieth century.

When Eastern European Jews migrated to Britain during the late nineteenth and early twentieth centuries, some were able to use their previous experience to open rooming houses and small boarding houses in the areas where they settled. A proportion of the Jewish boarding establishments in Britain's burgeoning seaside resorts were opened by people who had previously run rooming and catering establishments in urban settings, particularly London.

An analysis of advertisements appearing in the *Jewish Chronicle* during the latter part of the nineteenth century and the early years of the twentieth, reveals that providing hospitality was a respectable occupation for Jewish women, including unmarried women, to enable them to maintain their financial independence or to supplement the family income. Whereas at the beginning of the period we have been examining, the proprietors were fairly anonymous, by the second decade of the twentieth century, they had gained a much higher profile. The fact that an establishment was 'under the personal supervision' of a proprietor became a selling point. In addition, those running the various establishments became more professional in their approach, assessing their markets and promoting their accommodation accordingly. In the next chapter, we will see that the prominence of the individuals or the families who ran Jewish holiday accommodation in Bournemouth was to become even greater as the twentieth century progressed.

Notes

1. See https://www.frontiersin.org/articles/10.3389/fgene.2017.00087/full.
2. Rachel's Kolsky and Rosalyn Rawson, *Jewish London: A Comprehensive Handbook for Visitors and Londoners* (London: New Holland, 2012), p.11.
3. *Ibid.*, p.11.
4. V. D. Lipman, 'The Rise of Jewish Suburbia', *Transactions of the Jewish Historical Society of England* (London: Jewish Historical Society of England), Vol. 21 (1962-1967), p.80.
5. Gerry Black, *Jewish London: An Illustrated History* (Derby: Breedon Books Publishing, 2007), p.98.
6. '350 years of British Jewish Life'. See www.visitjewishlondon.com/uk-jewish-life/history.
7. See Kolsky and Rawson, *Jewish London*, p.11.
8. This brief history of Bournemouth is largely based on information available at: https://www.bournemouth.co.uk/explore/history-of-bournemouth and 'The Streets of Bournemouth: Tourism and the Town', https://www.streets-of-bournemouth.org.uk/wp-content/uploads/2018/02/Tourism.and_.Town_.pdf.
9. It now forms the central part of the Royal Exeter Hotel.
10. The mouth of the river has now disappeared, engulfed by the town.
11. Augustus Bozzi Granville, *The Spas of England and Principal Sea Bathing Places* (London: Henry Coburn, 1841).
12. It was located in what became St Stephen's Road, adjacent to the Mont Dore Hotel (also mentioned in the text).
13. *Jewish Chronicle*, henceforward *JC*, 26.7.1903.
14. See https://en.wikipedia.org/wiki/Henry_Drummond_Wolff.
15. In 1921, the Mont Dore became the Bournemouth town hall.
16. The station was known as Bournemouth East from 1885–99 and Bournemouth Central from 1899–1967.
17. See 'Streets of Bournemouth: Commerce and Industry', https://www.streets-of-bournemouth.org.uk/wp-content/uploads/2018/02/Commerce.Industry.pdf.
18. In 1888, storms damaged the pier, which was finally demolished in 1907.
19. Jackie Edwards, *A Bed by the Sea: A History of Bournemouth's Hotels* (Christchurch: Natula Publications, 2010), p.25.
20. *JC*, 12. 1872. Mr Touline gave his address as The Arcade, Bournemouth, which suggests that he owned a retail business or commercial enterprise of some kind in the recently opened arcade.
21. *The Western Gazette*, 30.8.1872.
22. *JC*, 20.3.1877. The family was not named.
23. *JC*, 12.12.1879.
24. *JC*, 26.11.1880.
25. *JC*, 7.2.1890.
26. *JC*, 5.2.1886.
27. *JC*, 7.1.1876.
28. *JC*, 23.6.1882.
29. *JC*, 26.3.1986.
30. *JC*, 28.1.1887.
31. *JC*, 13.12.1889.

32. *JC*, 20.12.1889.
33. *JC*, 13.6.1890.
34. *JC*, 25.9.1891.
35. *JC*, 12.1.1894.
36. *JC*, 22.10.1891.
37. *JC*, 27.7.1894.
38. It later became a non-Jewish guest house, first named the Seaways Hotel and then the Hedley Hotel.
39. *JC*, 4.11.1892.
40. *JC*, 28.9.1894.
41. *JC*, 13.7.1894.
42. *JC*, 24.8.1894. It was signed by Mr S. Levene (previously mentioned), Myer Silverman, formerly of Southampton (Treasurer) and Mr S. Levine (Hon. Sec.).
43. *JC*, 28.9.1894.
44. *JC*, 19.10.1894.
45. Just before the Second World War, it was renamed the Picardy Hotel, which was run by a non-Jewish owner. It was later to open as a Jewish establishment. See Chapter 4.
46. *Tisho-ba-Ab* (or *Tisha B'Av*) is an annual fast day in Judaism, on which a number of disasters in Jewish history occurred, primarily the destruction of both Solomon's Temple by the Neo-Babylonian Empire and the Second Temple by the Roman Empire in Jerusalem.
47. *JC*, 2.8.1895.
48. *JC*, 10.3.1899.
49. *JC*, 6.4.1898.
50. *JC*, 19.12.1899.
51. *JC*, 19.5.1899.
52. *JC*, 22.2.1901.
53. *JC*, 22.3.1907.
54. *JC*, 19.4.1901.
55. *JC*, 25.8.1905.
56. *JC*, 7.6.1935.
57. *JC*, 2.6.1905.
58. *JC*, 17.8.1905.
59. *JC*, 12.4.1996.
60. See https://www.streets-of-bournemouth.org.uk/wp-content/uploads/2018/02/Towns. Communities.pdf.
61. *JC*, 23.4.1908.
62. *JC*, 15.9.1909.
63. *JC*, 8.4 .1910.
64. *JC*, 6.9.1912. The foundation stone was laid by Chief Rabbi Hermann Adler, *JC*, 12.4.1996 and by Albert Samuel, whose brother Herbert later became a Cabinet Minister and subsequently the first British High Commissioner for Palestine under the Mandate. See http://www.bhcshul.co.uk/our-history/.
65. *JC*, 4.12.1912.
66. Yohanan Petrovsky-Shtern, *The Golden Age of the Shtetl: A New History of Life in East Europe* (Princeton NJ: Princeton University Press, 2015), p.129.

2

Jewish Hotels in Bournemouth, 1914–1945

Developments in Anglo-Jewry

The shift of the Jewish community to live in more salubrious environments, chiefly the suburban areas of the main conurbations and larger towns, gathered pace in the years immediately preceding the First World War. Those who had amassed enough money to secure a comfortable suburban home and to start climbing the social ladder tended to be the more determined and ambitious Jews.[1] The majority of Jews still lacked both the means and the inclination to leave familiar surroundings and their families, even though the places where they lived were becoming increasingly overcrowded. However, the dispersal of the semi-ghettoes was already becoming discernible.

The First World War had some positive side effects for the Jewish community. It was a period of sustained employment in the trades in which immigrants predominated. In addition, some Jews were able to secure government contracts, the so-called 'khaki boom'. Tailors and garment makers made uniforms for the armed forces and cabinet makers made ammunition boxes, pre-fabricated huts and furniture for barracks.[2] As a result, both the dispersal and assimilation of Jews into mainstream society gathered pace. These demographic and social changes were further hastened by the war-time bombing of many of the areas in which Jews had coalesced, especially the East End of London. By the end of the war, relatively few middle-class Jews remained in the first areas of settlement.

Despite the financial difficulties of the interwar years, notably the Great Depression of the early 1930s, the overall well-being of the Jewish community continued to improve. It evolved from a community dominated by immigrants with few skills and pursuing a limited number of occupations, to one in which Jews were mainly born in Britain (largely as an outcome of the Aliens Acts of 1905 and 1914, which limited immigration) and were able to access a wider range of employment opportunities and improve their socio-economic status. There was now a significant number of Jewish entrepreneurs whose businesses and personal wealth had expanded as the result of introducing modern methods of large-scale production and distribution and innovative business practices, such as credit arrangements.[3] In addition, with the support of their ambitious parents who had seen education as a means for improving the upward mobility of their offspring, a number of second-generation Jews had started to enter the professions. The new Jewish professionals tended to remove themselves both geographically and socially from the immigrant generation.[4]

During the 1930s, the size of Anglo-Jewry expanded as a result of the arrival of thousands of refugees fleeing Nazism, a large proportion of whom were professionals, academics, industrialists and artists, who had been thoroughly assimilated into the middle-class lifestyles of the central European countries in which they had lived. The continental refugees who arrived in Britain before 1938 generally fared better than those who came immediately before the Second World War, since they had been able to bring with them some of their assets. Some were also able to use their resources and European connections to establish successful businesses, in which they were able to employ those refugees who came later.

The bombing of Britain during the Second World War sounded the death knell of the immigrant areas that were already greatly depleted by the voluntary process of dispersal. In the face of the depressing sight of tracts of wasteland and empty spaces, the destruction of communal bodies and the replacement of acres of housing with warehousing offices and factories, yet more Jews left for other areas. Many Jewish evacuees and servicemen simply did not return to the areas where they had previously lived. As a result of their wartime experiences, they had developed a taste for a different environment and a new way of life.

In combination, these various changes in the Jewish community led to the almost complete absorption of Jews into the mainstream of British society and, more particularly from the point of view of this book, to an increasing demand for holiday accommodation. There remained wide variations in the type of holiday accommodation Jewish families could afford, and taking a holiday was still beyond the reach of many. Nevertheless, leaving one's normal abode to relax with friends and family in more congenial environments was no longer the preserve of the wealthier echelons of Anglo-Jewry.

The Evolution of Bournemouth as a Resort

Returning to the beginning of the period covered by this chapter, the holiday season in Bournemouth in 1914 started well.[5] With warm and sunny weather forecast, trains from London and elsewhere brought a rush of visitors to the town. It was reported in the local press that over 30,000 people had walked along the promenade over the May Bank Holiday weekend compared to 20,000 the previous year. The _Bournemouth Guardian_ commented: 'As far as Bournemouth was concerned, the black clouds of war starting to appear over the Continent did not exist. The town settled down, anticipating a bumper year.'[6]

The crowds were not so large during the August Bank Holiday, since by then war had been declared. People continued to visit Bournemouth throughout the First World War, but both the authorities and residents were preoccupied with the wounded soldiers who came to convalesce in the town. The Defence of the Realm Act of 1914 required 'aliens' to register at law courts and then they were asked to leave. This created problems for the hotel trade in Bournemouth, which employed over 12,000 aliens. Cutbacks in excursions, lack of cheap train tickets and petrol rationing also deterred people from visiting Bournemouth.

After the war ended in November 1918, the hotels found that by Christmas, bookings had returned to their pre-war levels. Over the next decade or so, Bournemouth became a leading holiday destination for families as well as those with health problems. It emerged as a two-season resort, catering for affluent, older visitors and invalids (as they were referred to then) in the winter and holidaymakers in the summer. This metamorphosis was facilitated by the commencement of paid holidays, the ending of segregated bathing that encouraged more families to take holidays,[7] and changes in social behaviour, such as the new fashion for sunbathing. Swimming in the sea had now replaced the therapeutic dipping and bathing rituals of the previous century.[8]

Local businesses, such as the Fancy Fair, the first shop of John Beale (a draper from Weymouth), which had opened in 1882, began to cater for the embryonic tourist industry as well as for Bournemouth's elite residents. The shop stocked buckets and spades and Japanese sunshades for the holidaymakers. In 1927, Charles Forte moved from Scotland to live in Winton and opened an ice cream parlour in Old Christchurch Road, the first of many.[9]

In the interwar years, many of the larger private homes in Bournemouth, particularly those on the East Cliff, were converted into hotels and boarding houses to accommodate the increasing number of visitors. In some instances, properties were knocked down to make way for newer, purpose-built hotels.[10] Several longstanding holiday establishments were refurbished and extended. The tourist trade was also boosted by the dismantling of some of the large estates (the Meyrick, Malmesbury and Cooper Dean estates) in order to meet death duties and as a result of inflation that had reduced real incomes from ground rent. New holiday accommodation was built on the land that was released.

The Bournemouth Improvement Commissioners (See Chapter 1) had sought to maintain the town as a resort for the elite that would rival the French Riviera. However, they had not catered for the democratisation of the Bournemouth holiday trade that commenced with the coming of the railways. The process of diversification was reinforced by when the entitlement to paid holidays was extended from professionals to other workers. Between 1925 and 1937, the proportion of workers who were entitled to paid holidays increased from seventeen to forty-seven per cent.[11]

In October 1910, a daily Manchester to Bournemouth railway service was introduced by the London & North Western Railway in conjunction with Midland Railway. From 1927 to 1967, this service ran under the name of the *Pines Express*, leaving Manchester's London Road station (now Manchester Piccadilly) at 10am and arriving at Bournemouth West some seven or eight hours later. There was also a service run by the London and South Western Railway and Great Western Railway from Birkenhead to Bournemouth. Together, these trains enabled many people from northern cities to visit the south coast.[12] One of the straplines used by the *Pines Express*, 'The seaside town in the pine forest', reflected Bournemouth's transition from a health resort to a destination for recreation. Another named train, the *Bournemouth Belle*, was introduced by Southern Railway in 1931. Except for a short break during the Second World War, it continued to run daily until 1947 operated by the Southern Railway. From 1947 until 1967, the service was operated by British Rail. It brought to Bournemouth visitors from London who did not own cars or who preferred to travel by train.[13] Although there were other, less expensive, trains that ran from Waterloo to Bournemouth, they did not have the same cachet as the *Bournemouth Belle* with its Pullman carriages.

While some tourism posters depicted 'bathing belles', young women clad in revealing swimwear, other advertisements for Bournemouth appearing during the interwar period depicted an elegant and fashionably dressed woman looking over an equally elegant and restrained Bournemouth, seeking to promote an image of refined leisure. There clearly remained a desire to appeal to visitors other than those who wanted sand, sea and fun.[14]

6. The early, year-round tourist trade at Alum Chine in 1927. Image courtesy of the Heritage Collection, Bournemouth Library.

During the early months of the Second World War, the number of visitors to Bournemouth fell only slightly.[15] The smaller hotels and the guest houses were affected more than the larger hotels. However, by the end of the year, bookings had returned to normal despite the wartime restrictions, which included debarring use of the beaches by enclosing them with barbed wire, laying mines, closing the two piers and cutting train services. The town's Hotel Association warned hotels not to reduce their prices, since the cost of food and utilities was likely to rise. Many of the larger hotels converted their basements to air raid shelters. J. B. Priestley, who stayed in Bournemouth in 1941, wrote: 'Nobody could call it a bad war in Bournemouth. Its frontline is negligible. The shops still look opulent, and thousands of well-dressed women seem to be flitting in and out of them: in short, a good time can be had by all.'[16]

However, as the war progressed and D-Day approached, conditions worsened and the town's efforts were again focussed on the its role as a centre for wounded and convalescent armed forces personnel. It also became a location for the rest and recreation of North American servicemen. The American Red Cross produced a booklet for those recuperating in the town, *Furlough in Bournemouth*, in which the town was described as 'unique in that it combined the sophistication of the city with the gaiety of a beach town and the quiet charm of country club life'. It even went so far as to suggest that Bournemouth could be compared to Miami

Beach, Atlantic City and Santa Monica.[17] Several of Bournemouth's larger hotels were requisitioned and became 'luxuriously furnished Red Cross Clubs' overlooking the sea. The Royal Canadian Air Force appropriated forty-three hotels for accommodation, including the Anglo Swiss and the Royal Bath hotels.

Several hotels were damaged by bombing during the war, including the St Ives, the Central, the Metropole and the Anglo Swiss. In March 1944, there was a ban on visitors to the south coast due to the build-up of troops in preparation for the D-Day landings. All hotels and boarding house were ordered by the police to cancel their bookings for guests who were not exempt. They reopened four months later. At the end of the war, hotels used by the Red Cross were easy to convert back into hotels, but those that had been used as billets needed considerable refurbishment. The hotels were gradually handed back to their owners and by mid-1946 only a handful remained requisitioned.

Bournemouth's Jewish Community

During the years between 1915 and 1945, many Jews came to live in Bournemouth where they made a significant contribution both to the local economy and to civic life. Several of the Jews settling in Bournemouth were tailors who had contracted tuberculosis as a result of their occupations. They had managed to escape the sweat shops of East London and to eke out an existence in Bournemouth. Some of their wives supplemented the family income by taking in paying guests and running small guest houses. Members of the community served in the armed forces in both world wars and in civil defence, including in the nursing and fire services, the ARP and the Home Guard.

When the purpose-built synagogue opened in Wootton Gardens in 1911, the congregation consisted of fewer than fifty families. The arrival of many young evacuees during the war meant that the *cheder* (religion school) had to be increased in size. In 1918, a Ladies' Guild was set up and in 1923, a social hall was added to the synagogue, where the recently formed Jewish Sports and Social Club, the Zionist Society and a Jewish Scout troop met. At this point, the community was largely made up of people who ran small businesses in the town, mainly clothes, fur and jewellery shops,[18] including the Kasmir family who gradually established a chain of shops across the region.

During the 1930s, the Bournemouth Jewish community, which by then had become an integral part of the local population, was shaken by instances of antisemitism, including at the local riding stables frequented by guests at the Jewish holiday accommodation in the town.[19] There was also in Bournemouth an active branch of the British Union of Fascists and in May 1937 public demonstrations were held in protest against the flying of a 'Blackshirt Flag'.[20] In April 1938, the *Jewish Chronicle* reported that a 'group of Nazis' had met at the Norfolk Hotel in the town, where they had shouted 'Heil Hitler' and sung the German national anthem.[21] In 1939, Rabbi Israel Brodie, then Public Relations Officer for the Board of Deputies of British Jews and later Chief Rabbi, met with the Jewish community to discuss antisemitism in the area.[22]

As tyranny in Europe threatened to plunge the world into another war, most Jewish families in Bournemouth provided accommodation for evacuees from other parts of the country and refugees from Nazism. The Jewish refugees who chose to settle in the town brought with them a strong desire to succeed and they added to the range of trades and employment in the town. One refugee was Ludwig Loewy from Bohemia (now part of the Czech Republic or Czechia). He arrived in 1933 and set up the Hydropress Company in 1935, which built extrusion presses used for aircraft production. The firm was to contribute significantly to the outcome of the Second World War.[23] In 1938, Rabbi Dr Winter, the former communal rabbi of Lübeck, moved to Bournemouth with his wife and opened a hostel for young adults and children, which was one of the many homes for *Kindertransport* children. Located in Westminster Road in Branksome Park, it called itself the 'strictly orthodox Dr Winter's home' and provided both short and long-term holidays.[24]

Refugees were welcomed by both non-Jews and the existing community, including by Jewish hotel owners such as the Pantels at the Marlborough Hotel, who in January 1939 entertained twelve refugee girls with tea and a concert at the hotel.[25] However, there were continuing reports of antisemitism. In June 1940, several members of the British Union of Fascists were arrested in Bournemouth because of their activities,[26] and in June 1943, a local resident wrote to the *Jewish Chronicle*, drawing attention to the existence of a branch of the New Order Group, which was distributing 'Ratcliffe's filthy anti-Jewish pamphlet' in the town.[27]

In the build-up to the D-Day landings in Normandy, the Jewish members of the Allied Forces stationed in Bournemouth enjoyed unlimited hospitality from BHC and the Ladies' Guild Forces Committee. In the autumn of 1944, the committee organised *Rosh Hashanah* (Jewish New Year) and *Yom Kippur* (Day of Atonement) services, and at *Pesach* 1945 it organised a *seder* (a ritual meal marking the beginning of *Pesach*, see glossary) for 600 servicemen, which was held in Bournemouth town hall.[28] Three hostels were set up for children rescued from the horrors of the concentration camps and the communal house in Wellington Road was used as a refuge for the homeless.[29]

Jewish Holiday Accommodation During the First World War

In Chapter 1, we saw that by the start of the First World War, a range of holiday accommodation was available to Jewish visitors to Bournemouth. During the war, the amount of accommodation seems to have remained fairly static, except for the opening of a few small boarding houses, such as Sunny View in Southcote Road run by Mrs Godfar, who had moved to Bournemouth from Edinburgh[30] and Argyle House run by Mrs A. Schlom (mentioned in Chapter 1), who had previously run apartments for rent in Old Christchurch Road.[31]

A larger boarding house that opened during the war, and went on to be very successful, was Hinton Court, which stood in its own grounds in Grove Road on the East Cliff. It was run by Edgar Steel, an experienced proprietor who also had a boarding house, the Oval Court, in Cliftonville. In the middle of the war, he was placing large advertisements in the *Jewish Chronicle* for what he described as 'the winter residence', clearly seeking to attract guests of means.[32] In 1917, Edgar Steel announced that his guests had contributed over £150 to the Comforts Fund for Jewish Soldiers[33] and Hinton Court was subsequently used to host a range of communal activities.[34] It also provided hospitality for Jewish soldiers stationed at camps near Bournemouth.[35] The smaller boarding houses generally fared less well than the larger establishments during the war. They advertised less frequently and usually closed over the winter months. With no established clientele, some of the boarding houses that had opened just prior to the war did not last for long, including The Breck in Kynveton Road run by Mrs H. Zolowski.[36]

With signs that the war might be coming to an end, during 1918 a number of new Jewish boarding houses opened in Bournemouth, including Granville House run by Mrs Goldstein, Lorraine House run by Mrs Cohen and Haywood House run by the Misses Barnett.[37] Some proprietors were also expanding their activities, including Mrs Schlom, who moved from Argyle House to Maison Leontine in St Peter's Road (changing her name to Mrs Annie Morris at the same time[38]) and Miss Magnus who opened Broadmead in St Michael's Road on the West Cliff.[39]

The Interwar Years

In the years immediately following the end of the First World War, some of the larger boarding houses changed hands, notably Merivale Hall which, having been run for several years by Fanny Twyman, was sold to Mr and Mrs J. Rosenthall. Following the death of Edgar Steel in 1922, ownership of Hinton Court passed to his son and daughter-in-law, Douglas and Mina Steel.[40] Several new and larger boarding houses also opened, such as Pinetown run by Mrs Parker, Bonavista run by Mrs Smullian and Ormsby run by Jacob Posalski.[41]

However, these changes were minor compared to what was to follow. During the interwar years, a growing demand for holiday accommodation and rising expectations about levels of comfort triggered a range of developments that together transformed the Jewish holiday scene in Bournemouth, setting the scene for what would be its heyday in the post-war years. One of the most obvious changes was a clearer differentiation between the boarding houses (now increasingly referred to as guest houses) and the new, larger and more luxurious establishments. The more upmarket accommodation was increasingly located on the East Cliff where it started to form a Jewish enclave.

Emulating Merivale Hall, which was now referring to itself as a hotel, some of the new establishments designated themselves as hotels rather than guest houses. The first to do so was Berachah (Hebrew for blessing). First listed in 1922, Berachah was located in Kerley Road on the West Cliff and was run by Isaac Grossman and his wife.[42] In April 1923, the Trouville Hotel (previously known as St Margaret's, owned by the Godfrey family) opened in Priory Road, also on the West Cliff, under the ownership of Hetty and Herman Polakoff. Herman was the son of the well-known London _mohel_ (a Jew trained to perform circumcisions), Rev. M. Polakoff, a relationship on which the proprietors of Trouville traded.[43] Herman Polakoff is said to have referred to his establishment as 'Mine Trouville'.[44] Both Berachah and Trouville were to become longstanding and prominent Jewish hotels in Bournemouth. They were noticeably more luxurious than the majority of the larger boarding houses of the pre-war years, boasting modern comforts such as central heating. Hilary Myers (née Levy), the niece of Herman Polakoff, often visited the Trouville as a child. She recalls thinking that it was 'the epitome of luxury'.[45] The Jewish holiday accommodation was catching up quickly with the non-Jewish establishments.

7. The Berachah Hotel (later the Kerley Hotel), 7 Kerley Road, West Cliff, Bournemouth, run by the Grossman family, *c.* 1950. Detail from postcard in the Flickr collection of Alwyn Ladell, https://www.flickr.com/photos/alwyn_ladell/46103073834.

8. The Trouville Hotel, 5 Priory Road, West Cliff, Bournemouth, run by Hetty and Herman Polakoff, *c.* 1925. Image in the Flickr collection of Alwyn Ladell, https://www.flickr.com/photos/alwyn_ladell/5330709300.

The year 1926 can perhaps be seen as a landmark in the development of Jewish hotels in Bournemouth. In December 1925,[46] Mrs Annie Morris (previously known as Mrs Schlom), 'proprietress' of Maison Leontine in St Peter's Road, took out a large advertisement in the *Jewish Chronicle*.[47] She announced that the following year she would be opening East Cliff Court guest house, a designation she quickly changed to private hotel, located on East Overcliff Drive. It is a moot point whether East Cliff Court, which was to become one of Bournemouth's largest and most luxurious hotels, was the first Jewish hotel in the town or whether that claim should go to the long-standing Merivale Hall, which described itself as such, or to either Berachah, the Trouville or East Cliff Court, which were clearly of a totally different ilk.

Preliminary Announcement

East Cliff Court

BOURNEMOUTH

This new and most luxurious Jewish Guest House will be ready for Passover.

SITUATED on the beautiful East Overcliff opposite the Cliff Lift, with magnificent sea views from every window; hot and cold water fitted to all bedrooms, HOT and COLD SEA WATER TO ALL BATHS, central heating throughout, electric lift to all floors. Spacious Ballroom.

LOCK-UP GARAGES FOR 20 CARS WITH CHAUFFEURS ACCOMMODATION IN GROUNDS.

Reasonable Terms.

EARLY BOOKINGS FOR PASSOVER ADVISABLE.

PROPRIETRESS:

Mrs. A. Morris, Maison Leontine, Bourremouth

[*Further Announcements Later*]

9. Announcement of the opening of the East Cliff Court Hotel, appearing in the *Jewish Chronicle* on 25 December 1925.

10. East Cliff Court Hotel (previously Lisle House), 23 (later 53) Grove Road, Bournemouth, *c.* 1927, shortly after its opening. Image in the Flickr collection of Alwyn Ladell, https://www.flickr.com/photos/alwyn_ladell/33540011541.

11. East Cliff Court Hotel (previously Lisle House), 23 (later 53) Grove Road, Bournemouth, *c.* 1927, showing the first extension to Lisle House, added during 1925. Image in the Flickr collection of Alwyn Ladell, https://www.flickr.com/photos/alwyn_ladell/32856146643.

East Cliff Court opened for *Pesach* in 1926. The story is that Annie Morris conceived the idea of opening a luxurious hotel while sitting on a bench on East Overcliff Drive, looking at a cottage with a large garden. This was Lisle House in Grove Road, which had previously been the home of Joseph Sebag as mentioned in Chapter 1. Annie Morris purchased and extended the property with the help of John Hayman, one of her permanent guests at Maison Leontine, who was to become her son-in-law.[48] The hotel was clearly aiming at a wealthy clientele. Early advertisements stated that it provided lock-up garages for twenty cars with chauffeurs' accommodation in the grounds, and it had a lift to all floors before any other Jewish hotel in Bournemouth. Annie Morris claimed that it was the 'most luxurious' establishment in Bournemouth.

The opening of East Cliff Court appears to have been the catalyst for other Jewish establishments to extend and to improve their facilities. During 1926, Hinton Court was enlarged, and in 1930 the Polakoffs announced that the Trouville had been rebuilt to make it 'the largest and most up-to-date orthodox hotel in the British Isles.'[49] The following year, Berachah added a 'Vitaglas' solarium to make it 'the only Jewish House in the country with a solarium facing the sun.'[50] In 1935, Daniel Rosenthall, owner of Merivale Hall, 'a Jewish communal favourite for forty-five years', added two floors, increasing the number of lettable bedrooms to sixty. He also added a sun lounge, a ballroom, a modern reception and enquiry hall and a passenger lift.[51] Not to be outdone, in the same year Annie Morris raised the game even further. She 'Enlarged', 'Renewed' and 'Transformed' East Cliff Court so that it became the 'most modern and up-to-date hotel'. For a while after the improvements were made, she marketed the hotel as the 'New East Cliff Court'.[52]

12. Annie Morris, proprietor of the East Cliff Court Hotel, dated 24 July 1935, standing in front of the newly-added wing. Image courtesy of Edward Hayman.

Another development was the greater number and range of guest houses. There was a wide variation in their prices and in the number of rooms available. Some offered a room or two for rent in a private home, while others were small hotels and were clearly catering for a very different section of the Jewish community. However, wherever they stood on the spectrum of accommodation, there was a continuous upgrading of the guest houses and smaller hotels. It was a completely different world from when the first Jewish boarding houses had opened in Bournemouth nearly fifty years earlier and merely offering hot and cold water in bedrooms and a sanitary licence was no longer sufficient. Many guest houses were installing central heating and had a garage, or at least a private car park. A few of the guest houses were now advertising that they were under rabbinic supervision, such as the (unnamed) guest house at 14 Carysfort Road, Boscombe, which was supervised by Rev. Fogelnest, a relative of the guest-house owners, Mr and Mrs Charles Fogelnest.[53] Several of the larger guest houses had ballrooms and resident bands, including Madeira Hall.

There was also an increasing level of competition between the proprietors, especially between the owners of the largest hotels. This can be seen in the advertisements placed in the *Jewish Chronicle* in the interwar years. The boxed advertisements became larger and wordier and there was a battle about where they appeared on the page, a battle that Annie Morris almost invariably won. Except for a few occasions, advertisements for East Cliff Court appeared at the top of the page listing the accommodation available in Bournemouth. Mrs Morris changed the descriptions of her hotel to suit the season and to appeal to different audiences. She never seemed to run out of superlatives. East Cliff Court was 'the acme of comfort', 'supreme among Jewish hotels', 'the most preferred of Jewish Guest Houses' and provided 'unsurpassed comfort'. Following her lead, advertisements for other establishments contained increasingly grandiose claims about the quality of their accommodation and the facilities they offered. Hinton Court provided 'Perfection' and the Trouville had a heated garage and also a night porter.

In addition, by the 1920s, the owners of the largest hotels had become even more prominent than they had been in the pre-war years. Several of the hotels and larger boarding houses were known by their owner's names, such as 'Steel's Hinton Court', 'Grossman's Berachah' and, in the case of the Trouville, simply 'Polakoff's'. The new generation of proprietors saw themselves as leading a fresh era in Jewish holiday accommodation. In an advertisement for Berachah, Isaac Grossman stated rather snootily, 'Boscombe is NOT Bournemouth and near the sea is NOT facing the sea'.[54] The exception to all of this was Merivale Hall, which generally maintained a lower profile. Since it was the longest standing establishment, it probably had a stable clientele and therefore had no need to compete for guests or broadcast the credentials of its proprietors.

Increasing competition in the interwar years was also reflected in the cost of staying in a Jewish hotel or guest house. Prior to the First World War, prices had been handled very discreetly. Advertisements usually stated that tariffs could be 'obtained on request'. By the 1920s, a few proprietors were beginning to advertise their charges and to mention varying rates for different times of the year ('inter-season rates', 'reduced terms', 'very special reduced inclusive terms in the month of July') and concessions for children.

As the demand for Jewish holiday accommodation continued to increase, there was a significant expansion in the number of establishments. There were now many more Bournemouth guest houses and hotels advertising in the *Jewish Chronicle* than those in the older seaside resorts. Local estate agents were regularly placing notices in the *Jewish Chronicle*, saying that they had properties on their books that were suitable for use as Jewish guest houses and hotels.[55]

Several guest-house proprietors took advantage of the booming market and invested in larger properties, such as Mr and Mrs Cress. Having let out a few rooms at their home in Wellington Road for several years, in 1932 they bought Holmleigh in Wimborne Road. Some of the owners of the larger guest houses expanded their premises and designated themselves as hotels. Astoria guest house in Westby Road run by the Risky family,[56] became the Astoria Hotel ('Risky's Astoria'), and started taking out boxed advertisements in the *Jewish Chronicle* alongside the larger establishments. During the 1930s, Mrs Stock refurbished and expanded Court Heath on the corner of Derby Road and raised its marketing profile.[57] Other larger establishments thriving at this time were Frogmore and Annerley Court, both in Christchurch Road on the East Cliff. Frogmore was run by a Mr and Mrs S. Cohen and Annerley Court was run by Woolf and Clara Galen (previously Galensky). Annerley Court was an Art Deco hotel, which Mr Galan, who had a number of other business interests in the town, built in 1934.[58] On the eve of war, Annerley Court was extended to provide forty bedrooms.[59]

13. Annerley Court Hotel, 38 Christchurch Road, run by Woolf and Clara Galen, *c*. 1935. Image courtesy of Bryan Galan.

The other way in which the stage was set for the postwar years was the emergence during the 1930s of the hotels run by proprietors who would be the 'big players' in future years. In 1930, Messrs Randolph and Balon took over Garthlands Court in Westby Road, Boscombe from Mrs B. Morris and upgraded it to make it the 'newest' and 'most modern hotel in Bournemouth'.[60] Although Mr Randolph seems to have dropped out of the enterprise, the Balon family went on to own another hotel in Bournemouth, Balon's Beacon Hotel on the seafront. In 1931, Elkan and Esther Shapiro opened the strictly orthodox Mayfair Hotel in Upper Terrace Road (close to Bobby's department store), in which they made a significant investment just before the outbreak of the Second World War.[61] In 1937, William and Fay Pantel opened the Art Deco Marlborough Hotel in Sea Road, Boscombe to provide accommodation for 'people of refined taste and modest means'.

14. The Marlborough Hotel, Sea Road, Boscombe, run by the Pantel family. Detail from image in the Flikr collection of Alwyn Ladell, https://www.flickr.com/photos/alwyn_ladell/6084934401.

However, even more significant was the opening of two 'luxury' hotels. In May 1932, it was announced that East Cliff Manor would be opening in Manor Road, managed by Ada Cohen, who had until now been running Southmoor guest house in Dean Park Road.[62] In the lead up to the Second World War, East Cliff Manor was renovated twice, including in 1935 when baths with hot and cold sea water, very fashionable at the time, were installed on all floors.[63] In 1936, Daniel Rosenthall, who in 1932 had taken over the management of Merivale Hall from his parents, announced that he was moving a short way along Meyrick Road to run the new, purpose-built Hotel Ambassador. The hotel, which would be opening in time for the December holidays would be 'far and away the largest, most luxurious and completely equipped Jewish Hotel in Europe.'[64] Within a few months, some very well-known Jews, such as Nathan Laski (the 'uncrowned king' of the Manchester Jewish community[65]), were staying at the luxurious hotel.[66]

15. East Cliff Manor Hotel, 30 Manor Road, Bournemouth (now Adelphi Court apartments), *c.* 1948. Image in the Flickr collection of Alwyn Ladell, https://www.flickr.com/photos/alwyn_ladell/14628690025.

16. Postcard showing the Ambassador Hotel, Meyrick Road, Bournemouth, *c.* 1960. Image in the Flickr collection of Alwyn Ladell, https://www.flickr.com/photos/alwyn_ladell/33501956651.

The Second World War

During 1938, the Polakoffs once again invested a large amount of capital to update and extend the Trouville, absorbing the neighbouring Garthlands Hotel. The improvements, announced in a full-page spread in the *Jewish Chronicle*, included an increased number of bedrooms (the hotel now had seventy-five bedrooms), extra dining space, a new games room, a lift to all floors and new bathrooms.[67] The Polakoffs might have regretted this major investment since, along with a number of Jewish hotels, it was soon to be requisitioned for most of the war. It was used initially to house government officials from the Home Office Aliens' Immigration and Nationality department, who had been evacuated to Bournemouth because of the bombing in London.[68] In 1942, the Trouvillle was taken over by the American Red Cross to provide a club for American soldiers 'on leave from distant points' to give them 'as near a home atmosphere as possible'.[69] Later that year, the Trouville was the venue for a large Thanksgiving Day turkey dinner.[70]

Another Jewish hotel that was requisitioned was the recently-built Hotel Ambassador, which became a club for American officers run by the American Red Cross. Towards the end of the war, the hotel was sequestered to accommodate American sailors who had survived the D-Day landings. The sailors, many of whom were former longshoremen from small American ports, were apparently startled to see how well affluent people lived.[71] In October 1942, Annie Morris announced that East Cliff Court had been requisitioned and that she had moved to accommodation where she was able to take a small number of paying guests.[72] The hotel furniture was placed in storage and the hotel was occupied by the Royal Canadian Air Force until the end of the war.[73] Some of the larger Jewish guest houses and smaller hotels were also requisitioned, including the newly-extended Annerley Court, which was used to accommodate American servicemen. D-Day planning is said to have taken place on the premises of this hotel.[74] The Miramar Hotel (previously Hinton Court) run by the Steel family was used to accommodate female personnel from the American forces. It provided breakfast in bed, a complete beauty salon and single bedrooms for nurses.[75]

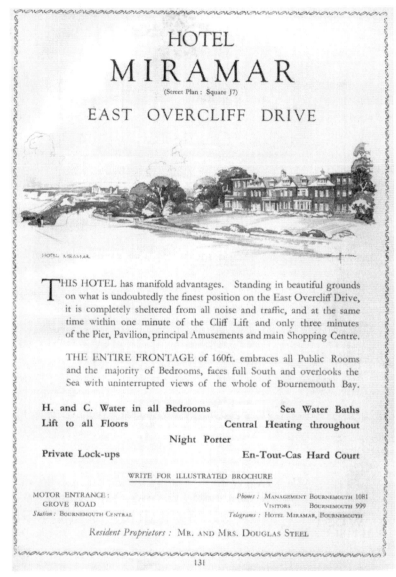

HOTEL

MIRAMAR
(Street Plan : Square J7)

EAST OVERCLIFF DRIVE

HOTEL MIRAMAR

THIS HOTEL has manifold advantages. Standing in beautiful grounds on what is undoubtedly the finest position on the East Overcliff Drive, it is completely sheltered from all noise and traffic, and at the same time within one minute of the Cliff Lift and only three minutes of the Pier, Pavilion, principal Amusements and main Shopping Centre.

THE ENTIRE FRONTAGE of 160ft. embraces all Public Rooms and the majority of Bedrooms, faces full South and overlooks the Sea with uninterrupted views of the whole of Bournemouth Bay.

H. and C. Water in all Bedrooms   Sea Water Baths

Lift to all Floors   Central Heating throughout

Night Porter

Private Lock-ups   En-Tout-Cas Hard Court

WRITE FOR ILLUSTRATED BROCHURE

MOTOR ENTRANCE :   *Phone* : MANAGEMENT BOURNEMOUTH 1081
GROVE ROAD   VISITORS   BOURNEMOUTH 999
Station : BOURNEMOUTH CENTRAL   *Telegrams* : HOTEL MIRAMAR, BOURNEMOUTH

Resident Proprietors : MR. AND MRS. DOUGLAS STEEL

131

17. Advertisement for the Hotel Miramar (previously Hinton Court), run by Mr and Mrs Douglas Steel, in the 1938 Bournemouth Guide. Image in the Flickr collection of Alwyn Ladell, https://www.flickr.com/photos/alwyn_ladell/4806135646.

The Jewish hotels and guest houses that were not requisitioned continued to operate for most of the war. There was a good market amongst Jews seeking respite from the hostilities, especially by those on leave from front-line roles. Madeira Hall offered hospitality for Canadian and American Jewish servicemen. Its owner, Miriam Lefcovitch, dubbed affectionately as 'Ma Lefco', was well known for her open door, the warmth of her welcome and her home-grown food. When she died in 1958, a former guest wrote: 'She was a real "Yiddisher Momma" to those boys, and her unfailing cheerfulness brightened the lives of many during their war service.'[76] The larger guest houses and hotels that remained open for business built air raid shelters in their basements or in their gardens. Some also had on-site air raid wardens.[77] Many of the hoteliers, such as Ada Cohen at East Cliff Manor, raised money for wartime and Jewish charities from among their guests.[78] Ada Cohen also opened East Cliff Manor to people whose homes had been destroyed by the bombing in London, some of whom subsequently became Bournemouth residents.[79] In March 1943, Lady Sassoon gave a dinner for Jewish men and women in the forces at the Jewish-owned Avon Royal Hotel in Christchurch Road, on the occasion of her birthday.[80]

However, in general, the Jewish holiday trade had a much lower profile than it had attracted in the pre-war years. Within a year of hostilities commencing, advertisements placed in the *Jewish Chronicle* by the Jewish hotels and guest houses became much smaller. The advertisements for the large hotels were the same size as those from the smallest guest houses and they were listed in alphabetical order rather than by the prominence of the establishment. This did not deter the Jewish proprietors from vying for attention. The names of the establishments were changed or the wording of the advertisements constructed so that a hotel or guest house appeared higher in the listings. One enterprising guest house worded its advertisement to commence 'A room …', which placed it at the top of the column. Towards the end of the war, the dimensions of advertisements in the *Jewish Chronicle* expanded again, but it would be a long time before the listings returned to the size of the pre-war advertisements, and before there was a clear distinction between the marketing of the large hotels and the guest houses.

As the war progressed, fewer establishments placed advertisements in the *Jewish Chronicle*. Like non-Jewish establishments, this was either because vacant space had been given over to housing evacuees and refugees, because they were filled to capacity providing accommodation for local residents who had been bombed out of their homes, or because they were taking guests from outside the town who now had to be accommodated in a smaller number of establishments. When the hotels and guest houses did have vacancies, they sometimes advertised at 'austerity prices'[81] and emphasised the opportunities that Bournemouth provided for rest and recuperation.

Despite the vagaries of war, between 1940 and 1945 a number of new Jewish establishments opened, including the Avonwood Hotel in Owls Road, Boscombe owned by Julia Cohen, who had previously run Meyrick Court,[82] and the Avon Royal Hotel in Christchurch Road, which opened at *Pesach* 1940.[83] It was run by Mr S. Fisher, previously the proprietor of the Oval Hotel in Cliftonville. He promised his guests 'assured healthy relaxation'.[84] By the end of the war, the hotel had been transferred to a Mrs Finch.[85] Several other people moved to Bournemouth to open guest houses, including Mr Gradel, proprietor of the Carmel Hotel in Margate. He opened the hundred-bedroom Grosvenor Court Hotel in St Michael's Road. Mr S. Deutsch, who had previously run the Textile Restaurant in Mortimer Street, London, opened the Harland Hotel in Derby Road.[86] Also arriving on the Bournemouth hotel scene towards the end of the war were Maurice and Fay Guild, who opened the 'strictly orthodox' Spa Hotel in Boscombe Spa Road.[87] Within two years they were to become the owners of one of the largest Jewish hotels in Bournemouth.

In the latter part of the war, the requisitioned hotels and guest houses started being returned to their owners. During 1944, the Grossmans announced that Berachah would be taking guests from the beginning of September.[88] However, it was some time before other properties were released. Annie Morris and the Hayman family were not reunited with East Cliff Court until December 1945. On seeing its dilapidation, Annie Morris cried. The garden had been dug up and was littered with sand bags. Inside the scene was even worse:

> The carpetless floor was covered with torn paper, sand and bits of old newspaper. The polished wooden counter of the reception office was scratched all over with names and drawings of hearts with arrows through them. Loose electric wires were sticking through holes in the walls and ceilings. In the lounges, the wallpaper was dirty, torn and scribbled on, with big holes eating into the plaster.[89]

Due to the state in which they found the hotel, the family was divided on whether or not they should revive the business, but Annie Morris insisted. Within two years, she had re-established the hotel so successfully that she was able to purchase the adjacent property, East Cliff Mansions (previously Kensington House and built in the same style as the former Lisle House), to use as overflow accommodation for East Cliff Court and for long lets.

18. East Cliff Mansions (previously Kensington House), 25 (later 55) Grove Road, Bournemouth, *c.* 1939. Image in the Flickr collection of Alwyn Ladell, https://www.flickr.com/photos/alwyn_ladell/8365548047.

Perhaps the most significant development during the war years was the opening in 1943 of the Green Park Hotel by Reuben (Ruby) Marriott, who had been running the Sandringham Hotel in Torquay and had developed a liking for the hospitality industry. The Green Park, which had been built during 1937 and run as a residential hotel by Saunders and Co. Ltd.,[90] was very expensive, but Ruby Marriott's accountant persuaded him that, situated on the cliff top and located close to the beach in fashionable Bournemouth, the hotel would be an excellent investment. He was to be proved correct. Ruby somehow raised the money from amongst friends, family and the banks. His son David Marriott comments: 'It was an extremely brave venture in the middle of a world war.'[91]

The hotel had been open for just a few months when the whole of what was designated as the 'Southern Area', which included Bournemouth, was closed to civilians for security reasons. Allied troops and their equipment were pouring in to the area in preparation for the forthcoming invasion of Europe. At the end of March 1944, hotels in Bournemouth were told to cancel bookings for visitors who were not exempt and to ask those who were already there to leave by 1 April.[92]

A Palace on breeze-swept cliff-top

" Palatial "—There is no fitter description of GREEN PARK, East Overcliff Drive, Bournemouth, the most delightful Jewish Hotel in all Europe, to be opened on the 1st November.

Inquiries which have already reached the proprietors (Mr. and Mrs. Reuben Marriott and Miss Helen Richman) from all parts of the country, disclose the keenest interest in this architectural gem, set in three acres of parkland and overlooking Bournemouth Bay.

The brief reference to Private Suites at GREEN PARK has evoked numerous inquiries. The fact, moreover, that each bedroom has its own private bathroom, toilet, telephone, and central heating may afford an idea of the superb standard aimed at, the deft merging of super-luxury with super-comfort in the fullest sense of the term.

And the cuisine? Be assured of its worthiness of the high standard the GREEN PARK has set itself—a magnet for the sophisticated and the exacting.

Until October 15th all inquiries to Sandringham Hotel, Torquay.

Green Park, East Overcliff Drive, Bournemouth
Tel.: Boscombe 2280 (3 lines)

19. Announcement of the opening of the Green Park Hotel, appearing in the *Jewish Chronicle*, 15 October 1943.

20. The Green Park Hotel, Manor Road, Bournemouth, *c.* 1950. Image courtesy of the Marriott family.

The Green Park had already made plans for *Pesach* and had purchased and started preparing for the *seder* on 7 April. Ruby Marriott hastily contacted the Jewish chaplains and invited British, Canadian and US Jewish servicemen stationed in the area to the Green Park for a *seder*.[93] Recalling the event, David Marriott says: 'The tables were all prepared when the troops entered the dining room. To the horror of the chaplains and before they could stop them, the troops ate all the *seder* dishes. Fortunately, they were quickly replenished. The servicemen made a real fuss of me, plying me with memorabilia.'[94]

Despite this initial setback and the suspicion with which the Green Park
was regarded by some of the longer-established Jewish hoteliers, especially
by Annie Morris at East Cliff Court who saw it as unwelcome competition,[95]
the hotel re-opened shortly after D-Day, signalling the beginning of the
'Golden Era' of Jewish hotels in Bournemouth.

Notes

1. Elaine Rosa Smith, 'East End Jews in Politics, 1918–1939: A Study in Class and
    Ethnicity' (PhD thesis, University of Leicester, 1990), p.24.
2. David Cesarani, 'A Funny Thing Happened on the Way to the Suburbs: Social Change
    in Anglo-Jewry Between the Wars, 1914-1945', *Jewish Culture and History*, Vol.1,
    No.1, p.8.
3. See Pam Fox, *The Jewish Community of Golders Green, A Social History* (Stroud: The
    History Press, 2016), p.186.
4. *Ibid.*, p.188.
5. This account of Bournemouth during the First World War is largely based on information
    provided in M. A. Edgington, *Bournemouth and the First World War, The evergreen valley,
    1914–1919* (Bournemouth: Bournemouth Local Studies Publications, 2013).
6. Quoted in *ibid.*, p.1.
7. Mate and Riddle wrote in 1910: 'mixed bathing, subject to regulation, has been one of
    the innovations of the last few years in Bournemouth'. Quoted in 'The Streets of
    Bournemouth: Tourism and the Town', https://www.streets-of-bournemouth.org.uk/
    wp-content/uploads/2018/02/Tourism.and_.Town_.pdf.
8. *Ibid.*
9. *Ibid.*
10. Both the converted and the new properties were held on long leases from the Meyrick
    Estate, which once restricted the East Cliff to residential properties.
11. See 'The Streets of Bournemouth: Tourism and the Town'.
12. See https://en.wikipedia.org/wiki/Pines_Express.
13. See https://en.wikipedia.org/wiki/Bournemouth_Belle.
14. See 'The Streets of Bournemouth: Tourism and the Town'.
15. Information on Bournemouth during the Second World War is largely based on
    accounts given in M.A. Edgington, *Bournemouth and the Second World War, 1939–
    1945* (Bournemouth: Bournemouth Local Studies Publications, 2013).
16. See 'The Streets of Bournemouth: Tourism and the Town'.
17. Quoted in *ibid.*
18. Manuscript, provided by Rhona Taylor, 8. 5. 2020.
19. *JC*, 9.4.1937.
20. *JC*, 21.5.1937.
21. *JC*, 28.4.1938.
22. 'The Streets of Bournemouth: The Town's Communities', https://www.streets-of-
    bournemouth.org.uk/wp-content/uploads/2018/02/Towns.Communities.pdf.
23. 'The Streets of Bournemouth: Commerce and Industry', https://www.streets-of-
    bournemouth.org.uk/wp-content/uploads/2018/02/Commerce.Industry.pdf.
24. *JC*, 3.2.1939.

25. *JC,* 13.1.1939.
26. *JC,* 7.6.1940.
27. *JC,* 18.6.1943.
28. *JC,* 12.4.1996.
29. See 'The Streets of Bournemouth: The Town's Communities'.
30. *JC,* 27.10.1914.
31. *JC,* 29.6.1917.
32. *JC,* 24.3.1916.
33. *JC,* 28.12.1917.
34. *JC,* 11.7.1919.
35. *JC,* 27.1.1922.
36. *JC,* 1.5.1914.
37. *JC,* 3.5.1918.
38. See Appendix 1 for information on the name change. Annie Morris might have called Maison Leontine after Lady Leontine Sassoon, a member of the 'Jewish aristocracy' who had a home, Keythorpe, 25 Manor Road at this time.
39. *JC,* 6.9.1918.
40. *JC,* 19.5.1922.
41. *JC,* 31.3.1922.
42. *JC,* 31 .3.1922.
43. *JC,* 19.3.1923.
44. Interview with Rhona Taylor, 6. 5. 2020.
45. Conversation with Hilary Myers, 30. 11. 2020.
46. *JC,* 25.12.1925.
47. *JC,* 25.12.1925.
48. Notes from Edward Hayman, sent by email, 24. 8. 2020.
49. *JC,* 17.5.1935.
50. *JC,* 5.7.1931.
51. *JC,* 7.6.1935.
52. *JC,* 25.10.1935.
53. *JC,* 20.7.1934.
54. *JC,* 24.6.1927.
55. For example, *JC,* 1.4.1932.
56. The family had previously run a smaller guest house called 'Seven' on the opposite side of Westby Road.
57. *JC,* 14.4.1933.
58. Email from Bryan Galan, grandson of Woolf and Clara Galan, 9. 7. 2020.
59. *JC,* 21.6.1940.
60. *JC,* 20.5.1930 and 3.7.1931.
61. *JC,* 15.9.1939.
62. *JC,* 27.5.1932.
63. *JC,* 17.1.1936.
64. *JC,* 21.10.1936.
65. See http://www.manchesterjewishstudies.org/nathan-laski/
66. *JC,* 9.4.1937.
67. *JC,* 30.12.1938.
68. See Edgington, *Bournemouth and the Second World War,* p.23.

69. *Ibid.,* p.63.
70. *Ibid.,* p.92.
71. Walter H. Diamond, *One of a Kind: Learning the Secrets of World Leaders* (Syracuse, NY: Syracuse University Press, 2005), p.66.
72. *JC,* 9.10.1942. They moved to a house called Fremington on the West Cliff.
73. See Edgington, *Bournemouth and the Second World War,* p.48.
74. Email from Bryan Galan, 9. 7. 2020. The hotel was sold after the war to a non-Jewish hotelier.
75. Vincent May and Jan Marsh (eds), *Bournemouth 1820–2010, From Smugglers to Surfers* (Wimborne Minister: Dovecote Press, 2010), p131. After the war, the Miramar continued to be run by the Steel family as a non-kosher hotel.
76. *JC,* 31.1.1959.
77. Information taken from advertisements in the *Jewish Chronicle.*
78. *JC,* 1.3.1940.
79. Email from Anne Filer, 1. 5. 2020.
80. *JC,* 19.3.1943.
81. *JC,* 18.12.1942.
82. *JC,* 19.2.1943.
83. It is reputed to have been visited by royalty in the nineteenth century. Jackie Edwards, *A Bed by the Sea: A History of Bournemouth's Hotels* (Christchurch: Natula Publications, 2010), p.136.
84. *JC,* 13.3.1940.
85. *JC,* 19.10.1945.
86. *JC,* 22.6.1945.
87. *JC,* 8.9.1944.
88. *JC,* 8.9.1944.
89. Ronald Hayman, *Secrets: Boyhood in a Jewish Hotel, 1932–1954* (London: Peter Owen, 1985), p.115.
90. From a listing in the *London Gazette* in December 1938, it appears that the hotel was open during that year but was probably not in operation when the 1939 Mates Guide to Bournemouth was published. It is first listed in 1940 Mate's Guide as the Green Park Residential Hotel. The guide books of these years also tell us that the hotel was built on land formerly occupied by a property named West Chevin. The hotel is listed under the name of J. W. Saunders. The Green Park is listed in Kelly's street guide for 1944 (which would have been compiled during 1943 before the hotel was put up for sale) as being owned by J. M. Saunders. This difference in the names might have been due to a typographical error in one of the guides.
91. Interview with David Marriott, 11. 5. 2020. At this time, most of the hotels located on the East Cliff were owned leasehold rather than freehold.
92. See Edgington, *Bournemouth and the Second World War,* p.87.
93. Ilana Lee, 'Diamonds at Breakfast', *Jewish Quarterly,* Vol. 54, No. 1, p.26.
94. Interview with David Marriott, 11. 5. 2020.
95. Notes from Edward Hayman, sent by email, 24. 8. 2020.

3

The Golden Era, 1945-1975:
The Larger Hotels

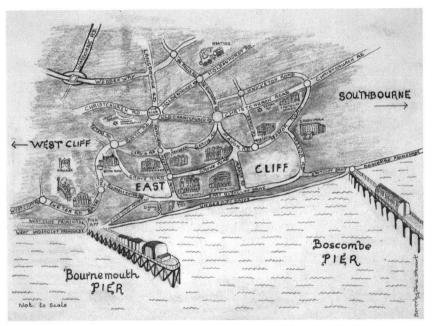

Illustration 1. Map showing location of the larger Jewish hotels and other important landmarks in Bournemouth. Drawing by Beverley-Jane Stewart.

The Anglo-Jewish Community in the Postwar Years

We have seen how, during the pre-war years, the Anglo-Jewish community experienced steady progress, becoming generally, although not uniformly, more affluent and middle class. By 1945, there was hardly a sphere of life to which Jews were not making a major contribution. Leadership of the community was passing into the hands of those whose parents had come to the country as immigrants instead of being dominated by a small group of acculturated grandees who had all but disappeared from public view. London Jewry retained its predominance in terms of numbers as well as influence, but it was now highly suburbanised.

During the immediate postwar period, the Anglo-Jewish community as a whole continued to flourish economically and socially, despite the years of austerity that followed the end of the war. However, the community was haunted by the Holocaust. The Jews of Britain now constituted the only intact Jewish community in Europe, and it was also the largest apart from the Jews remaining in the USSR. This leadership position weighed heavily on the community's shoulders.

Although there were things to forget, many Jews were soon ready to look to the future instead of the past. The community was fully committed to playing its part in rebuilding the country and set about doing so with great energy. Many Jews both prospered and played a pivotal role in revitalising the postwar British economy. Within a few years of the war ending, successful Jews were looking to relax and reap the benefits of their hard work. 'After the Blitz, here comes the Ritz' was a popular saying at the time.

During the 1950s, the Anglo-Jewish community rose to an estimated all-time high of 425,000.[1] Over the next two decades, the community spread geographically in urban centres, but began to decline in numbers. This decline was due to various factors: an excess of deaths over births, increasing intermarriage, which was making communal leaders concerned about the erosion of Jewish identity; and, towards the end of the period, emigration to Israel.[2] A predominantly middle-class, suburban Jewish lifestyle was now fully established. This was not the result of a merger between the rapidly shrinking 'old community' and the immigrant community, but a distinctive social formation forged by people with changed aspirations, who moved in new circles and made their living in different ways.

The 1950s were a very good decade for Britain in general and for its Jewish community. There was a new monarch on the throne, the National Health Service had been established and rationing finally ended in 1953. The mood was much more hopeful than it had been ten years earlier. It was an age of increasing affluence and Jews who had money to spend were enjoying the new luxuries now available, including car ownership and a greater range of leisure opportunities. By the mid-1950s, an ever-increasing number of Jews were taking holidays. Those families who could not immediately afford to holiday in Bournemouth continued to stay in places such as Westcliff-on-Sea, Brighton and Hove and Cliftonville in the

South East, in Whitley Bay in the North East and in Blackpool, St Anne's and resorts on the north coast of Wales for Jews living in the North West. However, as soon as possible, Jews made their way to the premier resort of Bournemouth, which became increasingly popular with Jews at the expense of other resorts.

The children of the postwar generation, the so-called 'baby-boomers', who came of age during the 1960s, had a very different outlook from their parents. They had not experienced first-hand the austerity of the postwar years and were caught up in the new ideas, fashions and music of the era, which Jews had helped to create. Jews were prominent in both the fashion and music industry, including the fashion stylist Cecil Gee (born Sasha Goldstein) and the music entrepreneur Brian Epstein, who were regular guests at the Jewish hotels in Bournemouth. The children of former continental refugees were particularly pivotal in developing the new technical and engineering industries that emerged in these years, and in the arts and culture. For the younger, more liberated generation, Bournemouth was a place to have fun, to socialise and, hopefully, find a partner.

However, the 1960s meant more to young Jews than mini-skirts and pop songs. There was an outpouring of support for Israel during the Six-Day War in 1967. Many Jews were apprehensive that there could be a second Holocaust and that what had become a place of refuge was under threat with armies massing on Israel's borders and the Egyptian president Nasser vowing to drive Israel into the sea. Ironically, the great pride in Israel that resulted from its 1967 victory, and which was reinforced by the outcome of the Yom Kippur War of 1973, was one of the factors that led eventually to the decline of the Jewish hotels in Bournemouth, as discussed in Chapter 5.

Bournemouth After the War

The guide sent out to prospective visitors to Bournemouth in 1946 was a reissue of the 1939 guide. Its publishers sought to reassure people that much of the pre-war entertainment had reopened, but stressed that visitors should bring their ration books with them.[3] It soon became evident that people were determined to have a holiday despite the somewhat neglected state of the beaches and short supply of accommodation. A number of hotels came on the market because their previous owners found it difficult to settle back into running them when they were returned to them, having been requisitioned during the war. The hotels were quickly purchased by people who were optimistic about Bournemouth's future as a holiday resort.

Repair of bomb damage commenced in 1947 and tourism picked up despite complaints from hoteliers about Bournemouth Corporation's apparent unwillingness to spend money on advertising holiday accommodation. By the 1950s, Bournemouth was boasting a million visitors a year. The general holiday trade was different both from the pre-war years and from the burgeoning Jewish holiday trade. Whereas many of the larger Jewish hotels were offering 'all-inclusive' packages and were catering for the increasingly affluent sections of the Jewish community, the non-Jewish hotels found themselves having to adapt to a changed market. The number of wealthy people, who had previously visited for extended periods during the late autumn and over the winter months, was significantly reduced. Instead, the hotels were now welcoming coach parties. In addition, the visitors were mainly seeking bed, breakfast and an evening meal rather than full board. As a result, there was a proliferation of smaller establishments and a reduction in the number of larger hotels.[4]

Whereas the quality of service and the facilities were of paramount importance in the newer Jewish establishments, a survey of holiday accommodation in the town conducted by the British Tourist Holiday Board in 1950 was critical of standards of service, comfort and amenities.[5] Visitors from abroad during the 1950s complained about the lack of private bathrooms, inadequate heating in the bedrooms and poorly-cooked food.[6] These deficiencies, together with rising prices resulting from increasing electricity, gas and staffing costs, meant that the non-Jewish postwar holiday trade was slow to take off.

The situation changed rapidly during the 1960s when entertainment in Bournemouth became plentiful. There were four theatres: The Pavilion (built in 1929) staging West End shows, ballet, opera, pantomime and offering a ballroom and a tea lounge; the New Royal presenting summer shows; the Palace Court specialising in modern plays; and the Hippodrome enacting variety performances. The Winter Gardens was home to the Bournemouth Symphony Orchestra and shows featuring radio and television stars. This, together with the improved financial climate, helped to attract large numbers of visitors to Bournemouth. As a result, there was now a shortage of accommodation and Bournemouth guidebooks were advising visitors to stagger their holidays instead of all arriving in the busy summer season.

Although more families were making Bournemouth their destination of choice, rising incomes and improved social conditions meant that the hotels and guest houses still had to find ways of attracting the attention of increasingly selective visitors. The hoteliers and guest-house owners offered inducements, such as modern bedrooms, spacious lounges, interior-sprung mattresses, efficient central heating and plentiful food.[7] Bournemouth was once again a prosperous resort and had one of Britain's best shopping centres. It had not been an easy journey for the town, but just as it was reaching the pinnacle of its popularity, forces were already at play that would have a major impact on its fortunes, to be discussed in Chapter 5.

Bournemouth's Jewish Community

By way of context for the evolution of Jewish hotels during the three decades following the end of the Second World War, this section looks at the development of the Jewish community in Bournemouth over that period.

With the war over, three young ex-servicemen who had returned to Bournemouth, started the 5705 Club (named after the Hebrew year in 1945), which met in the hall attached to the synagogue in Wootton Gardens.[8] For fifteen years it provided a full programme of social, cultural and sporting activities, mainly aimed at young people with the aim of preventing mixed marriages. Between 1945 and 1960, about sixty marriages resulted from club meetings.[9]

In the postwar years, BHC continued to thrive, and by 1960 its *cheder* was teaching over 100 children.[10] In 1962, the synagogue was rebuilt to house 1,000 worshippers and in 1973, the congregation purchased the neighbouring Windsor Hotel, which it demolished and built a second, larger synagogue hall and additional classrooms. The new building was named the Murray Muscat Centre.[11] The expansion of BHC resulted from an increasing number of people moving to Bournemouth, either to retire or because of the quality of life in the town. The Bournemouth community also included a number of Holocaust survivors, including the Austrian Jew Rudolf Schwarz, who in 1947 became Bournemouth's municipal director of music.[12] There were several Jewish social clubs in the town that helped the newcomers to put down roots.

Not all of the newcomers were orthodox in their Jewish outlook. In 1947, the first progressive services were held in Bournemouth. They took place in the hall of Trinity Church in Old Christchurch Road. The nascent community grew and the following year Rev. Charles Berg was appointed as the community's first minister. In 1958, a purpose-built Reform synagogue was consecrated in Christchurch Road, Boscombe.[13]

Illustration 2. The Bournemouth Synagogues, Bournemouth Hebrew Congregation and Bournemouth Reform Synagogue. Drawing by Beverley-Jane Stewart.

During the decades after the Second World War, the Bournemouth community became very self-sufficient. There was a wide range of communal bodies, covering all aspects of Jewish life. In 1950, additional burial space was obtained in Kinson and prayer houses were built both there and in the original cemetery in Boscombe.[14] The community (together with the kosher hotel trade, to be discussed later) was able to sustain three kosher butchers – Kays (Christchurch Road), Kesselmans (Curzon Road) and Zadels (Holdenhurst Road) – and its own abattoir, plus a number of Jewish bakeries and delicatessens (see Chapter 9).

The community was generally very Zionist in its outlook and there was a great deal of fundraising for Israel. Although the community became more prosperous overall, some families were less well off than others, which was reflected in the organisations to which they were affiliated and around which their social life was mainly organised. The more affluent families tended to belong to Bournemouth B'nai B'rith (Jewish lodge) and its youth chapter BBYO (B'nai B'rith Youth Organisation), while the less wealthy couples and their children were usually involved with the social (as opposed to the ceremonial) activities of AJEX (Association of Jewish Ex-Servicemen and Women) and HaNoar HaTzion (a Zionist youth movement).[15] Some families did not manage to make a living in Bournemouth and moved to other areas, such as to Ilford and other parts of Essex.[16] The more observant families enrolled their children in the Bournemouth branch of B'nei Akivah, which was run by Alec Kesselman, who was then a kosher butcher in the town.

As the community grew, it gradually relocated across the town. Whereas previously, Jewish families had largely lived in Winton and then Boscombe, a large proportion now lived on the fashionable East Cliff, often moving into the newly-built apartments that were gradually replacing the hotels. More wealthy families tended to live in Talbot Woods.

By the 1970s, many young people were leaving Bournemouth to go to university or to pursue careers elsewhere. There was now little interest amongst the younger generation in entering the family businesses that had been a feature of the town's economy for several decades.

The 'Big Eight' Hotels

In the previous two chapters we have seen how the first Jewish boarding houses in Bournemouth became larger guest houses, which in turn evolved into hotels that became ever more luxurious. After the Second World War, the largest hotels, East Cliff Court, the Ambassador, East Cliff Manor and the Green Park were joined by four other Jewish hotels to form what was retrospectively referred to as the 'Big Eight'. Located on the East Cliff, which became known as 'The Jewish Mile', these hotels gained a national (and international) reputation for being the epitome of luxury with their gracious living and sumptuous menus. By 1950, the eight hotels were offering a standard of excellence not seen anywhere outside the USA. According to one commentator, the hotels opened new horizons for Jews because they were 'so unique and so lovely'.[17] They were often compared to the legendary Jewish hotels operating at about the same time in the Catskill Mountains (referred to as the 'Borscht Belt' or the 'Jewish Alps') in upstate New York (see Chapter 10 for a detailed comparison between the Bournemouth hotels and the Catskill resorts).

The four hotels that joined the four pre-war luxury hotels were the Majestic, the Langham, the Normandie and the Cumberland. Having previously been run by Mr and Mrs Simcock, in 1946 the Majestic Hotel (then known as the Hotel Majestic), located on the corner of Derby Road and Manor Road, was purchased by a partnership that included the Shulman, Selby and Schneider families. In the same year, Maurice and Fay

Guild, who as previously mentioned had been running the Spa Hotel in Boscombe, purchased the Langham from the Mayger family. It was located on the corner of Meyrick and Grove roads, opposite the Ambassador. After Maurice's death in 1964, Fay Guild ran the Langham until 1968, when it became the Queens Hotel.[18]

21. Fay and Ben Schneider, proprietors of the Majestic Hotel, Derby Road, Bournemouth, *c.* 1948. Image courtesy of Shirley Davidson, Fay and Ben's daughter.

22. The Majestic Hotel, Derby Road, Bournemouth. Image in the Flickr collection of Alwyn Ladell, https://www.flickr.com/photos/alwyn_ladell/14473817039.

23. Fay and Maurice Guild, proprietors of the Langham Hotel, Meyrick Road, Bournemouth, *c*. 1955. Photograph courtesy of Andy Kalmus, Fay Guild's niece.

24. The Langham Hotel, Meyrick Road, Bournemouth, *c.* 1960. Image courtesy of Andy Kalmus, Fay Guild's niece.

Again in 1945, Robert (Bob) and Julia (Jules) Myers, who had previously run a hotel called Hotel Rivoli,[19] purchased the Normandie Hotel (then known as the Hotel Normandie), located on the corner of Manor Road and East Overcliff Drive. It had previously been owned by the Walker family. The last of the Big Eight to open as a kosher hotel was the Cumberland Hotel in Overcliff Drive. During the war, the hotel had been used by the Royal Army Pay Corps. It was purchased in 1947 by Joe Lipman, who soon afterwards went into partnership with the Feld family. The hotel opened as a kosher hotel under the direction of Bluma and Isaac Feld in 1949, with Joe Lipman as a sleeping partner. The Felds later went into partnership with their son-in-law, Howard Inverne.

25. Advertisement for the Cumberland in the classified section of the Yiddish newspaper *Di Zeit* in 1949. It notifies readers that the Cumberland has recently been acquired by the owners of Feld's Restaurant at 128 Whitechapel Road and encourages people to book for *Pesach* (Passover). Image courtesy of Jeffrey Maynard: https://jewishmiscellanies. com/2020/09/29/di-zeit-yiddish-daily-newspaper-london-1949-advertisements-and-classified/.

26. The Cumberland Hotel, East Overcliff Drive, Bournemouth, *c.* 1965. Image in the Flickr collection of Alwyn Ladell, https://www.flickr.com/photos/alwyn_ladell/5458282320.

27. Bluma and Isaac Feld, proprietors of the Cumberland Hotel, 20 East Overcliff Drive, Bournemouth, *c.*1950. Image courtesy of Geoffrey Feld.

The Ambassador, which had been requisitioned during the war, reopened in July 1946. At the reopening event, it was announced that the hotel was now owned by a board of directors headed by Bertram Levitus, who had been a prominent member of the Glasgow Jewish community and was hoping to contribute to the Jewish community of Bournemouth.[20]

The Trouville was vacated in November 1945, but by then its previous owners, the Polakoffs, had decided to sell it.[21] The hotel was placed on the market and purchased by Mr M. Lever and his partner Mr I. Woolf, who refurbished the hotel and received their first guests for *Pesach* 1946.[22] There were clearly difficulties with the partnership. In July 1946, it was announced that the hotel was to be sold.[23] Two months later, Mr and Mrs Woolf placed a notice in the *Jewish Chronicle* to say that the hotel was not for sale and they were now the sole owners.[24] However, by the end of the year, the hotel had been purchased by non-Jewish owners. Since the Trouville was a very large and luxurious hotel, had it remained in business as a kosher establishment, the Big Eight would have been the Big Nine.

Over the period between 1945 and 1975 some of the Big Eight hotels experienced changes of ownership and management. In 1969, the Majestic was purchased by the Feld family and run in tandem with the Cumberland until 1973 when it was sold to a development company. In 1958, ownership of the Normandie passed from the Myers family to Nathan (Nat) and Gertie Lee who managed it with the Lee's daughter and son-in-law, Belle and Louis (Lou) Keyne. Following the death of Nat Lee in 1968, the Keynes took over the hotel and ran it with their partners, Ron and Ann Fisher. In 1953, directorship of East Cliff Court transferred from Annie Morris to her daughter Sadie Hayman.

28. Gathering shortly after the Normandie Hotel, Manor Road, Bournemouth was sold by the Myers family to the Lee and Keyne families in 1958. From left to right clockwise: Nathan Lee, Robert Myers, Gertie Lee, Belle Keyne, Louis Keyne, Julia Myers. Image courtesy of Simon Keyne.

The ownership history of the Ambassador is more complicated. In 1948 the Levitus family sold the Ambassador to a consortium of owners that included non-Jews. A new company bought the hotel in 1958. In 1966, the hotel was purchased by Nat Lee, who owned it for just a year before selling it to Hyman (Hymie) Selby, who had previously part-owned the Majestic.

Hymie Selby changed the name of the hotel to the New Ambassador and ran it with his wife Nettie and his stepdaughter and her husband, Joy and Sefton Eagell. The hotel was sold in 1971 to Alfred (Alf) and Sadie Vickers (née Coren) and their partners, Max and Yvonne Green. The Eagells remained involved in the running of the hotel.

More detailed histories of each of the Big Eight hotels and their owners can be found in Appendix 1.

The Big Eight Hotels' Clientele

For over thirty years, the Big Eight hotels attracted thousands of guests each year, who often returned again and again to Bournemouth. Geoffrey Alderman comments:

> Once upon a time, if you were Jewish and you had a bit of money to spare, you would pop into a travel agent and ask to see all their brochures. You would carefully weigh up the options and then decide to go to one of the big kosher hotels in Bournemouth, just as you usually did.[25]

The regular hotel guests included numerous famous people – captains of industry, eminent business people, leading professionals, well-known rabbis and *dayanim* (religious judges), peers, communal and political leaders, and the top people involved in music, the arts and fashion. Others were less famous, but were nonetheless treasured and valued by the hoteliers.[26] The guests frequently stayed in the same rooms, at the same hotels and at the same time for several years in succession. They often came as part of extended or inter-generational family groups. Hettie Marks recalls:

> When the children were grown up and had families of their own, we sometimes rented a suite at one of the hotels so that we could be together. The Green Park had a particularly lovely suite with a delightful lounge with a sea view. It was large enough to take us all. Many of the hotels had tables in their dining rooms that were reserved for large family groups.[27]

Peter Fine from Manchester, who stayed at East Cliff Court on several occasions with his family, recalls that his parents occupied the same bedroom several times, a room at the front of the hotel that had the word 'Court' on its balcony.[28]

Each of the hotels became popular with people from particular parts of the country. For example, the Normandie became the rendezvous for families from Manchester and some from Hull, while families from Leeds tended to stay in the Majestic. One former visitor comments: 'It was all very tribal.'[29] The Ambassador was the favourite hotel amongst continental Jews due to the fact that the resident director for many years was the 'ebullient' Erwin Rubinstein ('Ruby'), himself a former German refugee from Konigsberg, and his wife Gertrud.[30] Peter Phillips recalls: 'My parents, who always went to the Ambassador, called him "Herr Rubinstein"!'[31] The hotel promoted its 'continental atmosphere' in the journal produced by the Association of Jewish Refugees (AJR).[32]

Although it was not a large proportion of their business, the hotels attracted guests from abroad, especially from Europe, the United States, South America and countries then forming part of the British Commonwealth. Foreign guests often stayed in the hotels during the main Jewish festivals and holidays. Joan Doubtfire (née White), who was a receptionist at the Cumberland (see later mention), recalls receiving a telegram from a French couple seeking to make a reservation for *Yom Kippur*: 'Something went a little awry in the translation because when it arrived, it read that they wanted to make a booking for someone called Tim Kipper!'[33] People from abroad also arrived at other times, often having disembarked from cruise ships docking at nearby Southampton. In his 1950 monograph documenting his stay at the Ambassador, Louis Golding commented rather tongue in cheek:

> Here they can recover (they learn with joy) from the ardours of a rough voyage. They can build themselves up after a gruelling year in preparation for a gruelling sight-seeing tour. Or here they can build themselves up again after one of those strenuous holidays of theatre and night-club in London, which can be much more devastatingly hard work than mere work. Here, moreover, they can be beautifully emancipated from the sort of slight to which Jews are sometimes subjected in similar hotels in less serene countries than ours.[34]

Later on, the Green Park set out specifically to attract guests from America. Barbara Glyn, the daughter of Ruby and Sarah Marriott, recalls that as a result of her parent's trip to New York in 1972, many prominent American families came to stay at the hotel.[35]

During the winter months, the hotels took group bookings from charities, synagogues, masonic lodges and other groupings. Stuart March recalls:

> For four years during the late 1960s, I stayed at the Majestic in February when market people from up and down the country gathered there for a week and had a whale of a time. The hotel organised a really good dance band for us. During the day it was a bit like a scene from *Dirty Dancing*. The men played cards and the women sat around talking or went shopping.[36]

Throughout the year, people stayed in the hotels to recuperate from illness, trauma or tragedy. Morella Kayman, who as a child stayed with her parents in several of the large hotels, recalls:

> Bournemouth had always been a very special place for me and I would go there for a week here and there – generally when I had split-up with a boyfriend. I'd take a little suitcase and a tapestry kit and shut myself away to take my mind off my broken heart. Judging by the number of cushions I made, I think my heart was broken far too many times![37]

Although the vast majority of their guests were Jewish, the hotels also welcomed non-Jewish people. They were usually people whom the hoteliers knew, or were the friends of their regular guests. Paul Harris comments: 'A member of the pop group *The Bachelors* sometimes stayed in the Majestic because he was a friend of Fay Schneider'.[38] David Marriott recalls: 'The non-Jewish guests at the Green Park respected and enjoyed Jewish traditions and were happy to join in with the atmosphere. They apparently also loved the food'.[39] Similarly, Richard Inverne remembers:

> We once had an enquiry at the Cumberland from a non-Jewish couple about staying at the hotel. They asked us to explain what was different about staying in a Jewish hotel. Searching for a simple answer, we said that the main difference was probably that there was no bacon for breakfast! They said that this wasn't a problem since they were vegetarians. When they came to stay with us, they were treated like celebrities and they loved it.[40]

However, other hotels were not as welcoming of people whom they thought were non-Jews. Michael Zeffertt recalls that when he and a group of friends arrived at the Langham in 1961, Fay Guild asked them if they realised that they had come to a strictly orthodox Jewish hotel: 'She was obviously concerned that I didn't look Jewish enough. I replied "Oh yes, I fully understand. Excuse me a moment", whereupon I ushered in one of my rather more acceptably Semitic-looking friends and everyone breathed a sigh of relief'.[41] Edward Hayman recalls:

> At one point we tried to get East Cliff Court included in the AA list of hotels, but failed to do so because they sent representatives incognito who, as non-Jews, were discouraged from staying by the longstanding receptionist Miss White! We did not refuse non-Jews, but very seldom had them to stay.[42]

Young Children and Teenagers

In the two decades following the Second World War, children and teenagers formed an important part of the clientele of the Big Eight hotels. Young people looked forward so much to their time in Bournemouth that they were prepared to change other plans to be there:

> I had my *Bar Mitzvah* photos taken in the *shul* at the Normandie, because we went away on holiday straight after my *Bar Mitzvah* service in Manchester. The date of the *Bar Mitzvah* was changed to fit in with our holiday. This meant that I had to learn a different *sedra* [portion of text], but I didn't mind because the summer holiday in Bournemouth was really important.[43]

However, while some of the hotels positively welcomed family groups and had arrangements for caring for and entertaining children (see Chapter 8), others were less 'child friendly'. The Green Park in particular was seen as being more welcoming of adults than of children. David Abrahams comments:

> The Green Park was definitely not geared up for children. It was for middle-aged and older people, who wanted to relax away from the hurly burly of their businesses. Although it was always full, it was very quiet. People came for the tranquility, not to cope with noisy children who might interrupt their card games, which were a big thing in the hotel. My parents, who ran a nightclub in Newcastle, valued the peace and quiet at the hotel.[44]

Similarly, Elissa Bayer recalls: 'The Green Park was very dignified, quiet and respectable, but not very comfortable for children. It was a bit like a library. People said "shush!" if anyone made too much noise.'[45] Apparently children were banned from some rooms. Frances Israel remembers: 'My brother once making his way into the Green Room (the hotel's main lounge), and running around with great excitement because he'd got in.'[46] Another interviewee commented: 'Children had to be seen and not heard or Mr Marriott would have a word with their parents!'[47]

At the Cumberland, during the summer months, Isaac Feld limited the number of children staying in the hotel. Geoffrey Feld tells us: 'He instructed the head receptionist at the beginning of the summer season how many could be accepted: twenty in June, fifteen in July and ten in August. There was a price to pay if his instructions were ignored!'[48]

By contrast, the Langham was very popular amongst families with young children. Marilyn Murray, who stayed at the hotel several times with her parents, her sister, her aunt and uncle and her two cousins, recalls that there were often dozens of children running around and making a lot of noise: 'On one occasion, the hotel owner Maurice Guild rounded up all the children and ushered them into the ballroom. He said that he would give a sixpence to the child who could stay quiet for the longest. As we sat in silence, our parents were peeping around the door, laughing at the spectacle of us being quiet.'[49]

Some of the families who stayed at the Langham brought their nannies with them to enable them to relax. The nannies did not stay at the hotel but at the smaller establishment, Gale's Private Hotel, run by Fay Guild's sister Golda and brother-in-law, Harry Gale (see Chapter 4).[50]

During the 1960s, the Normandie became more congenial for young people when its management passed from one generation to the next. Nat Lee, who ran the hotel with his wife Gertie until the 1966, was seen by young people as 'absolutely terrifying'. Paul Harris recalls: 'He did not seem to like children, which was unfortunate since the main clientele of the hotel was people with young families! His daughter Belle and son-in-law Lou Keyne had their own teenagers and were more understanding.'[51] Nat Lee's granddaughter confirms: 'He was of the opinion that children should be seen and not heard. He was very strict with us and his blue eyes didn't miss anything. If we were late for dinner, he wanted to know why.'[52]

Young people who stayed in the hotels with their families in the decades following the end of the Second World War frequently returned to the hotels when they were older and had families of their own. Many young people who holidayed in the hotels met their future partners there (see Chapter 8), and subsequently went back to Bournemouth for their honeymoons.

However, the hotels were popular with honeymooners wherever the couples met. During the 1950s and 1960s, more Jewish couples honeymooned in Bournemouth than anywhere else. Sheila Morris recalls that when she honeymooned at the Cumberland in November 1959, there were eight other honeymoon couples staying in the hotel at the same time: 'Towards the end of our week, we all got together in one of the bedrooms and drank champagne.'[53] One former hotelier says: 'To this day I still meet people who come up to me saying: "I had my honeymoon in your hotel".'[54]

Since people generally knew everyone else staying in a hotel, they were able to identify who the honeymooners were, and the honeymooners were often the object of a great deal of scrutiny. Sheila Samuels remembers: 'I stayed at the Cumberland for my honeymoon. One morning at breakfast, a woman leaned across to me and said, "I know you are newly married because your wedding ring is very shiny!"'[55] The honeymooners were warmly welcomed, but just occasionally the hotels fell short on meeting the honeymooners' expectations:

> I had my honeymoon at the Green Park in 1971. I went to pay the bill (£10 per day, all inclusive) and I gave the Richman sisters my compliments, but I had one reservation: since it was our honeymoon, I thought that they should have put a bowl of fruit or flowers in our room. The receptionist said, 'I'm sorry, I'll do it next time'. I laughed and laughed because she'd said it so deadpan, with no sense of irony.[56]

As the market began to change and the hotels started to compete for guests, enhanced facilities for children and young people were added, such as the children's playground, described as 'an amusement park in miniature', and the new games room installed at the Green Park.[57] The Cumberland shifted the focus of its entertainment programme from adults to children (see Chapter 8) and added a playroom: 'It was decorated with Muppet wallpaper and had arcade games so you could play Space Invaders for hours on end.'[58]

Bookings and Holiday Patterns

For twenty years or so, the Big Eight hotels were always full. Sometimes the hotels were so busy that they had to accommodate some of their regular guests in the annexes in their grounds, or in nearby guest houses. Jon Harris recalls:

One year, my family couldn't get into the Normandie for our normal
two weeks. We had to stay for the first few days at the nearby Fresh
Fields Hotel, which was used for overflow during the summer. We
went into the Normandie to eat and socialise since we were valued
customers. But it was still a big come down. We learned that to get
in and have the room you wanted, you had to book for the next year
as you were leaving at the end of your holiday.[59]

Life-long friendships were made at the hotels, and people often kept in
touch with each other between holidays. Families planned all year for their
next holiday in Bournemouth: 'Our annual trip took on an almost ritual
character suggestive of a pilgrimage. We sometimes went to other places in
between, but they were not the same as Bournemouth.'[60]

The bookings for the hotels ran from Sunday to Sunday. For religious
reasons, arrivals and departures could not take place on *Shabbat* (the Jewish
sabbath). An exception to the Sunday to Sunday bookings was made for
people who came from Scotland, as there were no trains travelling south
on a Sunday: 'We had a lot of people who came from Glasgow, Edinburgh
and Aberdeen. They had to book from Monday to Monday. We reserved
rooms for them.'[61] At this time, major towns had what was called 'factory
fortnights' which were staggered through the summer months. The visitors
therefore, arrived in Bournemouth on a phased basis and the hotels always
knew who was coming and when.

The hotels were full to bursting point over Christmas and New Year,
when the hotels took ten-day bookings. The guests arrived on Christmas
Eve and stayed until after New Year's Day. This was a very popular time,
not because people were celebrating in any way, but simply because people
were able to take a break then as everything was closed. The hotels went
into overdrive to organise star-studded entertainment for what was called
'the end of year holidays' (see Chapter 8).

While some people came to the hotels for their summer holidays, others
came regularly for the religious festivals, particularly for *Pesach, Shavuot*
and the autumn festivals and holy days (*Rosh Hashanah, Yom Kippur,
Sukkot* and *Simchat Torah,* collectively referred to as *Yamim Tovim,* see
glossary), when prices were higher: 'For several years my family used to
meet up for *Pesach* at the Cumberland with a crowd of their London friends.
They used to travel down to Bournemouth *en masse.*'[62] For those who could
afford to do so, it was far easier to stay in a kosher hotel than dealing with
the time-consuming preparations for *Pesach* and the comprehensive food
restrictions associated with the festival (see Chapter 7). Even when other

bookings were beginning to fall (see Chapter 5), the Green Park remained in demand over *Pesach*. In 1973, a visiting American journalist reported:

> For Passover it's almost impossible to win admission to Green Park without sterling recommendations. 'At *Pesach* we say no to everybody – and then we sort out the people we'd like to have,' explained Mr Marriott. He telephones the fortunate chosen people and asks them – with the air of a prince offering a baronetcy – if they'll be coming for Passover.[63]

The people who stayed in the hotels for Jewish festivals were generally older, more religious and wealthier than those who spent their summer holidays there, but there were exceptions. Barbara Glyn tells this story:

> One lady phoned up and spoke to my aunty Ray. She liked coming for the first two weeks in June. Aunty Ray pointed out that this year *Shavuos* would fall within that period and knowing this lady wouldn't want to be there for the festival and pay the extra cost involved, suggested she choose another time. After a prolonged argument, my aunt said rather sarcastically: 'Perhaps you'd like me to phone the Chief Rabbi and ask him to move the date of *Shavuos*.' The customer replied: 'Would you?'[64]

Pesach was a ten-day booking, but some families often stayed at the hotels for several weeks over *Yamim Tovim*. During this period, the men sometimes returned to London during the week to manage their businesses.
    Some people holidayed in Bournemouth several times a year, such as Hettie Marks. In the summer she and her husband went to Bournemouth with their children, but in February they had a week's holiday on their own:

> We ran a number of clothes shops in London, and we were very busy until 20 February, which was the end of our accountancy year. We left for Bournemouth after we had carried out the stocktaking. The hotel prices were lower in the winter, but the climate was still warmer than in London. It was a real break from the norm and being alone together allowed us to 'know' our marriage. We used to walk hand in hand along the promenade, chatting away to each other.[65]

When they first started taking holidays in Bournemouth, some people stayed at the more affordable hotels, especially when they had young children. However, as the children grew up and made their own holiday arrangements and as people became more affluent, they stayed in one of the more expensive hotels. The ultimate goal for many Jewish holidaymakers was to stay at the Green Park: 'We eventually worked our way up to the Green Park, which we couldn't afford when we were younger. It was *the* place to stay and a signal that you had arrived socially.'[66] However, some people stayed at the Green Park for more altruistic reasons: 'When I was younger, we stayed at the Cumberland because my father thought that the Green Park was a bit pretentious and a little "overdone", but when my parents were older, they stayed at the Green Park because by then my mother was very involved in a Jewish charity, Youth Aliyah, and the hotel was a good recruiting ground for committee members.'[67]

People who could not afford to stay at the Green Park and were staying elsewhere sometimes visited the hotel and tried to blend in with the people they perceived as the elite:

> You always had someone who wanted to impress his girlfriend by slipping into the Green Park to have tea in the dining room with other guests, in the garden, or by the swimming pool. They would come in dressed very smartly, and often you couldn't tell they weren't guests at the hotel. But there were certain things that would give them away, such as ordering just one pot of tea and two cups, thinking it would be too expensive to order two pots of tea, one each. Such frugality was rarely witnessed amongst regular Green Park guests, and by the time these visitors came to ask for their bill, they would usually have been unmasked.[68]

One interloper succeeded in fooling both staff and guests:

> In 1967, an unusually interesting American woman came to stay for a fortnight at the Green Park, even though she wasn't Jewish. Normally, when it was busy at Christmas, the hotel wouldn't let people they didn't know stay because the regular guests liked to stay in the rooms they usually occupied. The Richman sisters made an exception for her, as she said that she was a close friend of Brian Epstein, manager of *The Beatles*, who came to the Green Park each year. She was of a certain age but she had such a flamboyant style that you were left with the impression that she was a Hollywood actress. She befriended everyone and people talked about her constantly. She had travelled the world unlike most of us, had fantastic stories and was acquainted with many of the world's top acts

as her husband was a music agent in Los Angeles. Suddenly, one morning it was found that she had gone without paying her bill. People were up in arms. The police were called, and two weeks later the hotel received a call to say that they'd arrested her trying the same thing at the Dorchester.[69]

Some older people stayed at the Big Eight hotels for extended periods, such as Mr Potel, a clothing magnate, who was sent by his family to the Ambassador each winter to benefit from Bournemouth's mild climate: 'His chauffeur used to bring him down in his Rolls Royce in December and his family picked him up again just before *Pesach*. He came for the last time in 1969.'[70] A few people lived permanently in the hotels, such as the two older women who were cared for by Fay Schneider at the Majestic,[71] and the two women, Mrs Skolnick and Mrs Freedman, who lived permanently at the Green Park in rooms on the north side of the hotel.[72]

Marketing, Competition and Cooperation

Because they were so busy, in their heyday the Big Eight hotels did comparatively little marketing. Geoffrey Feld comments: 'There were no faxes, no internet, no mail shots. One advertisement in the *Jewish Chronicle* was enough to fill the hotel.'[73] At the commencement of the 1950s, the hotel advertisements appearing in the *Jewish Chronicle* were very understated, simply providing the name, contact details and a few words about the hotels, which was a big contrast to the pre-Second World War listings for the larger hotels (see Chapter 2). Advertisements for the Green Park were particularly minimalist. The words 'Green Park, Bournemouth' appeared in an otherwise blank box, possibly with the intention of conveying a sense of good taste.[74]

29. Advertisement for the Green Park Hotel, Manor Road, Bournemouth, appearing in the *Jewish Chronicle* several times during the early 1950s.

From 1952 onwards, the hotels started advertising in the newly-launched annual *Jewish Chronicle's Green Flag Travel Guide* as well as in the newspaper. By the end of the 1950s, the hotel advertisements in the *Jewish Chronicle* had become more elaborate, particularly those for the Normandie and the Ambassador. The advertisements for the Normandie emphasised its cuisine, while those for the Ambassador stressed its entertainment programme. As the 1950s proceeded, the boxed advertisements became larger, and were used to announce high-profile entertainers secured by each of the hotels (see Chapter 8), major refurbishments and new facilities.

In an informal understanding between the hoteliers, the most expensive of the hotels, the Green Park, set its prices and the others fixed theirs accordingly. Geoffrey Feld recalls that the Cumberland set its prices at ten shillings less than the Green Park, the owners of the Majestic and the Ambassador calculated theirs at ten shillings less than the Cumberland and the tariffs of the four other hotels were less than the Majestic and the Ambassador: 'None of the hotel owners tried to steal a march on the others in terms of their rates; they all knew their relative market position. There was no haggling; the differentials were always about the same.'[75]

The rates charged by the hotels were 'all inclusive', covering not only the accommodation but also all the meals, entertainment and room service. This meant that guests did not have to leave the hotel unless they wished to do so, and many did not. At the time that the hotels were operating, there were no credit cards and cheques did not become widely used until the late 1960s when cheque guarantee cards were introduced. People therefore settled their bills in cash. Geoffrey Feld tells this story:

> In my early days at the Cumberland, I worked on the accountancy side in the hotel. I worked from a little back office. When they checked out on a Sunday, guests had to come to the office to pay their bills. One day, an older woman came in and asked what she owed. I told her, and to my surprise she rolled up her skirt and peeled off notes from somewhere beneath it and handed me a bundle of £5 notes![76]

Guests staying in one hotel often knew people staying in another hotel, whom they visited. For a number of years, visitors were treated to free hospitality until the profit margins of the hotels became too tight to make this sustainable:

People began to abuse the system. I remember once noticing that a group of twelve people had ordered afternoon tea when only two of them were staying in the hotel. Several were staying in guest houses and non-Jewish hotels. We couldn't go on serving food for free. However, I couldn't change the situation unilaterally. So, I got the hoteliers together to talk about what we could do. Fay Schneider, Maurice Guild and Ruby Marriott all agreed that we should introduce a signing system. People didn't like it – there were squeals of protest – but they got used to it.[77]

Although the hotels cooperated on some matters, they competed fiercely with each other on the quality of their service, facilities, food and entertainment. Larry and Mandy Kaye recall: 'At one point they agreed amongst themselves to scrap the afternoon teas that they all offered to try and improve profit margins. It worked well until one of the hotels broke ranks and reintroduced free afternoon teas in a bid to attract more customers.'[78]

Travelling to Bournemouth

For people living in London and the Home Counties, as a large proportion of the hotel guests did, travelling to Bournemouth was relatively easy. As time progressed, more and more Jews from London travelled by car, the most affluent being driven by a chauffeur. However, some people still preferred to travel by train, especially on the celebrated *Bournemouth Belle*, with its Art Deco décor, well-sprung seats and tables laid out for three-course meals. It left London Waterloo mid-morning and reached Bournemouth two hours later. Hannah Jacobs recalls:

We went to Bournemouth several times with my grandparents. To begin with, we all travelled in my father's car, the men in the front and the women in the back. By the time I was seven, the luggage had increased so much that there was no longer room for everybody. So, my grandmother and I travelled down to the coast on the *Bournemouth Belle*. It took several hours, but we had refreshments on board. It was better than going in the car with my father, who refused to stop for a comfort break and who was tetchy if I was car sick.[79]

30. The *Bournemouth Belle*. Image by Ben Brooksbank, 1950, https://en.wikipedia.org/wiki/
Bournemouth_Belle#/media/File:Farnborough_Down_'Bournemouth_Belle'_geograph-
2620910-by-Ben-Brooksbank.jpg.

31. The *Pines Express*. Image by Ben Brooksbank, 1959, https://en.wikipedia.org/wiki/Pines_
Express#/media/File:Shoscombe_&_Single_Hill_Halt_'Pines_Express'_Relief_nearing_geog
raph-2671505-by-Ben-Brooksbank.jpg.

Marilyn Murray recalls to this day the distinctive smell of the carriages, the small blue glass lamps on the tables and the sense of anticipation as the train drew into Bournemouth station.[80] For many younger guests, the train journey from their homes to Bournemouth was one of the highlights of the holiday experience. Many people going from the north-west of England to Bournemouth travelled on another named train, the *Pines Express*. Paul Harris recollects:

> The first time we went to Bournemouth in the 1960s, my parents didn't tell us how they were going to get there or how long it was going to take. We boarded at London Road Station, which is now Manchester Piccadilly Station. We travelled first class and had both lunch and tea on the way. On our first trip on the *Pines Express*, we left the car at the station, but on subsequent occasions, the car was loaded onto a goods wagon at Mayfield Station in Manchester, and it was waiting for us when we arrived in Bournemouth West to use during our holiday.[81]

However, journeys to Bournemouth were not always so pleasant. Jackie Kalms (née Harris) recalls the occasion her family travelled from Hull to Bournemouth when she was aged eleven. At that time, there were no motorways or bypasses, and no air-conditioning in cars. It was a very hot day and tempers became a bit frayed. Jackie sat next to her father, reading the instructions sent by the RAC. After starting off at 7.15am, they arrived at East Cliff Court just in time for tea.[82] Families who travelled very long distances to Bournemouth often broke their journeys and stayed with relatives overnight or travelled on sleeper trains. David Abrahams recalls that the family took an overnight train from Newcastle to London and then transferred to an early morning train at Waterloo, which arrived in Bournemouth at about 11am.[83]

The Glamour

The 'dress code' in the hotels was very smart, especially for evening meals and during the Jewish festivals when guests wore their most expensive clothes. The women wore elaborate dresses (called 'gowns') with their best jewellery and fur stoles, and the men wore dinner jackets and bow ties. Mr Mimmo (Domenico Zacchia, see Chapter 6 for more information), the Italian maître d' at the Green Park kept a box of bow ties to hand out to men who arrived at the dinner table without one, and those men appearing at lunch without a tie or a jacket would be asked politely to return to their rooms and to put them on. Frances Israel recalls:

Hotel life was very grand. Everyone dressed up in their finery. It was very exciting to be part of it all. The hoteliers cultivated the rarefied atmosphere and the feeling of grandeur. It was all very different from the life we led in London, which was more relaxed and less formal. This difference made it feel very special being there.[84]

At the time, it was said that Green Park guests dressed as well as any of those to be seen at Claridge's and the other luxury hotels in London. The hotel was known for its daily fashion parades.[85] Many of the guests worked in the clothing trade and had ready access to smart and fashionable attire. There is a story that has often been told about a husband and wife, who were overheard through a bedroom wall at the Green Park:

> Wife: Maurice shall I put on my Dior or Balmain dress?
> Husband: The Dior.
> Wife: Maurice shall I put on my blonde or red wig?
> Husband: Your blonde wig.
> Wife: Maurice shall I wear my diamonds or my rubies?
> Husband: Your rubies. But hurry up or we will be late for breakfast![86]

One of the regular guests at the Cumberland was a woman who became known as 'Diamond Lil' (based on the 1928 play by Mae West) because of the amount of jewellery she brought with her to Bournemouth. Geoffrey Feld recalls:

> We had a bank of safe deposit boxes of various sizes. Diamond Lil had to have the largest one because she had so much jewellery. I have never seen so many diamonds in my life! For security reasons, the boxes had two keys, one for the guest and one for the receptionist. Diamond Lil always insisted that I should be there both when she took her jewellery out at the beginning of an evening and at the end of the entertainment when she put it back again. I sometimes had to stay up beyond midnight until she went to bed![87]

Barbara Glyn says that the hotel was a 'world apart' and tells this story:

> On one occasion, we had a call from a woman to say that she had left her jewellery in our safe. It was arranged that the family member who was next up in London, would deliver it to the guest's home. This turned out to be me. I was instructed to give the jewellery to

the woman in person rather than to anyone else who might answer the door. When I got there, the maid came to the door, and I asked to see the woman herself. When she came, I didn't recognise her. She was wearing no make-up and a dressing gown. She looked totally different from the glamorous person I knew at the Green Park.

Sheila Samuels recalls her parents telling her that when they stayed in the Cumberland shortly after it opened in 1949, they saw vans arriving from which were decanted the wardrobes of clothes to be worn during guests' holidays: 'There were rails and rails of dresses, enough for at least three changes of outfit per day, and racks of matching shoes and handbags. Those who worked in the gown trade were able to commandeer one of the firm's vans to transport everything down to Bournemouth.'[88] Sheila's mother also spoke of seeing the women in the hotel laundry room, ironing their dresses: 'She was a dressmaker and she was very interested in the quality of the dresses, especially their hems!' Betty Travis, the longstanding receptionist at the Green Park, recalls that some of the hotel's guests competed with each other, one arriving with twenty outfits and the next with thirty, and that one woman was notorious for her shoe collection: 'You knew instantly when she was going to stay in the hotel. She was always preceded by at least forty-two boxes of shoes, sometimes more. It was a big mystery to everyone – why did she need so many shoes?'[89]

Erev Shabbat (eve of the Sabbath) dinners were particularly 'dressy affairs'. On Friday afternoons, there was a mass exodus from the hotels with women going to the hairdressers in the town,[90] but one woman who stayed regularly at the Green Park, insisted that her husband drive her up to London so that she could have her hair done 'properly' and drive her back to Bournemouth in time for Friday night dinner.[91] Ronald Hayman describes evocatively a Friday night dinner at East Cliff Court:

The entrance of the visitors was like a parade past the mirror walls that multiplied the bright ceiling lights and picked up the sparkle from the dangling earrings, necklaces and bracelets. Permed hair glistened. Bosoms bulged under décolleté dresses. Diamond tie-pins and gold signet rings twinkled. I thought of the advertisement I saw in the London Underground showing six soldiers on parade: Six minds with a single thought – A Bravington ring and the girl is caught. Not these girls. I also liked watching rich men. Some looked immensely distinguished, with thick wavy, iron-grey hair, aquiline noses and delicate, fine-textured skin, as if they washed their faces in milk. Others looked tougher, more commanding, with coarse-edged voices, wide pores on their noses and confident eyes that made the waiters slightly frightened, transparently eager to please. Power endowed even ugly men with a glamour that clung like powder to their faces.[92]

Guests either brought their jewellery and furs with them or hired them from a local shop. The hotel guests included diamond merchants and couturiers, who used their holidays as an opportunity to conduct some business: 'My grandfather was a diamond merchant and he regarded the stays in the Bournemouth hotels as semi-holidays. Both my mother and my grandmother wore wonderful jewellery, enabling him to display his wares. As a result of staying in the hotels, he supplied a lot of couples with their engagement rings.'[93]

The glamour of the hotels was not confined to the adults. Marian Stern recalls: 'We used to catch the *Bournemouth Belle* at Waterloo Station at about 11.00am. Without fail, my mother would still be making me yet another outfit at 9.30am.'[94] Before going to Bournmouth, Hannah Jacobs had dresses made by Mrs Diamond in Anson Road, Cricklewood, who also made outfits for other children going to stay in the Bournemouth hotels.[95] David Abrahams recalls: 'When I went to stay at the Green Park when I was a child, I had to have my own suitcase to carry all the clothes I needed. I had several pairs of trousers – some velvet, some corduroy – for different occasions. I also had a suit and bow tie to wear for Friday night dinners.'[96]

32. David Abrahams, who stayed often at the Green Park in the late 1950s. He is pictured wearing his 'Bournemouth Suit'. Image courtesy of David Abrahams.

33. Hannah Jacobs at the Normandie Hotel, Manor Road, Bournemouth, c. 1960. Image courtesy of Hannah Jacobs (née Noorden).

The glamour of the hotels sometimes attracted the wrong kind of attention. Several times it was reported in the national press that there had been thefts of luxury items in the Big Eight hotels, including the reports of two burglaries at the Green Park in the early part of 1956. In January that year, jewellery and a mink coat, valued at a total of £9,000, were stolen from bedrooms,[97] and three months later, a burglar accessed bedrooms by climbing a drain pipe and stole jewellery and furs, including a mink coat valued at £1,000.[98] The robberies were not confined to the guest bedrooms. In 1962, it was reported that over £2,000 worth of furs had been stolen from the home of Isaac and Bluma Feld in Grove Road behind the Cumberland.[99]

The Hoteliers

Several of the Big Eight hotels were family owned and remained in the ownership of the same families for several decades. These families were very actively involved in the running of the hotels and made a point of getting to know their guests, who as a result often became close friends. Frances Israel comments: 'My uncle and my aunts [Ruby Marriott and the Richman sisters] knew everyone so well that when I went to stay at the Green Park, it was like being at a big house party rather than staying in a hotel.'[100] The hoteliers worked extremely long hours and had very little domestic life, especially those who lived on the premises, such as the Keyne family, who had a flat at the Normandie.

Many of the people who ran the hotels were powerful women, sometimes referred to as the 'Grandes Dames of Bournemouth'. They are said to have 'ruled the hotels with a rod of iron' and were 'the queen bees in an era when few women had top jobs'. While this might have surprised non-Jewish observers, their prominence was reminiscent of the role of women in the *shtetl* (Jewish village in Eastern Europe) where they were often the main breadwinners, sustaining the family while their husbands studied religious texts and kept the faith alive.

Some of the women hoteliers had experience of the hotel trade prior to managing one of the Big Eight hotels. Ada Cohen at East Cliff Manor had run the Southmoor guest house in Bournemouth; Annie Morris at East Cliff Court had been the proprietor of guest houses in both Bournemouth and Folkestone; and Sarah Marriott and Helen Richman at the Green Park had been involved in running the Sandringham Hotel in Torquay. According to one former guest, Sarah Marriott and the Richman sisters used to say that their previous 'hands-on' experience gave them confidence in managing the Green Park since it meant that they were not left in the lurch if a key member of staff was not available.[101]

Some of the other women proprietors had come to the hotels having been experienced business women in other spheres: Bluma Feld, described as 'a character of the old East End',[102] proprietor of the Cumberland, had run the very successful Feld's restaurant in Whitechapel Road whose clientele included many well-known people and which had rooms above that she used as a small boarding house.[103] Fay Schneider, owner of the Majestic, had managed a clothing factory in the East End of London; Nettie Selby at the New Ambassador had played a prominent role in the Hanover banqueting suite in central London; and Belle Keyne, co-owner of the Normandie,[104] had travelled widely, had a degree in English and had managed an engineering firm. Some young people found these powerful women 'quite scary'.[105]

The 'Grandes Dames' were always impeccably dressed: 'They never had a hair out of place and they didn't own a pair of jeans!'[106] They often ordered their outfits for the main Jewish festivals from couturiers in Paris and London. Fay Schneider's dresses were particularly legendary, and she frequently wore a fox stole. Fay Guild at the Langham wore beautifully tailored skirt suits, made for her by her brother-in-law, Harry Gale, the co-owner of Gale's Private Hotel in Frances Road (see Chapter 4), who had previously worked as a tailor in the East End of London.[107] Each morning, Sarah Marriott and her sisters rose very early to have their hair styled before the commencement of their long working day.[108] The women proprietors set exacting standards for their guests. Geoffrey Feld tells this story about his mother Bluma:

> In the Cumberland dining room, we reserved some tables for inter-generational groups. One year, sitting at one of these tables was a young man with hair down to his collar. My mother wanted to ban him from the dining room and send him to stay in the Majestic, which we had just bought. On *Shabbos*, hot water was accidentally poured over my daughter Juliet's arm at the lunch table. The young man with the long hair rushed over, saying 'I am a doctor, let me help'. He tended to my daughter's arm and kept an eye on it for the next few days. Afterwards, my mother kept saying: 'What a lovely man!' I said to her: 'You have been driving me mad with your *kvetching* [complaining]'. Without blinking an eye, she said: 'I never said a word against him!'[109]

Unlike the American women owner-managers of large hotels, the women hoteliers in Bournemouth did not refer to themselves as hostesses, but that is in fact the role that many of them played. They welcomed people to the hotels to help create a sense of community and ensured that their guests (they were never referred to as 'clients') enjoyed their stay by attending to the smallest of details. Hettie Marks comments: 'They were always walking around their hotels, making sure that everyone was happy and comfortable. They didn't just stay in the office and count the money they were making.'[110] This personal touch was pivotal in ensuring that guests returned to their hotels year after year.

> My mother, Bluma, was a human dynamo, the 'hostess with the mostest'. When she spotted someone she knew, she went across and greeted them by name. People said it made them feel like they were coming home. When she saw someone she didn't know, she knew their life stories within five minutes of meeting them: where they lived, what they did, who their relatives were![111]

Sheila Morris, who stayed at the Cumberland several times, recalls: 'Bluma Feld used to greet us: "Hello darlings! It is so lovely to see you again. You are looking wonderful." You knew that you were being *schmoozed*, but you still felt very welcome.'[112]

Between them, the women hoteliers knew everything there was to know about the hotel business: 'They were the tops in the hospitality trade at the time.'[113] They brought not only taste and style to Bournemouth, but also their friends and acquaintances. A significant number of guests at the Green Park, the Majestic and the Cumberland were friends of Sarah Marriott (née Richman), Fay Schneider and Bluma Feld from their days when they had lived in the East End of London (see Appendix 1).[114] In some of the hotels, the male proprietors were very prominent in running their business (Ruby Marriott at the Green Park, Maurice Guild at the Langham and Lou Keyne at the Normandie), but their wives were also fully involved. Sarah Marriott was highly skilled in organising entertainment (see Chapter 8). Fay Guild is remembered for her knowledge of cuisine and her accounting skills. Belle Keyne 'worked from early morning until late at night'[115] and the Normandie's success was largely due to her warm personality, wit and concern for detail.[116] Bluma Feld, Belle Keyne, Fay Guild and Fay Schneider all continued to manage their hotels after their respective husbands died. Although John Hayman had a financial interest in East Cliff Court, he played little part in its day-to-day management. It was run initially by his mother-in-law Annie Morris, and later by his wife, Sadie Hayman, who continued to run the hotel for several years after his death. Over time, some of the women proprietors became not just hoteliers but also well-known personalities, including Fay Schneider, who was renowned for her fundraising activities and her feisty character. Pat Cravitz recalls once seeing Fay Schneider standing on a chair 'shouting at people to be quiet'.[117]

However, perhaps the most memorable woman hotelier was Yetta (Bubbe) Richman, mother of Sarah Marriott and her sisters, who was 'from another Jewish world' and 'never lost her Yiddish ways'. She had little patience with the anglicised pretensions of the younger generation. She wore a *sheitel* (wig) and apparently she chain-smoked, drank a bottle of champagne in the evening and several brandies during the day, had a passion for watching wrestling (especially bouts involving Mick McManus) and cheated unashamedly at cards. Donald Sharpe recalls: 'She used to shout "Gin!", claiming that she had won within a minute of *Shabbos* ending and the card game commencing.'[118] For many years she was 'the driving force' behind the running of the Green Park.[119] David Marriott tells this story of his grandmother: 'My *Bubbe* had a sense of humour and had her own particular interpretation of English. A famous whisky distiller named Maurice Bloch often stayed at the hotel. She always used to refer to him as "Mr Maurice". One year he was knighted and she decided to call him "Mr Sir Maurice".'[120] Although she had not had much education, Yetta took a great interest in current affairs: 'Once television started, she became very interested in watching the world news.'[121]

34. Yetta ('Bubbe') Richman surrounded by her family, *c.* 1960. Front row, seated, left to right: Helen Lee, Judy Richman, Yetta Richman, Gertie Richman, Sarah Marriott (wife of Reuben Marriott). Back row, standing, left to right: Joseph (Joe) Richman, Ray Richman, Shir Richman, Hannah Richman, Meyer Richman. Image courtesy of the Marriott family.

Over the years, some of the hoteliers became quite prosperous and led wealthy lifestyles. Howard Inverne drove a Cadillac and Morella Kayman recalls that one year when she was staying in Bournemouth, Robert Myers, the then owner of the Normandie, took her for a flight in his helicopter and comments: 'How glamorous was that!'[122] Eliot Steinberg, a cousin of Lou Keyne, recalls that when he and his family stayed at the Normandie in the summer months, they would go out for the day in the Keyne's sailing boat.[123] During the 1960s, Nat Lee owned a Ford Thunderbird car. His granddaughter recalls: 'He once picked me up in his Thunderbird in London to take me down to Bournemouth. I was absolutely petrified all the way there. He was a terrible driver!'[124] Maurice Guild drove a Rolls Royce, and he and Fay took many exotic holidays abroad.[125] Clive Gold tells this story:

When my wife and I once went to stay at the Cumberland, as we were walking up the drive to the entrance, we noticed something shiny on the ground. It was a diamond earring, a very high-quality one with a three-carat stone. When we handed it in at reception, it turned out that it belonged to a family member, who presented us with a bottle of perfume worth about 2s 6d. We were not impressed and afterwards used to say to each other jokingly: 'We should have kept it!'[126]

Growing Up in the Hotels

Growing up in one of the Big Eight hotels has been described as 'a rarefied experience like no other'.[127] Some of the offspring of the hoteliers thrived on the experience, such as Barbara Glyn, the younger daughter of Ruby and Sarah Marriott, who says that when she was young, her life was 'inextricably bound up in the day-to-day life of the hotel'. Apart from school and visits to the local ice rink, the hotel was the centre of her life. Even when she went to the beach, she was usually accompanying young people staying in the hotel. After she married and moved away from Bournemouth, she regularly went to stay in Bournemouth with her daughters, and they spent all their time in the hotel. She recounts:

> About five years ago, nearly thirty years after the hotel closed, I was shopping in Stoller's fishmonger in Temple Fortune, when I noticed a woman staring intently at me. My reaction was to smile at her, but she continued to stare. Eventually, the light dawned and she called out to me: 'I know who you are. You're the Green Park's daughter'. 'Madam', I replied, 'That's exactly who I am, It's my very essence.' I was born a few years after the Green Park opened and the hotel shaped my life from day one.[128]

Her brother, David Marriott, says that when he was a young boy, he took the lifestyle for granted, and it is only now when he looks back that he realises how wonderful it was.[129] Simon and Jonathan Keyne, who grew up at the Normandie and who lived on the premises, mingled freely with the young guests staying there. They are reported as having revelled in a continuous supply of new acquaintances and friendships from around the country.[130]

35. Simon (left) and Jonathan Keyne, whose parents, Belle and Louis, owned the Normandie Hotel, *c.* 1958. Shown with 'Simon Four Legs', who was a popular part of hotel life during the 1960s. Image courtesy of Simon Keyne.

However, Ronald and Edward Hayman, whose grandmother, and then their mother, ran East Cliff Court, did not enjoy their childhood in the hotel. Edward Hayman believes that the hotel was not an ideal place to raise children: 'It was a comfortable place to be, but it was not a place where a family can really operate as a unit. Maybe other families did better in those circumstances, but I feel that it wasn't healthy for children.'[131] His older brother, Ronald, felt even more strongly about the matter. He became a well-known author and wrote a book about his childhood and teenage years at East Cliff Court. He said that the needs of the children were always secondary to those of the guests:

At the hotel, the most important people had been the visitors. I must never make too much noise or run along the corridors or do anything that might disturb them. I had always been conscious of their presence. I had lived a large part of my life in public, almost putting on a performance – the well-behaved little boy – while family life had been scattered all over the hundred-room building, with public corridors separating the nursery from the flat [the series of rooms in the hotel where his parents lived], the bedrooms from the dining room.[132]

36. Sadie Hayman, proprietor of East Cliff Court Hotel from 1953, and her sons Ronald (left), and Edward (right), taken by the prolific Bournemouth photographer Harry Taylor in 1949. Image courtesy of Edward Hayman.

However, there were some 'perks' of growing up in a hotel, such as being able to order your own food that was cooked specially for you by the chefs, like the shortbread baked by the pastry chef for Edward Hayman, which he 'gorged on while drinking Horlicks made by Nanny and reading Somerset Maughan short stories'.[133]

Hotel Staff

The hotels had a very high staff-to-guest ratio to maintain their reputation for offering a superb standard of service. David Abrahams recalls: 'My father was a larger than life character and he liked his creature comforts. He would often make a scene in hotels and restaurants if things didn't measure up to his standards. Real *nouveau riche*! At the Green Park in Bournemouth, there were no confrontations. Instead, there were generous tips all round.'[134]

The staff were highly valued, and the hoteliers invested in their training and took a personal interest in their welfare.[135] Chris Foster, whose father was a chef at the Langham for nearly twenty years, recalls that Maurice Guild collected his father in his Rolls Royce to take him to the hotel when no public transport was available and often gave Chris ten shillings to spend during his long school holidays (see Chapter 10 for further discussion of this generosity).[136] Many staff therefore remained with a hotel for long periods of time, often becoming part of the extended family.[137] The fact that they were paid well and earned substantial sums from tips, also encouraged them to stay.[138] Some of the longstanding staff are recalled fondly, such as John the porter, a war veteran from Southampton, who worked at the Normandie: 'Each year when we arrived, we had the same conversations with John. It was if we had never been away. He was the confidant to everyone.'[139] A memorable kitchen porter was Bill, who worked at East Cliff Court. Edward Hayman tells us: 'He had a broken nose, and possibly a cleft palate, which distorted his speech. Some of the other staff teased him, but Nanny was kind to him. He had the worst possible job – washing up all the greasy pans and dishes in the scullery and putting out the rubbish – but he remained even-tempered and obliging.'[140]

Other longstanding hotel staff remembered by many people include: Tim Standing, the Viennese hairdresser at the Cumberland, who trained at the famous salon in Knightsbridge, owned by the celebrity hairdresser Raymond Peter Carlo Bessone Raymond, known as 'Mr Teasy Weasy' and who also had a salon in Bournemouth;[141] Vivienne, who for many years looked after children staying at the New Ambassador on a Saturday afternoon and, when they went to bed, helped with the post-cabaret buffet: 'I first knew her when I was six or seven and she was still there when I got engaged in my twenties';[142] 'Auntie' Connie, the children's entertainer at the Majestic; Betty Travis, the receptionist at the Green Park, who knew the name of every single guest that stayed in the hotel, every detail of their stay, their likes and their dislikes and which room they usually took;[143] and Mr Olaf the 'hilarious' restaurant manager at the New Ambassador.

Over a nine-year period, Joan Doubtfire worked as a receptionist at three of the Big Eight hotels: the Cumberland, the Majestic and the New Ambassador. She recalls: 'People used to ring up and say, "It's Mrs Cohen", and I used to have to say, "Which Mrs Cohen?" After a while, I got to know their voices.'[144] Joan became so adept at her job, and so well known by the regular guests, that at one stage a photograph of her was used to promote the New Ambassador under the banner: 'I'm Jo…phone me. I'm the head receptionist at the New Ambassador Hotel and my job is to make sure that you and your family get what you want – **try me**.'[145] She loved being a receptionist in the hotels and 'bounced into work'. When she was working at the New Ambassador, Sefton Eagell loaned her his car and Alf Vickers arranged for her to take her honeymoon at the hotel in Marble Arch that the Vickers family owned.[146]

37. Joan (Jo) Doubtfire (née White), head receptionist at the New Ambassador Hotel. Advertisement in the *Jewish Chronicle*, 24 May 1974.

While many of the staff were recruited from Bournemouth or neighbouring areas (see Chapter 9), a significant number came from abroad. The Green Park recruited staff from Italy, Switzerland, Scandinavia, Spain and many other countries, some of whom took a while to gain a full grasp of the situation in which they were working. Barbara Glyn recalls: 'Our local Jewish chemist, Mr Fay, once phoned, saying: "Who have you got staying? One of your maids just came into the shop and asked for some aspirin for the Jewish Pope!" "Oh," came the reply from the receptionist. "Chief Rabbi Brodie is staying here and he has a cold."'[147] The Green Park provided accommodation for many of its staff from abroad. There were two annexes to the hotel, one of which was used to accommodate male staff and another, closer to the hotel, where the female staff slept, so that they didn't have to walk too far early in the morning or late at night.[148]

Many of the longstanding staff became very attached to the families for whom they worked. After the Green Park closed, David Marriott continued to speak frequently with Mr Mimmo, who managed the restaurant at the Green Park for twenty-five years until his death in late 2020: 'He always insisted on calling me Mr David!'[149]

38. Domenico ('Mimmo') Zacchia (second from right), maître d' at the Green Park Hotel, Manor Road, Bournemouth. To the right of 'Mr Mimmo' is Franco Corsi, the head waiter, to the left is Ray Richman and Reuben ('Ruby') Marriott, two of the hotels' proprietors. Image courtesy of the Marriott family.

The vast majority of staff in the hotels were non-Jewish, mainly due to the nature of the available pool of labour, but also out of necessity. To maintain the high standards of service expected by their guests, the hotels needed to employ people who could work on *Shabbat* and over the Jewish festivals. Joan Doubtfire comments: 'We used to refer to this as "working behind the curtain"'.[150] Jewish staff therefore had something of a rarity value. Mark Perl, who worked as a waiter in the Cumberland while he was at catering college, recalls: 'I used to wear my *yamulke* [skull cap]. It ensured that I got some very good tips!'[151]

Towards the end of the Golden Era, the hotels were beginning to experience a significant change in their clientele, and they had been reduced from the Big Eight to the Big Four. In 1973, Bournemouth's Director of Tourism made a public statement, regretting the changes taking place amongst the big Jewish hotels, for which the town had become famous.[152] However, worse was yet to come, as discussed in Chapter 5.

Notes

1.   Gerry Black, *Jewish London, an Illustrated History* (Derby: Breedon Books Publishing, 2007), p.165.
2.   Stanley Waterman and Barry Kosmin, *British Jewry in the Eighties, A Statistical and Geographical Study* (London: Board of Deputies, 1986), p.16. The loss was not just the people who emigrated to Israel, but also their children.
3.   Jackie Edwards, *A Bed by the Sea: A History of Bournemouth's Hotels* (Christchurch: Natula Publications, 2010), p.94.
4.   *Ibid.*, p.96.
5.   *Ibid.*, p.97.
6.   *Ibid.*, p.100.
7.   *Ibid.*, p.99.
8.   Manuscript, 'Growing up in Bournemouth', provided by Rhona Taylor, 8.5.2020.
9.   *Ibid.*
10.   Interview with Larry and Mandy Kaye, 11.6.2020.
11.   *JC*, 12.4.1996. It was named after the solicitor who was a prominent member of BHC who had contributed a great deal to its affairs.
12.   *JC*, 20.6.1947.
13.   *JC*, 12.4.1996.
14.   See https://www.streets-of-bournemouth.org.uk/wp-content/uploads/2018/02/Towns. Communities.pdf.
15.   Interview with Judi Lyons, 14.6.2020.
16.   *Ibid.*
17.   Interview with Kenny Arfin, 5.5.2020.
18.   It was sold by Fox and Sons for around £250,000. Interview with Andy Kalmus, 24.9.2020.
19.   *JC*, 22.3.1946.

20. *JC*, 26.7.1946. The other members of the board were Bertram Levitus's father and his uncle and aunt.
21. After the sale of the Trouville, Herman Polakoff became a diamond merchant. The hotel is still named the Trouville today.
22. *JC*, 22.3.1946.
23. *JC*, 26.7.1946.
24. *JC*, 27.9.1946.
25. Interview with Geoffrey Alderman, 27.4.2020.
26. Manuscript, 'The Green Park, 1943–1986', provided by Barbara Glyn, 22.5.2020.
27. Interview with Hettie Marks, 28.4.2020.
28. See https://eastcliffcourtmemories.wordpress.com/blog/.
29. Interview with Jon Harris, 4.5.2020.
30. Erwin Rubinstein was a teacher by profession who came to the UK in 1938 and obtained exemption from internment. He married in Bromley in 1939 and lived in St John's Wood before he moved to Bournemouth. Information from Peter Lobbenberg, 4.2.21.
31. Peter Phillips, 'London's Borscht Belt – Jewish Hotels in Bournemouth', *AJR Journal*, August 2014, p.11. Mr Rubinstein went on to purchase a hotel that was run along Jewish lines but was not kosher. Conversation with Brian Lassman, 1.12.2020. He died in 1969, aged 59. Information from Peter Lobbenberg, 4.2.21.
32. See, for example, *AJR Journal*, March 1964.
33. Interview with Joan Doubtfire, 13.5.2020.
34. Louis Golding, *Hotel Ambassador* (Bournemouth: Ambassador, 1950), p.13.
35. Interview with Barbara Glyn, 30.6.2020.
36. Interview with Stuart March, 21.9.2020.
37. Morella Kayman, *A Life to Remember* (London: John Blake Publishing Ltd, 2014), p.22.
38. Interview with Paul Harris, 1.5.2020.
39. Interview with David Marriott, 11.5.2020.
40. Interview with Richard Inverne, 6.7.2020.
41. Email from Michael Zeffertt, 30.8.2020.
42. Email from Edward Hayman, 24.8.2020.
43. Interview with Paul Harris, 1.5.2020.
44. Interview with David Abrahams, 25.8.2020.
45. Interview with Elissa Bayer, 30.4.2020.
46. Interview with Frances Israel (née Richman), 19.6.2020.
47. Anonymous interviewee, 16.5.2020.
48. Interview with Geoffrey Feld, 4.5.2020.
49. Interview with Marilyn Murray, 24.8.2020.
50. Interview with Stuart March, 21.9.2020.
51. Interview with Paul Harris, 28.4.2020.
52. Interview with Jenny Leigh, 27.1.2021.
53. Interview with Sheila Morris, 19.8.2020.
54. Talk given by Geoffrey Feld at Edgware United Synagogue, 6 March 2018.
55. Interview with Sheila Samuels, 11.5.2020.
56. Martin Levey, out-take from 'The Green Park', directed by Jack Fishburn and Justin Hardy, 2015.

57. *JC*, 20.5 1955.
58. Interview with James Inverne, 10.11.2020.
59. Interview with Jon Harris, 4.5.2020.
60. *Ibid.*
61. See talk given by Geoffrey Feld at Edgware United Synagogue.
62. Interview with Sheila Davies, 29.4.2020.
63. Israel Shenker, 'On the British Seafront, Kosher Cuisine With an English Accent', *New York Times*, 6.1.1973.
64. See manuscript, 'The Green Park'.
65. Interview with Hettie Marks, 28.4.2020.
66. Interview with Sheila Morris, 19.8.2020.
67. Interview with David Latchman, 5.11.2020.
68. Ilana Lee, 'Diamonds at Breakfast', *Jewish Quarterly*, Vol. 54, No. 1, p.28.
69. *Ibid.*, p.28.
70. Interview with Brian Lassman, 14.5.2020.
71. Interview with Geoffrey Feld, 4.5.2020.
72. Interview with Barbara Glyn, 1.6.2020.
73. See talk given by Geoffrey Feld at Edgware United Synagogue.
74. *JC*, 18.6.1952.
75. See talk given by Geoffrey Feld at Edgware United Synagogue.
76. *Ibid.*
77. *Ibid.*
78. Interview with Larry and Mandy Kaye, 11.6.2020.
79. Interview with Hannah Jacobs (née Noorden), 12.5.2020.
80. Interview with Marilyn Murray, 24.8.2020.
81. Interview with Paul Harris, 1.5.2020. The links from the north to the south west came via the Somerset and Dorset Joint Railway.
82. Memory shared on the website https://eastcliffcourtmemories.wordpress.com/blog/.
83. Interview with David Abrahams, 25.8.2020.
84. Interview with Frances Israel, 2.6.2020.
85. Commentator in 'The Green Park', directed by Jack Fishburn and Justin Hardy.
86. Harry Michaels in *ibid.*
87. Conversation with Geoffrey Feld, 29.11.2020.
88. Interview with Sheila Samuels, 11.5.2020.
89. See Lee, 'Diamonds at Breakfast', p.27.
90. Interview with Paul Harris, 1.5.2020.
91. Anonymous interviewee, 16.5.2020.
92. Ronald Hayman, *Secrets, Boyhood in a Jewish Hotel, 1932-1954* (London: Peter Owen, 1985), p.126.
93. Interview with Hannah Jacobs, 12.5.2020.
94. Conversation with Marian Stern, 19.11 2020.
95. Interview with Hannah Jacobs, 12.5.2020.
96. Conversation with David Abrahams, 20.11.2020.
97. *Northern Daily Mail*, 31.1.1956.
98. *Liverpool Echo*, 28.4.1956
99. *Aberdeen Evening Express*, 19.3.1962.
100. Interview with Frances Israel, 2.6.2020.

101. Interview with David Latchman, 5.11.2020.
102. *JC*, 25.1.1983.
103. Recordings of interviews with Bluma Feld, carried out by her grandson, Richard Inverne, in 1996, Disc 4, kindly provided by Geoffrey Feld.
104. At this point the Normandie was owned by Belle and Lou Keyne and Ron and Ann Fisher. Ron and Ann Fisher had previously owned a non-kosher hotel near the pier, which they sold in order to buy into the Normandie. Conversation with Janeen Shaw (née Fisher) 22.11.2020.
105. Interview with Judi Lyons, 14.6.2020.
106. Interview with Elissa Bayer, 30.4.2020.
107. Interview with Andy Kalmus, 24.9.2020.
108. See Lee, 'Diamonds at Breakfast', p.26.
109. See talk given by Geoffrey Feld at Edgware United Synagogue.
110. Interview with Hettie Marks, 28.4.2020.
111. See talk given by Geoffrey Feld at Edgware United Synagogue.
112. Interview with Sheila Morris, 19.8.2020
113. Interview with Kenny Arfin, 5.5.2020.
114. See talk given by Geoffrey Feld at Edgware United Synagogue. Some of the women hoteliers knew each other from London, including Bluma Feld, Fay Schneider and Fay Guild.
115. Interview with Eliot Steinberg, 14.5.2020.
116. *JC*, 17.4.2002.
117. Interview with Pat Cravitz, 30.4.2020.
118. Interview with Donald Sharpe, 7.12.2020.
119. Commentary, 'The Green Park', directed by Jack Fishburn and Justin Hardy.
120. Interview with David Marriott, 11.5.2020.
121. Interview with Frances Israel, 2.6.2020.
122. See Kayman, *A Life to Remember*, p.22.
123. Interview with Eliot Steinberg, 24.5.2020.
124. Interview with Jenny Leigh 27.1.2021.
125. Interview with Andy Kalmus, 24.9.2020.
126. Interview with Clive Gold, 23.9.2020.
127. Interview with Barbara Glyn, 1.6.2020.
128. See manuscript, 'The Green Park'.
129. Interview with David Marriott, 11.5.2020.
130. Interview with Paul Harris, 1.5.2020.
131. Quoted in 'It was a Golden Era: Memories of the East Cliff Court as a Jewish Hotel', *Bournemouth Daily Echo*, 4 October 2017.
132. See Hayman, *Secrets*, p.60.
133. Email from Edward Hayman, 25.8.2020.
134. Conversation with David Abrahams, 24.11.2020.
135. Interview with Joanna Benarroch, 19.6.2020.
136. Chris Foster, response to author's post on Memories of Old Poole and Bournemouth Facebook Group, 21.11.2020.
137. Interview with David Marriott, 11.5.2020.
138. Interview with David Latchman, 6.5.2020.
139. Interview with Jon Harris, 4.5.2020.

140. Email from Edward Hayman, 25.8.2020. A kitchen porter was not uniformed as were the front of house porters.
141. Conversation with Dawn Waterman, 6.8.2020.
142. Interview with Jonathan Perlmutter, 26.8.2020.
143. The Richman sisters, out-take from 'The Green Park', directed by Jack Fishburn and Justin Hardy.
144. Interview with Joan Doubtfire, 13.5.2020.
145. *JC*, 24.5.1974.
146. Interview with Joan Doubtfire, 13.5.2020.
147. See manuscript, 'The Green Park'.
148. Anonymous, out-take from 'The Green Park', directed by Jack Fishburn and Justin Hardy.
149. Interview with David Marriott, 11.5.2020. A reference written by Judy Richman at the time that the Green Park closed explained that Mr Mimmo had started work at the Green Park in 1961, but within a few years he was promoted to became the restaurant manager, 'through his ability and his personality'. He had full responsibility for the organisation of the restaurant including staff recruitment. Copy of letter, dated 25.12.1986, provided by Kim Bomford, 5.2.2021.
150. Interview with Joan Doubtfire, 13.5.2020.
151. Conversation with Mark Perl, 14.1.2021.
152. See Edwards, *A Bed by the Sea*, p.135.

4

The Golden Era, 1945-1975: The Smaller Hotels and Guest Houses

When people speak about the Jewish hotels of Bournemouth, they usually mention the largest hotels, the 'Big Eight' that dominated the Jewish hotel scene in the postwar years. However, as Jews living in the town during these years were well aware, there was also a wide range of Jewish-owned and run smaller hotels, guest houses and bed and breakfast establishments. They were very popular amongst the postwar generation of holidaymakers, who wanted to be in fashionable Bournemouth, but who were unable to afford to stay in the larger hotels. At any one time during the 1950s and 1960s, there were between fifteen to twenty of these smaller establishments, but the number began to decline noticeably during the 1970s. Jewish holidaymakers also rented flats, apartments and holiday homes. This chapter looks at how these various types of holiday accommodation operated in the three decades after the Second World War.

Since this chapter refers to so many different establishments and their owners, to assist the reader, Appendix 2 provides a list of all of the establishments mentioned with salient details.

The Smaller Hotels and Larger Guest Houses

Only a few of the guest houses and smaller hotels had been requisitioned to contribute to the war effort. Several of the establishments that had opened in the 1920s and 1930s therefore emerged from the war intact and with the same owners. Those that survived the war included Berachah, Marin Court, the Mayfair guest house, the Mayfair Hotel, the Rosemore Hotel[1] and Madeira Hall. The well-known Marlborough Hotel in Sea Road, Boscombe not only survived the war but appears to have prospered. In September 1946, its owners Fay and William Pantel opened a second, larger hotel, the Palm Bay, immediately opposite the Marlborough. The Pantels occupied the new hotel and appointed Mr and Mrs Robinson to manage the Marlborough.[2]

They sold the Marlborough after they had extended the Palm Bay, which stood in its own grounds and had direct access to the beach.[3]

Illustration 3. Rosemore Hotel run by Rose and Maurice Millman. Drawing by Beverley-Jane Stewart.

However, some of the hoteliers and guest-house owners no longer had the heart to continue running their businesses. Towards the end of the war and immediately afterwards, several Jewish establishments were sold to new owners, including Frogmore, which was purchased by Mr Sumroy and renamed Alexander,[4] and the Avon Royal Hotel, which was sold to Frederick Marshall.[5] Due to Elkan Shapiro's illness, from June 1946 the Mayfair Hotel was temporarily run by a non-Jewish owner.[6] The Grosvenor Court, which was purchased by Betty Retter in 1945, was resold within a year.[7] By March 1947, it had again been placed on the market.[8] As far as the smaller hotels and larger guest houses are concerned, the situation in the immediate postwar years was therefore a very fluid one.

During 1946 and the early part of 1947, the columns of the *Jewish Chronicle* frequently contained advertisements not only for holiday accommodation for sale,[9] but also those placed by people looking for partners to purchase hotels and guest houses.[10] As a result, by the end of 1946 a number of new establishments were listed in the *Jewish Chronicle*, including the Chine Court Hotel in Boscombe, run by Mr and Mrs Acker, who had moved to Bournemouth from Southport; the fifty-two-bedroom Brownswood Hall Hotel on the seafront, close to the pier; the Carmel Hotel in St John's Road, Boscombe; and Debonnaire in Sea Road, Boscombe.

Some of the new establishments, including Eaton in Madeira Road, Lebonville in Frances Road and Lewbess in York Road, continued for several years. One of the longest enduring of the new tranche of guest houses was the Oxford guest house in Frances Road, the owners of which, Dot and Benson Stieber, were very well known in the local Jewish community. Dot Stieber was the daughter of the Grossman family, owners of the Berachah hotel discussed in Chapter 3, where Dot had worked prior to her marriage.[11] Apparently, Dot Stieber was 'very smart and looked like Audrey Hepburn'. She was also a very hard worker, 'a little dynamo',[12] and after her husband died, she expanded the guest house to make it a more substantial establishment.[13]

Several of the newer hotels and guest houses did not survive for very long, including the Harland Hotel acquired in 1945 by Mr S. Deutsch. By March 1946, it had been sold to a non-Jewish hotelier.[14] However, new establishments continued to open. Several of those who opened guest houses at this time were people whom had been bombed out of the East End of London and had moved to Bournemouth for a better life. Others were set up either by people whom had been evacuated to Bournemouth during the war and had decided to stay, or by soldiers stationed in the area who had married local women and had settled in Bournemouth when they were demobbed. Several of the guest-house owners started by letting out one or two rooms in their homes before moving to larger premises, usually one of the big villas that had been built in Bournemouth in the late nineteenth century (see Chapter 2). Initially, some of the guest-house owners lived a hand-to-mouth existence. Judi Lyons tells us: 'They only ate chicken when they had a bit of money to spare.'[15]

Interestingly, there was a number of guest houses run by refugees from Germany and Vienna, who had arrived in Britain before and during the Second World War. The first continental guest house to open was Ashdale in late 1946.[16] Located in Beaulieu Road, Westbourne, it was run by Emil and Hilde Bruder from Linz in Austria.[17] The other guest houses that followed were Simar House, the 'new continental guest house', in Herbert Road, which opened in 1956. Boasting a large sun lounge, Simar House was run by Simon Gustav and Margot Smith. Simon died in 1959, but Margot carried on running the guest house alone.[18] The twelve-bedroom Continental Hotel in Church Road, Southbourne, was run by Mr and Mrs Schreiber,[19] its origins being betrayed by the name, even though it offered traditional English pursuits such as golf, riding and fishing.[20] The Schreibers had previously run Schreiber's Guest House in Blenheim Gardens, Willesden where German had been spoken.[21] The guest-house owners emphasised that their establishments were 'run along continental lines', provided their guests with continental food and advertised in the journal published by the Association of Jewish Refugees (AJR) to attract other former refugees. Rabbi David Hulbert recalls staying with his father at Simar House several times when he was a child: 'I was the youngest guest by far, and I revelled in all the attention that I received from the middle-aged Germans staying there. My nostalgic and lonely German father just loved being with other Germans. It was the perfect holiday for him. The food was all very Germanic and whenever I smell *sauerkraut*, I think about Simar House.'

The largest of the new establishments opening in the late 1940s was Hotel Rubens at the top of Bath Road. It had been first listed as the Knyveton boarding house in 1890 and was subsequently known as the Essilmont and then the Bourne Hotel. It was conveniently close to the two synagogues, the town centre and the railway station. It had been purchased by Joseph Grower, a local business man and prominent member of BHC. His son Ben Grower comments: 'When I am asked what he did, it is quicker to say what he didn't do. He was an insurance broker, and estate agent, a property developer, a furrier and the rest.'[22]

39. Hotel Rubens, Bath Road, Bournemouth (later the Bourne Hotel), run by Joseph and Helena Grower, *c.* 1950. Image courtesy of Ben Grower.

Joseph Grower ran the hotel with his wife Helena, who owned well-known furrier and millinery businesses in Old Christchurch Road, above one of which the Grower family lived before they moved into the hotel. The hotel was popular amongst families with young children because it had a garden with play equipment.[23] Most of its guests came from London. Mr Nash, who was not Jewish, was a silent partner in the hotel, which was sufficiently successful for the Grower family to run a Daimler car and to employ a nanny to look after the children.

In the early 1950s, the property was marketed as the 'Bourne Holiday Flats and Apartments' and by the late 1950s had become the Bourne Vegetarian Hotel.[24] The renamed hotel continued to be advertised in the *Jewish Chronicle,* but fewer of its guests were Jewish. After the untimely death of Joseph Grower in 1961, Helena Grower continued to run the hotel as a bed and breakfast establishment with her son Ben. The hotel was compulsorily purchased in about 1963 and was demolished to make way for the Bath Road roundabout.[25]

The number of establishments continued to expand over the next few years to include some hotels and guest houses that became an integral part of the Jewish holiday offering in Bournemouth, including Filora guest house in Campbell Road and Hotel Splendide in Sea Road, Boscombe. The Hotel Splendide was owned by Lou Simmons and his wife Hannah. Although he was blind, Lou helped to make the beds and with the washing up. Prior to running the hotel, Lou had led a band in which he was the drummer. The band had played in several of the Jewish hotels, including the Trouville, the Alexander and the Avon Royal.[26]

In the immediate postwar years, the listings for Jewish holiday accommodation in Bournemouth remained quite low key. The advertisements for the largest hotels continued to be the same size as those for the smallest guest houses and there was very little space for the owners to vie with each other about their respective comforts and facilities. The first boxed advertisement to appear was for the Picardy Hotel in Meyrick Road on the East Cliff (previously Merivale Hall), which had been operating under non-Jewish ownership for a few years after being de-requisitioned in 1945. It was the first Jewish vegetarian hotel to open in Bournemouth. The advertisements for the hotel stated that neither fish nor meat were served 'in any circumstances'.[27] The hotel's proprietors claimed that it had all of the advantages of a 'Nature Cure' facility, combined with the luxuries of a first-class hotel.[28] Two years later, the business transferred to the property in Kerley Road that had been run for many years as the Berachah Hotel until Isaac Grossman's retirement in 1947. The Picardy Hotel continued to operate for several years as a combined vegetarian hotel and hydro resort.[29]

Following the lead provided by the Picardy Hotel, by the end of 1948, several of the smaller hotels and the larger guest houses began to take out boxed advertisements in the *Jewish Chronicle*, including Chine Court, which was now owned by Mr and Mrs Tanner.[30] These prominent advertisements mainly appeared in advance of *Pesach* and also in the run up to the summer season.

In 1948, the Mayfair Hotel (to be distinguished from the Mayfair guest house, known as 'Russells', in Westby Road run by the Russell family) returned to the ownership of Elkan and Esther Shapiro.[31] Elkan Shapiro, who had recently recovered from a long illness, was now advertising that he spoke fluent Hebrew.[32] Rita Eker, Elkan and Esther's niece, who often stayed at the hotel at weekends and for the Jewish festivals, remembers the Mayfair as a busy hotel and that its clientele were mainly very orthodox families from across England.[33] Bertram (Bertie) Levitus, who had part-owned the Ambassador (see previous chapter), ran the Embassy Hotel in East Overcliff Drive for three years before it was sold to a non-Jewish owner.[34]

40. The Mayfair Hotel, Upper Terrace Road run by Esther and Elkan Shapiro. Advertisement appearing regularly in the *Jewish Chronicle*.

By the early 1950s, the Jewish hotel scene was more stable than it had been in the years immediately following the end of the Second World War. However, a number of new establishments continued to open, the first of which was the Brenhar Hotel in Owls Road. It was particularly welcoming of children and, in comparison to the Big Eight hotels at this time, offered weekend breaks as well as seven-day holidays during the summer months. Other notable new establishments were the Queen Hotel in Landsdowne Road on the East Cliff run by Lionel Cowen, who had moved to Bournemouth from Cardiff[35], and the sixty-bedroom Grosvenor Court Hotel, which was purchased by Mr and Mrs Salmon in 1953 after it had been operating under non-Jewish ownership for six years.[36] The Grosvenor Court Hotel offered free holidays for children under the age of six years, saying that the hoteliers would look after children to allow their parents to enjoy their holiday.[37]

One of the most prominent medium-sized hotels opening in the early 1950s was Hotel Florence in Boscombe Spa Road, which had originally been a sea captain's house named Blenheim Towers.[38] It was owned by Jules and Fay Segal, who had moved to Bournemouth from Cliftonville, where they had previously run a boarding house with another couple, and then a hotel on their own.[39] Both businesses had failed to take off, and the Segals had therefore decided to move to Bournemouth, which they perceived had become the Jewish community's favourite seaside town. Hotel Florence initially had fifteen bedrooms, but over the years the Segals added to the premises, such as in 1958 when they doubled the number of bedrooms enabling the hotel to accommodate up to sixty guests.[40] The Segals' son, Lennie, recalls that the clientele of Hotel Florence was very different from that of the larger hotels: 'They were mainly the workers rather than the governors, people working in the garment trade in the East End and taxi drivers from Ilford and other parts of Essex.'[41] In comparison to the owners of the larger hotels, the Segals were very 'hands on'. Fay, who had very high standards, did most of the cooking with the help of a chef, while Jules was 'front of house'. In October 1971, when Fay Segal became ill, Hotel Florence closed at the end of the summer holiday season.

41. The Blenheim Towers Hotel that became Hotel Florence, Boscombe Spa Road, *c.* 1935. Image in the Flickr collection of Alwyn Ladell, https://www.flickr.com/photos/alwyn_ladell/6089977180.

Over the next decade, the smaller hotels and larger guest houses began to offer a greater range of facilities, reflecting the higher expectations of their guests. Several were now advertising games rooms, weekend dancing, cabarets, centrally-heated bedrooms, a 'liberal table', private suites and telephones in each of the bedrooms. In the early part of 1952, the Pantels made a major investment in the Palm Bay Hotel to update its bedrooms, add a sun terrace and library and extend the dining room so that it could seat a hundred people and be used as a ballroom.[42] By the mid-1950s, the Palm Bay had sufficient custom to remain open throughout the year.

However, while the Big Eight generally stressed luxury, excellence of service and fine dining in their advertisements, the smaller hotels and guest houses continued to emphasise their affordability ('moderate terms', 'inexpensive') and described their premises as 'comfortable' or 'cosy'. The Palm Bay Hotel, which appears to have regarded itself as being towards the top of the second division of Bournemouth's Jewish hotels, was something of an exception. During 1950, it took out boxed advertisements alongside those for the Big Eight hotels, saying that it offered 'every possible luxury'.[43] It is interesting to note that, as the decade progressed, the list of smaller establishments became noticeably shorter, since all but the smallest guest houses, of which there were fewer, were taking out boxed advertisements on the same page as those for the Big Eight hotels.

During the mid-1950s, several establishments changed hands, including the Picardy Hotel, which became what was described as a 'strictly kosher' hotel under the combined supervision of Mrs Moisa, who had previously run Marin Court, and Mr and Mrs David Fieldgrass. Although the hotel was no longer a hydro resort, physiotherapy was still available and salads were a speciality.[44] However, within two years the hotel was back on the market and left Jewish ownership for a few years.[45] It was acquired in 1958 by Eric and Rose Kerpner, who had previously run hotels in Vienna and London. They carried out major building works, reducing the number of bedrooms so that each now had a private bathroom.[46] Offering 'continental cuisine', this hotel was a larger and more upmarket version of the continental guest houses discussed above. It offered reduced terms for AJR members.[47]

In 1955, the Grosvenor Court, which had also had a chequered history, came on the market again and was sold to a non-Jewish owner.[48] After eight years of being run by the Jacobs family, Mountain Ash guest house in Argyll Road was sold to Rose and Tony Ricklow, who changed its name to Mount Aishel.[49] Tony Ricklow, who was born in the East End of London, had worked in his family's cap-making business before serving in the Royal Engineers during the war.[50] After he was demobbed, he ran his own

business in London for several years. In 1958, he and Rose moved to
Boscombe where they ran Mount Aishel for fourteen years. It operated as
a strictly kosher dairy hotel (serving no meat). Several of the postwar
establishments continued in the ownership of the same families for several
more years, notably the Mayfair and Oxford guest houses.

During the 1960s, a number of the medium-sized hotels closed their
doors. The first to do so was the Mayfair Hotel following the death of Elkan
Shapiro in 1959. The Mayfair Hotel was sold to a non-Jewish owner in
1960,[51] as was the Hotel Splendide. The Palm Bay ceased trading at the end
of the summer season in 1963 and the Picardy Hotel closed as a Jewish
Hotel in 1964.[52]

However, these hotels were replaced by a number of new
establishments, including Gresham Court (previously known as
Neilghewerries) in Grove Road, which opened in May 1961. It was initially
run by the Rivlin and Weimar families,[53] and subsequently by Meyer
(sometimes Meir) and Marjorie Rivlin alone. Marjorie Rivlin was diverted
from a musical career by the outbreak of the Second World War, which
prevented her from taking up a place at the Royal Academy of Music. After
working at the Ministry of Shipping, she volunteered for the Women's Royal
Naval Service, where she was selected to work on the programme that
cracked the German Enigma Code. While a 'Wren', she met the extrovert
Meyer Rivlin, who came from a very distinguished family in the Palestine
Mandate. They married in 1939 and a few years later moved to
Bournemouth. The Gresham Court had forty bedrooms, a kosher kitchen
and a ballroom.[54] The hotel became the focal point for Israelis visiting
Bournemouth.[55] In the winter, its clientele was mainly older people, but
during the summer it offered special packages to attract younger people.
One of the people who took advantage of these packages was Michael
Zeffertt, who stayed in the hotel with a group of friends in 1961. They found
the hotel quite run down and were not impressed when, shortly after their
arrival, they were asked to change rooms:

> On our return in the early evening, we discovered we had been
> moved to the basement where beds had been erected in what was
> nothing more than storage space. No one really knew what to do, so
> it was decided we would sleep on it. The following morning, I noticed
> cockroaches crawling over the floor of the basement. I captured one
> of these insects and placed it in an empty matchbox. We had a
> conference and it was decided the matter had to be reported to the
> Borough of Bournemouth Public Health Officer.[56]

The group were able to obtain a refund and decamped to the Langham. The Rivlins carried out a major refurbishment of the hotel in 1968 to add a 'luxurious cocktail bar' and to create *en suite* bedrooms.[57] The hotel gained a reputation for being 'a bit of a gambling den' (see Chapter 8) and people staying there who did not play cards felt somewhat excluded.[58] The Rivlins retired in 1978.

42. Gresham Court, 4 Grove Road, Bournemouth (later the Green House Hotel), run by Marjorie and Meyer (Meir) Rivlin, *c.* 1960. Image in the collection of Alwyn Ladell, https://www.flickr.com/photos/alwyn_ladell/35742012775/. Photo credit: Michael J. Allen.

Over the course of the 1960s, the Jewish guest houses generally moved up market, adding new facilities, such as televisions and play areas for children. For example, in 1960, Golda and Harry Gale purchased a guest house in Frances Road, which the following year they extended by acquiring an adjacent property. They added a ballroom and private suites and re-designated the expanded establishment as Gale's Private Hotel.[59] It was upgraded and extended again in 1968.[60] Golda Gale (née Danieloff) was the sister of Fay Guild, owner of the Langham Hotel and often took overspill guests when the Langham was full. Andy Kalmus, (née Forman), the niece of both Fay Guild and Golda Gale, often spent her holidays in Bournemouth walking backwards and forwards between the two hotels.

The regular guests at Gale's Hotel included several families from Manchester and black cab drivers from Essex.[61] When Golda died in 1975, Harry continued to run the hotel alone, but in 1979 it was sold and converted into flats.[62]

Similarly, in 1967 the Gutsteins purchased a house at 96 Lowther Road, where they ran the Carmel guest house under Kedassia supervision, which being a branch of the Union of Orthodox Hebrew Congregations was stricter than the United Synagogue's Kashrus Commission (see Chapter 7). The Gutsteins had originally moved to Bournemouth when French-born Armand Gutstein was appointed to the role of *shammas* (salaried sexton) at BHC, but he eventually managed to set up his own business. The Carmel was advertised under Mr Gutstein's given name of Armand, but he and his Israeli wife were known locally by their Hebrew names of Noson and Yudit: 'She wore a *sheitel* [wig], which was rare in Bournemouth in those days.'[63] A year after the Carmel opened, the Gutsteins moved their business to 22 Florence Road, Boscombe where they opened what they named the Carmel Hotel (referred to as 'Gutstein's'), which became known for its strict orthodoxy. Advertisements for the Carmel stressed that *Shabbat* and *Yamim Tovim* were 'really upheld', but that the Gutsteins also catered for 'the modern person's fullest requirements'. The bedrooms had private bathrooms and there were TV and other lounges and a games room.[64] However, while the Gutsteins welcomed guests of all denominations, they were apparently more comfortable with the regular *charedi* (ultra-orthodox) guests. Hazel Green recalls:

> One day, my father, also a hotel owner, had a call from the Gutsteins to say that they had some 'English guests' staying at the hotel and they weren't quite sure how they should be catering for them. It turned out that the people to whom they were referring were middle-of-the-road Jews from Hendon whereas most of their regular guests were from Stamford Hill.[65]

Frances Kahan, who worked in the hotel as a teenager, recalls how crowded the hotel always felt because the *charedi* guests had large families.[66]

Also, newly opened in the 1960s was Stevra House in Southern Road run by Stephen and Golda Corren, who became widely known in the Bournemouth community. However, one of the best-remembered guest houses operating during the 1960s is Villa Judi. As a newly-married couple in 1946, Sylvia and Henry Kay purchased a property in Harcourt Road. Henry Kay was 'an old-time Jewish barber' with a shop in Boscombe and Sylvia let out two rooms in their home, providing a useful second income. In 1961, the couple moved to a larger property in Roseberry Road in Boscombe, which they named after their daughter Judi, who recalls that most of the guests were mainly working-class people who did not have the money to stay in a larger hotel, former refugees and Holocaust survivors. They usually arrived in Bournemouth by train rather than by car. She also remembers one particular family from London who stayed at Villa Judi on a regular basis: 'They were real scallywags! They ran market stalls and used to pay my mother in threepenny pieces.'[67] People came to Villa Judi from as far away as Glasgow, travelling to the south coast on an overnight coach. The guests were very aware of differences between the guest houses and the Big Eight hotels. Judi Lyons (née Kay) again recalls: 'Some of our guests and those in other guest houses sometimes went to the big hotels and "borrowed" some of their headed notepaper, which they used for writing to friends so that they would think they were staying there.'[68]

43. Villa Judi, Run by Sylvia and Henry Kay, 33 Hamilton Road, Boscombe, Bournemouth. Image courtesy Judi Lyons (née Kay).

44. Sylvia and Henry Kay (left and middle), who ran Villa Judi at 33 Hamilton Road, Boscombe, Bournemouth, *c.* 1980. They are on holiday with Golda Corren, who ran the Stevra House guest house in Southern Road, Bournemouth. Image courtesy of Judi Lyons (née Kay).

At this time, running a guest house was 'unremitting hard work', and for comparatively little gain. Judi Lyons tells us:

> The margins were very tight indeed and if a guest cancelled at the last minute or a table cloth became so soiled a new one had to be used, this had a significant impact on Villa Judi's profit margins. My parents tried not to worry me with their financial affairs. I remember that they sometimes found errands for me when they were poring over their budgets.[69]

In those days, there were no automatic washing machines or dish washers, and the bedding and linens had to be sent out to a professional laundering service: 'Our table cloths and sheets all had a laundry mark. We were "Kay15". We used to count the items in and out of the laundry boxes.'[70] The other washing was taken to a local launderette on a Sunday morning. Sylvia Kay had a maid to help her clean and make the beds and Judi helped when she could. Judi recalls: 'I have a vivid memory of singing away with friends in the kitchen as we did the washing up for my mother. It was a good way of catching the attention of male guests. It was also a good way of earning a bit of money.[71]

Over the years, the Kay's financial situation improved and in 1968 they were able to move to a larger house in Hamilton Road in Boscombe. The new property had nine guest bedrooms, some of which were large enough to accommodate two double beds. The income from the larger guest house enabled Henry Kay to reduce his hours gradually and to retire earlier than he had anticipated.[72] However, running the guest house eventually became too much for Sylvia Kay, as she was no longer able to go up and down two flights of stairs several times a day. After operating for twenty-five years, Villa Judi was sold in 1986 to non-Jewish owners.[73]

Most of the small guest houses were only open from *Pesach* until *Rosh Hashanah* (Jewish new year) because there were not enough guests to make it economic to remain open over the winter months. It was while the guest houses were closed that the families took their own holidays and carried out any necessary renovation works. The guest-house owners all knew each other, communicated regularly and had reciprocal arrangements for dealing with difficult guests:

> They were a community within a community. They all knew each other from meeting at the hairdressers, at *shul*, at the butchers, etc. Each of the guest houses had their longstanding clientele, who returned year after year. If there was a falling out with a guest, when they booked into another establishment, the owner was forewarned of the problems. There was also a common approach for dealing with complaints. If people said a guest house wasn't *frum* [orthodox] enough, then the response would be: 'Go and stay with the Gutsteins then.' If they said there wasn't enough choice of food, the reply would be: 'Then go and stay at the Green Park.'[74]

In the 1950s and 1960s, there were a number of hotels and guest houses operating in Bournemouth that were Jewish-owned but not kosher. They nevertheless attracted mainly Jewish clientele, including the upmarket, seventy-bedroom, Cliffeside Hotel, located in East Overcliff Drive, run by Philip and Valerie Nyman,[75] and Sunnyside Court Hotel in Florence Road run by Josef and Sylvia Perl for five years between 1969 and 1974. Josef, who originated from Velicky Bockov in Czechoslovakia, was a Holocaust survivor. He had been imprisoned in several extermination camps and had a lifelong limp as a result of a gunshot wound that he sustained when escaping from one of them.[76] Sunnyside Court started out as a kosher hotel, but quickly changed to being non-kosher. Hartford Court, which had opened in 1958 at 48 Christchurch Road, was run by Ben and Elsa Lateman. Ben was an immigrant from Belarus and Elsa was a refugee from Bavaria. Ben had been to a holiday camp just outside Bournemouth in the 1920s and he had promised himself he would one day live in the town, which he succeeded in doing thirty years later. Hazel Green recalls: 'My parents had a limited catering background, but it was acceptable in those days to open a hotel without any relevant experience or training.'[77] Hartford Court was located close to the Majestic, and was used for overflow accommodation when the Majestic was overbooked.

Although they were non-kosher, both Sunnyside and Hartford Court were part of the network of Jewish guest-house owners mentioned above. Ben Lateman regularly referred clients to kosher guest houses, especially to the JoAnna bed and breakfast establishment in nearby Annerley Road, run by Hannah and Joe Levy (who was also a chef at the Majestic), which was also sometimes used for overflow accommodation when the larger hotels were full.[78] Ben Lateman also helped the proprietors of kosher establishments in a number of other ways, such as assisting Armand Gutstein when staff let him down. One task he sometimes performed was slicing the smoked salmon, a very skilled task, for the *kiddushim* (food served to accompany blessings on *Shabbat*) held at the Gutstein's hotel.[79] When Gutstein's was full, it used Sunnyside Court for boarding guests who ate all their meals at the Carmel Hotel. They were very different from Sunnyside's normal clientele and were very conspicuous.

The main development during the early 1970s was the opening in March 1972 of the Grosvenor Hotel, formerly the Redroofs Hotel, in Bath Road. It was run by Sydney and Rhoda Lukover and Johnnie and Pearl Michaels, all of whom had extensive experience in the catering industry. Sydney Lukover had previously run a chain of fish restaurants in various parts of London, and Johnnie Michaels had run the Grosvenor Rooms banqueting suite in Willesden. The owners invested significant resources in updating and redecorating the hotel's fifty bedrooms, several of which were reserved for families. The hotel, which was licensed by the United Synagogue's Kashrus Commission and the London Beth Din (see Chapter 7), had its own synagogue. It also had a sun lounge, a dance floor, a card room and a games room.[80] Sydney and Rhoda Lukover were the resident directors, while Johnnie Michaels was the licensee. Rhoda Lukover was the sister of Alf Vickers, owner of the New Ambassador Hotel (see Chapter 5).

By the mid-1970s, there were more medium-sized hotels and far fewer small guest houses than there had been two decades earlier. The less expensive hotels were taking guests both from the larger, more luxurious hotels (which people were visiting less frequently for reasons we will see in Chapter 5) and also from smaller establishments that could not provide the facilities that had now become *de rigueur*, especially *en suite* bedrooms and *à la carte* menus.

Other Jewish Holiday Accommodation

In addition to the small and medium-sized hotels and the guest houses, during the postwar years there were a number of households who let out a room or two during the summer season, usually only providing breakfast, or even just a bed. This was how some people managed to survive.[81] For example, Mrs Tibber accepted 'a few visitors' in her 'lovely private house' in Chessel Avenue, Boscombe and an unnamed woman advertised that she could receive paying guests in her 'refined orthodox home'.[82] Mrs Gold offered bed, breakfast and afternoon drinks in her home in Hillbrow Road, Southbourne.[83] Some of the people offering bed and breakfast also welcomed long-term paying guests, such as Mrs Haimovich in Aschem Road.[84]

This type of accommodation was often used by Jews who were visiting the town for a short length of time to visit friends and relatives, or to attend a celebration taking place in one of the larger hotels, where they took their meals during their stay in Bournemouth. It was also used by those who simply could not afford to stay elsewhere. Geoffrey Alderman recalls:

> The Hackney-based, cash-limited Alderman household could never have afforded to stay or even eat in any of the upmarket establishments, but we did spend several summer vacations in Bournemouth, bivouacking in sundry, nondescript bed-and-breakfasts. One year, in the late 1950s, we stayed in such accommodation but, courtesy of a rich relation, we ate at the Green Park for an entire *Shabbat*.[85]

From the beginning of the 1950s, the *Jewish Chronicle* began to include listings for flats, apartments and other self-catering accommodation, which was available during the summer and for the Jewish festivals. Initially, the self-catering properties being advertised were quite basic, but over the years the range increased to include both affordable accommodation and luxurious apartments, and sometimes even houses with access to a swimming pool.[86] The self-catering properties were offered both for rental and for sale. The advertisements were usually strategically placed alongside the advertisements for the hotels. A large proportion of the accommodation was purchased or rented by people who had previously holidayed at one of the hotels or guest houses.

In 1951, the Branksome Dene convalescent home in Alumhurst Road, Westbourne, was consecrated by Dayan Grunfeld and declared open by the Jewish MP Barnett Janner. It had been set up by the Grand Order of Israel and Shield of David Friendly Society. Branksome Dene was a large house, which had been built in 1860 for Lord Wimborne. It was the first house to be completed in what became Westbourne, standing in five acres of park land and overlooking Bournemouth Bay. From 1930 until 1950, Branksome Dene had been used as a hotel. When it became a Jewish convalescent home, most of the accommodation was arranged in wards, but there were also a number of 'tastefully furnished' private bedrooms and Branksome Dene was increasingly advertised as an ideal holiday destination and a venue for seminars and lectures.[87]

45. Postcard of Branksome Dene Jewish convalescent home, Alumhurst Road, Westbourne, Bournemouth, *c.* early 1950s. Image in the Flickr collection of Alwyn Ladell, https://www.flickr.com/photos/alwyn_ladell/4868310318.

Mr and Mrs Brand were the longstanding managers of Branksome Dene. By the early 1970s, many of the guest rooms at Branksome Dene had *en suite* facilities, which were accessed via a lift, and the holiday accommodation it provided was advertised alongside the Big Eight hotels and other substantial holiday establishments.[88] However, by the late 1970s, the home had obviously outlived its main purpose as a convalescent home. In 1980, it was purchased by the Royal Masonic Benevolent Institution and reopened as the Zetland Court Masonic Residential Care Home, which is still operating today (2021).[89]

In 1957, the Jewish Blind Society announced that it would be transferring the Dolly Ross Holiday Home, which had been opened by Aneurin Bevan in 1950, from Devonia Hall in Cliftonville to larger premises in Grand Avenue in Southbourne. It was consecrated on 19 October 1958 by Rev. Ephraim Levene and Rev. Joseph Indech (later Rabbi Indech),[90] With the generous support from the Yager family, the society had purchased the Braemar Royal Hotel. It consisted of four buildings, interconnecting on the ground floor, which were able to accommodate over sixty people.[91] Although its official name was the Braemar Royal Holiday Home, it was always referred to as the Dolly Ross Holiday Home. From the outset, it had a number of permanent residents, but most of its bedrooms were given over to holiday accommodation.

46. The Braemar Royal Holiday Home (known as the Dolly Ross Home for the Blind), Grand Avenue, Southbourne. Image in the *Bournemouth Daily Echo*, 21 October 1958, recording the opening of the home.

Visitors came from all over Britain, and also from continental Europe to stay in the home. From the mid-1960s, the home held annual (and later biennial) fêtes, which were well attended by the local Jewish community. There are fond memories of the cakes and pastries that were provided by the home's Austrian cook.[92] The Dolly Ross Holiday Home was later run by Jewish Care and closed in 2000.

In May 1962, the Jewish Association for the Physically Handicapped (JAPH), opened Carlton Dene holiday home at 21 Stourwood Avenue, Southbourne, in a former hotel.[93] It provided twelve-day holidays for children, teenagers and adults with disabilities, mainly from London but later also from other parts of Britain and France. The carers and family of those staying in Carlton Dene were often accommodated in and helped to sustain the nearby Jewish guest houses. Between 1983 and 1985, the home was refurbished, modernised and extended. Guests were now mainly accommodated in single bedrooms.[94] When it opened in 1962 it had been consecrated by Chief Rabbi Israel Brodie. On its reopening in 1986, it was re-consecrated by Chief Rabbi Immanuel Jakobovits. The home was supported by a cross-communal local committee, Bournemouth Friends of Carlton Dene. It was later administered first by the Jewish Blind Society, which had acquired the home from JAPH, then by Jewish Care after the Jewish Blind Society was absorbed into Jewish Care when it was formed in 1990. Carlton Dene closed in 1997 as by then it became uneconomic and was replaced with flats.[95]

During the summer months, Bournemouth was the destination for group holidays and camps arranged by a variety of organisations. Some operated on a commercial basis, while others were arranged by Zionist bodies and youth organisations. Starting in 1946, for many years students from the orthodox Hasmonean Grammar School in north-west London holidayed in Bournemouth. They camped at Talbot Heath School, where a variety of daily activities were arranged, including daily trips to the beach.[96] In 1960, Mr Price of Salford organised his thirty-first 'personally supervised and conducted' holiday in Bournemouth for Jewish boys and girls. The holiday included kosher food and a 'full programme of activities and excursions'.[97] In 1969, Mr and Mrs Palace from Golders Green advertised in the *Jewish Chronicle* for Jewish girls to join a group holiday, staying at a girls' school in Bournemouth.[98] The grounds of Branksome Dene convalescent home (see above) were used for the activities of summer camps arranged by various Zionist youth organisations.[99] When young people came to Bournemouth for summer camps, some of the guest-house owners offered them free accommodation.[100]

While some of these alternative forms of holiday accommodation were to become less fashionable, others, as we will shortly see, were to become more popular.

Notes

1. The Rosemore Hotel consisted of two properties, one in West Cliff Road and another in St Michaels Road. It was run by Maurice and Rose Millman who had previously run a guest house in Stafford Road. The two properties together provided twenty bedrooms. Between them, Maurice and Rose had nine children who helped in the running of the hotel.
2. *JC*, 13.9.1946.
3. *JC*, 8.8.1947.
4. *JC*, 20.4.1945.
5. *JC*, 22.6.1945. It was sold again in January 1948. See *JC*, 9.1.1948. It was subsequently demolished, along with the neighbouring Hazelwood Hotel, to make way for a Travelodge.
6. *JC*, 2.6.1946.
7. *JC*, 13.9.1946,
8. *JC*, 14.3.1947.
9. See for example, *JC*, 21.12.1945.
10. See for example, *JC*, 12.4.1946.
11. Berachah ceased trading in about 1947, and Isaac Grossman died in 1953. See *JC*, 4.9.1953.
12. Conversation with Hilary Myers, 30.11.2020.
13. Conversation with Judi Lyons, 14.5.2020.
14. *JC*, 22.3.1946.
15. Interview with Judi Lyons, 4.5.2020.
16. *AJR Journal*, November 1946.
17. Interview with Ruth Shire, 27.8.2020. After Hilde Bruder died in 1951, Emil Bruder employed a local, non-Jewish woman, who had been taught about Jewish dietary requirements, to do the cooking. Emil died in 1960.
18. Anthony Grenville, *Jewish Refugees from Germany and Austria in Britain 1933–1970* (London and Portland OR: Vallentine Mitchell, 2010), p.233.
19. See for example, *AJR Journal*, August 1963.
20. *AJR Journal*, July 1959.
21. See Grenville, *Jewish Refugees from Germany and Austria*, p.232.
22. Interview with Ben Grower, 22.11.22.
23. Interview with David Abrahams, 25.8.2020.
24. *JC*, 7.3.1958.
25. Information for much of this paragraph was provided by Joseph and Helena's son, Ben Grower. After the CPO was served on the hotel, the family lived for a year in a flat in the Normandie. The Growers were related to the Keyne family who then co-owned the hotel.
26. Barrie Sondack in reply to author's post in Memories of Old Poole and Bournemouth Facebook Group, 21.11.2020.

27. *JC*, 23.6.1950.
28. *JC*, 2.4.1948.
29. *JC*, 24.10.1952.
30. *JC*, 20.8.1948. These two establishments advertised in the main section of the paper rather than in the hotels section of the classified advertisements.
31. *JC*, 27.2.1948.
32. *Jewish Travel Guide*, 1952, p.37.
33. Interview with Rita Eker, 20.10.2020.
34. *JC*, 23.2.1951. Bertram Levitus went on to be the managing director of the non-kosher Melford Hall Hotel in St Peters Road.
35. *JC*, 12.12.1952.
36. The number of bedrooms had decreased as result of a renovation to make more rooms *en suite*.
37. *JC*, 20.2.1953.
38. By the early twentieth century it had become a guest house, Blenheim Towers, and then an annexe to the Gorse Cliff School opposite. It reverted to being a hotel named first the Blenheim Hotel and then the Chester Hotel. Its name was changed to Hotel Florence when it was purchased by the Segals. It is now a block of flats called Florence Court.
39. Interview with Lennie Segal, 15.6.2020.
40. *JC*, 13.6.1958.
41. Interview with Lennie Segal, 15.6.2020.
42. *JC*, 11.4.1952.
43. *JC*, 24.10.1952.
44. *JC*, 18.2.1955.
45. *JC*, 15.1.1957.
46. *JC*, 20.6.1958.
47. *AJR Journal*, March 1964.
48. *JC*, 6.5.1955.
49. *JC*, 2.5.1958.
50. *JC*, 24.6.1994.
51. *JC*, 2.12.1960.
52. Information for this paragraph is taken from various issues of the *Jewish Chronicle*.
53. *JC*, 28.4.1961.
54. Interview with Lennie Segal, 15.6.2020.
55. *JC*, 15.4.1988.
56. Email from Michael Zeffertt, 30.8.2020.
57. *JC*, 28.6.1968.
58. Louise Goldschmidt, post on Facebook, Jewish Britain Group, 7.10. 2020.
59. *JC*, 28.4.1961.
60. *JC*, 28.6.1968.
61. Interview with Andy Kalmus, 25.9.2020.
62. *Ibid.*
63. Interview with Hazel Green, 1.9.2020.
64. *JC*, 13.8.1971.
65. Interview with Hazel Green, 1.9.2020.
66. Conversation with Frances Kahan, 14.1.2021.

67. Interview with Judi Lyons, 4.5.2020.
68. *Ibid.*
69. Conversation with Judi Lyons, 10.8.2020.
70. *Ibid.*
71. Interview with Judi Lyons, 4.5.2020.
72. *Ibid.*
73. *JC*, 7.3.1986.
74. Interview with Judi Lyons, 4.5.2020.
75. In 1980, the Nymans sold Cliffeside to the non-Jewish Young family, who operated it in tandem with the Queens Hotel. Four years later, they purchased East Cliff Court, which after being sold in 1960, had been running as a non-kosher hotel by the Jewish Rosenthal family. *JC*, 24.8.1984. It welcomed Jewish guests and organised activities designed to appeal to them, including kalooki weekends.
76. See https://45aid.org/064/ and http://www.josefperl.com/introduction/.
77. Interview with Hazel Green, 25.8.2020.
78. *Ibid.*
79. *Ibid.*
80. *JC*, 31.3.1972.
81. Interview with Judi Lyons, 16.6.2020.
82. *JC*, 9.5.1947.
83. *JC*, 8.7.1955.
84. *JC*, 9.5.1947.
85. Interview with Geoffrey Alderman, 27.4.2020.
86. Various issues of the *Jewish Chronicle*.
87. See for example, *JC*, 26.9.1969.
88. See for example, *JC*, 29.9.1972.
89. See https://www.flickr.com/photos/bournemouth_grant_too/8268032404.
90. *Bournemouth Echo*, 21.10.1958.
91. *JC*, 29.11.1957.
92. Interview with Kenny Arfin, 5.5.2020.
93. *JC*, 11.5.1962.
94. *JC*, 16.8.1985.
95. *JC*, 21.11.1997.
96. *JC*, 7.2.1958.
97. *JC*, 31.5.1960.
98. *JC*, 21.2.1969.
99. Interview with Judi Lyons, 4.5.2020.
100. *Ibid.*

5

Holidaying in Bournemouth: 1975 to the Present Day

By the mid-1970s, the social and economic topography of Anglo-Jewry was undergoing very significant change. We have seen that in the decades that followed the Second World War, Anglo-Jewry grew substantially, especially in London. After a decade of relative stability, the number of professed Jews living in Britain decreased dramatically, and by 1996, it was estimated that the Jewish community had fallen from over 400,000 to around 283,000.[1] The two main causes of the decline were a falling birth rate[2] and increasing intermarriage. In 1976, the Board of Deputies of British Jews estimated that the level of assimilation through intermarriage was about twenty per cent, which looked set to increase due to the disproportionately high numbers of Jews going to university. Equally worrying to communal leaders was the decreasing number of Jewish marriages and increasing rate of divorce and separation of Jewish couples, which were seen as threatening Jewish family life.[3]

As well as these demographic trends, which reached their zenith in the 1980s, the outcome of changes in the religious life of the community was now fully apparent. The number of synagogues had increased, as had the rate of synagogue membership. However, attendance at services had reduced significantly and the regular worshippers tended to be older people. Other signs of reducing religious observance included a major decline in the consumption of kosher meat, a reduction in the number of households keeping a kosher kitchen and a rise in the number of Jews who were willing to drive on *Shabbat* and Jewish festivals.[4]

However, other forces were at play during the last two decades of the twentieth century that eventually not only counter-balanced but reversed the impact of the trends described above. The first of these did not come from within the community, but from developments in the non-Jewish world. Prior to the 1960s, Jews had been the main minority group in Britain and as such, they had been the principal target of discrimination. The arrival in Britain of immigrants from Africa, Asia, the Caribbean and the

Middle East gave rise to an increasingly multi-cultural society, which meant that the focus of discrimination was no longer on Jews alone and ethnic separatism became respectable. Although antisemitism, resulting largely from the growth of Muslim influence in Britain, still gave Anglo-Jewry grounds for concern, there was sufficient respite to enable the community to make the transition from 'would-be-English' to a successful cultural grouping proud of its distinctive Jewish life. Whereas in previous decades the practice of Judaism had been a private affair and one confined to 'safe' spaces, the public display of Judaism, such as the wearing of *kippot* (skull caps), was now more commonplace.[5]

The other main countervailing trend was the sharp rise in the number of Jewish day schools. In 1975, for every child in a Jewish day school there were 1.5 children in a part-time *cheder*. By 1997, the pattern had completely reversed: for each child in a supplementary school, there were 1.7 children in a Jewish day school.[6] The growth of Jewish schools increased the Jewish identity both of the children attending the schools and that of their families.

While the community generally became more observant in the latter part of the twentieth century, Anglo-Jewry also became more polarised and less cohesive than it had been in the postwar years. There was a growth in the progressive movements (Liberal Judaism and the Reform Movement), and what is now called the *charedi* community made up of various denominations of ultra-orthodox Jews. These gains at either end of the spectrum of Judaism were achieved at the expense of the mainstream orthodox congregations that collectively made up the United Synagogue and the Federation of Synagogues, which until this time had formed the backbone of Anglo-Jewry.[7]

By the end of the twentieth century, the traditional picture of the Jewish community being predominantly proletarian and engaged in a narrow range of employment had been superseded by a community engaged in an ever-expanding variety of middle-class occupations. Over the last fifty years, the Jewish community has also become increasingly affluent. Official Labour Force Surveys (LFS) carried out in the first decade of the twenty-first century showed that Jews had the highest median gross hourly wages and median total wealth in the general population. In addition, the LFS also showed that Jews were the most educationally qualified population group, and more likely to be self-employed, especially within the *charedi* community, which is generally not as affluent as other sections of Anglo-Jewry.[8]

At the beginning of the twenty-first century, statistical information became available on the Anglo-Jewish community when a question on religious affiliation was included in the 2001 Census. The information this provided on the community became even richer following the 2011 Census, which yielded comparative information. The data confirmed that, compared with other religious groups, Jews were relatively old but that between 2001 and 2011, the community became younger. Given that Anglo-Jewry had been ageing from the 1950s onwards, this was a major turnaround. The key driver of this change was the growth of the *charedim*. Although *charedi* Jews account for less than fifteen per cent of the Jewish population, at least twenty-nine per cent of Jewish children were being born to *charedi* parents. This makes the profile of the *charedi* section of Anglo-Jewry, which according to the 2011 Census had an average age of twenty-seven, quite different from the Jewish community in general with its average age of forty-four years.[9] As we will see, these changes in Anglo-Jewry had a profound impact on the Jewish holiday trade in Bournemouth.

Bournemouth in the Late Twentieth and Early Twenty-First Centuries

Like many other coastal resorts, by the 1970s, Bournemouth was faltering as a tourist destination. Fewer people were visiting the town and when they did, they were spending less money.[10] People who had previously holidayed in the more luxurious hotels now preferred to vacation in places such as Majorca and the Spanish coastal resorts with their promise of guaranteed sunshine. This was made possible by the lifting of currency restrictions, the growth of package holidays and the advent of cheap air flights. Despite the electrification of the main line railway service from London to Bournemouth in 1967, which reduced the journey time to ninety minutes, ever-increasing car ownership meant that most visitors were arriving by road using the improved road system. This had a significant impact on the holiday trade. Instead of staying by the sea in expensive hotels, some car owners were now staying inland at caravan parks and campsites and cheaper hotels, and travelling to the beach for the day. As a result, many hotels either closed at the end of the summer holiday season and did not reopen until Easter (apart from briefly at Christmas and New Year), or were sold for redevelopment as apartments.

The small hotels, guest houses and bed and breakfast establishments generally fared better than the large hotels. During the winter months, they had started to provide accommodation for students attending degree and diploma courses at what became Bournemouth University in 1992. The burgeoning language schools also needed affordable accommodation for their students. However, the small hotels and guest houses in Boscombe suffered when the new Wessex Way, which was completed in 1975, cut them off from the rest of the town.

In 1974, Bournemouth became part of the county of Dorset rather than Hampshire and the local authority gained new powers enabling it to respond to the town's declining tourist trade. The main initiative was to build a large conference centre, Bournemouth International Centre (BIC) and to market the area as a year-round conference destination.[11] It took fourteen years from the conference centre being proposed until it opened in 1984. Five hotels were demolished to make way for the conference centre. The BIC was expanded in 1990 when the Purbeck Hall was added and again in 2005 when the much larger Windsor and Solent Hall were opened. By 2009, the BIC and the Pavilion were together contributing £15 million to the local economy.

The BIC had a positive impact on the hotel trade. Those hotels that had previously been closing in September were now open throughout the year, and there were fewer staff reductions over the winter months. Several of the larger hotels, such as the Royal Bath and the Carlton, made substantial investments in refurbishing their premises, hoping to cash in on the conference trade. However, some smaller hotels and guest houses closed and became residential or care homes since their owners were unable to afford the *en suite* facilities that were now expected by guests. A number of the larger hotels were continuing to be replaced by blocks of flats, which were often snapped up as second homes by people living and working in other parts of Britain. With the advent of the recession of the late 1980s, an increasing number of hotel owners sold their properties to developers. Fearing that the loss of hotels would undermine Bournemouth's position as a leading conference centre, town planners stepped in to curtail the redevelopment of hotels and clamped down on the conversion of the larger guest houses to nursing homes. The East Cliff, where a large proportion of the Jewish hotels were located, was designated as a conservation area.

As a result of these changes, in 2000 Bournemouth was voted 'Resort of the Year' by *Holiday Which?* The profile of the Bournemouth tourist trade was very different from a hundred years earlier. The majority of holidays taken in the town were now in addition to people's main holidays, with nearly a third of visitors coming for weekends and short breaks. As a result, the distance travelled by visitors had declined since people were less inclined to travel many miles for short periods of time. The visitors were predominantly from London, the South East, the South West and the West Midlands and fewer people than previously from the North East, the North

West and Scotland. Booking patterns had also seen a dramatic change. Whereas in the past people had booked their accommodation months before their arrival, the internet had made it possible for people to book their stays a short while in advance, depending on the weather forecast. Another significant change was that instead of being mainly family owned, a large proportion of Bournemouth hotels was now owned by powerful hotel chains, with which the independent owners, including Jewish hoteliers, found it hard to compete.

In the latter part of the twentieth century, Bournemouth had gained a reputation for being a resort where older people took their holidays. During the early part of the twenty-first century a number of attractions opened, including the artificial surf reef near Boscombe and the Urban Reef Restaurant, which placed Bournemouth on the UK surf map. Between 1970 and 2006, there was also a major investment in replenishing Bournemouth's beaches and revitalising its seafront area. These developments increased Bournemouth's attractiveness to young people, families and mid-week visitors. As a result, the town began to lose its 'God's waiting room' image.

Today, Bournemouth is once again regarded as a premier holiday resort, relying on its traditional offer of sea, beaches, cliffs and gardens. However, while it is recognised that Bournemouth has a strong tourist image and has extensive experience of providing holiday accommodation, it has increasingly been marketed as part of the South East Dorset conurbation that includes Poole and Christchurch as well as Bournemouth. This combined marketing strategy has intensified since the recent amalgamation of the three local authorities governing the area.

Bournemouth's Jewish Community from 1975-2020

During the last quarter of the twentieth century, the Jewish community of Bournemouth continued to grow as people retired to the town. Many of the new residents were people who had stayed in the Jewish hotels in Bournemouth. They arrived in waves from various cities: London initially and then Birmingham, Leeds and Liverpool. A number of families also arrived from places such as Cardiff, Dublin and Sunderland. The retirees often left behind waning communities, heading for one that was flourishing. Bournemouth's Jewish population was also boosted by the arrival of people with young families who moved to Bournemouth in search of a better quality of life. As a result, there was a growth in both BHC and the Reform congregation and an expansion in the number of organisations focusing on matters of Jewish interest, such as the very active branch of the Women's Campaign for Soviet Jewry, known as 'the 35s'. Ruth Soetendorp comments: 'People in Russia thought that Bournemouth was a real metropolis because of the amount of support that came from the group.'[12]

In 1975, BHC established the Yavneh kindergarten. It was held several mornings a week in the Gertrude Preston Hall at the Wootton Gardens Synagogue and was open to all Jewish children in the area. Owing to the zeal of Rabbi Sydney Silberg, in 1976 the community was able to install an 'on-the-site' *mikveh* (ritual bath used by observant Jewish women) at the synagogue. In 1980, the *Beth Hamedrash* (house of study), in which the community held weekday morning and evening services, was refurbished. In 1995, a new cemetery was opened in the nearby village of Throop.

From 1975 until the present day, the social centre at Wootton Gardens Synagogue has been used for a variety of events and regular activities, including those organised by the Ladies' Guild, which has now been operating for over 100 years. It is also the base for a number of independent bodies, such as Bournemouth Action for Israel and the local branches of the JIA (Joint Israel Appeal), WIZO (the Women's International Zionist Organisation), British Emunah (an organisation that raises money for vulnerable children in Israel) and AJEX (the Association of Jewish Ex-Servicemen and Women). During the 1980s, there was a brief revival in youth activities at the synagogue, but today the community does not have a *cheder* and *Bar* and *Bat Mitzvahs* (coming of age celebrations for boys and girls, see Glossary) are a rarity.[13] Since 2009, Sephardi services have been held on some *Shabbat* mornings and at Jewish festivals.

From humble beginnings, Bournemouth Reform Synagogue (BRS) developed into a thriving community, attracting members from across Hampshire and Wiltshire. During the thirty-three-year leadership of the Dutch Rabbi, David Soetendorp, there were several developments, including the founding of the South Hampshire Jewish Community under the auspices of BRS and the setting up of a burial society and a prayer house. Rabbi Soetendorp was succeeded in 2005 by Rabbi Neil Amswych. Today, the 320-member congregation is led by Rabbi Maurice Michaels.

During the early years of the twentieth-first century, BRS went through turbulent times and a group of congregants split off from the community to form what became Wessex Liberal Jewish Community (WLJC) under the auspices of Liberal Judaism. WLJC has now been operating for over ten years and has a solid membership of around ninety people. It does not yet have its own building, but holds services fortnightly and for the Jewish festivals at venues in Bournemouth and East Dorset. Once a month, the

Shabbat evening and morning services are led by Rabbi Rene Pfertzel. Congregants are involved in local Jewish and non-Jewish activities, including a food bank and a multi-faith initiative with Safe Haven Wessex. Attracted by a burgeoning Jewish community, Chabad of Bournemouth[14] was first established in 1988 by Lubavitch UK at premises in Gordon Road, Boscombe. Its aim was to cater to the spiritual needs of Jews in Bournemouth and the entire south-west region. In 1989, American-born Rabbi Yossie Alperowitz and his wife Chanie were appointed to serve as the directors of Bournemouth Chabad. Since their arrival, a wide range of educational and social activities for all segments of the community has been established and gained widespread recognition.[15]

In addition to the activities and services provided by the individual congregations, there are a several cross-communal bodies, including some that provide welfare services for the ageing Jewish population of Bournemouth, such as the Jewish Council for Social Services, the League of Jewish Women and, until very recently, the Hannah Levy House care home.[16] All Jewish bodies in the area are represented on the Bournemouth Jewish Representative Council (BJRC), which was set up in 1976. It embraces the local branch of the Council for Christians and Jews and is a source of information about Jewish activities in Bournemouth. In addition to a communal diary, BJRC publishes a quarterly newsletter, *Wessex Jewish News*, which was set up by Helena Greene in 1994. BJRC also organises social and cultural activities. While some cross-communal activities have endured for many years, others have been short-lived, including the Jewish Day School that operated in the BHC *cheder* classrooms for just seven years. It closed due to falling numbers and rising costs.[17]

Until recently, the Bournemouth Jewish community was continuously augmented by new retirees, but in the last few years the influx has not kept pace with the number of deaths. Based on census results, the Institute for Jewish Policy Research (JPR) estimated that the number of people in Bournemouth identifying themselves as Jewish in 2011 stood at 1,343, less than one per cent of the total population and that thirteen per cent of the community was aged over eighty-five compared to three per cent in the town's general population.

The various congregations in Bournemouth are enlarged by Jews visiting the area to stay in their second homes (often bought as future retirement homes), or to take holidays or breaks in the area. However, a significant number of Jews living in or visiting Bournemouth on a regular basis, including some Israeli families, are not involved in any of the congregations.[18]

Over the last fifty years, Jews have been very involved in Bournemouth civic life. Many Jews have served as councillors and six have been appointed as mayor: Dr Gabriel Jaffe, Michael Filer, Anne Filer, Ben Grower, Barry Goldbart and more recently Lawrence Williams. There have also been a number of Jewish magistrates and people who have been celebrated for their contribution to Jewish and non-Jewish bodies, such as Thelma Cowan, who in 2006 received Bournemouth's Volunteer of the Year award.[19]

The Decline of the Jewish Hotels

When East Cliff Court and East Cliff Manor hotels were both sold in 1960, the *Jewish Chronicle* took the optimistic view that this was not a particularly worrying development. It was suggested that the remaining kosher hotels were expanding and could therefore cater more economically under fewer roofs for the Jewish holiday trade.[20] This optimism proved to be misplaced. Although the Jewish hotels continued to invest in ambitious modernisation programmes and several were to operate for another decade or more, by the late 1960s the cracks had begun to appear. During the 1970s and 1980s there was a gradual but seemingly irreversible decline in their fortunes.

By the mid-1970s, like the population as a whole, Jews were taking more frequent, shorter holidays in Bournemouth. However, instead of booking into hotels and guest houses, an increasing proportion of visitors were staying in other types of accommodation, mainly self-catering flats and apartments, which they rented or owned. For families, renting an apartment was a cheaper option than staying in a hotel and it gave them more private space and greater independence.[21] The self-catering accommodation in which they stayed had often been created from the conversion of former guest houses and hotels, including several that had been Jewish owned. Before they closed, some of the guest houses operated as a hybrid of 'demi-pension' and self-catering accommodation, such as the Mayfair guest house, which advertised that it had several self-catering suites in its new extension. Judi Lyons explains:

> People gradually realised that there was more money to be made from renting out property and it wasn't nearly such hard work as running a hotel or a guest house. The owners didn't have to do much except collect the money. A number of people had inherited flats and decided to let them, while others bought them with the specific purpose of renting them to Jewish visitors.[22]

For those Jews with the means to purchase holiday homes, especially sought after were the apartments in Dorchester Mansions and the Albany where several of the Jewish hoteliers lived. These apartments were advertised prominently in the *Jewish Chronicle*.

The impact of this development was not nearly as damaging as the advent of cheap foreign travel. During the late 1960s, it had become noticeable that Jews in the UK were taking more holidays abroad than the non-Jewish population. This was partly a result of their comparative affluence mentioned above, but also because kosher hotels were now opening in popular destinations, such as Majorca. Elissa Bayer comments: 'Jews quickly developed a liking for playing kalooki in the sun!'[23] Reading the signs, in 1968, Alec Kesselman, who had run one of the butcher's shops in Bournemouth, moved to Majorca to preside over the kosher section of the five-star De Mar Hotel at Illetas, just outside Palma, where he greeted many former clients of the Bournemouth hotels. Since childhood, he had been enthralled by the history of the Jews of Spain and Majorca and once said that he had been 'guided by a power higher than myself to make my way to Majorca and set up a living expression of the Jewish people.'[24] During the peak summer season, Jewish clients at the De Mar Hotel paid a supplement for kosher food, but the package holidays offered by the hotel still cost less than the all-inclusive Bournemouth hotels. Mr Kesselman introduced several innovations that helped to attract British Jewish families, including special kosher meals for children and provision for Jewish celebrations such as *Bar Mitzvah* parties.[25]

The trend gained momentum with the introduction of affordable holiday packages that included air travel as well as accommodation and board. While the coastal resorts in mainland Spain were favoured by younger Jewish travellers, Jewish families tended to gravitate towards the more established fashionable resorts, such as Knokke le Zoute in Belgium with its prominent kosher Grand Hotel Motke. As air fares continued to fall in price, holidays in North America, especially in Florida, also became affordable. Geoffrey Alderman comments:

> Florida became to Anglo-Jewry what Bournemouth was a generation previously. It had sand, sun, Jews in abundance, a language that was approximate to ours and, most excitingly of all, Mickey Mouse. Other places paled into insignificance when compared with all this.[26]

Wealthier Jews were now booking holidays in the more expensive kosher hotels, such as the Grand Hotel in Rimini and the Liberty Hotel in Milan, and also in the various kosher hotels located on the French Riviera, such as in Juan-les-Pins and Cannes. They also took winter cruises to South Africa and holidayed in more exotic locations, including the Bahamas.[27]

In addition to the reducing cost of foreign travel and the increasing number of kosher hotels abroad, the growth in Jewish foreign travel was also an outcome of the Six-Day War of 1967. With Jerusalem reunited, large numbers of Jews started to travel to Israel. Over the next few decades, several luxury hotels, often modelled on the kosher hotels in Bournemouth, began to open there and air fares to Israel, which had previously been prohibitively expensive, dropped in price. People who had previously not been interested in holidaying abroad, became very comfortable with the idea of taking holidays in Israel, which as a result became known as 'Bournemouth-on-the-Med'.[28] Sheila and Jack Morris, who holidayed in Bournemouth several times a year for over twenty years, decided that they wanted to do something special for their twenty-fifth wedding anniversary in 1974: 'We went to Jerusalem, our first ever holiday abroad and after that, we took all our main holidays in Israel and only went to Bournemouth for short breaks.'[29]

As a consequence of these developments, the Bournemouth hotels, especially the larger ones, found it increasingly difficult to fill their bedrooms. In a bid to retain trade, the luxury hotels continued to refurbish and expand their premises, offering even greater comforts for their guests. They also became more flexible in their booking arrangements. Geoffrey Feld recalls: 'The Sunday-to-Sunday bookings became seven days, starting at any time of the week. Later, we began accepting five-day bookings and then any bookings at all. It didn't work. Gaps appeared in our reservations, both during the summer and for Jewish holidays. I had to start marketing the hotel proactively.'[30]

Towards the end of their heyday, the hotels began splitting the bookings for some of those times when they had once been at their busiest – Christmas and New Year and for several of the Jewish festivals – since people no longer wanted to stay for extended periods. Richard Inverne explains:

> First, we had to split the 'end of year' holiday period – people came for either five days over Christmas or five days over New Year. Then people stopped coming for the period covering *Rosh Hashanah* and *Yom Kippur*. We started to take bookings for three days over *Rosh Hashanah*, when quite a few people came, but fewer were interested in coming over *Yom Kippur*. We also had to split *Sukkot* into 'Sukkot

One' and 'Sukkot Two' (*Sukkot* and *Simchat Torah*). Apart from the peak summer period, weekends and the now-split 'end of year' holidays, the only time that the hotel was still full to capacity was over *Pesach*. This slow but steady decline was all very different in my grandparents' time, when a fortnight was generally the minimum expected booking. Clients who could only manage a week were requested to find friends to fill their second week.[31]

The hotels also began to diversify their customer base and their holiday offering, displaying great ingenuity in enticing guests: taking bookings at reduced rates for group holidays; introducing special packages, such as golfing holidays and card tournaments, children's weekends and singles' weekends; offering family rates; providing a venue for conferences, seminars and lectures; and hosting commercial ventures, such as fashion and jewellery sales.

As the years progressed, an increasing number of older people, many of whom had been hotel guests in their younger days and were now too frail to travel abroad, came to stay in the hotels for long periods over the winter months, and even permanently. As a result, out of season, some of the hotels came to resemble sheltered housing and Bournemouth was described as 'the geriatric wonderland of the South Coast'.[32] Elissa Bayer recalls that when she once stayed in the Cumberland in the 1980s, the heating was always turned up high to ensure that the older guests were kept warm: 'The hotel had a revolving door and when people got outside, they just carried on walking back into the hotel as the cool air was too much to bear by comparison to the overheated hotel.'[33] Barbara Glyn recalls: 'In the Green Park's declining years, Esther and Max Astaire were resident at the hotel. They didn't have to do anything themselves. All their meals were provided and they had the company of other guests. They loved dancing and were always first up to dance.'[34]

Some contemporary social commentators thought that this was not a positive development. In a *Jewish Chronicle* article subtitled 'Don't Send Grandma to Bournemouth', Barry Kosmin, executive director of the Research Unit of the Board of Deputies of British Jews, said: 'Community support or placement does not mean shifting the responsibilities by placing the problem in someone else's community. Merely sending an old parent to Hove, Bournemouth, Southport or wherever is no solution.'[35] Some of the Bournemouth hoteliers agreed. In 1980, Geoffrey Feld explained why the Cumberland was not enthusiastic about having permanent guests: 'The main reason is that we don't like the attitude of a lot of their children, who think they can put all their responsibilities onto us, and feel marvellous if they come down for lunch with the kids once in three months and then disappear again. They tell their parents: "Don't worry, Mrs Feld will look after you."[36]

However, other hotels advertised proactively for permanent guests, including the Normandie.[37] Particularly popular as a retirement hotel was the Grosvenor. Several permanent guests stayed on even after the hotel relinquished its kosher licence in 1980.[38] After a gap of nine years, in 1989 Sydney and Rhoda Lukover, who had previously run the Grosvenor, returned to the hotel business in Bournemouth to run the fourteen-bedroom Grove House Hotel in Grove Road. Their clientele was mainly permanent and long-stay guests. Although it was run as a kosher establishment, for financial reasons it was not under rabbinical supervision.[39]

During the 1970s, two of the Big Eight began operating as non-kosher hotels. In 1973, the Majestic was sold by the Feld family to Metropolitan Estates (owned by Mr Taubman), which had hoped to demolish it and build flats on the site, but a property slump prevented the company from doing so. Instead, the hotel was sold on to the Specialist Leisure Group, owners of the Shearings coach company,[40] which carried out an extensive renovation of the hotel. Its reopening was advertised prominently in the *Jewish Chronicle* and the hotel attracted mainly Jewish visitors, despite the fact that it no longer held a kosher licence.[41] The new manager was Armand Rosier, who ran the hotel 'along continental lines': guests paid for a bedroom and could 'please themselves where they ate'.[42] On occasion, the hotel was taken over for large conventions of *Chassidic* Jews (members of sects originating in Eastern Europe), who brought with them their own equipment and supervising rabbis. These events provided a great deal of learning for the non-Jewish staff.[43]

From 1976 until 1980, the Normandie Hotel (known at that time as the Normandie International), operated under the same management as previously (Belle Keyne and Ron and Ann Fisher), but as a non-kosher hotel. Again, the hotel continued to advertise in the *Jewish Chronicle*. Seventy-five per cent of the guests were Jewish and *latkes* (hash browns) and *lokshen* (noodle) pudding were still staple fare on the hotel's menus. Its clientele included groups of *Chassidic* Jews, who self-catered.[44] When Belle Keyne retired in 1980, the Normandie was sold to International Hydro Hotels, which refurbished it, added a hydro facility and reopened it as the four-star New Normandie International.[45] Although its owners, Isaac and Bertha Klug, were Jewish, they did not run it as a kosher hotel. Advertisements for the hotel welcomed Jewish guests and stated that it specialised in vegetarian food.[46]

One of the main reasons for the two hotels becoming non-kosher, was the spiralling cost of kosher catering. Operating as non-kosher establishments was the only way in which the hotels were able to make a profit. David Latchman comments: 'Although it was religiously incorrect, it was probably quite a good business decision if these hotels still attracted Jewish clientele even though they no longer had a licence. It would have saved them a lot of money and also a lot of hassle, like the soup being declared as unfit five minutes before it was due to be served.'[47]

The remaining large kosher hotels reduced their prices further and further in a bid to retain guests. Kenny Arfin comments: 'The Green Park, once the most expensive Jewish hotel in Bournemouth, was now amongst the cheapest and just managed to cover its costs.'[48] Despite the repeated urging of *Jewish Chronicle* travel writers for readers to remember the kosher hotels in Bournemouth when making their holiday plans, during the 1980s two more of the Big Eight closed. In 1984, the Feld family sold the Cumberland to the non-Jewish entrepreneur Rick Wright, part-owner of the Majestic Hotel, sold by the Feld family eleven years previously. He immediately sold it on to two hoteliers who owned hotels in Torquay. For the first year after the sale, the new proprietors switched to being kosher during *Pesach* under the supervision of the Sephardi licensing authorities.[49] However, owing to a scandal, this initiative proved to be a one-off event.[50] The hotel subsequently changed hands several times and is now owned by an Arab company, the Oceana hotel group, which has other hotels in Bournemouth, including the Hotel Royale.[51]

By the mid-1980s, the Green Park had lost the lustre it once had. David Latchman comments: 'The family stopped investing in the fabric and furnishing of the hotel and in its last few years it looked and felt a bit neglected.'[52] Having run the hotel for forty-three years, in 1986 the Marriotts and the Richman sisters decided to call it a day: 'Ruby was well into his eighties, they were tired and wanted to sell. A businessman approached them with an offer they couldn't refuse.'[53] The Green Park was sold to non-Jewish owners, Majestic Holidays. After the closure was announced, the business was wound down and the hotel office apparently became a haven for distressed staff who were comforted by the Richman sisters. On the last day of trading, there was a big farewell party. Hettie Marks recalls:

> My husband and I were there for the 'Last Hurrah' at the Green Park. It was held over a weekend and the hotel owners recreated the atmosphere of its heyday. We danced like we had always danced

when we stayed at the hotel over the years. My husband was a wonderful dancer. A couple came over to talk to us, saying that they remembered seeing us dance many years before when they had been staying in the hotel at the same time as we were.[54]

The new owners of the Green Park operated it as a non-kosher hotel, but continued to advertise in the *Jewish Chronicle*, until they eventually obtained planning permission to erect an apartment block on the site. At this point, the hotel was sold to the developers, Manway Homes. The Green Park was the last hotel on the East Cliff to be granted planning permission for redevelopment. Despite the protests of the local civic society, demolition commenced in September 1988.[55] Due to sentiment for the longstanding hotel, a large proportion of the eighty Green Park apartments were purchased by Jews. David Latchman comments:

> To begin with, the vogue for Jews to buy flats in Bournemouth, either as retirement or holiday homes, helped to stave off the demise of the hotels since the part-time residents continued to frequent them for eating or entertainment, but eventually the demand for flats hastened their closure because the proprietors realised that they could make loads of money by selling off their hotels for development as flats.[56]

The fate of the smaller, less expensive hotels followed a similar trajectory. During 1976, the Carmel embarked on a major modernisation programme, making most of its bedrooms *en suite*.[57] Although its owner, Armand Gutstein, emphasised that the hotel was open not only to the most orthodox Jews, it did not offer dancing and other forms of entertainment available elsewhere, foreshadowing the future *charedi* holiday trade in Bournemouth (see below). Despite its loyal clientele, the Carmel closed in April 1980 and the Gutsteins moved to Edgware where they ran a successful delicatessen named Pelters.[58]

By the mid-1980s, the Bournemouth section of the hotel listings in the *Jewish Chronicle* was dominated by advertisements placed by non-kosher establishments. These advertisements were not only for hotels that had previously been kosher but also hotels that were not Jewish owned. Richard Inverne comments: 'Their owners appeared to sense that with the closure of the large kosher hotels, they might be able to attract Jewish clientele.'[59] These non-Jewish-owned hotels included the most luxurious hotels, such as the Royal Bath and the Palace Court. In the early 1980s, the prestigious, five-star Carlton had so many Jewish guests that its managers were seriously considering opening a separate kosher kitchen to cater for them and for Jewish conferences and functions.[60] When some of the non-Jewish hotels found it increasingly difficult to fill their bedrooms, they converted their upper floors, sets of rooms or even wings into apartments, for sale or rent, some of which were taken up by Jews. These upmarket, non-Jewish owned hotels were promoted by *Jewish Chronicle* travel writers, especially those establishments that were willing to provide vegetarian or fish meals by arrangement.

As the number of kosher hotels decreased, Jewish families seeking a cheaper option began staying in some of the other non-Jewish hotels in Bournemouth, such as the Cliff End Hotel, which had a private path leading to Boscombe Chine.[61] When the Feld and Inverne families sold the Cumberland, they purchased from the Lanz family four non-kosher hotels in Bournemouth – the Anglo Swiss, Heathlands, Cecil and Durlston Court – which they brought together for marketing and purchasing purposes as the Quadrant Group.[62] To their surprise, they discovered that the Heathlands, located in Grove Road and the largest of the group, had a substantial number of Jewish guests, who had been staying in the hotel year after year, mainly during the summer months. They wanted to continue coming to the hotel so that they could meet up with other Jews with whom they had become friendly. The hotel had 115 bedrooms, extensive conference and banqueting facilities, an outdoor pool and a large restaurant and coffee shop. Richard Inverne recalls: 'Until then, I had been under the somewhat-blinkered view that Jews only stayed in kosher hotels. It was a totally different world meeting Jews who were comfortable holidaying with non-Jews and mainly sticking to fish and vegetarian diets.'[63] A number of guests who had previously stayed at the Cumberland joined the existing Jewish clientele at the Heathlands and, to a lesser extent, at the Anglo Swiss Hotel.

Bucking the trend, in March 1985 it was announced that a new kosher hotel would be opening for *Pesach*, the thirty-three-bedroom Glencairn Manor in Manor Road, opposite the Majestic Hotel. It had been purchased by Paula and Jack Bright. Paula Bright was the daughter of Rabbi Jonah Indech, emeritus rabbi of BHC, and had previously taught in London.[64] Jack Bright was an accountant. During their ownership of the hotel, the Brights placed an emphasis on activities for young people. They established a singles' club that met monthly at the hotel and held singles' weekends twice a year, as the result of which several marriages took place.[65] A number of guests returned to the hotel several times, including a family from Ireland with whom the Brights became friendly.[66] However, this venture was to be relatively short-lived. In 1990, ownership of the hotel passed from the Brights, who had sold it 'for personal reasons', to the Sephardi Amdur family,[67] who reopened the hotel as the New Glencairn Manor. The hotel went into receivership in August 1992.[68]

GLENCAIRN MANOR HOTEL,
MANOR ROAD, BOURNEMOUTH.

Tel. Mangt. 27636
Visitors. 20473

47. The Glencairn Manor Hotel, 19 Manor Road, Bournemouth, *c.* 1970. Image in the Flickr collection of Alwyn Ladell, https://www.flickr.com/photos/alwyn_ladell/14648631303.

The smaller guest houses were unable to offer either the standard of comfort required by some guests, or the higher levels of *kashrut* (see Chapter 7) required by others as they were unable to pay for the requisite supervision. As a result, by the late 1970s there were no more than a handful of kosher guest houses. Only one of these – Villa Judi – endured into the 1980s and closed as a kosher guest house in March 1986.[69] During the 1980s, two new guest houses opened for short while – Sharon in Fisherman's Avenue run by Gillian Ross, and Wyndsmere run by Annie Lewis. This type of accommodation had become unfashionable and no new kosher guest houses opened subsequently.

Throughout all of these changes, the New Ambassador continued in business under the ownership of Alf and Sadie Vickers. The partnership between the Vickers and Max Green was dissolved, but Joy and Sefton

Eagell remained as general managers of the hotel. During the 1980s and
1990s, the hotel received a steady flow of bookings from families during
the summer and from older guests for the Jewish holidays and during the
winter months. David Latchman comments: 'The clientele continued to be
mainly mainstream United Synagogue type Jews, who were not particularly
religious.'[70] The hotel took many group bookings at weekends, especially in
the winter, and for wedding parties (see Chapter 8). The hotel was also
frequently used for conferences and seminars, mainly for communal
organisations ranging from WIZO and the League of Jewish Women to the
annual AJEX gathering and conventions of European rabbis.[71] Jewish hotels
in other coastal resorts attempted to enter the profitable conference market,
but the New Ambassador gained an outstanding reputation for catering for
Jewish gatherings.[72] One of the organisations that met at the hotel on several
occasions during the 1990s was the Masorti movement. Michael Alpert
recalls that those present at the conferences were given permission by the
resident minister, Rev. Camissar, to hold a service, providing the men and
women sat separately.[73] Geoffrey Alderman also recalls: 'There was a
Shabbat morning service. Rabbi Louis Jacobs was there. I was given an
Aliyah [called up to read during the service] and I asked Louis Jacobs to
leyn [chant from the scroll] for me. Afterwards, I said to Louis, "This is a
first time that I have asked a real live heretic to *leyn* for me". Quick as a
flash, he replied, "This is the first time that I have been asked by a real live
heretic to *leyn*!"'[74]

However, by the 1990s, the hotel was struggling to fill its bedrooms
out of season, especially after a staff wing had been converted to create
additional guest bedrooms. Whereas in the past the Big Eight hotels had
competed with each other, the New Ambassador's main competition now
came from non-Jewish hotels, particularly those that were Jewish-owned
but non-kosher. They were able to offer cheaper accommodation since
they did not have to buy expensive kosher food, meet licensing costs or
pay the fees for a *shomer* (religious supervisor, see Chapter 7). The non-
kosher hotels, many of which were part of hotel chains, could also deploy
their staff more flexibly. Roger Vickers, who directed the New Ambassador,
explains: 'Because of *kashrut*, and the many other requirements of our
religion, staff were specially trained to understand what they should and
what they should not do. We had to keep sufficient staff all year to cover
peak periods as we couldn't easily bring in extra staff just for the busy
times.'[75] Although its market had reduced, the hotel continued to invest in
repair and maintenance programmes. The hotel had fewer, mainly older,
guests, but its overheads remained the same. By the beginning of the

twenty-first century, it had become more and more difficult for the hotel to remain afloat. It was sold to the Britannia hotel chain[76] and closed as a Jewish hotel in January 2006.

The void was partly filled by the opening the previous year of a new kosher hotel. At the beginning of 2005, David Bright,[77] a kosher chef and son of Paula and Jack Bright, who had owned the Glencairn Manor, purchased the Bourne Dene Hotel in Manor Road in partnership with his brother-in-law, Barry Berlyn. It was renamed Acacia Gardens and was completely refurbished. The existing forty-two bedrooms were reduced to twenty-two with *en suite* facilities. The hotel also had a seventy-seat restaurant open to the public, and conference and banqueting facilities in its grounds.[78] Announcing its opening, David Bright described it as 'a small, upmarket kosher hotel with five-star facilities'.[79] Judy Silkoff, who visited the hotel in 2006, wrote in the *Jewish Chronicle*:

> Unlike some other kosher hotels' 'like it or lump it' style, Acacia Gardens has paid lots of attention to décor. The entrance hall has swag curtains, plush carpets and chintzy sofas, which create an atmosphere of cosy opulence. Indeed, signing in at the reception desk (a huge polished wood affair) it almost felt as though we were visiting a friend's country house. Each guest room has a name instead of a number, and although the refurbishment of the hotel above the ground-floor level still seemed to be ongoing, the most important comfort factors have been attended to.[80]

The hotel struggled to sustain a trade throughout the year and also experienced problems with the licensing authorities (see Chapter 7). It became a non-kosher hotel in 2006, and plans to open a second kosher hotel were abandoned by the partners.[81]

The Normandie was the only other Big Eight hotel to remain open beyond the 1980s. It had a very different clientele from the New Ambassador. During 1987, the hotel was purchased by a partnership between the Chontow brothers, who were property dealers, and the Mozes family, who were of Dutch origin and owned the largest Jewish travel agency, Goodmos Travel, a pioneer in travel to Israel. Brian Lassman comments: 'The travel agency connection worked well for bringing people to stay in the hotel.'[82] The partnership ran the hotel along strictly orthodox lines and it was supervised by Kedassia operated by the Union of Orthodox Hebrew Congregations (see Chapter 7). Since it had been run as a non-kosher hotel for a number of years, major changes had to be made before the hotel reopened for *Pesach* in 1988. Brian Lassman, previously the general manager at the New Ambassador, was appointed as managing director. After the Green Park closed, a number of the staff went to work at the Normandie. Since the Green Park had been the most orthodox of the Big Eight hotels, the staff had little difficulty in adhering to the stricter rules set by Kedassia.[83]

48. Owners of the Normandie Hotel from 1988. From left to right: Sidney Chontow, Modcha Mozes, David Chontow, Shampi Mozes, Michael Chontow. Image courtesy of Brian Lassman.

The Normandie was marketed as being '*glatt* Kosher' and as a place for orthodox wedding celebrations (*sheva brachos,* see Chapter 8). As a result, the hotel attracted mainly *charedi* customers. Lashings of Kedassia-supervised food and an atmosphere in which children were not just tolerated, but positively pampered, proved to be a winning formula. Beverley-Jane Stewart recalls: 'The people in the hotel were wonderful with our children, although they did tend to feel sorry for us because we only had two!'[84] By this time, the hotel was far less glamorous than it had been a decade or so previously. David Latchman comments: 'While most guests wore *sheitels* and *kippot,* it was no longer expected that they would wear dinner jackets or long dresses. In fact, modest dress was *de rigueur.*'[85] James Inverne, who as a child spent much of his time at the Cumberland (his family's business), and later worked as a porter at the Normandie, recalls that it was popular hotel, but it did not have quite the same atmosphere as the Cumberland, perhaps because it missed the personal touch that family ownership can bring. He says: 'I used to see many former Cumberland guests in the Normandie, who wanted to reminisce about days gone by.'[86] As a result of events in the Gulf during the early 1990s (the invasion of Kuwait by Iraq), bookings at the Normandie increased significantly for several years as a result of people deciding not to go to Israel.[87]

Despite its popularity, particularly with the *charedi* community, over the years, the owners of the Normandie invested less and less in its upkeep, and in 2005 they applied for planning permission to demolish the hotel in order to develop the site for flats. Planning permission was refused, the hotel's owners lost an appeal and the hotel remained in business.[88] In 2008, it was rumoured once again that the Normandie was going to close, but in fact it stayed open.

Illustration 4. The growth in *charedi* holidaymakers in Bournemouth. Drawing by Beverley-Jane Stewart.

During the last decade, Bournemouth has seen something of a revival as a Jewish holiday destination, but the clientele has changed radically. The days of huge meals and non-stop entertainment have been consigned to history. The Normandie is now largely the preserve of *charedi* Jews who use the hotel mainly for summer holidays and celebrating Jewish festivals. It is also the location for rabbinical conferences. After *Yamim Tovim*, it is only open for group bookings. The hotel, which was becoming quite dilapidated, changed hands in January 2020 and is now owned by a *charedi* New York property dealer. Renovation works are said to have commenced.[89]

A new kosher hotel, the Water Garden in Annerley Road (formerly named Southcombe and later the Britannia), opened in 2015 with the help of a Chabad supporter's legacy.[90] It is open throughout the year and has an attached not-for-profit delicatessen named Chabadeli. The delicatessen transferred to the hotel from its initial location at Chabad House on Lansdowne Road (see Chapter 6). The hotel is very busy when it is catering for school parties, but at other times it can be quite quiet. Lillian Gonshaw comments: 'I remember staying there once with my brother and we sat alone at a table in the middle of the dining room.'[91]

Since the end of the twentieth century, but during the last ten years in particular, there has been a rapid growth in the number of *charedi* Jews who either rent or buy large properties in Bournemouth. They have been drawn to the area like generations of other Jewish holidaymakers before them, by the climate and Jewish facilities in the town: 'The *mikveh* [ritual bath] is vital. You can bring food with you but you can't bring a *mikveh*.'[92] The *charedim* travel to Bournemouth from London and Manchester and also from Switzerland, New York and Israel. One commentator said: 'Israelis go to Bournemouth because they can get three things there that are not available at home: carpets, rain and the chocolate buttons that are sold in Asda. My daughter just loves Asda!'[93]

The favoured location for *charedi* families is the Manor Road area of the East Cliff where there are many purpose-built apartment blocks, such as Crag Head and Dorchester Mansions. The property dealer and financier Willy Stern (the son-in-law of Osias Freshwater mentioned in Chapter 7), had a luxury penthouse in Dorchester Mansions, at which the Bobover Rabbi and his followers were often guests.[94] In 2008, Willy Stern's son-in-law, the wealthy philanthropist Rabbi Benzion Dunner, referred to as 'God's Postman' because of the amount of money that he gave to charity, was killed in a car crash on the outskirts of Bournemouth on his way to his holiday home on the East Cliff.[95] Many other *charedim* now visiting Bournemouth were the offspring of people who a generation earlier had been amongst the most orthodox guests staying at the Green Park Hotel and then the Normandie. They are therefore used to the idea of holidaying in Bournemouth and feel comfortable there.[96]

Today, the East Cliff is once again something of a Jewish enclave and it is often referred to as 'Golders-Green-On-Sea'. Recognising the changing market, from the 1980s onwards, listings for flats to rent or buy were often described as 'kosher' and sometimes the advertisers stated that adjacent apartments were available, understanding that this might be of interest to large *charedi* families. The Carlton Hotel has added an extension of timeshare apartments, which have mainly been sold to *charedi* families.[97]

When Bournemouth first started becoming popular with *charedim*, polite questions were asked at meetings of the local branch of the Council of Christians and Jews about their clothes and their customs.[98] The late journalist and author Michael Freedland once told the story of a *charedi* family sitting on a bench overlooking the sea in Bournemouth, eating *matzah* (unleavened flat bread that forms an integral part of *Pesach*). They were joined by a blind man who, on hearing the munching, leaned towards them to try and discover what was afoot. The kindly mother offered him a piece of *matzah*, which he touched appreciatively, running his fingers backwards and forwards over its surface. Eventually, he said: 'Forgive me for saying so, but I don't think much of this writer.'[99]

The presence of the *charedim* is now taken for granted by Bournemouth residents. Where hundreds of wealthy and well-known guests staying at the kosher hotels once came to promenade in their finery (see Chapter 8), *charedi* families are now often to be seen strolling in their traditional garb:

> I was told a story the other day about a man and his son who were walking along the promenade in Bournemouth dressed in Jewish apparel. Another Jewish man walking in the opposite direction and wearing 'normal' clothes, stopped to say hello. He wished them '*Gut Shabbos*'. As he was walking away, he heard the young boy saying to his father in Yiddish: 'Is that man even Jewish?'[100]

Many of the less orthodox Jews who previously self-catered in Bournemouth have increasingly bought second homes in Jerusalem, Netanya and Herzliya. However, with the advent of the COVID-19 pandemic, there appears to be a resurgence of interest in holidays in Bournemouth by non-*charedi* Jews who are no longer able to travel freely to Israel. While some are staying in self-catering accommodation, others are staying in non-Jewish hotels, such as the Queens Hotel (formerly the Jewish-owned Langham).

On this positive note, we now move on to the second part of this book to examine in detail particular aspects of hotel life.

Notes

1. Marlena Schmool and Frances Cohen, *A Profile of British Jewry, Patterns and Trends at the Turn of the Century* (London: Board of Deputies, 1998), p.5.
2. A survey conducted among Jewish mothers giving birth in 1971 showed that Jewish families with an average of 1.72 children per family were less prolific than the general population, which had an average of 2.16 children per family. The same survey indicated that at this time, Jewish women had a shorter child bearing period than the general population. Quoted in Lionel S. Kochan, 'Anglo-Jewry Since World War II', *The American Jewish Year Book*, Vol. 78 (1978), p.339.
3. *Ibid.*, p.341.
4. *Ibid.*, p.346.
5. Geoffrey Alderman, 'British Jews or Britons of the Jewish Persuasion', in S. Cohen and S. Horenczyk, *National Variations in Jewish Identity* (New York: State University Press, 1999), p.133.
6. See Schmool and Cohen, *A Profile of British Jewry*, p.21.
7. V. D. Lipman, *A History of the Jews in Britain Since 1858* (Leicester: Leicester University Press, 1990), pp.242–243.
8. See http://www.brin.ac.uk/economic-inequality-and-religion/.
9. David Graham, *A Tale of Two Jewish Populations, Census results 2011* (England and Wales) (London: Institute for Jewish Policy Research, 2013), p.9.
10. This section is largely based on 'The Streets of Bournemouth: Tourism and the Town', https://www.streets-of-bournemouth.org.uk/wp-content/uploads/2018/02/Tourism. and_.Town_.pdf and Jackie Edwards, *A Bed by the Sea: A History of Bournemouth's Hotels* (Christchurch: Natula Publications, 2010).
11. The BIC was officially opened by the Jewish Mayor, Michael Filer.
12. Conversation with Ruth Soetendorp, 6.7.2020.
13. *JC*, 15.4.2016.
14. See Glossary.
15. For a time, Rabbi Alperowitz served BHC on an informal basis. There was dissent about whether or not he should be appointed as senior minister when the position became vacant. He eventually withdrew his application to concentrate his attention on the Chabad congregation, which some BHC members joined. This detracted from BHC's centenary celebrations and created discord in the community.
16. The Hannah Levy House care home was originally run by the Jewish Board of Guardians and subsequently by a local board of trustees. It closed in late 2020.
17. *JC*, 26.9.2003.
18. *JC*,15.4.2016.
19. *JC*, 9.6.2006.
20. *JC*, 2.12.1960.
21. Interview with Richard Inverne, 6.7.2020.
22. Interview with Judi Lyons, 4.5.2020.

23. Interview with Elissa Bayer, 30.4.2020. Kalooki is a form of contract rummy originating in Jamaica. At one point, it was an integral part of Jewish life.

24. *JC*, 18.7.1997.

25. *JC*, 25.2.1972. The kosher section of the De Mar Hotel closed in 1978.

26. Interview with Geoffrey Alderman, 27.4.2020.

27. *JC*, 7.1.1977.

28. Interview with David Latchman, 6.5.2020. There were a number of other reasons for Jews to take holidays in Israel apart from the weather, including to see friends and relatives who had gone there to live, as a way of showing support for Israel, to interest children in their Jewish roots, etc.

29. Interview with Sheila Morris, 19.8.2020.

30. Talk given by Geoffrey Feld at Edgware United Synagogue, 6 March 2018.

31. Interview with Richard Inverne, 6.7.2020.

32. *JC*, 27.8.1982.

33. Interview with Elissa Bayer, 30.4.2020.

34. Interview with Barbara Glyn, 30.6.2020.

35. *JC*, 4.1.1980.

36. *JC*, 28.11.1980.

37. *JC*, 23.10.1981.

38. *JC*, 28.11.1980.

39. *JC*, 23.6.1989.

40. The company went into administration in the early part of 2020. The Majestic was closed and the staff all made redundant. See: https://www.bournemouthecho.co.uk/news/18472133.bournemouth-hotels-savoy-majestic-close/.

41. *JC*, 11.11.1977.

42. *JC*, 16.7.1976.

43. Conversation with Paul Millington, who was then a manager at the hotel, 27.11.2020.

44. *JC*, 24.6.1977.

45. *JC*, 6.6.1980.

46. *JC*, 5.6.1981. Mrs Klug pioneered alternative therapies in Bournemouth, founding the Wessex Health Living Foundation.

47. Interview with David Latchman, 5.11.2020.

48. Interview with Kenny Arfin, 5.5.2020.

49. *JC*, 1.3.1985.

50. In 1986, Alfred Litman was found guilty of fraud and declared bankrupt, owing money for the event at the Cumberland. *JC*, 6.6.1986.

51. Email from Geoffrey Feld, 17.8.2020.

52. Interview with David Latchman, 5.11.2020.

53. Ilana Lee, 'Diamonds at Breakfast', *Jewish Quarterly*, Vol. 54, No. 1, p.29.

54. Interview with Hettie Marks, 28.4.2020.

55. *JC*, 9.9.1988.

56. Interview with David Latchman, 5.11.2020.

57. *JC*, 18.6.76.

58. *JC*, 6.9.2020.

59. Interview with Richard Inverne, 6.7.2020.

60. *JC*, 3.6.1983.

61. *Ibid.*
62. The hotels were divided for tax and accounting purposes. Howard Inverne ran Durlston Court and the Anglo Swiss and Geoffrey Feld ran the Cecil and the Heathlands.
63. Interview with Richard Inverne, 6.7.2020.
64. Sadly, she died in a car accident in 2010, *JC*, 22.10.2010.
65. *JC*, 23.6.1989.
66. Conversation with Loraine Berlyn, née Bright, 2.9.2020.
67. *JC*, 21. 4.1990. It was purchased by Simon and Val Amdur, but Simon ('Sid') died shortly afterwards and the hotel was run by Val and other family members.
68. *JC*, 14.8.1992. The Amdur family also owned the non-kosher Treetops Hotel in Boscombe.
69. *JC*, 7.3.1986.
70. Interview with David Latchman, 5.11.2020.
71. *JC*, 4.6.1982.
72. *JC*, 3.6.1983.
73. Email from Michael Alpert, 28.11.2020.
74. Interview with Geoffrey Alderman, 27.4.2020.
75. Interview with Roger Vickers, 27.5.2020.
76. *JC*, 20.1.2006. Britannia Hotels is Jewish owned, but does not run kosher hotels.
77. See *JC*, 31.5.1996.
78. *JC*, 28.10.2005.
79. *JC*, 7.1.2005.
80. *JC*, 31.3.2006.
81. *JC*, 3.11.2006.
82. Interview with Brian Lassman, 14.5.2020.
83. Interview with David Latchman, 5.11.2020.
84. Interview with Beverley-Jane Stewart, 29.5.2020.
85. Interview with David Latchman, 5.11.2020.
86. Interview with James Inverne, 10.11.2020.
87. *JC*, 8.2.1991.
88. *JC*, 20.1.2006.
89. The Normandie is said to have been purchased by the Meisels family who are related to the Rabbi, Chaim Meisels, a Satmar follower who lives in Stamford Hill.
90. *JC*, 15.4. 2016.
91. Interview with Lillian Gonshaw, 25.9.2020.
92. Anonymous interviewee, 16.6.2020. The *charedi* visitors now have their own *mikveh* located behind what was once Mon Bijou guest house in Manor Road.
93. Anonymous interviewee, 16.6.2020.
94. *JC*, 27.2.1987.
95. *JC*, 8.8.2008.
96. Interview with David Latchman, 5.11.2020.
97. Interview with Stuart March, 21.9.2020.
98. *JC*, 27.2.1987.
99. *JC*, 14.8.2006.
100. Anonymous interviewee, 16.6.2020.

PART TWO

Aspects of Life in the Hotels and Guest Houses of Bournemouth

6

Food and Catering in the Bournemouth Jewish Hotels

The Anglicisation of Jewish Food

It has long been recognised that food is a central feature of Jewish existence. However, due to Jewish history, there is no such thing as a typical Jewish diet. As Jews have moved around the globe, escaping from persecution and economic and social discrimination, they have taken with them the regional flavours they absorbed in the countries they left behind. They acquired a fresh diet as they assimilated into their new homelands. For example, bagels are derived from a Polish baked bread, originally created for Lent and later embraced by the Jews, while gefilte fish stemmed from a German dish adopted by Jewish cooks. *Cholent* (a stew prepared in advance of *Shabbat*)[1] and *charoset* (a sweet paste made of fruit and nuts eaten at *Pesach*) have both surfaced in different forms in every land in which Jews have lived. As Claudia Roden has written: 'Every cuisine tells a story. Jewish food tells the story of an uprooted, migrating people and their vanished worlds.'[2]

By the mid-nineteenth century, those Jews who had arrived in Britain since the Readmission of the Jews in 1656 had incorporated the norms of mainstream society, including its diet. The existing community was vastly expanded by the great tide of Jewish migration from Eastern Europe, which commenced during the late nineteenth century. Initially, the newcomers remained wedded to the diets they had adopted in Eastern Europe as a means for retaining their links to the countries from which they had fled, but also because they were accustomed to the food. Adherence to their existing diet was also a mechanism for preserving their identity, a phenomenon discussed by the culinary philosopher Jean-Anthelme Brillat-Savarin, who wrote: 'Tell me what you eat: I will tell you what you are.'[3] There were variations in the diets of the new arrivals depending on the different countries from which they emanated,[4] and also differences between their everyday food and the food that they ate on Jewish festivals and holy days.[5]

At the beginning of the twentieth century, what Hasia Diner refers to as a 'foodway'[6] and what Panikos Panayi calls 'food transfer',[7] that is the process by which migrants adapt to the availability of different foods in their lands of settlement, was evident. The changes taking place were particularly obvious amongst those Jews who had achieved a degree of social mobility and amongst the offspring of the immigrants who had been educated in Britain and were rapidly acculturating. The process was accelerated by geographical mobility. As Jews left the first areas of settlement and moved to the suburbs, they quickly adopted the lifestyles of wider society, including the consumption of food similar to that of their new gentile neighbours, adjusted where necessary to meet Jewish dietary rules (see Chapter 7).

Recipes appearing in the *Jewish Chronicle* and Jewish cookery books and manuals published during the first three decades of the twentieth century illustrate the dietary transition that was occurring. For example, Estella Altrutel's *An Easy and Economical Book of Jewish Cookery Upon Strictly Orthodox Principles*, included recipes that did not differ significantly from those that appeared in general cookbooks. The menus for kosher restaurants are also a useful source of information. For example, the menu for Stern's Hotel and Restaurant in Mansell Street, Whitechapel, which catered for a wide range of Jewish social groups, served dishes available in any interwar British restaurant, such as egg mayonnaise, grapefruit, sardines, roast beef and roast lamb, alongside recognisably Jewish dishes, including *lokshen* (noodles), fried *worsht* (salami-style sausages) and pickled herrings.[8]

Dietary change became even more evident in the decades after the Second World War as a result of the break-up of the semi-ghettoes in London and other places where Jews had settled in significant numbers. With the rapid assimilation of the majority of Jews into mainstream British society, their diet became less distinguishable from that of non-Jews. However, the process was not straightforward. As the dishes were being transferred, the nature of the British diet was also changing. With European travel becoming more popular, the British diet acquired continental overtones, aided by cookery writers such as Elizabeth David. In addition, as other ethnic groups settled in Britain, particularly those from the Indian Sub-Continent and the West Indies, the British diet became ever more international. These changes were absorbed by the assimilated Jewish community, as can be seen in places such as Golders Green where there is a wide range of restaurants – kosher Chinese, Japanese, Indian, Italian and so on – but few Eastern European Ashkenazi restaurants.[9]

Again, the progress of food transfer after the Second World War is indicated by the contents of cookery books. In the postwar years, the best-known Jewish cookery writer was Florence Greenberg, the culinary correspondent for the *Jewish Chronicle*. The 1988 edition of her *Jewish Cookery Book* (or simply 'FG'), includes recipes such as spaghetti with Bolognese sauce. There are also references to curry, boiled tongue with sweet and sour sauces and sausages with savoury noodles. However, some meals of Eastern European origin remain and there are also separate sections on 'The Seder Table', 'Passover Cookery' and 'Traditional Jewish Dishes'. There is an obvious absence of dishes involving pork and shellfish.[10]

By the beginning of the twenty-first century, books such as the *Jewish Princess Cookbook* show that the process of food transfer had advanced even further. In respect of this book, Panikos Panayi concludes that 'while traces of Eastern European Jewish foods may remain, such volumes clearly suggest that Jewish diet has changed dramatically since the late nineteenth century', mirroring the integration of Jews into mainstream British society.[11]

The Prominence of Food in Hotel Life

In earlier chapters we have seen that when Jews first started to visit Bournemouth for the purposes of health or relaxation, there was no provision for their dietary requirements but, as their numbers increased, the issue began to be addressed. By the end of the nineteenth century, both convalescent facilities and boarding houses were catering for Jewish diets. As small Jewish boarding houses evolved to become larger and more comfortable guest houses, which in turn were superseded by ever more luxurious hotels, food became an important selling point in the marketing of the various establishments.

However, it was not until after the Second World War that food moved centre stage and became a legendary feature of Jewish hotel life in Bournemouth, particularly in the largest hotels, the Big Eight (see Chapter 3). Even during the years of austerity and rationing that followed the end of the war, the large hotels were able to acquire all the food and produce they needed to feed the Jewish visitors now flocking to Bournemouth. On their arrival, the guests handed over their ration books to the hoteliers, who pooled the food purchased with the coupons to produce meals that were far better than those that people had become accustomed to eating during the years of austerity. According to the *Jewish Chronicle*, the hotels were able to serve 'wholesome and varied fare, even if the meat ration is dwarfed by offal and poultry served in many attractive and palatable forms'.[12] Sometimes the hotels (like some of their non-Jewish counterparts) resorted to less legitimate means to feed their guests. Edward Hayman, who was brought up at East Cliff Court, recalls:

> When meat was still rationed after the war, my mother supplemented the legal supply by every so often driving to a black-market (supposedly kosher) butcher in Southsea. She would take me with her, though my father disapproved. My grandmother, Annie Morris, who owned the hotel, must have known what was happening, but I do not know how she felt about it.[13]

In 1947, the Levitus family, owners of the Ambassador, were summonsed for allegedly buying and selling eggs at above the legal price and for serving meals of more than three courses, which was illegal at the time.[14]

Within a few years of the war ending, the hotels had gained a reputation for their lavish meals and for round-the-clock eating. Geoffrey Alderman comments: 'It was a mind-exploding, waist-line-expanding experience, almost a practically non-stop, eat-athon.'[15] Since a large proportion of the hotel guests were observant and were unable to eat elsewhere in Bournemouth, the hotels offered packages that included all their meals. This encouraged people to eat whatever was on offer since it had been paid for,[16] and some people were loath to leave the hotels because they feared that they might miss a meal. Francine Wolfisz recalls her parents telling her about a guest staying at one of the hotels just after the war, who so engorged himself with the generous portions on offer that he had to be carried out of the dining room by the waiters.[17] Hazel Green remembers being told about a GP practice located on the East Cliff, which in the summer months received numerous calls from the hotels to treat guests with angina and digestive problems caused by overeating.[18] Some guests complained about the amount of weight they gained while staying in the hotels and said that they wouldn't be coming again, but they usually did.[19]

By the 1950s, a pattern of daily life in the hotels had been established that revolved almost entirely around food. Hannah Jacobs comments: 'The modern equivalent of the top Jewish hotels in Bournemouth after the

Second World War is the upmarket cruises where there is barely a pause between meals.'[20]

Schedule of meals

Tea and biscuits in bed.

Breakfast, served in the dining room. It was a 'milk' meal (i.e. no meat was served, see Chapter 7 for explanation). It consisted of eggs, fruit, cereal, kippers, haddock and rolls or toast. There were huge trolleys of preserves, including many different varieties of marmalades.

'Elevenses': Coffee and biscuits, served in the lounge.

Lunch was served at 12.30pm. This was another 'milk' meal (except on *Shabbat* when *cholent* was served). There would be a choice of starters (e.g. vol-au-vents or salad) followed by soup. The main dish was fish. There was usually a choice of three, such as bloaters, dab and local plaice, which were served grilled, fried or with a sauce, together with potatoes and vegetables. Dessert would include a choice of five or six fruit dishes, a dessert trolley with fresh gateaux and cheesecakes and a hot pudding. Because lunch was a milk meal, there would often be an ice cream dish, such as peach melba.

Afternoon tea of beverages, cakes and sandwiches, available between 4 and 6pm and served in the lounge or on the veranda.

Dinner was served at 7.00 or 7.30pm. This was a 'meat' meal. There would invariably be a choice of hors d'oeuvre, such as pickled herring and Russian salad, followed by a choice of soups, one of which was often chicken soup with *kneidlach* (dumplings) and an entrée, which might be mushrooms or chopped liver. The main course would be veal, chicken or beef, again with potatoes and vegetables. On Saturday evenings in the summer when *Shabbat* was not out until late, the hotels served cold meals, such as cold poached salmon with a sauce. The dessert – fruit, gateaux and cakes and sorbets – was followed by lemon tea and coffee (served with a milk substitute) and petits fours, such as glazed grapes, which in some hotels would be taken in the lounge.

Refreshments at 10.00pm: Tea, sandwiches and cakes were served for those who felt that they could not survive through the night until breakfast or had difficulty falling asleep after the kalooki and other entertainment (see Chapter 8).[21]

In addition to the regular meals, guests could order food from the room service menu at any hour, or additional teas and coffees at no additional cost. However, one commentator pointed out that the hoteliers were 'on a good wicket' in making this offer 'because nobody had any strength to eat between meals'.[22]

Angela Epstein recalls staying at the Ambassador and watching with horror as the post-dinner crowd stampeded the evening tea trolley, having recently devoured 'three cholesterol-laden courses'.[23] This scene was obviously quite notorious since a similar description was included in the fictional account of Bournemouth hotel life in Gerda Charles's satirical novel, *The Crossing Point*:

> Brought into the lounge too early by an inexperienced waiter, the rattle of cups on the evening trolleys was heard, at first by only a few at the back. With that fine community of interest that Micky [the evening entertainer] had so far been begging for in vain, those within ear shot at once dived rapidly for the next room. Within seconds, the news spreading, Micky found himself singing to scurrying backs. A swell like an ocean wave swept across the ballroom. Mrs Freiwinkel dropped her mink cape and was nearly trodden underfoot herself. Three chairs overturned. Sammy-boy, struggling against the tide to retrieve his wife's spectacle case, got swept out to sea again.[24]

People speak with amusement about the particularly lavish buffets served after the Saturday evening dancing and cabaret shows, referred to as 'light refreshments'.[25] In some hotels, the waiters apparently formed a cordon in a vain attempt to hold back the tide of guests heading for the late-night refreshments.[26] The Cumberland was famed for the bagels and Vienna sausages it served late on Saturday evenings.[27] After its Saturday dances, East Cliff Court served (non-pork) sausage rolls and savoury pies.[28]

The four-course lunches were beyond the appetites of some people. Hettie Marks says: 'I used to get Mr Mimmo [see below] to bring me a smoked salmon salad because I just couldn't cope with four courses.'[29] However, the rich cakes served by the hotels in the afternoon were especially appreciated by young people. Jon Harris recalls: 'There was a group of us, who met up year after year at the Normandie. We ran a book on who was able to eat the most chocolate eclairs or doughnuts. We used to stuff them in our pockets. My brother usually won. I think his record was twelve!'[30] Despite the fact that the hotels served generous afternoon teas, disorderly queues would start to form half an hour before the dining room doors opened for dinner.

Those guests who went for a morning walk after breakfast to work off a few calories often met up with people they knew who were staying in other hotels (see Chapter 8). A common topic of conversation was the quality of the breakfasts they had been served. Geoffrey Feld comments: 'Even when they were not actually eating, the guests were thinking or talking about food!'[31] Although the meals in the large hotels followed roughly the same pattern, they each had their specialities. The Green Park was renowned for its outstanding dessert trolley and the selection of thirty-five jams and marmalades available at breakfast, and the Ambassador for its afternoon cream teas. The Normandie's sweet trolley often featured an iced swan. Jon Harris recalls: 'It was made of choux pastry filled with cream and topped with chocolate sauce. It was a heart attack just waiting to happen.'[32]

One hotelier recalls that, notwithstanding the huge quantities of food available and the finesse with which meals were prepared and served, he once overheard a woman complaining that the food was terrible and the portions were too small. He comments: 'You can't win them all!'[33] Julia Wagner, who holidayed with her family at the New Ambassador recalls: 'We had a family joke, saying between ourselves: "The food is too hot, the food is too cold, haven't you got anything SMALLER?", copying the fussy clientele seated around us in the dining room.' Her observation is echoed by Jonathan Perlmutter, who stayed in the same hotel in the 1960s and early 1970s: 'If you serve Jews chicken, they want meat. If you serve them fish, they want chicken. There is simply no pleasing them!'[34]

Shabbat Kiddushim

The Big Eight kosher hotels became particularly famous for their *kiddushim*, the informal buffets served after the *Shabbat* morning services held in the hotels (see Chapter 7). They were arranged on tables that stretched from one side of the room to the other. At the Cumberland, the preparation for *kiddushim* started early on a Friday morning. Richard Inverne, former director of the Cumberland recalls: 'We made all the food from scratch – the gefilte fish, chopped liver and chopped herrings. We prepared enough to feed a full hotel of around 200 people.'[35] The *kiddushim* were primarily intended for people who had attended the services in the hotel *shuls*, but they attracted many who had not done so. Hettie Marks recalls: 'Often you would see people arriving who had been shopping in

Bournemouth. They came into the hotel clutching their Marks and Spencer carrier bags and bags from the clothes shops. They rushed upstairs to their rooms to drop their purchases and then came into the *kiddush*.'[36]

New guests to the Bournemouth hotels were sometimes taken by surprise at the size of the *kiddushim*, which were served just an hour or so before the four-course lunches. They soon learned they needed to pace themselves or to skip courses at lunch. If the size of the *kiddushim* was a surprise for Jews, it was even more mesmerising for non-Jews. Richard Inverne comments: 'One *Shabbat* we had to warn a non-Jewish couple who were staying with us about not eating too much *kiddush* because it would spoil their lunch. They were astounded. When they had seen the *kiddush* they had thought that it was lunch!'[37]

Illustration 5. The famous *Shabbat kiddushim*. Drawing by Beverley-Jane Stewart.

Despite the fact that there was only a short gap between the *kiddushim* and lunch, people crowded around the tables. If the *shomrim* (religious supervisors, see Chapter 7) took too long in saying the blessings, the assembled throng would become restless. One hotelier apparently warned first-time guests to stand back to avoid being trampled in the stampede to reach the food. Hettie Marks recalls:

> So many people crowded round the *kiddush*, it was sometimes difficult to get to the food. Once, when we were staying at the Majestic, my husband managed to squeeze his way in to try and procure a fishcake for me. Just as he was putting his hand towards the plate, an arm reached across him and almost speared him. He escaped injury, but after that he stood well back until those hungrier than he was had taken what they wanted.[38]

The *Shabbat kiddushim* were particularly appealing for children and young people, who descended on the buffet tables with great relish. Hannah Jacobs, who stayed at the Normandie for several years as a child, recalls her excitement at being able to eat food that was not on offer at home, including cold tinned spaghetti and Heinz Russian Salad.[39] There are also stories of children who hid beneath long tablecloths that covered the groaning buffet tables, periodically stretching out their hands to 'steal' the food, and those who gorged themselves on the reserve supplies of smoked salmon secreted under the tables.[40] Teenagers were not at all fazed by the large quantities of food. Jon Harris recalls: 'While the adults sat around looking a bit bloated and as if they could sleep for a week, we starved ourselves for an hour before moving onto lunch; we just loved it!'[41] Jonathan Perlmutter comments: 'Our parents were not keen for us to go swimming afterwards. I think they were worried that we might sink!'[42]

At the Cumberland, the Feld and Inverne families had a round table set up in the *shul* after the *Shabbat* morning service. Favoured guests would be invited to join the family at this table where they were served by the waiters rather than joining the throng jostling around the *kiddush* table. At the beginning of the *kiddush*, family members stood behind the buffet, helping to serve and chatting with the guests.[43] Richard Inverne recollects that his grandmother, Bluma Feld, never became proficient at silver service: 'Instead of using spoon and fork to serve the smoked salmon to the guests, she used a fork and her thumb!'[44]

When the Normandie became more orthodox in the late 1980s, the sumptuous *kiddushim* remained a key aspect of hotel life and the enthusiasm of guests continued unabated. Michael Alpert recalls: 'The staff were lined up behind a long row of tables. The crowd of guests was lined up like horses waiting for the gate to open in a race. Then there was a sudden charge. The staff looked alarmed by the army rushing towards them, looking as if they hadn't eaten for a week.'[45]

Alcohol

Although alcoholic beverages were readily available for those who desired them, the hotel guests were generally quite abstemious. Jon Harris comments: 'The old saying goes: "Gentiles drink and Jews eat".[46] At the Cumberland, it was not unheard of for the longstanding Spanish barman, Francisco, to fall asleep due to lack of custom.[47] Geoffrey Feld recalls that the wine served with meals at the hotel often went unfinished: 'When they were young, Gary Kopfstein [son of the catering manager Alex Kopfstein, see below] and my nephew Richard Inverne, were charged with going around the *seder* tables after the guests had departed to pour the left-over wine into jugs. We provided several bottles of free kosher wine for each table, but rarely were they all drunk. We used what was left for hot puddings and sauces. Waste not want not!'[48] Peter Phillips remembers that even amongst the younger guests there was very little drinking: 'A beer for us chaps and perhaps a naughty Babycham for the girls.'[49]

However, the situation appears to have been a little different when drinks were complimentary. According to her daughter Shirley Davidson, Fay Schneider often remarked on how Jews flocked to the free bars at events held at the Majestic, but only bought Coca Cola at the permanent bar she had taken the trouble to install at the hotel.[50] Similarly, even some of the normally abstemious guests partook of the complimentary drinks, especially the brandy and whisky, provided as part of the *Shabbat kiddushim*. Geoffrey Feld recalls:

> I once saw Mr Cohen coming into the hotel bar and invited him to have a drink with me. He said that he wasn't a big drinker. However, on the following *Shabbat*, I noticed that as soon as the rabbi had said the blessings, Mr Cohen headed with some speed for the drinks table where he asked for a whisky. 'Make it a double', he said to the waiter.[51]

As a child growing up around the Cumberland, James Inverne recalls that he was sometimes allowed to help pour the drinks for the *kiddush*: 'I loved the range of colours of the different drinks, including the yellow Advocaat, which no one drinks anymore. It was a rush to get all the drinks poured in time for the blessings.'[52]

When they were first established, the Big Eight hotels were not licensed and some of the hoteliers were summonsed for selling alcohol illegally. The first hotel to be in trouble with the law was East Cliff Court. Alexander Harris recalls: 'It became known to Bournemouth police that alcoholic drinks could be bought at East Cliff Court by non-residents who were not taking meals, which was illegal. Two Jewish police officers were sent round to investigate.'[53] In 1953, the proprietors of the Green Park were fined £200 plus £130 19s costs for selling whisky and sherry without a licence. Ruby Marriott defended himself by saying that he did not sell the drinks, but gave them away since drinks were included in the daily tariff. The court was not persuaded by this argument and the magistrate said that it was known to the police that 'there were other hotels in Bournemouth with similar ideas about getting around the licensing laws. The police are not going to tolerate it and action will be taken if it is not stopped.'[54]

One-by-one, the hotels obtained drinks licences and opened licenced bars that enabled them to sell alcoholic drinks both to their guests and to people who were not staying in the hotels. Once East Cliff Court had a full drinks licence, a wine waiter called Gini was appointed, who became known not only for his knowledge of wines, but also for his crêpe suzette flambé, which he prepared in front of the guests on a trolley that he wheeled into the dining room.[55] The other hotels followed East Cliff Court's lead and appointed their own wine waiters. As the proprietor of a first-class hotel, Ruby Marriott felt that it was incumbent upon him to establish a well-stocked wine cellar, managed by the wine waiter Mr Franks. Writing in the *Jewish Chronicle* in 1985, one of its regular columnists, Chaim Bermant, noted that although the Green Park had the 'best wine list he had seen in a kosher establishment anywhere', Ruby Marriott openly admitted that he had little knowledge of its contents. Bermant attributed this to the fact that few of the hotel's patrons were wine connoisseurs.[56] This view is supported by a story told by Simon Keyne:

> After the services in the *shul* at the Normandie on *Shabbat*, my mother, Belle, used to help with the *kiddush* by pouring the sherry. She asked people if they wanted sweet, medium or dry sherry. Whatever their response, she poured the drink from the same bottle. She realised that most of her guests were not big drinkers and were unlikely to know the difference. She explained with a smile that it was more important with Jews to offer them a choice. She was a clever business woman![57]

At this time the wine served in the hotels was *yayinnesech* (literally poured wine but meaning wine handled by non-Jews in its making).[58] This situation was to change in later years (see Chapter 7).

Mr Franks, the wine waiter at the Green Park, was later the barman at the New Ambassador, where he apparently conducted more trade selling Coca Cola and orange juice to adults and mixing non-alcoholic fruit cocktails for the young people than serving alcoholic drinks.[59] At one point, Trading Standards officers from the local authority took their trainees to the New Ambassador. When they asked to test the pumps, the trainees were always surprised to be told that the hotel did not have any pumps since Jews drank so little beer and they were therefore not needed.[60]

After the Majestic was sold, the Feld family purchased the Spider's Web motel in Elstree. Geoffrey Feld, a former director of the Cumberland and Majestic hotels, quickly discovered that the takings at the licensed bar of the motel were far higher than at the kosher hotels in Bournemouth: 'At the Cumberland the bar takings were £2,000 per year while at the Spider's Web the takings were £1,500 per weekend!'[61]

Changing Fare

Initially, the food served in the Bournemouth hotels was very reminiscent of the Eastern European Ashkenazi dishes that most of their guests would have known as children, with the hoteliers using recipes that had been passed down through generations of the families who owned the hotels. These recipes were refined and much loved. At that time, the traditional food was regarded as a 'cuisine that could hold its own with any in the world'.[62] However, in retrospect, it sounds less appealing to many people. One former guest at the Green Park recalls: '*Cholent* was served on *Shabbat*. It had been left to cook overnight on Friday. It was made of beans, meat, carrots, potato and cooked till all the goodness had been sucked out of it'.[63] Catering at the Green Park was initially overseen by Helen Richman, who was well-known for her *bubalehs* (pancakes made of *matzo* meal, usually served during *Pesach*). Nino Benedetto, former head waiter at the Green Park, recalls: 'They were made of chopped liver with egg and fried butter. They were a cholesterol time bomb!'[64] Vegetarian options were a rarity in those days and vegetarians were seen as rather 'cranky'. Edward Hayman comments: 'Guests would be served vegetarian food, or have any other dietary need met, but only if they gave the hotel advance notice of their requirements'.[65] The menu at East Cliff Court in the postwar years was noticeably less extravagant and more anglicised than those at the other hotels. It included dishes such as shepherd's pie and Irish stew.[66]

In the *shtetlach* (small Jewish towns or villages) of Eastern Europe the diet had been very simple – a herring and a piece of bread during the week and *challah* (plaited bread loaf used to welcome *Shabbat* and festivals) and a chicken on *Shabbat*. Generations later, as the hotel guests became more affluent and assimilated, their concern was not just with the quantity of food, but also with its quality, variety and modernity. The hoteliers were quick to respond to this shift in tastes. As the *Jewish Chronicle* noted in 1952: 'There is no man [*sic*] in the world so ingenious in the preparation of satisfying meals as the British hotelier. If the food is not right, no *kasher* [kosher] place ever stays open very long.'[67] Different foods, such as avocados, were introduced gradually and in small portions to allow guests to become acquainted with them. A former guest comments: 'It was an educational experience. Remember England wasn't known for its gastronomy.'[68]

By the early 1950s, continental influences were detectable. The Marriotts and the Richman sisters travelled across Europe, staying in leading hotels to gather inspiration for the menus at the Green Park, which they self-described as 'kosher international cuisine'.[69] One former Green Park guest recalls: 'We ate crème caramel twice a day. There was both French and Italian food but not Chinese, which wasn't yet fashionable.'[70] Interviewed by the *Jewish Chronicle* in 1953, Robert Myers, then the proprietor of the Normandie commented: 'At the Normandie the standard has always been very high, and has now developed to a fine art. Our chefs are famous for their flair for combining Jewish cooking with French finesse, and have proved that strictly kosher meals and traditional dishes can be served most attractively.'[71]

Over the next decade, the hotels started to give food exotic names, using French or Italian terminology (for example, *hors d'oeuvres* rather than starters), and the menus were printed in French. Over time, the menus became a parody of themselves. At the Green Park, guests were offered 'Le pickled brisket' and 'potage de kreplach'.[72] On election night in 1964, the Cumberland served a special menu that included 'Grimond Grapefruit', 'Election Meatballs á la Wilson', 'Candidate's Consommé with Floating Voters', 'Tory Tart' and 'Common Market Fruit'.[73] Although they took great care in the presentation of their menus, the hotels stressed that they were just suggestions and guests were free to order any dishes they pleased.[74] Menus varied from week to week, but some dishes became enshrined in tradition. At the Green Park, smoked salmon was usually served for dinner on a Saturday evening and borscht was a Sunday evening special. A story is told that when a guest, who was staying in the hotel for a month, was asked by a fellow guest how much longer he was there for, he replied: 'Two more smoked salmons and a borscht.'[75]

In the postwar years, some foods were less of a delicacy than they are nowadays, such as Dover sole, which was readily available and cooked to order. Other dishes were more expensive and regarded as more of a luxury than they are today, including smoked salmon.[76] It is therefore an indication of the lengths that the hoteliers were prepared to go to impress their guests that one former Green Park guest recalls a lunch when a huge table was placed in the centre of the dining room, on which upturned glasses had been arranged to form a pyramid. Smoked salmon was draped from glass to glass to create a smoked salmon fountain.'[77]

By the end of the 1960s, with the advent of organisations such as Weight Watchers, women in particular were becoming more conscious about what they ate. The late Mimmo Zacchia, former maître d' at the Green Park recalled: 'Suddenly people were wanting "fat-free" this and "low-cal" that. We used to end up with so much wasted food.'[78] Belle Keyne at the Normandie was quick to pick up on the trend and in 1965 started to advertise 'slimming' menus, inspired she said 'by popular demand'. Breakfast at the Normandie during 'Health Month' consisted of a small portion of scrambled egg with mushrooms, a non-starch roll or crisp bread, fruit juice and a cup of tea or coffee. However, the big 'tuck-in breakfast' (porridge, eggs, fish, doughy rolls, stewed fruit and endless tea and coffee) was still available for those who wanted it. Sophie Levine, the *Jewish Chronicle* columnist reporting on the development, commented pithily that she was intending to visit the hotel for a day or two so she did not 'miss the sight of Jewish people who flocked to a kosher hotel NOT JUST FOR THE EATING.'[79] However most guests at the Big Eight hotels continued to eat the same highly calorific food, even if it meant that they went straight from a Bournemouth hotel to Grayshott Hall Spa in Surrey to lose weight.[80] Elissa Bayer recalls:

> As a young married woman, I went to stay at the Green Park with my husband and some of our friends who hadn't stayed there before. They didn't know what to expect and one of them made the mistake of asking for a salad, which resulted in a shocked reaction from the waiter.[81]

The chef at the Cumberland appears to have been ahead of his time in experimenting with serving lighter and healthier food. Ruth Shire, who stayed at the hotel in the late 1960s, recalls eating 'sensibly-cooked vegetables' and 'excellent salads with the chef's own very special mayonnaise, as well as the lightest and fluffiest *latkes* [hash browns] I had ever tasted.'[82] However, Richard Inverne recollects the traditional Jewish food that was also served in the Cumberland. He comments: 'There was so much food that we now know to be unhealthy (Did we actually kill anyone?), but it was wonderful!'[83]

In their declining years, the food at the Big Eight hotels became less extravagant. Naomi Taub recalls: 'By the late 1960s, people were already saying that the Green Park was going downhill because at the 10.30pm snack time, the hotel was serving tinned salmon sandwiches instead of smoked salmon.'[84] The food at the hotel also reverted to being more traditional to cater for the mainly older clientele now staying at the hotel (see Chapter 5), and most of the hotels were now offering more flexible meal packages, such as half board or bed and breakfast only.

The two Big Eight hotels that remained open beyond the 1980s – the New Ambassador and the Normandie – continued to serve large, well-cooked meals, but the food was fairly traditional. Elissa Bayer recalls: 'At the New Ambassador the tables still almost buckled under the weight of the food, but its menus were a bit of a throwback, they didn't move with the times. I remember being served tinned fruit with a glacé cherry on top.'[85] Brian Lassman, who managed the hotel, does not recall ever serving a vegetarian meal there.[86]

The food served at the New Ambassador appealed to the many young families staying there during the 1980s and 1990s. Hannah Jacobs comments: 'Nouvelle cuisine wouldn't have gone down very well there, but my two growing sons just loved the copious amounts of food.'[87] Those guests looking for something less calorific were treated as something of a rarity. Carole Reggel, a former guest at the hotel, recalls: 'We once asked for fresh fruit for dessert. The waiter brought us an orange on a plate covered with serviettes. He put his finger to his lips as if to say: "Shh, don't tell anyone".'[88] The regular dishes on offer at the hotel at this time included Chicken Forestier served on Mondays, which was made of chicken left over from the previous Friday's dinner with a sauce, and the regular dish on Sundays was giblet pie, made with a thick layer of pastry and served with a generous helping of gravy, which people either loved or hated. It has been described as both 'luscious'[89] and 'resembling road kill with a pastry top – vile!'[90] Roger Vickers, who directed the New Ambassador, recalls:

The hotel once had an entry in *The Good Food Guide* and as a result many non-Jewish guests came to the hotel for a meal, often on a Friday night. As you can imagine, this caused all sorts of confusion and complications, for example, trying to explain why we wouldn't serve milk with tea or coffee after a meaty meal. In the end, I rang *The Good Food Guide* and asked for the hotel to be removed from their guide. I couldn't get the person taking the call to understand what I was asking or get them to believe I was serious. He said that he often received calls from people wanting to get into the guide and this was the first time ever that anybody had wanted a listing to be removed![91]

Unlike many of the non-Jewish hotels that bought in a high proportion of their meals, the New Ambassador cooked most of its food from the raw ingredients. Roger Vickers again recalls: 'Bournemouth Catering College was always extremely pleased to place their catering students with the hotel. They received a good all-round experience with us, and with the other kosher hotels, as in all departments in the kitchen we always made everything from scratch.'[92]

At the Normandie, which was now under the supervision of the strictly orthodox Kedassia (see Chapter 7), apparently the food was also 'plentiful but not very memorable.'[93] Laurie Rosenberg recalls that when he asked about a salad bar, he was 'met with incredulous looks.'[94]

Today, the two Jewish hotels in Bournemouth, the Water Garden and the Normandie, are both *glatt* kosher. During the week, the Water Garden does not provide dinner, but guests are able to buy hot take-away meals from the on-site delicatessen, Chabadeli (see below), which can be eaten in the hotel lounge. Traditional, well-cooked Jewish fare is available at the Water Garden on *Shabbat*. The Normandie offers strictly kosher meals on weekdays, which are served in its dining room during the summer season. The choice of food is quite limited and reviews suggest that the menu is not the main reason for people staying at the hotel. However, the food provided on *Shabbat* and for special events held at the hotel appears to be prepared with more care.[95]

Kitchen and Dining Room Staff

The diversification of the food available at the kosher hotels was hastened by the employment of kitchen and dining room staff from European countries, including the well-known Italian waiters, who from the late 1950s worked at the Green Park. When the Richman sisters were once staying at the Excelsior Hotel in Venice, they were approached by the proprietor to ask if they would be willing to employ some of his waiters so that they could learn English. The British holiday trade was beginning to take off in Italy and he thought that it would be helpful if his staff were able to speak English.[96] The arrangement worked well for the hotel, adding glamour and style to the dining experience that appealed to a generation that in general rarely ate out. The simple gestures of having their chair pulled out and their napkin placed on their lap were regarded as 'a delightfully foreign treat'.[97] The arrangement also worked well for the Italian waiters:

> The Italian boys came to England for the girls, not just to learn English! It was more relaxed in England than in Italy. There you couldn't touch a girl; it was very strict. So, it was very liberating to be able to talk to a girl with no commitment or a chaperone. The Italian waiters used to change partners every couple of days. The boys would come for six months and have a wonderful time in the nightclubs. The Royal Ballrooms in Christchurch Road was one of their favourite haunts.[98]

Many of the Italian waiters met their future partners while working at the Green Park. Some married English women whom they met in the town, while others married colleagues working in the hotel, including the Swedish maids.

During the 1960s, the Normandie employed several Spanish waiters. Simon Keyne, son of the Normandie's proprietors, recalls: 'Spain was going through a very bad patch. The Spanish waiters worked extremely hard and were really good at their jobs.'[99] The trainee waiting staff were closely managed by the various head waiters in the hotels: 'Mr Coles, the dapper head waiter, lined up the novice waiters before each meal to make sure that their hands were clean!'[100] Later on, the hotel employed several Italian waiters, including Adriano Brioschi, who was the head waiter at the hotel for nine years. He explains:

> I was working at the well-known San Marco restaurant in Holdenhurst Road run by the Longi family. One night, the owners of the Normandie came in for a meal and we got talking. I told them about my experience of working in top hotels and restaurants in Europe, such as those in St Moritz and Davos, and they hired me to work in the hotel. When I started working at the hotel there was only one other Italian waiter, but I recruited more using an Italian agency. Eventually, eight of the

fourteen waiters were Italian, several of whom lived in a villa in the hotel grounds. They used to meet up with the Italian waiters working in the other hotels. I often had coffee with Mimmo, the maître d' at the Green Park but was closer to the then headwaiter, Franco Corsi. Some of the waiters just came for the summer season but many stayed. If staff worked hard and showed commitment, they were well rewarded and became part of the family.[101]

However, many of the waiters were recruited locally, including the popular waitress Marjorie, who worked for many years at the Cumberland. Richard Inverne, who was taught by Marjorie to handle a silver-service spoon and fork when he was attending catering college, recalls:

> She would speed dangerously into the car park on her yellow motor-scooter, three times a day, about twenty minutes before meal-service, charge into the restaurant, whirl around her station of tables, long-hair flying everywhere, apron flapping, getting ready. Woe betide anyone getting in her way, whether guest, staff-member, or even Mrs Bluma Feld herself! Up would go the hair, on would go the smile, in would come the guests and Marjorie the Completely Professional Waitress would be calm, collected and ready to serve 'her people'. They don't make them like Marjorie any more![102]

The waiters were generally very polished, including the head waiter at East Cliff Court:

> ...[he] could carry four plates of fried fish in each hand, would whirl round like a ballroom dancer, probably sidestep to let another waiter pass him with a loaded tray, deposit his fried fish on one of the high serving tables and glide over to greet the newcomers, 'Good evening, sir', 'Good evening madam' and lead them off. Another waiter would pull out the chairs, and Tonks with a flap and a flourish would unfurl the starched linen napkins and flaunt them towards the newcomers' knees...Everything about Tonks was creased, from his voice and his smile to his trousers and his patent leather shoes.[103]

Moishe, a longstanding head waiter at the Ambassador, is remembered for having worn a tailcoat at breakfast, lunch and dinner. He worked for over twenty-five years at the hotel, during which time there were many changes of ownership and managers (see Chapter 3).[104]

The waiters were trained to provide a personal service to the hotel guests and to respond to their individual dietary tastes, even when they were outlandish, such as the guest who insisted on having celery, served in a tall glass, on her table at each meal, and a woman who asked for her *matzah* to be toasted. Barbara Glyn recalls: 'We had to go out and buy a new toaster each *Pesach*!'[105] Nino Benedetto, a longstanding head waiter at the Green Park, recalls: 'You would find yourself serving one night and flat fish would be on the menu. Flat fish has two sides and two colours of skin: one is white and one is dark. Needless to say, nobody wants the dark skin. If you had ten orders for flat fish, you had to have twenty fish because everybody wanted the white part.'[106]

The longstanding waiters, who served the same guests year after year, knew exactly what they would want to eat and how they wanted their meal to be served. A former guest recalls: 'We used to go down once or twice each year and they would always remember us. For instance, my husband always had to have a lemon with everything and it had to be cut in half. They would bring it out without even being asked, even after a year's gap.'[107] However, sometimes the personal service did not go quite to plan. Nino Benedetto recalls:

> I remember once when Mimmo was on holiday and Mario and I were left in charge. A customer came up to me and said: 'Nino, I am coming in September and I want a birthday cake, but please don't wait for us to finish dinner; bring the cake as soon as we sit down and give our order.' So, I went to the pastry chef and told him that I needed the birthday cake for six people for September. On the day of the birthday, the restaurant was full and I said to Mario: 'Go and get the cake straight away.' He went off, but he didn't come back. I went to see what was happening, which I shouldn't have done because I was in charge. I found Mario in the patisserie. He said: 'I can't find the cake; its nowhere to be seen!' I said to myself: 'Oh God, what do I do now!' I went into the kitchen, where the Polish chef Nicki was working. He wasn't too bad with cakes. I told him: 'Nicki, drop everything, you are going to make a cake.' I left him to it and returned to the restaurant. Time passed but the cake didn't arrive. I went back to the kitchen to find out what was happening and Nicki told me he didn't know how to write Happy Birthday. So, I showed him how to melt chocolate and use the icing tube to write Happy Birthday, but he forgot the H. and wrote 'Appy Birthday'. With a palette knife I removed the lettering and spread on another layer of butter cream and I wrote Happy Birthday

on a piece of paper for him to follow. Back in the restaurant, people were starting to leave. Still the cake didn't arrive and I went back to the kitchen once more to see if the cake was ready, which it was. Mario picked it up, opened the door and dropped the cake on the floor. I was now sweating with panic! We put the cake back together and took it to the restaurant. The band was having a break and the room was deserted apart from the table of six people waiting for the cake. The guest who had ordered the cake looked at it and said: 'It looks like it has been on the floor.' I said 'How did you guess?' He laughed otherwise he would have had to kill me! [108]

The personal service in the dining rooms ensured the waiters received good tips. David Latchmen recalls: 'My father had a little black book in which he made a note on the tips he had given to "our" waiter the previous year.'[109] The longstanding waiters often found themselves serving several generations of the same family.[110] James Inverne recalls that the Cumberland employed a toastmaster called Mr West: 'He was tall and thin and used to walk round the hotel announcing "Dinner is being served in the dining room", or "Tea is being served in the lounge". It was all very theatrical!'

Not all the waiters were exemplary in their behaviour. Joan Doubtfire recalls that when she was head receptionist at the New Ambassador, Olaf the Polish restaurant manager was once found drunk in the broom cupboard,[111] and Edward Hayman recalls that, after the Second World War, East Cliff Court employed a head waiter named John, who was 'handsome in a Spanish-looking way and a favourite of my mother's'. He once had a fight with the assistant head waiter named Hall, cutting the latter's cheek so badly that he had to be taken to hospital: 'According to Nanny one or both were drunk and the large ring John wore was specifically used for such occasions!'[112]

The Big Eight hotels all employed top-class chefs and under chefs. Several of the early chefs were continental refugees. The first chef at the Green Park was Mauritz Kuflik, a refugee from Germany, who arrived in England during the Second World War and had made his way to Torquay. Barbara Glyn recalls: 'He made contact with my father, then running the Sandringham Hotel in the town, who trained him as a chef. He transferred with the family to Bournemouth and worked at the Green Park until he retired. He married Muriel, the hotel's housekeeper, who had converted to Judaism encouraged by my mother, Sarah Marriott.'[113] Later, Mauritz's children and his father all worked in the hotel. The early chefs at the Green Park also included twin sisters from Hungary who were known as 'Tweedledum and Tweedledee'. The hotel chefs usually moved backwards and forwards between the meat and the milk kitchens, only one being open at any time, but the Hungarian twins,

Aranka and Helen, split the duties, one was the meat chef and the other was the milk chef.[114] This was apparently not only for religious reasons, but also because they did not get on well together.

The head chef at the Majestic was Max Colman (previously Kollmann), who trained as a pâtissier before leaving Austria for England just two weeks before the gates were closed to Jewish emigration. On arrival in Dover, he was sent to the Kitchener refugee camp at Richborough, near Sandwich in Kent. He signed up for the Pioneer Corps in the British Army and became a cook at a base camp, preparing meals for a Royal Engineers unit and was praised for his 'exemplary work'. He was released from the army in 1946 and went to Torquay where in 1946 he found a job at the Sandringham Hotel, previously been owned by Ruby Marriott. When Fay Schneider took over the Majestic (see Chapter 3), she recruited Max to become the head chef at the hotel. Miriam Marcus (née Colman) recalls: 'Fay Schneider was considering running the hotel as a non-kosher establishment to attract as many guests as possible, but my father said he would only work in a kosher hotel, so she changed her mind.'[115] Miriam recalls going to watch her father at work in the kitchen at the Majestic: 'He rolled out hundreds of pastry circles, which he filled with meat and shaped to make *kreplach*.'[116]

49. Max Colman (originally Kollmann), head chef at the Majestic Hotel, Derby Road, during the 1940s and 1950s, c. 1954. Image courtesy of his daughter, Miriam Marcus.

Later on, one of the trainee commis chefs at the Green Park was Luke Matthews, who today is the executive chef at the Chewton Glen Hotel, which is consistently included in the list of the top ten country hotels in Britain. Other well-known chefs at the Big Eight hotels included the Turkish Cypriots, Emil and Costa, and Dennis Eden at the Normandie, and the Italian chef Franco, who worked at the New Ambassador for over thirty-five years. Jonathan Perlmutter, who supplied the hotel with meat recalls: 'When I went to the hotel to take the meat order, I used to go into the kitchen to chat with Franco and he gave me a good breakfast. His English was awful, even after many years in the country, but he made the most wonderful chicken soup. For an Italian he was a very good traditional Jewish chef!'[117]

Like the waiters, some of the chefs were memorable for less positive reasons. Richard Inverne recalls a chef who became very drunk on New Year's Eve and picked a midnight fight with one of the head waiters: 'My late father, Howard Inverne, my uncle, Geoffrey Feld and I had to hold them apart and restore order before a very full hotel's worth of guests became too interested and too involved. Needless to say, the chef was gone before 1am and instructed never to return!'[118] Richard Inverne also recalls:

> In the late 1970s, we employed an Egyptian chef, in the spirit of playing our part in the peace process begun by Sadat and Begin. Unfortunately, whilst competent and happily-understanding of *kashrut*, he was rather temperamental and must have thought of himself as some kind of celebrity chef in the days long before Gordon Ramsay became famous. He gradually alienated virtually all his kitchen staff, many of whom had been with us for years. Let's just say that it was necessary for me to terminate his employment when, on a busy summer night and upset by something, he decided to go home in a huff *before* dinner, having unforgivably told several of his mystified colleagues to do the same. I thus found myself as the stand-in head chef, leading only two or three loyal remaining chefs, instead of about eight, through a hectic meal service. We managed somehow![119]

The experiences of former hotel guests indicate that standards might have slipped somewhat in the hotels' declining years. Hazel Green recalls eating a celebratory meal with her parents at the Cumberland in the early 1980s: 'The plates were whipped away from us before others on the table had finished eating, and I remember one of the waitresses explaining rather resignedly to my Dad (who had asked if the steak was tender): "Sir, kosher steak is always tough!'"[120] Carol Reggel tells a similar story about her stay in the New Ambassador:

> Dinner was served at 7pm until 8.30pm. We came down for dinner one evening at about 7.20pm. An elderly lady at the next table pointed to her watch and said: 'You are going to be in trouble', implying that dinner was served promptly at 7pm. The waiters were always out of there by 9pm. We thought that they must have had other jobs to go to![121]

Illustration 6. Kitchen life in the large hotels. Drawing by Beverley-Jane Stewart.

Anne Filer, who was born in Bournemouth and has remained resident in the town, suggests that sometimes the service at the New Ambassador was similar to that at Blooms in Golders Green: 'It was rumoured that the waiters put their thumbs in the soup to hold the bowls steady and made slightly risqué remarks such as "Do you want leg of lamb today or a Dolly Parton?"'[122]

The hotel kitchens were usually split into a number of areas, which were used for different purposes and which were managed by different staff members. At East Cliff Court the kitchen complex formed an open suite with partitions between the meat kitchen, the milk kitchen (see Chapter 7), the pastry kitchen and the stillroom where hot drinks, sandwiches and toast were prepared. Edward Hayman, grandson of the hotel owner recalls: 'The stillroom was ruled by a formidable lady called Daisy, who kept a caged parrot there.'[123]

Although the hotels employed large teams of staff to assist with the preparation and serving of food, most of the hoteliers were closely involved in overseeing the catering arrangements. At the Green Park, Hannah Richman, who followed her sister Helen as the hotel's catering director, was assiduous in maintaining an overview of the hotel's kitchens and dining room. Even though she was vegetarian, she personally supervised all of the ingredients that were used and the processes that were followed to produce the dishes served to the guests, asking others to taste them if necessary before they were served.[124] However, she was not as directly involved as her grandmother, Bubbe Richman, who in the Green Park's early days, did some of the cooking herself. Her grandson, David Marriott, recalls: 'She made butter cakes, using her cupped hands rather than scales to weigh the ingredients. On Fridays, she prepared the chopped fish with a bowl in her lap and a cigarette in her mouth. I don't think the ash ever fell into the bowl, but I can't be absolutely certain.'[125] Edward Hayman recalls that his grandmother, Annie Morris, was often in the kitchen, talking with the chef 'as with a friend' and tasting the dishes being cooked: 'I thought it unhygienic the way in which she tasted the soup being kept hot in the kitchen, dipping a spoon into the large pot in the bain-marie.'[126]

When she first became a hotelier, Fay Schneider had no catering experience and apparently hardly knew how to cook an egg. However, she came to be regarded as the 'doyenne of kosher caterers'. After she retired from running the Majestic, she took over the kosher catering at the Royal Lancaster Hotel in London with her daughter, Shirley Davidson, and became well known for her interesting and adventurous menus.[127]

Festival and Holy Day Food

A great deal of time and effort went into planning and preparing for meals served during *Pesach*, especially for the *sedarim* (plural of *seder*) when the hotels were full to bursting point. The hotels catered for 200-300 guests, some of whom stayed in nearby guest houses. People came to the *sedarim* from around the world, which meant that the catering managers had to accommodate many different tastes.[128]

Despite the dietary restrictions in force during *Pesach*, food was in great abundance during the eight-day festival (seven in Israel), except it seems at East Cliff Court, which had a more anglicised clientele than the other Big Eight hotels. Hilary Myers, a longstanding Bournemouth resident, recalls a *seder* at East Cliff Court, at which two slices of boiled egg were served in salt water, instead of the one or two whole eggs she was accustomed to eating at her grandparents' home.[129] However, other guests have rather different memories, including Anthony Winston, who stayed at East Cliff Court several times during the 1950s with his grandfather Rev. Solomon Lipson, who conducted festival services at the hotel (see Chapter 7): 'One of the special treats for myself as a young child was to be able to order my own afternoon tea in the lounge. On *Pesach* afternoons, I remember being served round *matzahs*, which were apparently buttered using a brush. I also especially enjoyed the meringues, which were sandwiched with real cream!'[130]

Food was especially abundant over the Christmas and New Year period, when the hotels went into overdrive. Martin Levey recalls: 'We used to have a Jewish Christmas meal, which included kosher turkey, until the Chief Rabbi said that it had to stop!'[131] On each evening during their ten-day stay in the hotels, guests were treated to a particularly extravagant evening buffet following the entertainment (see Chapter 8). On the stroke of midnight on New Year's Eve, breakfast was served. This was also the case at the other hotels.

50. Midnight banquet at the Normandie Hotel, Manor Road, Bournemouth, New Year's Eve, 1961. From left to right: 'Peter the pâtissier', Mr Coles the head waiter, Nathan Lee (one of the hotel proprietors), Dennis Eden, the head chef, Bert (surname unknown), the sous chef. Image courtesy of Simon Keyne.

At East Cliff Court, the fare over the holiday period was a little less lavish. Edward Hayman recalls: 'On New Year's Eve, there was free punch and a cold buffet at midnight, and on Christmas Day we served a chocolate yule log and plum pudding (without holly) at dinner time.'[132]

The Dining Rooms

51. Dining room at the Green Park Hotel, Manor Road, Bournemouth, *c.* 1955. Image courtesy of the Marriott family.

The hotels were renowned not just for their food, but for the whole dining experience. Much of hotel life centred around the dining rooms. To begin with, the dining rooms were quite traditional, such as that at East Cliff Court, which had heavy mahogany furniture, embroidered curtains, 'a blue carpet with whirly patterns' and 'mirrored walls designed to make it appear even larger than it was'.[133] The dining room at the Cumberland, which led off the ballroom and the large lounge, also had a traditional décor of rosewood-panelled walls and chandeliers, but it was made 'warm and cheery' with the use of 'subtle spotlighting'.[134] The hotels used the best table linens, fine china and high-quality cutlery.[135] The dining chairs were deeply upholstered. At the Green Park, each of the covers of the dining room chairs were lovingly stitched by hand by the Richman sisters.[136] The efforts made by the hotels were not always appreciated. When the Green Park upgraded its expansive dining room and replaced the carpet with marble, an older woman guest is reported to have declared: 'You'd think they could afford carpet!'[137]

Over the years, the dining rooms became ever larger and more luxurious. By the 1960s, most were air conditioned and were brighter and more modern in appearance, such as the split-level dining room at the Majestic, which was seen as being 'chic'. The Cumberland added an extension to its dining room, overlooking the terrace and the swimming pool. At the Normandie, Lou Keyne, who had trained as an artist, painted murals on the walls of the hotel dining room, assisted by his son Simon, to accompany the entertainment taking place in the hotel.

During the early 1960s, the Guilds bought an adjacent property and demolished it to add a large banqueting suite to the Langham (referred to by Maurice Guild as 'The Guildhall') and introduced silver service. This involved the head waiter serving the fish or the meat and other waiters following behind him to serve the accompaniments item by item. Larry Kaye recalls that on the opening evening, local residents were invited to eat in the new banqueting suite. Things did not go well:

> The waiters were so intent on serving the food that they did not notice that whoever had set the tables had failed to provide empty plates at one of the tables and they served the food straight onto the pristine tablecloth. Maurice Guild spotted what was going on and rushed across to the table. Red-faced, he scooped everything up in the tablecloth. It put rather a damper on the whole evening.[138]

At several of the hotels, regular guests were allocated their 'own' tables and vied with each other to be seated in cherished spots. Marian Stern recalls: 'When we stayed at the Cumberland, we always sat on Table Two. Table One was always allocated to the Bloom family famous for their restaurant in the East End of London.'[139] At East Cliff Court, the dining room was situated between the kitchen complex and the hotel's drive, which was overlooked by tall windows. Favoured guests were seated at the window tables.[140] A former guest recalls that there was a hierarchy in the Green Park dining room: 'The top spots were closer to the window and towards the back. This was very important to many people. They used to bribe Mr Mimmo to get a better table, or just be extra nice to him. People always respected him, there was never a bad incident.'[141]

However, obliging the guests was sometimes very difficult. Nino Benedetto recalls: 'You wouldn't get a regular's table unless he died. For example, Mr Fisher always sat at Table One, and if the Green Park was still there, he would still be sitting at Table One. That was his table and if someone else wanted to sit there, they were told: "You can't. It's already been given."'[142] Sometimes it was not about securing a prime location, but rather who people wanted to sit next to in the dining room. Nino Benedetto again recalls: 'People used to bribe Mr Mimmo to sit them next to Mr or Miss so-and-so!'[143] Although the maître d's were usually in charge of where people sat, at the Majestic, Fay Schneider made it a personal priority to ensure that her guests were seated at their preferred tables. Her granddaughter Dawn Kaffel recalls: 'And woe betide the restaurant manager that chose to change her seating plans!'[144]

In their heyday, the Big Eight hotels took differing approaches to children eating in their dining rooms. At East Cliff Court, children were definitely not welcome in the dining room at dinner time. Edward Hayman comments: 'I don't know if there was a particular cut-off point, but youngsters would only have been allowed in if they were controllable.'[145] Eileen and Cyril Mincovitch stayed at East Cliff Court in the 1950s with their elder daughter Gail, then aged three. They wanted Gail to eat with them in the evenings, but it was made clear to them that this was not an option. They cut short their visit, found alternative accommodation and never returned to East Cliff Court.[146]

The Cumberland, Majestic, Ambassador and Normandie were apparently more 'child friendly'. Hannah Jacobs recalls that when she stayed in the Cumberland as a young girl, she was allowed to stay up for dinner. She felt very special sitting in the dining room wearing her smart clothes: 'It made it so much more exciting than when you sat down to dinner at home.'[147] However, although children were welcome, the dining rooms did not specifically cater for them. Anne Leach recalls that when she stayed at the Ambassador with her young daughter, there was no such thing as a child's portion: 'She was just served the same huge meals as the rest of us!'[148] Some of the hotels, such as the Langham, organised special children's teas ('high tea'), which were served at about 6pm and either overseen by the children's entertainers or served in the hotels' bedrooms. This meant that the children could be sent to bed early, leaving their parents to enjoy a 'child-free' dinner and the entertainment that followed.[149] At the Green Park, children ate dinner with their parents, but since relatively few small children stayed at the hotel, this was probably not viewed as detracting from the 'grown up' atmosphere that prevailed in the dining room.[150]

By the 1980s, the hotel dining rooms had become less formal and some, including the Cumberland, were experimenting with buffet service. Richard Inverne recalls: 'In our latter years we often had a lunchtime hors d'oeuvres buffet for guests to help themselves. The trouble was that many took so much food (like at the *Shabbos kiddush*) that they sometimes (only sometimes mind you) wasted half their main course.'[151]

In most of the hotels, the families who owned and ran them ate their meals in the dining rooms alongside their guests, reinforcing the family atmosphere of the hotels. However, the presence of the proprietors also enabled them to keep an eye on matters. In his account of growing up at East Cliff Court, Ronald Hayman described how his grandmother, Annie Morris, apparently regarded the hotel dining room as her personal domain: 'From the head of the family table in the corner, her pale grey spectacled eyes moved as if the glinting lenses could send out rays to make the waiters bustle faster down the runways, black coat tails flapping, trays crammed with steaming silver dishes.'[152] She was treated with great respect by the waiters:

> 'Madam' they all called her. When Mummy, who sat next to her, ordered: 'A baked apple for Madam', the waiter would respectfully repeat: 'A baked apple for Madam', before he disappeared through the swishing door to shout: 'Baked apple for Madam', as if the apple had to be bigger and better than the others, with a thicker crust of sugar scorched onto the skin.[153]

However, Ronald's younger brother, Edward Hayman, maintains that while the family had their meals at the same time as the guests and chose from the same menu, the guests took priority in respect of both the service and the food: 'If there was a shortage of a particular food, the motto I learned at an early age was "FHB", meaning family holds back.'[154] Annie Morris's daughter, Sadie Hayman, who took over the running of the hotel in 1953, had clearly been taught well by her mother. A visitor to the hotel in 1956, who sat at the family table, has recorded:

> What I did notice was Mrs Hayman's unbroken surveillance of the dining room. From our table, she surveyed everything and everyone – guests and staff – and, although the manager was in evidence, it seemed that Mrs Hayman was the one who really kept an eye on what was going on and, if she spotted any deficiency, made sure that a member of staff dealt with it immediately. The hotels I've stayed in since that period have never been owner-managed, and I have to admire the impeccable way that Mrs Hayman ran hers. Most of her guests were 'regulars' who clearly appreciated her care and vigilance.

Bluma Feld made a point of speaking to each and every guest eating in the
Cumberland dining room, both at lunch and dinner times, to check that they
were comfortable and were not experiencing any problems.[155] At the Green
Park, the family, especially the Richman sisters, circulated around the dining
tables at meal times, talking to their guests and sometimes sitting down to
eat a course with them.[156] Particularly favoured guests were invited to dine at
the family table on a Friday night.[157] Well-known, regular guests were often
placed in close proximity to the family tables. This was also the situation at
the other hotels. Simon Keyne recalls: 'Denis Norden's family were frequent
guests at the Normandie. He always sat close to our family table.'[158] James
Inverne recalls that when he was growing up around the Cumberland: 'It was
second nature to go into the dining room and to sit at the family table to eat
nice meals, such as chicken, duck, and trout and lovely desserts.'[159]

Hotel staff, such as the front-of-house porters and the receptionists,
also ate in the dining rooms and from the same menus. Joan Doubtfire
recalls that she especially liked the 'Jewish food', such as *lokshen* and
cholent.[160]

Food Supplies

Acquiring food for the Jewish hotels was a complicated affair, especially the
purchasing of kosher meat. The hoteliers could not simply go out and buy
the food they needed to feed their guests, it had to be sourced from the
limited number of firms certified for selling kosher goods and produce.
Each of the hotels had their favoured suppliers, a large proportion of which
were located outside Bournemouth.

Feld's restaurant in the East End of London, run by Isaac and Bluma
Feld, was the first establishment to be licensed by the Kashrus Commission
(see Chapter 7).[161] They developed a number of trusted suppliers and when
they purchased the Cumberland in Bournemouth, they used many of the
same suppliers. Alex Kopfstein (a refugee from Austria and former internee
of the Kitchener camp), who had previously worked at Feld's restaurant in
the East End, became the catering manager at the Cumberland after the
restaurant closed.[162] On his arrival in Bournemouth, some of the hotel's
original suppliers were replaced by other firms, including Luton Kosher
based in Hertfordshire, which was part-owned by Ossi Pressburger, whom
Alex Kopfstein had known in Vienna. The same firm also supplied the
Majestic where the head chef, Austrian-born Max Colman (see above), was
another friend of Ossi Pressburger. Later, the firm went on to supply some
of the food required by the Green Park.[163] By the 1960s, when Bournemouth

had three kosher butchers, and an abattoir in Blandford Forum that supplied them, the hotels did start to buy more of their meat locally, negotiating hard to obtain the best prices.[164] Before the Feld's moved to Bournemouth to run the Cumberland, their successful restaurant in Whitechapel Road had supplied the Ambassador. The hotel sent a van up to the East End each Thursday to collect the meat – salt beef, sausages made at the restaurant and tongue -and continued to do so until they sold the restaurant in 1951 (see Appendix 1).[165]

As mentioned in Chapter 3, in 1971 the New Ambassador was taken over by Alf and Sadie Vickers who lived in Muswell Hill. They usually purchased their meat from Alf Perlmutter, a well-known and highly respected local kosher butcher in Palmers Green. When the Bournemouth kosher butchers closed, the hotel was supplied by Alf Perlmutter, who arranged for a weekly delivery to Bournemouth. This arrangement lasted until the hotel was sold and no longer kosher.[166] Jonathan Perlmutter, who made some of the regular deliveries to the hotel, says: 'Since we were a large firm, we could supply meat at more competitive prices than the local kosher butchers.'[167] The quantities of meat that Perlmutters supplied were huge. A typical weekly order for the New Ambassador included two hundred chickens, ten seven-bone ribs each weighing twenty kilos, ten boulas (shoulders of cut beef), ox and chicken liver, fifty kilos of diced beef, twenty pickled tongues and seventy kilos of minced beef. Jonathan Perlmutter again comments: 'The hotels had the top chefs and they only wanted the best meat.'[168] Since Perlmutters were regularly sending a van to Bournemouth with the meat, they also delivered a range of produce, including smoked salmon, fruit, eggs and other kosher groceries. Perlmutters also supplied some meat to the Green Park. *Pesach* was a particularly busy time for deliveries. Jonathan Perlmutter again recalls: 'We could never go away at that time. We had to make three deliveries over three days.'[169]

When the Normandie became strictly orthodox in 1988, it was supplied by the Kedassia-licensed Frohwein's butcher in London's Temple Fortune.[170]

Controversy sometimes arose about the sourcing of meat and poultry by the large Bournemouth hotels. The argument was about whether those hotels using suppliers located in London and elsewhere should pay a fee to the Bournemouth Shechita Board (see Chapter 7). Before his death in 1969, Isaac Feld steadfastly refused to do so, saying that he was entitled to obtain his produce from his established sources without paying a local surcharge.[171] He referred to his ongoing argument with Bournemouth Hebrew Congregation as 'The Kashrus Wars.'[172] The matter came to a head again in 1978 when the National Council of Shechita Boards considered a complaint that some of the Bournemouth Jewish hotels supplied by London butchers were not paying their dues to the Bournemouth Shechita Board. After a heated discussion, it was agreed that the London Shechita Board would pay a fee to the Bournemouth Board for supplies delivered to Bournemouth hotels from firms they licensed.[173]

Over time, the larger hotels became more self-sufficient, especially when the local kosher shops began to close down. They opened their own bakeries, which were attached to their kitchens or housed in outbuildings. During the 1950s, the Green Park had a German pâtissier named Paul Simeoni. Nino Benedetto recalls: 'He made everything; the hotel never had to buy anything. Rolls, croissants, sponge cakes, butter cake, petits fours, you name it, he made it.'[174] East Cliff Court employed a longstanding pastry chef called Dolan, with whom Sadie Hayman worked very closely. According to Edward Hayman: 'He was really skilful, making his own ice cream and sorbets as well as cakes and the usual puddings.'[175]

During the 1960s, the owners of the Cumberland purchased Ballon's kosher bakery in the town centre (the bakery was in Verulam Place and the retail outlet was in St Swithun's Road), which they gradually relocated to a hotel annexe that had previously been used as a maintenance shed. Having its own bakery proved especially beneficial for the Cumberland at *Pesach*. Geoffrey Feld comments: 'It meant that within a short while of *Pesach* ending, Alex Kopfstein was able to serve salt beef sandwiches oozing with mustard.'[176] The Cumberland bakery also provided baked goods for some of the other hotels until they set up their own bakeries. It was later extended to include a delicatessen, which was open to the public. Richard Inverne recalls: 'We made so much food for the *Shabbos kiddush*, it was no effort to make extra to sell to others. It was a nice little earner for us!'[177] Until it caught fire in the mid-1970s, the Cumberland also had its own smokehouse for smoking the salmon.[178] When the Cumberland closed, the bakery and delicatessen were transferred to the New Ambassador. Most of the large hotels also had their own butcheries, usually attached to their kitchens: 'They purchased big slabs of meat and carried out their own preparation, overseen by the *shomrim*' (see Chapter 7).[179] At the Green Park, fruit and vegetables were grown in its lower garden and were used in the hotel.

The Smaller Hotels and Guest Houses

When Jewish guest houses and smaller hotels first began to proliferate in the interwar years (see Chapter 2), they generally stressed that they provided home-cooked food. Only the larger establishments, such as Merivale Hall, suggested in their advertisements that they offered more adventurous menus. However, during the 1920s, the larger establishments, especially those that were now calling themselves hotels, started to refer to the quality of their food and to adopt terminology, such as 'cuisine' and 'fine food'.

In the decade after the Second World War, the food served at the smaller guest houses was still generally less elaborate and more 'homely' than in the Big Eight hotels, and in some it was still quite basic, since the guest houses were disproportionately affected by rationing and did not have the buying power of the large hotels. Diane Langleben tells this story:

> My parents went to Bournemouth on honeymoon in 1946. They stayed in one of the guest houses there. My father was deaf, but one of his great pleasures in life was eating. The food in their accommodation was awful and he decided that they couldn't stay there. My parents went upstairs and my father asked to borrow my mother's lipstick. He used it to paint spots on his face and neck. He went back downstairs to explain to the owner that they had to leave because he wasn't well. Seeing the spots, the owner was only too pleased to let them go! They packed their bags and moved to the Green Park. The following night, they went down to dinner in the dining room. While they were eating, to their horror, they noticed that the guest-house owner was also dining there. They were quite embarrassed, but it was clear that the guest-house owner didn't like his food either![180]

Most of the smaller guest houses offered breakfast (usually eggs and cereal) and an evening meal but not lunch. Judi Lyons recalls: 'At Villa Judi, my mother started out offering lunch as well as dinner, but after a while she stopped because serving three meals a day was just too much for one person.'[181] Visitors staying in the guest houses usually found something to eat at midday at one of the shops in the town. Dinner was served at around 6.30pm. It was often a set menu, which the guest-house owners found difficult to vary to suit individual tastes, or a menu that offered few options. Judi Lyons again comments: 'It really used to faze my mother when a guest arrived saying that they could only eat chicken breast.'[182] However, most of the establishments had their specialities, which were sometimes traded between the different guest houses: 'My mother's speciality was macaroons and it was my job to take some to Aunty Golda [Mrs Corren], who ran

Stevra House. In return, Aunty Golda would send us some of the coconut pyramids that she made for *Pesach*. The guest-house owners trusted each other's *kashrut*.'[183]

Sam Russell, who ran the Mayfair guest house in Boscombe, was the president of the Boscombe and Southbourne Sea Fishing Club, which meant that his guests could usually be assured that fresh fish was on the menu.[184] His wife Addie is said to have been an excellent cook. At Hotel Rubens, the Grower family raised chickens for the table and the long-standing Polish-Jewish chef was Mr Epstein. Ben Grower, son of the owners recalls: 'He often got drunk, which made my mother very cross.'[185] While the food at Gresham Court was 'well cooked', the service was apparently a little aggressive. Michael Zeffertt recalls: 'For example, if you ordered roast beef, the waiter came to the table with a platter and demanded, "Who is rozzbiff?" A positive response resulted in the roast beef in question being unceremoniously dumped on one's plate.'[186] At the Carmel Hotel ('Gutstein's'), the kosher cuisine was said to be 'unique in its cooking and presentation'.[187] However, the strictly orthodox guests who stayed at the hotel were quite particular about what they ate. According to Hazel Green: 'Some guests complained if they didn't get two meat meals a day and if the Gutsteins served up fish for lunch for a change.'[188] By comparison, in 1970 Mount Aishel run by the Ricklows, also a very observant guest house, became meatless and served only fish and vegetarian meals.

At Villa Judi, there was a weekly cycle of traditional Jewish food, described by Judi Lyons: 'On Sundays it was salt beef (which my mother prepared herself); Monday it was meat balls; on Tuesday it was *pureg* (a Polish dish of raw meat wrapped in pastry or dough and then fried); on Wednesday it was chicken; on Thursday it was fried fish.'[189] There was also a starter, which was often home-made soup or smoked salmon and a dessert with *lokshen* pudding being a firm favourite. Like the other small guest houses, Villa Judi was not licensed to serve alcohol. Judi Lyons recalls that her mother started cooking the *Shabbat* meal on a Thursday, which was *Gedempte*, an Ashkenazi pot roast dish. The meat (a *boula*) and the vegetables were all placed together in a huge cooking pot so large that it took two people to lift it. It was placed in the large, double-oven Aga, where it simmered for two days. Judi's father said that the meat melted in his mouth, but Judi recalls that the vegetables were not so palatable, having been cooked for so long: 'My mother was a good cook, but vegetables, often called by their Jewish names like *kugel* for potatoes, were perhaps not her forte.'[190] In the high season, when most of the Jewish guest houses were full, Sylvia Kay cooked dinner for Jewish people staying at nearby non-Jewish establishments. In comparison to the larger hotels, the Kays ate later in the evening once the dining room and kitchen had been cleared, although a family member was usually present when people were eating.[191]

The smaller hotels and guest houses generally purchased the food they required in Bournemouth from the local butchers and other kosher shops. Judi Lyons recalls: 'The regular delivery of chickens from Kesselman's butchers arrived on Wednesdays. The delivery man used to come down the side of the house and throw the chickens through the open kitchen window, directly into the *fleisch* [meat] sink.'[192]

Although there tended to be less choice of dishes and the quantities were not as lavish as in the Big Eight hotels, food was still plentiful in the guest houses and smaller hotels. After he left school, Lennie Segal, the son of the owners of the Hotel Florence in Boscombe Spa Road (see Chapter 4), obtained a catering qualification and worked in the hotel as a waiter. He recalls: 'I used to have a banter with the guests. At breakfast time, I asked them if they would like prunes, fruit, juice cereal or porridge and they used to say: "Yes please". They wanted it all!'[193] Both the lunches and dinners served at Hotel Florence were four-course meals.[194]

We have seen that by the 1980s, there were far fewer guest houses and smaller hotels (Chapter 5), but those that were still operating or had recently opened, were offering a much better standard and range of food. One of the selling points for the Glencairn Manor, which opened in 1985, included its 'fully-licensed bar' and 'luxurious dining room', with their 'carefully chosen kosher wine list' and à la carte menu. These facilities were open to the public.[195] All the food served in the hotel was prepared on the premises by a Cordon Bleu chef and vegetarian food was a speciality.[196] When the Glencairn Manor was taken over by the Amdur family in 1990, they stressed that, despite their Sephardi background, they served Ashkenazi food in their restaurant and in their garden café, Boobie Ettie's Eatery. The hotel employed its own pâtissier, Mr Gordon.[197] The hotel's Spanish head waiter was named Jesus. David Weitz comments: 'You can imagine the fun the guests had asking, "Jesus, do this" and "Jesus, do that" can't you?'[198] Paul Newman remembers eating at the hotel one *Shabbat* lunchtime: 'The owner's family sat at their own table and were served first and had better food and much bigger portions. Needless to say, we didn't return.'[199]

Gourmet food was often on the menu at the Dolly Ross Holiday Home run by the Jewish Blind Society, and later by Jewish Care (see Chapter 4), where John Liddle, who had trained at leading catering colleges, served 'featherweight *kneidlach* and meltingly delicious *latkes*'. For the knowledgeable eaters, he also introduced twice-baked cheese soufflé and smoked haddock roulade. The roulade so enthused a distinguished jury which included Evelyn Rose, that John was unanimously voted Kosher Chef of the Year in 1995.[200]

Self-Catering

In Chapter 4 we saw that from the 1960s onwards, more and more Jewish visitors to Bournemouth began to self-cater. One of the reasons for this was that people had become increasingly health conscious. A former Bournemouth resident comments: 'People wanted to take more control of what they ate and when.'[201] It was also a reflection of the increasing number of *charedim* taking holidays in Bournemouth for whom the Jewish hotels and guests houses were not sufficiently observant, even when they were licensed by one of the religious authorities. The most orthodox visitors usually brought their food with them. Miriam Levene recalls:

> We had many holidays on the south coast, including in Bournemouth, always self-catering. I remember us taking lots of food and Mum kashering the cooker as soon as we arrived. Dad didn't always have annual leave left, as so much was taken for the *Yamim Tovim*, so he drove us down, went back to London and joined us at weekends, bringing with him more food, such as chicken from Frohwein's butchers in Temple Fortune.[202]

Although the most orthodox Jews brought food with them, or arranged for it to be delivered, a number of businesses grew up in Bournemouth to supply those who were self-catering. Kenny Arfin, who in 1978 bought Zadel's butchery, regularly advertised in the *Jewish Chronicle*, encouraging people not to *schlep* (carry) food to Bournemouth and to buy locally when they arrived. Providing for the self-catering market proved to be a good business and Kenny later opened a delicatessen attached to the butchery, run by his parents-in-law, where people could buy fresh bread and kosher groceries. The delicatessen was initially supplied by the Cumberland.

Following the closure of Kenny Arfin's delicatessen, there were a series of delicatessens, including Louise's in Old Christchurch Road, which was later taken over by Rev. Ian Camissar, former *chazan* at Harrogate Synagogue and son of Solomon Camissar, the *shomer* at the New Ambassador (see Chapter 7), who specialised in 'veggie' hot dogs,[203] and the delicatessen ('The Deli') run by Lise Rossano and her husband Roger, which opened in 2003. Lise had previously run a catering business licensed by BHC that was absorbed into the delicatessen. The delicatessen was licensed by the Kashrus Commission. Lise did all of the cooking herself . with the help of an Israeli cook, who prepared Israeli and Moroccan-style food. However, the main produce was traditional Ashkenazi dishes. The clientele was largely *charedim* from Golders Green and Stamford Hill now staying in self-catering accommodation (see Chapter 5). Lise Rossano recalls: 'I used to purchase thirty-five kilos of fish to make fishballs. That is a lot of fishballs! My children used to refuse to travel in the car with me after I had been frying them on a Tuesday.'[204]

While those who self-catered initially relied on the specialist kosher stores, as they closed, the self-caterers started to shop at the mainstream supermarkets, such as Tesco, Asda and Sainsbury's, which stocked an increasing range of kosher foods.[205] Some self-caterers managed to arrange with one of the large hotels to buy bread and cakes from them and booked into one of the hotels or guest houses that was open to the public for *Shabbat* dinner. [206] David Latchman comments: 'One of the reasons why people had bought flats was because they had liked the experience of eating kosher food in the Bournemouth hotels. As flat owners, it was appealing just to book a table at one of the hotels rather than to go to the trouble of making Friday night dinner themselves.'[207] When the Normandie became strictly orthodox, the *charedi* flat owners were very comfortable with eating at the hotel.

Today, a large proportion of those Jews who self-cater in Bournemouth are *charedim,* who largely bring their own food with them or who arrange large deliveries from *glatt* kosher[208] shops in London, which are then distributed amongst other families when they arrive.[209] During Jewish festivals, Kosher Deli in Golders Green delivers food to Bournemouth free of charge. The *charedim* usually stay in flats that are kosher, but if this is not the case, they bring with them their own cooking equipment and disposable crockery and cutlery. Ready-made meals are available for 'drive through pick up' at Chabadeli at the Water Garden hotel in Annerley Road, which is supplied by the commercial kitchen based at the hotel. Particularly popular with its *charedi* self-catering customers are Chabadeli's fried fish, *latkes*, schnitzel, chopped liver, soups, salads, dips and freshly baked bagels and the excellent *challot* (plural of *challah*) made by the manager Chanie Alperowitz. One regular *charedi* visitor comments: 'Its shelves are always fully stocked and excited customers are drawn in by the wonderful aroma of freshly baked bread.'[210]

Since 2010, a kosher shop, Shop@theShul, run by volunteers at the Wootton Gardens Synagogue, has been serving visitors to the town (as well as local residents) with groceries, frozen meat, home-cooked, ready-made meals and baked goods, including fresh *challah*. It is open on a Thursday and Friday. People often email their requirements in advance of a stay in Bournemouth and pick them up on their arrival.[211] The shop also provides food for Jewish guests staying at non-Jewish hotels, such as the Queens Hotel (formerly the Langham). Lillian Gonshaw comments: 'My son and his family ate *Shabbat* dinner obtained from Bournemouth *shul*, which the Queens Hotel were happy to heat and serve.'[212] Two other non-Jewish hotels (the Bournemouth Highcliff Marriott and the Orchid Hotel[213]), say that they are 'kosher friendly' and are able to provide their guests with 'kosher items'. Over the summer months, when many *charedi* families stay in Bournemouth for long periods of time, the chef at the Normandie makes additional take-away meals for those staying in nearby flats and apartments, which are sold from a kiosk in the car park.

Notes

1. According to *The New Jewish Holiday Cookbook* by Gloria Kaufer Greene, the word *cholent* may have come into usage in medieval Europe, being derived from the French *chaud-lent*, meaning 'warm slowly', or, less likely, from the Yiddish *shul ende*, describing when the *cholent* is eaten – at the end of *shul*.
2. Quoted in Panikos Panayi, 'The Anglicisation of Eastern European Jewish Food in Britain', in *Immigrants & Minorities*, 30: 2, p.294.
3. Quoted in *ibid.*, p.295.
4. For example, Jews with Polish backgrounds served *lokshen* as a pudding, while those with Lithuanian or Ukrainian backgrounds served *lokshen* as a savoury main course.
5. Panayi, 'The Anglicisation of Eastern European Jewish Food in Britain', p.295.
6. Hasia Diner, *Hungering for America: Italian, Irish and Jewish Foodways in the Age of Migration* (London: Harvard University Press, 2001).
7. See Panayi, 'The Anglicisation of Eastern European Jewish Food in Britain'.
8. *Ibid.*, pp.298–301.
9. Pam Fox, *The Jewish Community of Golders Green: A Social History* (Stroud: The History Press, 2016), pp.136-139.
10. See Panayi, 'The Anglicisation of Eastern European Jewish Food in Britain', pp.306-307.
11. *Ibid.*, p.310.
12. *JC*, 30.5.1952.
13. Email from Edward Hayman, 15.10.2020.
14. *Lincolnshire Echo*, 25.2.1947.
15. Geoffrey Alderman, 'Abundant Southern Comforts', *JC*, 29.9.2014.
16. Interview with Jenny Green, 19.5.2020.
17. Francine Wolfisz, 'A Bournemouth Summer Just Like the Old Days', *Jewish News*, 21.8.2014. See https://jewishnews.timesofisrael.com/bournemouth-summer-just-like-old-days/.

18. Interview with Hazel Green, 25.8.2020.
19. Sarah Marriott speaking in 'The Green Park', directed by Jack Fishburn and Justin Hardy, 2015.
20. Interview with Hannah Jacobs, 12.5.2020.
21. This indicative schedule of meals is compiled from out-takes from 'The Green Park', directed by Jack Fishburn and Justin Hardy, information included in a talk given by Geoffrey Feld at Edgware United Synagogue, 6 March 2018 and an email from Edward Hayman, 25.8.2020.
22. Israel Shenker, 'On the British Seafront, Kosher Cuisine with an English Accent', *New York Times*, 6.1.1973.
23. *JC*, 16.7.2010.
24. Gerda Charles, *The Crossing Point* (London: Eyre & Spottiswoode, 1961), p.201.
25. See Alderman, 'Abundant Southern Comforts'.
26. Interview with Norman Shapiro, 23.10.2020.
27. Interview with Elissa Bayer, 30.4.2020.
28. Email from Edward Hayman, 25.8.2020.
29. Conversation with Hettie Marks, 20.11.2020.
30. Interview with Jon Harris, 4.5.2020.
31. Talk given by Geoffrey Feld at Edgware United Synagogue, 6 March 2018.
32. Interview with Jon Harris, 4.5.2020.
33. See talk given by Geoffrey Feld.
34. Interview with Jonathan Perlmutter, 26.8.2020
35. Interview with Richard Inverne, 6.7.2020.
36. Conversation with Hettie Marks, 20.11.2020.
37. Interview with Richard Inverne, 6.7.2020.
38. Conversation with Hettie Marks, 20.11.2020.
39. Email from Hannah Jacobs, 4.8.2020.
40. See talk given by Geoffrey Feld.
41. Interview with Jon Harris, 4.5.2020.
42. Interview with Jonathan Perlmutter, 26.8.2020.
43. Recordings of interviews with Bluma Feld, carried out by her grandson, Richard Inverne, in 1996, Disc 5, kindly provided by Geoffrey Feld.
44. *Ibid.*
45. Email from Michael Alpert, 26.11.2020.
46. Interview with Jon Harris, 4.5.2020.
47. See talk given by Geoffrey Feld.
48. *Ibid.*
49. Peter Phillips, 'London's Borscht Belt – Jewish Hotels in Bournemouth', *AJR Journal*, August 2014, p.11.
50. Interview with Shirley Davidson, 25.8.2020.
51. See talk given by Geoffrey Feld.
52. Interview with James Inverne, 10.11.2020.
53. Anecdote submitted by Alexander Harris to eastcliffcourtmemories.wordpress.com/blog/.
54. *Portsmouth Evening News*, 8.1.1953.
55. Notes from Edward Hayman sent by email, 24.8.2020.
56. *JC*, 29.3.1985.

57. Conversation with Simon Keyne, 27.1.2021.
58. Kosher wine arrived first from Israel and then from other countries where it was made under rabbinical supervision.
59. Interview with Jonathan Perlmutter, 26.8.2020.
60. See talk given by Geoffrey Feld.
61. *JC*, 29.3.1985.
62. Louis Golding, *Hotel Ambassador* (Bournemouth: Ambassador, 1950), p.12.
63. Jennifer Stanton and Carol Santaub, out-take from 'The Green Park', directed by Jack Fishburn and Justin Hardy.
64. Out-take from *ibid*.
65. Email from Edward Hayman, 25.8.2020.
66. *Ibid*.
67. *JC*, 30.5.1952.
68. Out-take from, 'The Green Park', directed by Jack Fishburn and Justin Hardy.
69. Ilana Lee, 'Diamonds at Breakfast', *Jewish Quarterly*, Vol. 54, No. 1, pp.26-27.
70. Jennifer Stanton and Carol Santaub, out-take from The Green Park', directed by Jack Fishburn and Justin Hardy.
71. *JC*, 11.9.1953.
72. See Lee, 'Diamonds at Breakfast', p.27.
73. See talk given by Geoffrey Feld.
74. See Shenker, 'On the British Seafront'.
75. *Ibid*.
76. See talk given by Geoffrey Feld.
77. See Lee, 'Diamonds at Breakfast', pp.27-28.
78. Out-take from, 'The Green Park', directed by Jack Fishburn and Justin Hardy.
79. *JC*, 22. 10.1965.
80. Talk given by Dawn Kaffel, Fay Schneider's granddaughter, at Hampstead Garden Suburb Synagogue, 'Majestic Days at the Majestic'. See https://docplayer.net/amp/138128447-These-were-the-words-of-a-shul-member-on.html.
81. Interview with Elissa Bayer, 30.4.2020.
82. Interview with Ruth Shire, 27.8.2020.
83. Email from Richard Inverne, 19.8.2020.
84. Naomi Taub, out-take from, 'The Green Park', directed by Jack Fishburn and Justin Hardy.
85. Interview with Elissa Bayer, 30.4.2020.
86. Conversation with Brian Lassman, 1.12.2020.
87. Interview with Hannah Jacobs, 12.5.2020.
88. Carole Reggel, post on Facebook, 28.8.2020.
89. Interview with Jonathan Perlmutter, 26.8.2020.
90. Laurie Rosenberg, post on Facebook, 25.8.2020.
91. Interview with Roger Vickers, 29.10.2020.
92. *Ibid*.
93. Interview with Beverley-Jane Stewart, 29.5.2020.
94. Laurie Rosenberg, post on Facebook, 24.8.2020.
95. Information taken from various reviews available online.
96. Interview with David Marriott, 12.5.2020.
97. See Lee, 'Diamonds at Breakfast', p.27.

98. Mimmo Zacchia, maître d' at the Green Park, out-take from 'The Green Park', directed by Jack Fishburn and Justin Hardy.

99. Interview with Simon Keyne, 15.6.2020.

100. *Ibid.*

101. Interview with Adriano Brioschi, 4.1.2021.

102. Email from Richard Inverne, 19.8.2020.

103. Ronald Hayman, *Secrets: Boyhood in a Jewish Hotel, 1932*-1954 (London: Peter Owen, 1985), p.12. Although Ronald Hayman referred to the head waiter as Tonks, his name was Jones.

104. Interview with Brian Lassman, 14.5.2020. His surname is unknown; he was always just 'Moishe'.

105. Interview with Barbara Glyn, 1.6.2020. A toaster would be difficult to rid of leaven, which was mandatory at *Pesach*. See Chapter 7.

106. Nino Benedetto, head waiter at the Green Park, out-take from 'The Green Park', directed by Jack Fishburn and Justin Hardy.

107. Mrs Gottlieb, out-take from *ibid.*

108. Nino Benedetto, head waiter at the Green Park, out-take from *ibid.*

109. Interview with David Latchman, 6.5.2020.

110. Nino Benedetto, head waiter at the Green Park, out-take from 'The Green Park', directed by Jack Fishburn and Justin Hardy.

111. Interview with Joan Doubtfire, 13.5.2020.

112. Email from Edward Hayman, 20.8.2020.

113. Interview with Barbara Glyn, 30.6.2020.

114. Mimmo Zacchia, maître d' at the Green Park, out-take from 'The Green Park', directed by Jack Fishburn and Justin Hardy.

115. Interview with Miriam Marcus, 20.10.2020.

116. *Ibid.*

117. Interview with Jonathan Perlmutter, 26.8.2020.

118. Email from Richard Inverne, 19.8.2020.

119. *Ibid.*

120. Interview with Hazel Green, 1.9.2020. The tenderest steak are taken from the hind quarters of a cow, but Jewish dietary rules forbid the use of hind quarters unless the sciatic nerve is removed and there are few shochets that have the skill to do this. As a result, the removal of the sinew and sale of cattle hind quarters was increasingly controlled and eventually banned by the Jewish religious authorities. See Geoffrey Alderman, *British Jewry Since Emancipation* (Buckingham: The University of Buckingham Press, 2014), p.359.

121. Carol Reggel, post on Facebook, 29.8.2020.

122. Interview with Anne Filer, 30.4.2020.

123. Notes from Edward Hayman.

124. Interview with Kenny Arfin, 5.5.2020.

125. Interview with David Marriott, 12.5.2020.

126. Notes from Edward Hayman, sent by email, 24.8.2020.

127. *JC*, 6.11.1981.

128. See talk given by Geoffrey Feld.

129. See eastcliffcourtmemories.wordpress.com/blog/.

130. Anthony Winston, memory submitted to the above website.

131. Martin Levey, out-take from 'The Green Park', directed by Jack Fishburn and Justin Hardy.
132. Email from Edward Hayman, 23.9.2020.
133. See Hayman, *Secrets,* p.11.
134. Email from Richard Inverne, 19.8.2020.
135. See Hayman, *Secrets,* p.24.
136. See Lee, 'Diamonds at Breakfast', p.30.
137. *Ibid.,* p.30.
138. Interview with Larry and Mandy Kaye (née Kasmir), 11.6.2020.
139. Interview with Marian Stern, 11.5.2020.
140. Notes from Edward Hayman, sent by email 24.8.2020.
141. Anonymous, out-take 'The Green Park', directed by Jack Fishburn and Justin Hardy.
142. Nino Benedetto, head waiter at the Green Park, out-take from *ibid.*
143. *Ibid.*
144. See talk given by Dawn Kaffel.
145. Email from Edward Hayman, 25.8.2020.
146. See eastcliffcourtmemories.wordpress.com/blog/
147. Interview with Hannah Jacobs, 12.5.2020.
148. Anne Leach, post on Facebook, 24.8.2020.
149. Interview with Marilyn Murray, 24.8.2020.
150. Interview with David Abrahams, 25.8.2020.
151. Email from Richard Inverne, 19.8.2020.
152. See Hayman, *Secrets,* p.11.
153. *Ibid.,* p.11.
154. Notes from Edward Hayman, sent by email, 24.8.2020.
155. Recordings of interviews with Bluma Feld, carried out by her grandson, Richard Inverne in 1996, Disc 4, kindly provided by Geoffrey Feld.
156. Interview with David Abrahams, 25.8. 2020.
157. *Ibid.*
158. Interview with Simon Keyne, 15.6.2020.
159. Interview with James Inverne, 10.11.2020.
160. Interview with Joan Doubtfire, 13.5.2020.
161. Isaac's bother, Benny, also ran a smaller restaurant called Feld's in Commercial Road.
162. Interview with Richard Inverne, 6.7.2020.
163. Yanky Fachler, *The Vow: Rebuilding the Fachler Tribe After the Holocaust* (Victoria, Canada: Trafford Publishing, 2003), p.265.
164. One of the butchers was closed following a scandal resulting from the shop supplying the Green Park with non-kosher meat.
165. Recordings of interviews with Bluma Feld, carried out by her grandson, Richard Inverne, in 1996, Disc 5, kindly provided by Geoffrey Feld.
166. Interview with Roger Vickers, 29.10.2020.
167. Interview with Jonathan Perlmutter, 15.5.2020.
168. *Ibid.*
169. *Ibid.*
170. Interview with Brian Lassman, 14.5.2020
171. See talk given by Geoffrey Feld.

172. *Ibid.*
173. *JC,* 7.4.1978.
174. Nino Benedetto, head waiter at the Green Park, out-take from 'The Green Park', directed by Jack Fishburn and Justin Hardy.
175. Email from Edward Hayman, 25.8.2020.
176. See talk given by Geoffrey Feld.
177. Interview with Richard Inverne, 6.7.2020.
178. *Ibid.*
179. *Ibid.*
180. Interview with Diane Langleben, 17.6.2020.
181. Conversation. with Judi Lyons, 10.8.2020.
182. *Ibid.*
183. Interview with Judi Lyons, 4.5.2020.
184. *JC,* 2.6.1978.
185. Interview with Ben Grower, 22.11.2020.
186. Email from Michael Zeffertt, 30.8.2020.
187. *JC,* 13.8.1971.
188. Interview with Hazel Green, 25.8.2020.
189. Conversation with Judi Lyons, 10.8.2020.
190. *Ibid.*
191. *Ibid.*
192. *Ibid.*
193. Interview with Lennie Segal, 15.6.2020.
194. *Ibid.*
195. *JC,* 12.4.1985.
196. *JC,* 14.2.1986.
197. *JC,* 26.10.1990.
198. David Weitz, post on Facebook, Jewish Britain Group, 7.1.2020.
199. Paul Newman, post on Facebook, Jewish Britain Group, 7.1.2020.
200. *JC,* 11.10.1996.
201. Conversation with Ruth Soetendorp, 6.7.2020.
202. Email from Miriam Levene, 30.4.2020.
203. *JC,* 27.8.1993.
204. Interview with Lise Rossano, 8.12.2020. The *shomer* at The Deli was Yossi Stauber, who had been the *shomer* at the New Ambassador before it closed.
205. Interview with Richard Inverne, 6.7.2020.
206. Email from Judi Lyons, 23.6.2020.
207. Interview with David Latchman, 5.11.2020.
208. The term *glatt* is used to refer to a product processed under a stricter standard of *kashrut.*
209. Interview with Elissa Bayer, 30.4.2020.
210. Anonymous interviewee, 16.6.2020.
211. Conversation with Loraine Berlyn, 2.9.2020.
212. Interview with Lillian Gonshaw, 25.9.2020.
213. See https://trip101.com/article/kosher-hotels-bournemouth.

7

Religion in the Jewish Hotels
and Guest Houses

In the years following the end of the First World War, major changes took place in the nature of the areas where Jews had first settled on their arrival in London and elsewhere. While at the beginning of the twentieth century the vast majority of Anglo-Jewry had been born abroad, by the interwar years, the majority of the community had been born in Britain. This was mainly due to immigration control, the Aliens Act of 1905 and the more restrictive Aliens Act of 1914. As a result, a gulf opened up between the older generation of Jews, who had come to the country from Eastern Europe, and the younger generation, who had been raised and educated in Britain. The generational differences were evident in the decline of Yiddish as the main spoken language, a reduction in religious observance and a decrease in membership of the friendly societies and *chevrot* (small places of worship) that had sustained newly-arrived immigrants.[1] These generational differences were reinforced as Jews moved to the suburbs and integrated into wider society.

The discernible trend towards secularisation was a matter of concern for both religious and lay leaders, but most Jews who left the first areas of settlement did not abandon their faith entirely. Although they did not seek to recreate the *chevrot* to which the previous generation had belonged, they did set up new synagogues, many of which became affiliated to the United Synagogue. For the new suburban dwellers, membership of the mainstream United Synagogue was a symbol of respectability and of upward mobility. By the end of the Second World War, with a large proportion of the Anglo-Jewish community now living in suburban locations, membership of the United Synagogue was growing exponentially.[2]

Over the next two decades, the United Synagogue continued to grow. Denominations of Anglo-Jewry to both the left and right of the United Synagogue were also beginning to expand, partly as a result of the influence of the progressive and *charedi* rabbis who came to Britain to escape persecution in Central and Eastern Europe. While the level of Jewish observance and synagogue attendance varied greatly amongst members of the United Synagogue, during the period between 1945 and 1970, Anglo-Jewry was at its most homogeneous. Geoffrey Alderman comments: 'People generally observed the same things and generally broke the same rules, although they didn't do anything that would offend anyone or deviate too far from the rules.'[3]

As already mentioned in Chapter 5, in the latter part of the twentieth century Anglo-Jewry became increasingly polarised and fragmented and Anglo-Jewry overall moved to the right. These changes in religious outlook were reflected in the rise and decline of Jewish hotels and guest houses in Bournemouth and elsewhere. The heyday of the Jewish holiday establishments coincided with the period when membership of the United Synagogue was at its zenith and their popularity waned as 'middle-of-the-road orthodoxy' declined. Some former customers of the kosher hotels were now staying in the non-kosher hotels, while others sought accommodation that was more orthodox. Changes in the religious nature of Anglo-Jewry was not the only factor in the demise of the kosher hotels in Bournemouth, but they were an important one.

As well as the shift in religious outlook, there were also developments in Jewish eating habits. The rules governing Jewish diet have their origins in several books in the Bible, particularly Leviticus, which have been interpreted, elaborated on and expanded by Jewish sages and commentators, whose remarks are debated in the Talmud. The dietary rules, referred to as *kashrut*, determine what is fit to eat (kosher), and what is forbidden (*treif*). The most important rules relate to the meat that can be eaten (the meat of cud-chewing animals with fully cloven hooves) and the way in which both meat and poultry must be killed (*shechita*) by a professional slaughterer (*shochet*). Only fish with fins and scales may be eaten and milk and meat cannot be cooked or consumed together. Observant Jews use different plates, crockery and cutlery for meat and non-meat ('milk') dishes as well as waiting several hours after eating meat before consuming milk dishes. While there were several aspects of hotel life that made the kosher establishments specifically Jewish, the keeping of *kashrut* was the most significant manifestation.

In 1804, the London Shechita Board was established to supervise religious slaughter and to issue a seal (*hechsher*) to butchers who carried out these practices correctly.[4] Over time, *shechita* boards were established in a number of other localities as immigrant communities became more self-assertive.[5] When the Anglo-Jewish community began to disperse and opened new synagogues and other facilities necessary to support Jewish

life, the communal authorities began to consider how the purveyors of
kosher produce might be regulated. This had not been a problem when
Jews had lived mainly in small geographical areas alongside the communal
authorities. Another stimulus to increased supervision was a series of
scandals relating to *kashrut* at public and communal events.[6] In 1920, the
Kashrus Commission was set up as a division of the London Beth Din,
operating under the auspices of the Chief Rabbi. The purpose of the new
body was to ensure that those institutions claiming to sell or serve kosher
food adhered fully to Jewish dietary laws.

Initially, the Kashrus Commission was quite 'light touch' in its
supervision and was subject to a great deal of criticism by the more
orthodox elements of Anglo-Jewry. The situation changed dramatically
during the 1930s when Chief Rabbi Joseph Hertz appointed the ultra-
orthodox Rabbi Yechezkel Abramsky as a *dayan* (religious judge) to the
London Beth Din. Abramsky, who was a Talmudic genius, had a profound
impact on the Beth Din, especially in respect of *kashrus*.[7] He established
customs and policies that are still being followed by the London Beth Din
and the Kashrus Commission (now referred to as the Kosher division of
the London Beth Din, KLBD). During the Second World War, certain
leniencies were tolerated due to wartime conditions, but in the postwar
years there was a renewed determination to tighten up regulation of
kashrut, including dietary standards in the high-profile hotels that were
opening in Bournemouth. The advent of these religiously licensed hotels
led to the public becoming more *kashrut* conscious, which in turn
contributed to the boom in the kosher hotel industry in Bournemouth
during the 1950s and 1960s.

By the late 1940s, the Kashrus Commission was carrying out its
regulatory role more rigorously, supported by the London Beth Din. Unlike
in Israel where the state attends to such matters, the Beth Din extended its
role to include not only the supervision of dietary standards but also other
aspects of hotel life, such as the keeping of *Shabbat,* the conduct of religious
services and practices during religious festivals and the tone of
entertainment in the hotels (see Chapter 8).[8] One of their main
requirements was that the hotels should employ *shomrim* to oversee day-
to-day adherence with *kashrut.* Since the hotels were regulated by arms of
the United Synagogue and the local supervisors had to be approved by
them, the hotels became in effect a Hampshire constituent of the United
Synagogue.[9]

Over the years, differences of opinion began to arise on the way in
which *kashrut* should supervised. Just after the war, the *charedi* Union of

Orthodox Hebrew Communities set up Kedassia, which imposed stricter standards of adherence to dietary laws. Later on, the Federation of Synagogues and the Sephardic community set up their own *kashrut* boards[10] (in 1967 and 1969 respectively). Smaller *kashrut* boards were also established in Gateshead and Manchester. However, the Kashrus Commission remained the main body for regulating the Bournemouth hotels.

As the century progressed, the various licensing bodies all became increasingly rigorous. In 1983, the Green Park lost its licence for a week due to the Kashrus Commission's concerns about lack of proper supervision. A *shomer* had been dismissed by the hotel and had left before a replacement was appointed. The hotel's directors placed an advertisement in the *Jewish Chronicle* assuring the public that its *kashrut* status had not been affected by the temporary withdrawal of the licence.[11] Geoffrey Feld recalls that at about the same time, he had a disagreement with Rabbi Silver, the examiner for the Beth Din:

> The Kashrus Commission had decreed that licensed hotels must serve kosher wine. I said that we couldn't do this because kosher wine was not readily available at the time and the small amount that was on the market cost a lot of money. Nowadays of course you can get kosher wine from across the world and it is much more reasonably priced. I told Rabbi Silver that our guests would not be prepared to pay for kosher wines and our income would be reduced at a time that we were already losing customers. In the end, he agreed to let me go on selling non-kosher wines, but that stopped during the 1980s.[12]

Not only did the list of foods and ingredients that must be certified steadily grow longer, the religious authorities also became more stringent on a number of related matters, such as food hygiene. For example, by 1990, the Kashrus Commission was requiring licensed caterers, including hotels, to provide a certificate of hygiene issued by an independent inspector.[13]

Religious Variations Between the Hotels

One of the prime purposes of establishing a synagogue in Bournemouth was concern for the religious needs of Jewish visitors to Bournemouth. In 1894, a letter was published in the *Jewish Chronicle* stating that: 'These poor creatures [the visitors] cannot enter the synagogue to pray for relief; if they require kosher meat it cannot be obtained, for there is no *shochet*, and when they are seriously ill there is no Jewish priest to give them consolation, and in case of death, the bodies must be taken long distances for sepulture [burial].'[14] The existence of an embryonic community led to an almost immediate increase in the number of Jewish boarding houses in Bournemouth. This growth became even more noticeable when the congregation was placed on a formal footing in 1905. One of the first priorities of what was named Bournemouth Hebrew Congregation (BHC) was to appoint a *shochet* to ensure a supply of kosher meat.

In the three decades prior to the Second World War, there were variations in the extent to which the Jewish-run hotels and guest houses adhered to dietary laws. At that time, none of them operated under any form of religious supervision. However, it was understood by those Jews to whom it was important that the proprietors possessed the requisite skills and knowledge and could be relied upon to keep a kosher kitchen; it was a matter of trust and word of mouth.

After the Second World War, when the Big Eight hotels became prominent, being kosher was a major selling point. However, the degree to which Jewish customs and practices were observed continued to vary significantly between the hotels. Ruby Marriott, proprietor of the Green Park, was a deeply religious man, setting an example for his guests, and the hotel became recognised as the most orthodox amongst the large Jewish hotels in Bournemouth. Barbara Glyn recalls: 'The religious aspect of life in the hotel was my father's uppermost concern.'[15]

The London Beth Din recognised that Ruby Marriott and the Richman sisters, who between them managed the hotel, knew all that they needed to know about running a kosher establishment. Joanna Benarroch comments: 'My grandfather taught the religious authorities a lot because he had the practical experience of running a kosher hotel in Torquay while they just had the theory.'[16] However, according to family sources, although for several years the Green Park was not required by the London Beth Din to have a *shomer*, Ruby Marriott was encouraged to apply for a licence so that other hotels would follow suit.[17] Some of the hotels – the Cumberland, the Majestic and eventually the Langham – did so, but the others established their own arrangements for maintaining *kashrut*. The Normandie and the Ambassador appointed a *shomer* and advertised that they were strictly kosher, but neither hotel was licensed by the Kashrus Commission, nor by any other religious body until much later (see below).

East Cliff Court was not licensed, nor did it have a *shomer*. Edward Hayman recalls:

> My grandmother, Annie Morris, was adamant that she wasn't having a rabbi in her kitchen. She decreed that her food was kosher regardless of whether there was a rabbi there or not. This meant that some people were not prepared to stay at the hotel, but it still did a very good business and the policy may even have gained the hotel the patronage of some guests.[18]

Kashrut was strictly controlled at the hotel. Ronald Hayman recalls:

> In the dining room, all the meals were either milk meals or meat meals. For milk meals the table cloths were checked with blue or brown lines; for meat meals [they were] plain white. For milk meals the plates and cups and saucers had black edges and the knives, forks and spoons had round handles; for meat meals the edges were blue and the handles were pointed. Breakfast was always a milk meal because you couldn't eat meat if you were going to have milk in your tea or coffee; at meat meals no one could have butter on their bread or cream on their stewed fruit. When it was a fish lunch or dinner, tables were laid with the milk table cloths, milk crockery and milk cutlery, which meant that ice cream would be one of the puddings. But if a waiter made a mistake when he was laying the tables, or used a round-edged spoon to serve vegetables during a meat meal, Mummy would be very angry and call Tonks [the head waiter] over to tell him off for being careless.[19]

Annie Morris, who had done her own catering when she had run boarding houses,[20] took a 'hands on' approach to *kashrut*. Ronald Hayman again recalls:

> At the hotel, her closest contact had been with the meat, for even meat bought from a kosher butcher had to be koshered in the home [not as now by a Jewish butcher], and it had always been Grannie who marched through the swing doors into the kitchen, to take charge of the soaking and salting. The idea apparently was to remove all traces of blood. It was very wrong to eat blood.[21]

Later on, Annie's daughter, Sadie Hayman, also closely supervised the kitchen staff. According to her son, Edward Hayman:

My mother stood in the kitchen corridor during a large part of the time when the main meals – lunch and dinner – were being served to guests. Most of the time she stood in silence, feeling that her presence alone was enough to instil conscientiousness in the staff. Occasionally, she would intervene if the aggression natural to working kitchens seemed to be growing too loud, or if a waiter was mixing milk and meat products.[22]

Maintaining a licence involved a great deal of effort as well as expense. Geoffrey Feld recalls the stress that resulted when the Feld and Inverne families purchased the Majestic and were running two large hotels simultaneously: 'Can you imagine two rabbis, two *shuls*, two lots of *Yamim Tovim*, two licences to renew each year?'[23]

As discussed in Chapter 5, by the mid-1980s, most of the Big Eight hotels had either closed or had shifted in their religious orientation. After it was sold in 1973, the Majestic operated as a non-kosher hotel. For several years during the 1980s, the Normandie also operated as a non-kosher hotel before becoming *glatt* kosher. David Latchman comments: 'Whereas in the past hotel guests had been satisfied to drink ordinary pasteurised milk, the milk used at the Normandie was now one hundred per cent kosher.'[24] David also recalls: 'When my parents stayed at the Normandie in the 1990s, they were somewhat to the left of the hotel's *charedi* clientele and my mother was once asked by a *charedi* child if she was really Jewish!'[25]

Some of the entertainment, for which the hotel had previously been well known (see Chapter 8) was replaced by religious activities, such as talks by high-profile religious leaders, *shiurim* (lessons on a Torah subject) and study sessions. When he was the managing director of the Normandie, Brian Lassman organised an eight-day *yarcheikallah* (intensive learn-in). He recalls: 'It was attended by people from all over the world. Sessions ran from 7am on one day until 1am the next day. Very famous lecturers came to the event from Canada, South America, Europe. The travel was arranged by Goodmos Travel and the Chomtovs knew many of the prominent *rabbanim* [plural of rabbi] who were invited.'[26] The event was particularly aimed at *charedim*, who due to their work commitments had limited time to study on a regular basis. The men listened to lectures in Yiddish and the women learned in English. James Inverne (the great-grandson of Bluma and Isaac Feld), worked as a porter at the Normandie in the early 1990s and recalls that there were often large rabbinical conferences at the hotel: 'When the visiting rabbi was particularly famous, all of the guests went out to the front of the hotel to greet him.'[27]

It took some former guests a little while to catch up with the changes that had taken place at the Normandie:

I had often stayed in the kosher hotels in Bournemouth when I was a child. So, one year, I decided to have a holiday there with my own children. We booked into the Normandie. This was in 1989, by which time the hotel was very orthodox and it was nothing like two decades earlier. We drove down from London on a very hot day and arrived frazzled. I was dressed in shorts and a sleeveless T-shirt. We were ushered into the dining room for lunch to be greeted by a sea of black hats. I was mortified, but a man in the centre of the room came across and invited us to sit at his table. It turned out that he was Rabbi Bubu Eiselmann from Israel, the first cousin of my husband's father. He remembered having met my husband when he was young. After that everyone in the hotel accepted us, but for the rest of the holiday I dressed more modestly.[28]

For over two decades after the Second World War, the Ambassador did not have a licence, possibly because it was owned by a board of directors that included non-Jews. However, when the hotel (now known as the New Ambassador) was taken over by the Selby family in 1967, it operated under the supervision of the London Beth Din and the Kashrus Commission. It continued to do so, under the ownership of the Vickers family until the beginning of the twenty-first century. Today, only one of the Big Eight hotels, the Normandie, remains in business as a kosher hotel, supervised by Kedassia.

The *Shomrim*

The *shomrim* appointed by the Big Eight hotels came to their roles from across the country and having previously held a variety of positions. Some were former congregational leaders, mainly ministers, who had trained as 'reverends' at Jews' College rather than the more recently ordained United Synagogue rabbis, who were often *yeshiva* (a college for the advanced study of Torah and rabbinic traditions) graduates with a more intensive training in the Talmud. Others had been *chazanim* (cantors) or employed as educators. An appointment as a hotel *shomer* was a retirement job rather than for those who were setting out on their career. Geoffrey Alderman comments: 'Being a *shomer* in a luxurious hotel in beautiful Bournemouth would have been an attractive proposition for retirees.'[29] Norman Lebrecht recalls: 'The strictest Bournemouth hotels had a rabbi. He sat in the lobby looking as if he had found heaven on earth.'[30]

The *shomrim* spent much of their time in the hotel kitchens, inspecting the ingredients that were being used and ensuring that there was no cross-contamination between milk and meat products.[31] Jonathan Perlmutter comments: 'The *shomrim* had the key to the fridge to make sure that the food was not tampered with overnight.'[32] They also watched to make certain that non-Jewish staff did not bring *treif* food into the kitchens.[33] Some of the hotel *shomrim* combined their supervisory role with other religious functions, such as acting as a *chazan* and leading services in the hotel *shuls* (see below) and also informal activities. Geoffrey Alderman tells us: 'They were also called upon to carry out low profile welfare work and to chat to the guests as well as making sure people didn't use the lifts or switch on a light over *Shabbat*.'[34]

While the *shomrim* were able to train and oversee those directly employed by the hotel, they had less control over the tradespeople who visited the hotels on an occasional basis, such as delivery people. Roger Adsworth, who worked for M&J Seafood, recalls:

> I used to deliver to the Green Park Hotel in the mid-1980s. The delivery included jars of capers that had to go to a dry store outside the hotel, but the fish had to go inside to the kitchen via the rear entrance. My very first delivery was a carp (quite unusual) encased in a two-stone box. I took it into the kitchen where I had to get someone to sign for it. As it was lunchtime, there was mayhem, so I put the box down on a near-by meat block. Well that got everyone's attention! A rabbi appeared and went mad and the staff all went crazy. l legged it without bothering to get the invoice signed. I found out later the meat and fish should never meet. I knew better next time.[35]

Several of the *shomrim* at the largest hotels remained in post for many years and became well known by the regular guests, including Aaron Segal, who was the *shomer* (sometimes referred to as 'the administrator') at the Cumberland for twelve years. He moved to Bournemouth from Manchester where he had been the minister at the Central Synagogue for thirty-five years. His father, and later his brother, was the head of the *yeshiva* in Manchester. As well as supervising *kashrus*, he was a skilled *chazan*.[36] Other *shomrim* at the Cumberland were the refugee Mr Irsai, who was not a trained rabbi but who was a very religious man and, from 1973, the very popular Rev. Lewis (pronounced Louis) Wyatt (originally Wykanski). Rev. Wyatt had previously been the minister at the Old Hebrew Congregation in Newcastle where he had taught Susan Gould who married Geoffrey Feld, a director of the Cumberland.[37] According to his daughter, Simone, although it had taken some persuasion by Bluma Feld for Rev. Wyatt to make the move to Bournemouth, he soon discovered that he 'adored working in the hotel'.[38]

Supported by his wife Dollie (with whom he had honeymooned at the Trouville Hotel many years earlier and had subsequently holidayed at the Cumberland), he became an integral part of hotel life. The Wyatts had a flat in nearby Marchwood in Manor Road, but they apparently hardly spent any time there because of the long hours that Rev. Wyatt worked, and because he and Dollie (referred to by some younger people as 'Aunt Dollie') socialised with people they knew at the hotel, especially guests from Newcastle.[39] Rev. Wyatt was 'fastidious about *kashrus*, but he was prepared to be flexible on some matters for the sake of *sh'lombayit* (literally peace in the home, but meaning to maintain harmony), such as his willingness to commence *sedarim* (plural of *seder*) early so that the children could go to bed at a reasonable time.[40] He was meticulous about practising the *sedra* to be read at *Shabbat* services, even though he 'knew the text inside out'. On *Shabbat*, children were invited to sit with Rev. Wyatt at his table in the dining room when he said 'Grace After Meals'. James Inverne recalls: 'He did funny things with his hands, which made it interesting and often hilarious for the children.'[41]

52. Dollie and Lewis (pronounced Louis) Wyatt, *c.* 1979. Lewis Wyatt was the *shomer* at the Cumberland Hotel during the 1970s. Image courtesy Simone Halfin (née Wyatt).

The longstanding *shomer* at the New Ambassador was Josh Rose (previously Rosenblueth), whom Brian Lassman describes as 'a really gentle man who worked sixteen hours a day'.[42] He was succeeded for a short time by Rev. Nathan Rockman, previously the minister at Nottingham Hebrew Congregation and then by Rev. Solomon Camissar, previously the headmaster of the Talmud Torah at Springfield Synagogue in Upper Clapton Road and who later taught at the Hasmonean School and the Jews' Free School. At the Normandie, the *shomer* for many years was Rev. Phillip Isaacs, formerly the minister at Southampton *shul*. The Langham was not licensed by the Kashrus Commission until 1963. The religious supervisor who was then appointed was Rev. A. I. Burland from Manchester.[43]

Two well-known *shomrim* at the Green Park were Rev. Samuel Wolfson and Alec Kesselman. Rev. Wolfson was a retired minister from Greenbank Drive Synagogue in Liverpool, who was renowned for his sense of humour[44] and for being 'a master of *nusach* (form of text or prayers), his *chazanut* (cantorial singing) and *leyning* (reading of the scroll)'.[45] Alec Kesselman, studied at the *yeshivot* (plural of *yeshiva)* in Liverpool and Manchester, where he had gained a thorough knowledge of meat and poultry *kashrut*.[46] Prior to becoming the *shomer at* the Green Park, Alec Kesselman had been a minister at the Higher Boughton and Aguda synagogues in Manchester, run a butchers shop in Bournemouth, managed the kosher section of the De Mar Hotel in Majorca, and been the *shomer*/manager at the Carmel Hotel (Gutstein's).[47] After the Green Park closed, he became the *gabbai* (warden) at the *Ahavat Re'im Bet Hamidrash* (house of study) at the, by then, very orthodox Normandie.[48]

One of the best remembered *shomrim* was Rev. Herman Fenigstein, a Holocaust survivor, who was employed by the Normandie during the 1960s. He was 'a much-loved personality' and had a 'fine tenor voice'. He led 'homely traditional services' and had a 'warm and friendly manner'. He started his career as a leading light in the Yiddish theatre before becoming a prominent *chazan* in the Glasgow Jewish community.[49] Paul Harris, who holidayed at the Normandie for twelve years remembers Rev. Fenigstein as 'a very human character' and tells this story:

> We were staying at the Normandie during the 1966 World Cup final between England and West Germany. The hotel never had the television switched on during *Shabbat,* but that day they had sets on in two separate rooms. Observant and non-observant guests alike

assembled to watch the game. Even Rev. Fenigstein was watching from the back![50]

Rev. Fenigstein is also remembered for involving children in religious activities. Eliot Steinberg recalls:

> The children in the hotel were asked to hold the candles when he did the blessings on Friday nights. The candles often deposited hot wax on their hands and it was hard to cry out when it did. So, I always went prepared in case I was asked to hold the candles. I took with me one of my sister's white evening gloves. When I was selected and I brought out the glove, everybody applauded with merriment.[51]

For a short time before his retirement, Rev. Fenigstein was the minister/ *shomer* at the Green Park. He was replaced at the Normandie by Samuel Wolfson who had previously been the *shomer* at the Green Park.

The *shomrim* worked very closely with the chefs and often struck up a good relationship based on mutual respect. Miriam Marcus recalls:

> Years later in Jerusalem we met Rabbi Reich who was the *mashgiach* [another Hebrew word for religious supervisor] when my father Max Colman was head chef at the Majestic Hotel. He told us that although it was common in those days for the *mashgiach* to help in the kitchen to earn a few more pounds, our father would never let him lift a spoon and paid him the utmost respect while the hotel paid the rest.[52]

Some of the hotel proprietors were not willing to delegate supervision entirely to the *shomrim*. At the Green Park, each of the directors saw it as their responsibility to oversee adherence to all aspects of *kashrut*. David Marriott recalls: 'Their view was that one *shomer* wasn't enough. All family members looked out to make sure *kashrut* was observed. There was not a moment when the kitchen was not being supervised by a family member. My grandmother and my aunts were super-vigilant.'[53] At the age of seventy-three, Bluma Feld was still examining the kitchens at the Cumberland each day.[54]

In addition to the supervision carried out by the *shomrim* and the hoteliers themselves, there appears to have been an informal network of informers, who took it upon themselves to report perceived breaches of dietary standards to the religious authorities. For example, in 1961 Mr S.

Cherkoff from Stamford Hill wrote to the London Beth Din following a stay at the Majestic. He alleged that he had been served Brussel sprouts that had not been sliced in half for examination before they were cooked to check whether or not they contained worms.[55]

Kashrut in the Smaller Hotels and Guest Houses

In the immediate postwar years, most of the smaller hotels and guest houses continued to describe themselves as either 'kosher' or 'strictly kosher'. By the 1950s, a wider range of practices was becoming evident. While some establishments maintained that they were strictly kosher, others stated that they were non-orthodox, including the Chine Court Hotel in Boscombe, Mon Bijou in Manor Road and the Bourne Hotel (previously Hotel Rubens) in Bath Road (see Chapter 4).

Due to the cost involved in obtaining a licence and employing a *shomer*, most of the smaller hotels and guest houses were not supervised by a religious authority, although some were able to call on friends and relatives with a religious training to provide guidance on *kashrut*. When the Hotel Rubens first opened in Bath Road under the direction of Joseph and Helena Grower, Wolf Siefert, Mrs Grower's father, who was one of the founders of the Great Garden Street Synagogue in the East End of London, lived with the family. Advertisements for the hotel placed in the *Jewish Chronicle* suggested that he provided *kashrut* supervision at the hotel.[56] However, his grandson, Ben Grower, comments: 'I wasn't aware of him providing any supervision. It was probably my father looking to encourage people to come to the hotel!'[57] However, Wolf Siefert's reputation did attract to the hotel a number of orthodox rabbis, such as Rabbi Leslie (Eliezer) Turetsky from Newcastle Hebrew Congregation.[58] Ben Grower recalls that the hotel had a kosher kitchen: 'I remember seeing my father sitting in the kitchen with a file, marking the cutlery. Those to be used for meat were marked with a "1" and milk cutlery was marked with a "2". I still have a set that I use for barbecues!'[59] The smaller establishments were also able to take the advice of the rabbi from BHC. Judi Lyons recalls:

> Rabbi Jonah Indech was extremely flexible and pragmatic. One *Pesach*, my mother brought a supply of *matzos*, but when she went to bring them in from the garage where all her supplies were stored, she discovered that the wrong *matzos* had been delivered – they were not stamped 'Kosher for Passover'. My mother was in a real flap as the *seder* was about to take place. She called in Rabbi Indech, who

advised her to take the *matzos* out of the box and serve them on a plate. His view was that she had purchased the *matzos* in the belief that they would be kosher for Passover and that they would therefore be good enough for her to use for a few days until she could procure replacements.[60]

One of the exceptions to the general lack of direct supervision was the Mayfair Hotel in Upper Terrace Road run by the very observant Elkan Shapiro, who had studied at Etz Chaim Yeshiva in the East End of London before moving to Bournemouth in 1928, when he married his wife Esther.[61] The Mayfair Hotel was licensed by the Kashrus Commission and the London Beth Din, but because of Elkan Shapiro's standing as a Talmud scholar, the hotel was not required to employ a *shomer*.[62] Norman Shapiro recalls that many distinguished rabbis stayed at the hotel and studied with his uncle Elkan in his hotel office: 'I remember once meeting Rabbi Rabinov on the stairs in the hotel and I stood back to let him past. However, he insisted that I should go first, even though I was just a humble *yeshiva* student at the time. His humility left an indelible impression on me.'[63] The Mount Aishel in Argyll Road, Boscombe run by the Ricklows, was also supervised by the Kashrus Commission and the London Beth Din. The Ricklows initially advertised that it had separate meat and milk kitchens, but it later became a 'milk' hotel. The ultra-orthodox Carmel Hotel in Florence Road, Boscombe run by the Gutsteins, was supervised by Kedassia.

Although the other smaller establishments were not supervised by a religious authority, their clients, most of whom were regular visitors, were prepared to trust the proprietors in respect of *kashrut*. At Villa Judi, Sylvia Kay maintained a kosher kitchen. Judi Lyons recalls: 'We used separate table cloths and crockery for milk and meat meals. The table cloths were a checked-pattern for milk and plain white for meat. The crockery was not colour coded, but we knew which was which.'[64] Judi also tells us that the ingredients used in the food served in the guest houses were not scrutinised to the same extent as they are today:

I don't think we were so kosher in the 1960s. Bread and cheese were not required to be kosher. Things started to change in the 1970s. Personally, I have always had kosher bread, but unless you were really *frum* [orthodox], there was nothing wrong with Hovis bread and Dairylea cheese triangles when my parents had the guest house.[65]

The Kays employed a maid, who carried out the tasks they were unable to perform on *Shabbat*, including removing the large cooking pot containing the *Shabbat* meal from the oven.[66]

The owners of some of the smaller hotels were enterprising in finding ways of maintaining *kashrut* while keeping costs to a minimum. Judi Lyons recalls: 'I was once told that Sydney Lukover, who ran the Grosvenor Hotel in Bath Road, was seen reversing his trailer into the sea at Boscombe. It was filled with a new set of crockery for the hotel. It was cheaper and just as effective to dip the crockery in the sea than to take it to the *mikveh*.'[67] The extensive kitchens at Branksome Dene convalescent home, which also offered holiday accommodation, were designed to conform to Jewish orthodox requirements, but the establishment was not run under the supervision of a religious authority.[68]

The *kashrut* status of the smaller hotels and guest houses was placed on a more transparent footing in June 1961, when the *Jewish Chronicle* introduced a classification system for those establishments advertising in the newspaper. Each establishment now had a symbol by its name: 'SKO' denoted an establishment under the supervision of a religious authority; 'KO' identified those establishments that were not operating under official supervision but which used kosher produce, separated meat and milk in their kitchens and at the table and observed *Shabbat* and Jewish festivals; the letter 'K' was allocated to establishments serving kosher meat but which did not observe other Jewish religious duties; and the classification 'O' was given to establishments offering no assurances about religious observance. The descriptions in the advertisements for the hotels and guest houses often differed from the *Jewish Chronicle* classifications.[69]

By the time that the Glencairn Manor opened in 1985 under the ownership of Jack and Paula Bright, the religious outlook of British Jews was very different from the postwar years. The hotel was licensed by the stricter Kashrus Board and the Beth Din of the Federation of Synagogues. The hotel was orthodox in its orientation and attracted some very observant guests and people to eat in its restaurant. Both the male managers and male guests wore *kippot* (skull caps) in the dining room, which until this time had been rarely seen in the Bournemouth hotels except during the in-house services (see below) and the blessings on *Shabbat*.[70] The *shomer* at the hotel was Rev. Lewis Wyatt, previously the *shomer* at the Cumberland. With his wife, Dollie, he is said to have been 'instrumental in making the Glencairn Manor a popular place to stay'.[71]

When ownership of the Glencairn Manor passed to the Amdur family, it was supervised for a short while by Rabbi Yechiel Weiss.[72] However, when the hotel obtained a licence from the Sephardi Kashrut Authority, its resident *shomrim* over the two years that it operated were Rabbi Wyatt (who had worked with the Brights), Rabbi Bernard Susser (formerly the rabbi in Plymouth) and Rev. I. Cohen.[73]

In 2005, Jack and Paula's son, David Bright, opened the Acacia Gardens in Manor Road. It provided the base for the activities of the Chabad (Lubavitch) community led by Yossie and Chanie Alperowitz.[74] However, David Bright experienced problems with both the Manchester Beth Din, which initially licensed the hotel, and then with the Sephardi Kashrut Authority. In November 2006, he announced that the Acacia Gardens would no longer be run as a kosher hotel.[75]

Today, the Chabad-run Water Garden offers a wide variety of social and educational opportunities, particularly those involving *limmudeikodesh* (study of Jewish texts). The Water Garden's *glatt* kosher kitchen is supervised by Rabbi Alperowitz.

Religion Amongst the Hotel Guests

As well as varying degrees of orthodoxy between the hotels and guest houses, there was also a range of religious observance amongst the guests who stayed in them. While the most religious guests gravitated towards the more orthodox establishments, less observant guests also stayed at these establishments. Some guests who were not particularly religious or regular synagogue attenders often found themselves caught up in the religious atmosphere of the hotels. Louis Plotkinoff, a regular visitor from Scotland, is quoted as saying: 'Most people here [at the Green Park] have *Shabbos* jackets. They keep wearing them out from putting their hands in their pockets to get their cigarettes – and then remembering its *Shabbos*.'[76]

Others stayed away from the kosher hotels altogether or chose not to participate in the religious aspects of hotel life, nor to adhere to the rules governing *Shabbat* and the Jewish festivals. Even at the Green Park, the most orthodox of the Big Eight hotels, there was a gambling culture (see Chapter 8) and some guests continued betting on *Shabbat* afternoons. A former guest recalls: 'Everyone knew what was going on, but because it was taking place in the bedrooms, no one said anything. You could see plumes of smoke rising from underneath the doors.'[77] Peter Phillips, who stayed at the Ambassador in the late 1950s, shares this memory: 'Not being religious, I was amused by the number of men who slid out of their hotels after their Friday night meal to stroll up and down the East Cliff on which the hotels stood, smoking their cigarettes furtively and walking in typical Jewish

fashion with their hands on their bottoms!'[78] Joan Doubtfire recalls that
when she worked as a receptionist at the Cumberland, guests sometimes
approached her to place bets for them on *Shabbat*: 'I used to tell them, "You
should know better than that on *Shabbat*!"'[79] The fact that some people did
not stay at the kosher hotels for religious reasons is illustrated by an
anecdote that appeared in the *Jewish Chronicle*: 'While having a meat lunch
at a kosher hotel in Bournemouth, a guest asked the waiter for some butter.
Another guest told her that it was not permitted to have butter with meat.
"Oh", came the reply, "But it's not *Shabbos*!"'[80]

However, there was an unwritten understanding that the rules would
be followed in the public areas of the hotels and guest houses. Barbara Glyn
recalls that, at the Green Park: 'No notices asking people not to smoke on
Shabbos were ever necessary. Nor were guests ever requested not to drive
into the car park on that day. No doubt the surrounding streets were used
instead, but in public they respected the way the hotel was run, according
to our family's religious way of life.'[81]

There were some guests for whom the levels of *kashrut* maintained by
the directors of the Green Park were not sufficient. David Latchman recalls
that one of the regular guests at the hotel, Osias Freshwater, insisted on
having kosher milk delivered to the hotel for his consumption 'at a time
when most hoteliers were satisfied that the Milk Marketing Board were
taking sufficient precautions to ensure that milk was not contaminated.'[82]
Rev. Isaac Livingstone, the longstanding minister at Golders Green
Synagogue, who also often stayed in the hotel, 'made a point of not using
the lift on *Shabbat* or *Yom Tov*, even when he was aged over ninety.'[83]

Like the Green Park, the Cumberland was also strict about observing
Shabbat. Jack Morris, a regular guest at the hotel had 'a bit of a falling out'
with Geoffrey Feld, one of the directors of the Cumberland, when he had
to return home to Portsmouth one Saturday to deal with an urgent business
matter.[84] The religious atmosphere of the hotel was enhanced when Bluma
Feld's parents, Berish and Alta Posner, moved from London to live in
Bournemouth and spent a great deal of time in the Cumberland. Berish
Posner often led *shiurim*. During the *Yom Kippur* services held at the hotel,
Alta stood for the whole day. Her grandson, Geoffrey, recalls that when she
was older, he once suggested to her that she did not have to stand for hours
on end: 'She told me in no uncertain terms in Yiddish, "I know what I have
to do", and the matter was never raised again.'[85]

Although the guests who stayed at East Cliff Court were generally not
particularly observant,[86] Annie Morris was not pleased when her guests
openly ignored *Shabbat*. Martin Slowe recalls:

My parents told me that they once stayed at East Cliff Court and they wanted to leave to go home on a Saturday evening before the end of *Shabbat*. The hotel owners were none too pleased as they could not accept payment on *Shabbat*. They had to rely on my father's promise that he would pay them at a later date, which of course he did.[87]

Although Annie Morris apparently turned a blind eye to guests who used the lift on *Shabbat*, she would not allow smoking in the hotel.[88]

Observance also varied widely amongst the guests staying at the smaller hotels and guest houses. The Carmel Hotel in Boscombe was particularly noted for its *heimische* (traditional Jewish) atmosphere. A contemporary travel writer commented: 'There, amid ultra-modern surroundings, one is taken back to the world of Sholem Aleichem for especially on *Shabbat* the *Chassidic* guests wear the *streimels* and other appurtenances reminiscent of life in Eastern Europe under the Tsars.'[89] Hazel Green recalls: 'The Carmel Hotel was often referred to by my family as "the cowboy ranch" because of the hats worn by its guests.'[90] Hazel also tells this story: 'Davina, a Spanish maid, who had previously worked for years at my parent's hotel, went to work at the Carmel Hotel. She told us how difficult it was to clean there because everywhere she went men were always davening away in the public areas like the dining room and the lounge as well as in the bedrooms. She accompanied this statement with an energetic impression of the "shockelling" clientele.'[91]

In Chapter 3 we saw that during Bournemouth's heyday as a Jewish holiday destination, many visitors arrived by train, including the 'named trains' – the *Pines Express* and the *Bournemouth Belle* – in which tea and other meals were served. The food was not kosher. While some families took care to avoid consuming milk and meat together,[92] others avoided the refreshments altogether.

Religious Services in the Hotels

The Big Eight hotels all had synagogues where *Shabbat* and other services could be held.[93] Initially, the synagogues were established in rooms that were used for other purposes. At the Green Park and the Langham, *Shabbat* services were held in part of their ballrooms, and during the week the *shul* (alternative word for synagogue) at the Cumberland was used as a card room. David Latchman recalls that the room that was at first used for services at the Green Park did not resemble a *shul*. It was a quite a bare room with two columns. However, this didn't prevent those who used it from having their favourite spots for services: 'Once when we were staying at the hotel, a German-Jewish guest got quite cross with my father and me because we had taken "his place" next to one of the columns. We noticed that for the next service, he had gone into the room early and had placed his *tallit* [prayer shawl] on a chair close to one of the columns!'[94] At the Normandie, the room used as a *shul* also accommodated a juke box, around which young people gathered during the week to listen to the latest hits. Jon Harris recalls: 'Even though it was covered on *Shabbat*, I still worried sometimes that it might start playing during the service.'[95]

The rooms where religious activities took place were quite small and could not hold many people: 'They were mainly an amenity for people who couldn't or who didn't want to move far on *Shabbat*.'[96] John Colvin comments: 'When I visited my grandmother during her stays in the Majestic in the late 1950s, she wasn't mobile enough to leave the hotel and she really appreciated the in-house *shul*.'[97]

Those who attended the services were usually (but not always) the most religious guests and were mainly men. Marilyn Murray recalls: 'My father and uncle always went to the services while my mother and aunt took us four children to the beach.'[98] Those attending services in the *shuls* were sometimes aware of people continuing with their holidays while they worshipped. Beverley-Jane Stewart recollects: 'When we were in the *shul* at the Cumberland, you could hear people enjoying themselves in and around the swimming pool. It was all a bit distracting.'[99] Some of the hotels reserved a few places in their *shuls* where women could pray separately from the men, or they listened into services from adjacent rooms. At the Green Park, the lounge known as the 'Green Room' acted as part of the ladies' section of the *shul*. Frances Israel, niece of Ruby and Sarah Marriott, recalls: 'I used to sit there with my aunts, the Richman sisters, and it felt like being involved in the service even though we weren't in the *shul* itself. The services were very melodious and warm.'[100]

The services in the hotels generally followed the format of the United Synagogue worship and used the same *siddurim* (prayer books) and *machzorim* (the special prayer books used for *Rosh Hashanah* and *Yom Kippur*), a supply of which the hotels kept for guests who arrived without them.[101] Rabbi Jonathan Romain, who as a child attended services in the synagogue at the Normandie, recalls that they were almost identical to those that he attended at Wembley United Synagogue: 'It felt like a home from home.'[102]

After the *shul* at the Cumberland was enlarged in 1969, the hotel was presented with an Ark (the cupboard in which the scrolls of the Pentateuch are housed) by an appreciative guest, Louis Shor of Westcliff, in memory of his sister, Golda Werner,[103] and the Feld family donated a *Sefer Torah* (scroll) in memory of Bluma Feld's parents, Berish and Alta Posner. It was consecrated in July 1969 by Dayan Lew, a relative of the Felds.[104] In the *shul*, which led off from the bar, the men sat facing the Ark and the women sat sideways onto the men.[105]

When the dedicated synagogue at the Green Park was established in what had previously been the ballroom, a *mechitzah* (partition) was erected to separate the men and the women worshipping there.[106] Hettie Marks recalls that the rabbi who presided at the services when she stayed in the hotel said that she was his 'best customer' because she laughed at his jokes. Her husband looked forward to attending services because he enjoyed meeting people there.[107] The *shul* had a wonderful sea view and was Ruby Marriott's 'pride and joy'[108] and, according to a journalist, had the most comfortable seating in any place of worship he had visited.[109] When the hotel closed in 1986, some of the fittings were given to Borehamwood United Synagogue, but the family retained the scrolls.[110] During the 1960s, the Keynes added an extension to the Normandie that included a new, larger dining room where dancing could be held after the evening meal and the original ballroom became the *shul*.[111]

53. The first synagogue at the Green Park Hotel, Manor Road, Bournemouth. Image courtesy of the Marriott family.

As they entered their teenage years, some boys started to attend the services held in the hotels, often with their grandparents. Rabbi Jonathan Romain recalls: 'I remember one particular service at which my grandfather said *kaddish* [Jewish prayer for the dead] for his father. My grandfather cried. This is the one and only time I saw him cry.'[112] However, not all young people were enamoured with the experience of attending services. Stuart March comments: 'We went to the *shul* in the Langham out of respect for my grandmother, not because of any religious conviction. It was the thing then, you did it for your parents.'[113] Jon Harris recalls: 'At the time we thought that the services were dire. They seemed to go on for ever when in fact they were probably not much more than an hour long.'[114]

In some of the hotels, guests were invited to participate in leading services. Paul Harris recalls that his father Frank Harris, proprietor of the Manchester-based *Jewish Telegraph*, had a good singing voice and without prior warning he was often asked to recite *maftir* or the *haftarah*[115] during a *Shabbat* service held at the Normandie: 'Having spent five years studying at the Etz Chaim Yeshiva in the East End of London in his youth, he was well-placed to be able to do this.'[116]

In 1950, the writer Louis Golding described the services held in the Ambassador as 'becoming to a holiday hotel, not services of frightening formality, but warm and simple services, which bring a glow to a Jewish heart'.[117] Two decades later, services at the New Ambassador commenced at 9am and finished at about midday. There was a break at around 10.15am for people to eat breakfast. Some men and most of the women who attended the services only went for the second part of the service.[118] A Friday night *minyan* (a group of ten men or more, who come together informally to pray) was also convened in the hotel.[119]

At the Cumberland, the *Shabbat* services always ended on time so that the staff could set up for the *kiddush* (see Chapter 6), which started at midday 'on the dot'. Bluma Feld apparently became stressed if the services overran.[120] East Cliff Court did not hold regular services at the hotel. On *Shabbat* and for weekday *minyanim* (plural of *minyan*), some East Cliff Court guests attended services at BHC, where John Hayman, Annie Morris's son-in-law, was a prominent member (see Chapter 9).

Many guests made a conscious decision to opt out of the *Shabbat* services held in the hotels. Sheila Morris recalls: 'Our holidays in Bournemouth were a break from *shul* as well as from our business.'[121] Others found that there were more exciting things to do, or preferred to worship alongside the resident community at BHC. David Abrahams recalls: 'We went to Friday evening services at the Green Park, but on *Shabbat* morning we always went to Wootton Gardens because it felt more like being part of a community.'[122]

On weekdays, some of the hotels aimed to hold early morning services (*shacharit*), but they sometimes found it difficult to form a *minyan* as even the most observant Jews were not always enthusiastic about rising early when they were on holiday, especially when they'd had a late night being entertained (see Chapter 8). However, the *shomrim* were always available to form a *minyan* if a hotel guest wanted to say *kaddish*, although some guests again preferred to say *kaddish* at one of the local synagogues.

While some visitors who stayed in the smaller hotels and guest houses attended services at BHC, others went to the regular services held at the Dolly Ross home (see Chapter 4), which had its own synagogue, the scroll for which was provided by the Yager family,[123] or services held at the Hannah Levy House care home. Branksome Dene also had its own synagogue.[124] The Carlton Dene holiday home in Southbourne, which was strictly kosher, held services on a Friday night in its lounge, where an Ark was installed.

More orthodox guests staying in guest houses worshipped at the Carmel Hotel. Judi Lyons recalls: 'When we had *frum* guests staying who wanted to *daven* my father took them to Gutstein's for *mincha* or *ma'ariv* [afternoon and evening services]. If the Gutsteins were short of men to make up a weekday *minyan*, Dad would grab some men and drive them round to assist.'[125]

In some of the hotels, the proprietors and other family members played a prominent role in services. For many years, services at the Green Park were led by Ruby Marriott. He was often assisted by his brother-in-law, Joseph Richman, and later by his son David Marriott. During the winter months, Ruby Marriott led the blessings before and after Friday night dinners in the hotel dining room.[126] It was only when he was no longer able to read from the *Sifrei Torah* (plural of *Sefer Torah*) that Ruby was prepared to delegate the *davening* to a minister or *chazan*. His daughter Barbara Glyn explains: 'Even though he knew the Torah by heart and could have read it without seeing it, according to Jewish law, he could not *leyn* without reading the text.'[127]

Although he took little part in the day-to-day running of East Cliff Court, John Hayman organised all the religious ceremonies that were held at the hotel. He also led the *kiddush* before meals and 'Grace After Meals' on *Shabbat*.[128] Before he died in 1950, Ben Schneider enjoyed the religious side of the Majestic, and helped the resident minister to run the *shul* in the hotel.[129] In addition to leading the *Shabbat* and weekday services held at the Carmel Hotel, its owner Armand Gutstein led regular *droshes* (religious talks), which were attended by people staying at other smaller hotels and guest houses and by the local Jewish community. Judi Lyons recalls: 'My father used to *daven* at Gutstein's and he sometimes stayed on for the *droshes*, which were given in Yiddish. He was sometimes away for a long time, which worried my mother.'[130] The Glencairn Manor, which opened in 1985 under the ownership of the Bright family, had its own *shul*, where *Shabbat* services were held, often led by their son, Alan, who was the part-time *chazan* at Dollis Hill and then Wembley Synagogues.[131] During the short time that the Amdur family ran the Glencairn Manor, it became known for the Friday night dinners at which the Amdurs sang beautifully.[132]

One of the reasons why the *charedim* started holidaying in Bournemouth in increasing numbers during the latter part of the twentieth century (see Chapter 5), was the religious infrastructure that existed in the town, especially the in-house *shul* at the Normandie, which had by then become very orthodox. As a result, at one point the Normandie *shul* became very crowded, and it was sometimes very difficult for hotel guests to find a seat, a matter of concern to the older guests staying in the hotel. David Latchman comments: 'The Normandie *shul* became very popular with the *charedim* staying in nearby flats, who would certainly not have been happy in *davening* at BHC, which would have been too United Synagogue for them.'[133]

Today, *charedim* staying in Bournemouth have limited interaction with the resident Jewish community. They either *daven* in the *shul* at the Normandie and join *minyanim* in the hotel when it is open, or form *minyanim* elsewhere. An interviewee said: 'In the apartment blocks on the East Cliff there is always a *minyan* going on somewhere, which is a welcome option for those who want a bit more privacy.'[134]

Festivals

We have seen that, even in their declining years, the Big Eight hotels were at their busiest during the main Jewish festivals, each of which was observed scrupulously and attracted a core group of guests. The hotels were especially busy during *Pesach*, when visiting rabbis and *chazanim* would usually be in residence for the duration of the festival, and at *Rosh Hashanah*. The hotels would close down for up to a week before *Pesach* to enable them to make the necessary preparations, which involved ridding the kitchens and dining rooms of any trace of leavened food (*chametz*). It was a major operation. A former chef recalls: 'The rooms were scrubbed and repainted. All of the cutlery and pots were boiled, the bench tops were steamed and new Passover crockery, cutlery and table cloths were used.'[135] Brian Lassman tells us that when he managed the Normandie and was meeting the stringent requirements of Kedassia, it took a full seven days to prepare for *Pesach*, whereas at the New Ambassador he had streamlined the preparation time to three and a half days.[136] Ronald Hayman recalls:

> You had to go without bread for eight days, but you could spread *matzah* with butter and marmalade at tea time. All the usual plates, cups and saucers were hidden away somewhere and were replaced by special Passover crockery that was never used except for these eight days each year. The meat plates had thick blue bands round the edge, but the milk plates and cups and saucers were my favourite because the edges were gold.[137]

At the Majestic, Fay Schneider was highly skilled at planning for major events, but sometimes things went wrong, including a near disaster one *Pesach*:

> Each year we ordered new crockery for *Pesach*, a different design for meat and milk meals. One year, they didn't turn up and we were ringing the suppliers for several days trying to track them down. They were eventually found in a van sitting in a lay-by somewhere. They arrived just an hour before the *seder* was due to start and they were still being washed as people were taking their seats. We were tearing our hair out![138]

Preparing for *Pesach* was particularly demanding for the *shomrim* who oversaw the whole process. Rev. Wyatt's wife, Dollie, used to worry about how fatigued he became in the run up to *Pesach*, and sometimes said that 'the stress and effort of it would be the death of him'. Coordinating the *sedarim* was also quite complicated with different groups of guests singing different songs and using different tunes for the many songs included in the *Pesach* narrative.[139] In the large hotels, *sedarim* were held on the first two evenings of *Pesach*. They were hosted by the families who owned the hotels. The family atmosphere was apparently particularly evident at the Green Park: 'It felt like the guests had been invited to Ruby Marriott's private family celebration, which he led. When he had finished eating, he said "Grace After Meals" regardless of whether or not other people had finished their eating. You got the impression that you were paying Mr Marriott for the privilege of joining in his celebration.'[140]

For many years, Joseph Richman, who had a lovely melodious voice, 'sang all the special traditional tunes so beloved by all' at the Green Park *sedarim*. As the youngest child, Barbara Glyn recited *Mah Nishtanah* ('The Four Questions' that form part of the *seder* service, usually recited by the youngest child present).[141] The family *Pesach* table grew ever larger as the children married and brought their own offspring to the hotel for *Pesach*: 'When the family table got to over fifty places, the guests began to complain in jest that we were taking up too much space and the dining room was becoming cramped.'[142]

David Latchman recalls that the *sedarim* at the Cumberland were so large that they spilled over from the dining room into the ballroom. One year, when he was aged about nine, he was selected to sing *Mah Nishtanah*: 'My father made cards for me to read from. I was very nervous and can still recall the sea of faces around me as I sang, standing on a chair. Everybody was dressed up to the nines in black tie and long dresses. I wore the full black tie outfit that I'd had made for me for a family wedding – a black dinner jacket and trousers with white dress shirt and black bow tie.'[143] After attending a *seder* held at the Ambassador in 1950, Louis Golding wrote:

> At the *seder* night festivities a number of guests were present who had not attended a *seder* since their childhood, and perhaps not then. Of these guests, several told me that they would think the years left to them incomplete without the celebration of the *seder*, either in Bournemouth, or in their own home. And, of course, it is easier in Bournemouth.[144]

Although Annie Morris would not entertain religious supervision of her kitchen, she did allow services to take place at East Cliff Court during the main Jewish festivals. In the early days, these services were led by Rev. Solomon Lipson, formerly the minister at Hammersmith Synagogue, to which John Hayman, her son-in-law, had previously belonged. Her grandson, Ronald Hayman, recalls: 'He was a big old man with shrivelled skin under his eyes, blotchy pink cheeks and a white beard like a goat's. He hugged me and kissed me wetly, saying he'd married Mummy and Daddy.'[145] Rev. Lipson and his family stayed in the hotel and mixed freely with the other visitors. One of his grandsons was Robert, who became the well-known professor, scientist and television presenter, Lord Robert Winston. Robert Winston often accompanied his grandfather at the hotel when he was a child. Rev. Lipson made a point of encouraging those present to participate in the reading of the services and keeping his sermons to a minimum so that the guests could enjoy the sunshine before lunch.[146] When Rev. Lipson became too frail to lead services at East Cliff Court, his role was gradually taken over by Edward Hayman's university friend from Oxford, David Weitzman. The festival services at East Cliff Court were conducted 'according to orthodox rituals', but Edward Hayman found them 'fairly relaxed and short compared with those at BHC'.[147]

The hotels were generally less busy at *Yom Kippur*, which a former hotelier ascribes to the fact that less food was available. However, although there was no breakfast, lunch or afternoon tea, the meals immediately before and after the fast were very substantial.[148] Joan Doubtfire recalls that *Yom Kippur* was the busiest time for the room service staff at the hotel. They took orders for food from older people who were not fasting for health and other legitimate reasons, and also those who were not so observant. They were 'running up and down stairs all day'.[149] This apparently amused the kitchen staff, but Bluma Feld was less sanguine about the behaviour. Joan Doubtfire again recalls:

> During the first year that I worked at the hotel, I learned a lot about Jewish festivals and practices. I decided that at *Yom Kippur* I was going to fast along with the guests. I stopped eating at 5.45pm on the eve of *Yom Kippur* and didn't eat again until 6.45pm the next day. When Mrs Feld got to hear about this, she led me into the dining room and told the guests to note the example that had been set by this non-Jewish woman, saying: 'She is more committed than many of you whom I have seen coming into the hotel with bags of food to eat in your rooms.' It was all very embarrassing![150]

However, on *Kol Nidre* (the eve of *Yom Kippur*), guests 'fell over themselves' to give generously to the hotel's *Yom Kippur* appeal.[151] One former Cumberland guest recalls: 'People gave far more generously in the hotel than elsewhere. They were away from home and relaxed. Guests stood up and said what they were going to pledge, which spurred others on.'[152]

Sukkot was also a popular time for staying in the large hotels in Bournemouth. Each of the hotels had their own *sukkah* (temporary structures roofed with foliage, in which Jews eat during the eight-day festival of *Sukkot*), providing seating for men. Edward Hayman recalls that at East Cliff Court, the *Sukkot* services were held in the ballroom on the lower ground floor:

It was converted into a synagogue with a reading-desk in the centre and an 'Ark' for the scrolls of the law (*Sifrei Torah*) at the eastern end. Part of the veranda outside the ballroom was converted into a *sukkah* by means of fence-like panels constructed from wooden slats and wire and connected to each other by bolts and more wire. Each year, fresh foliage was acquired to weave into the panels. The roof, which had to be open to the sky, had more foliage and fruit suspended from it. There were also bunches of glass grapes (from my father's shop), within which there were light bulbs that were connected to the main electricity supply and switched on at night.[153]

When he was older, Edward took on responsibility for making sure everything was in order, and for bringing down from the Oak Room (the private family sitting room in the hotel) the prayer books and *Sifrei Torah* used at the services.[154] In his memoir of growing up at the hotel, Edward's older brother, Ronald, remembered *Sukkot* in the hotel because everyone had a *lulav* (made of palm, myrtle and willow leaves) to shake and the *etrog* (a citron fruit) to smell. Guests were given a glass of red wine and could help themselves to salted almonds and biscuits spread with chopped liver.[155] Ronald Hayman also enjoyed *Simchat Torah,* a service that follows *Sukkot* when the last and the first section of the Pentateuch are read:

> …everyone was in a jolly mood, and all of the Scrolls of the Law had to be taken out of the Ark and to be carried in procession around the *Shool* [sic] until all of the men had had a turn. I was too small to hold one from the Ark, but Daddy bought a very small one with all Five Books of Moses on the scroll in tiny Hebrew letters. The rollers were silver, and it lived in a little Ark of its own. I walked behind the procession carrying my own scroll, and gave all the other little boys a turn afterwards.[156]

The Green Park had a large *sukkah*, located adjacent to the dining room. The roof was composed of sections, which could be lowered using a system of pulleys to enable it to be decorated. There was also an electrically operated sliding roof that was pulled over the top of the *sukkah* if it rained. Growing up around the Cumberland, James Inverne recalls: 'I was entranced by the *sukkah*, which was created by a large portion of the hotel's roof being rolled back so you could see the stars. This seemed like magic to me as a small child.'[157]

For many years, Ruby Marriott blew the *shofar* (a musical instrument, made from a ram's horn blown on important Jewish public and religious occasions) on *Rosh Hashanah* and *Yom Kippur* until he was advised to stop doing so by his doctor.[158] His place was taken by Leslie Curzon, who organised kosher package holidays for the Goodmos travel company.[159] Because of the length of the services, it was essential for the *shomrim* and visiting rabbis to have additional support. At the Cumberland Rev. Wyatt was assisted by the *chazan* Robert Brody.[160] Henry Kesselman recalls that he was paid £15 to blow the *shofar* at the Cumberland. He comments: 'That was a lot of money in those days.' [161]

Although the profile of the Jewish holidaymakers has changed over the years (see Chapter 5), *Pesach* remains a popular time of year for Jews of all denominations to visit Bournemouth. In 2006, the well-known London caterer, Steven Wolfisz, began organising nine-day *Pesach* package holidays in Bournemouth, which were supervised by the London Beth Din. Worthy of the finest traditions of the kosher hotels in their heyday, the packages included all meals, two communal *sedarim* and entertainment for all ages. Over the eight years that Steven Wolfisz organised these *Pesach* events, they took place at various non-Jewish hotels around Bournemouth: the Menzies Carlton, Queens, Heathlands, Cumberland and Cliffeside hotels. The rabbi who regularly led the *sedarim* and oversaw the holidays was Jeremy Conway from the London Beth Din.

Since 2014, Brian and Judy Lassman have taken over the Queens Hotel for *Pesach*, acting as consultants to the hotel. They organise the *sedarim*, the kosher meals, the services, and various other activities, such as guest lecturers, children's entertainment and outings. The all-inclusive, nine-day holidays are supervised by the Kashrut Division of the London Beth Din (KLBD). The hotel closes for a week before *Pesach* for a 'deep clean' that is overseen by Rabbi Jeremy Conway and Rabbi Hillel Simon, the KLBD 'non-kosher places' expert. Services that take place in the in-house *shul*, which holds 180 people, have been led by Rabbi Geoffrey Shisler, who also gives a daily *shiur*. The *chazzan* has been Colin Dworkin, who brings with him his sons to form a choir, and the leading *shomer* has been Chaim Azulay of the London Shechita Board. These *Pesach* packages have proved very popular and have been attended by up to 250 people, many of whom have come for several years running.

The *Pesach* holidays appeal particularly to older people who are no longer able to travel to Israel for *Pesach*, but they have also attracted a significant proportion of younger people who do not wish to use the airports when they are busy with Easter holiday passengers. People come to the Queens Hotel from far and wide: from Dublin, Belfast, Scotland, Leeds, Liverpool, Manchester and London and also from Canada and Paris. However, a significant number of Jewish people resident in Bournemouth also participate in the activities at the Queens Hotel. The holidays were suspended during the COVID pandemic of 2020, as was everything else.

The *Pesach* holidays organised by Brian and Judy Lassman attract mainly 'United Synagogue-type of people' rather than 'Kedassia-type people',[162] but *Pesach* and other Jewish festivals (especially *Purim*) are also popular times for *charedi* Jews to visit Bournemouth.

Before they became less fashionable, the smaller hotels and guest houses were often filled to capacity during *Pesach*. Some of their guests attended services at BHC, but most attended the services held at the Dolly Ross home (see Chapter 4), which over several decades were led by Mark Woolfson, a local resident, who owned Southbourne Jewellers and was the local agent for Venus Travel, a well-known Jewish travel firm organising holidays in Israel for Bournemouth Jews. Mark Woolfson also led *sedarim* held at Stevra House in Southern Road run by the Correns (see Chapter 4).[163]

For several years, the Kays at Villa Judi hosted *sedarim* for forty people, some of whom were staying at other guest houses. This entailed a great deal of preparation by Mrs Kay who, unlike the larger establishments, had few staff to help her. The Russells at the Mayfair guest house in Westby Road also held *sedarim*. Hazel Green recalls going to these *sedarim*, which were led by a former minister, who lived full time in the guest house (what was known as 'a perm'): 'He made an excellent job of explaining the story. He really engaged my attention. It was a pity that some of the guests disappeared after the meal. They had only come for the food!'[164] The *sedarim* at the Grosvenor Hotel were sometimes led by Josef Perl from Sunnyside Court Hotel (see Chapter 4), who had a very orthodox background.[165]

At *Rosh Hashanah* and *Yom Kippur* Mark Woolfson led services at the Dolly Ross home, assisted by his two teenage sons. Jonathan Woolfson recalls: 'My brother blew the *shofar* whereas I, the younger one, was "the finger". What is "the finger"? While my father read from the Torah, I stood next to him and followed his words in a *Chumash* [the first five books of the Bible] with my finger, so that he could look over and see the vowel sounds and recite correctly.'[166]

A large proportion of the guest houses closed before *Rosh Hashanah* and therefore did not need to make special arrangements for the High Holydays. An exception was the strictly orthodox Mount Aishel guest house run by the Ricklows, which took bookings for *Sukkot* and erected a *sukkah* in its grounds.[167] One of the regular guests at the larger Hotel Florence in Boscombe Spa Road was a religious leader from London, who led the *sedarim* at *Pesach* and also services during *Yamim Tovim*.[168]

Later on, over *Pesach*, the Glencairn Manor was often over-subscribed and arrangements were made for people to stay at the Majestic opposite the Glencairn Manor. The *sedarim* were sometimes led by the Brights' son, Alan. Until his emigration to Florida in 1989, Rev. Bright also led a number of other festival services in the hotel's *shul*. When ownership of the hotel passed to the Amdur family, it offered special packages at *Pesach*, *Rosh Hashanah* and *Sukkot*, during which services were led by the resident rabbi (see above). The Amdurs stressed that the *Pesach* meals would be Ashkenazi style, and that there would be 'no *kitniot*' (that is, no rice and pulses, the eating of which is however customary for Sephardi *Pesach* meals).[169]

Staff

As previously mentioned, the hotels and guest houses employed mainly non-Jewish staff, who were vital in enabling them to maintain their high standards of service over *Shabbat* and Jewish festivals. Rotas were organised so that Jewish staff did not work over *Shabbat*. This meant that the non-Jewish staff had to be thoroughly trained in *kashrut* and other religious laws (*halachah*) governing the Jewish way of life. According to a former employee at the Green Park, new recruits were not left to work alone for the first month of their employment; they were always paired with an experienced colleague. It sometimes took a while for new staff to absorb all of the rules that needed to be followed. Another former employee comments: 'The milk and the meat separation was the most difficult thing to learn.'[170] However, Jewish customs and practices eventually became second nature. Joanna Benarroch (née Marriott) recalls: 'The staff were so well trained that they told us children what we should and should not do in respect of *kashrus*. Some of the staff even learned to speak a few words of Hebrew and Yiddish!'[171] In 1977, the following story was related in the *Jewish Chronicle*:

> Rev. Samuel Wolfson, Religious Supervisor of the Green Park Hotel, Bournemouth, where the crockery and kitchen utensils are marked in red or blue for milk and meat separation, was talking to one of the directors in the hotel lounge when water suddenly poured down from the ceiling from an overflowing bath. Mr Wolfson told a porter to bring some bowls from the kitchen to catch the water. The man

came back empty handed and said: 'Kitchen wants to know, sir, do you want red bowls or blue bowls?'[172]

The staff training included what to do on Jewish festivals. At East Cliff Court, the porters knew how to put the furniture in place and construct the *sukkah* and at the Green Park, the hotel's waiters were trained to operate the sliding roof if necessary, as observant Jews were unable to do so on the first two and last two days of *Sukkot*.

Notes

1. Elaine R. Smith, 'Jews and Politics in East End London, 1918–1939', in David Cesarani (ed.), *The Making of Anglo-Jewry* (Oxford: Basil Blackwell, 1990), p.145.
2. See Aubrey Newman, *The United Synagogue 1870–1970* (London: Routledge Kegan Paul, 1976).
3. Interview with Geoffrey Alderman, 20.8.2020.
4. See https://www.shechita.org/about-us/e.
5. Bill Williams, *The Making of Manchester Jewry, 1740–1875* (Manchester: Manchester University Press, 1985), p.332.
6. Interview with Geoffrey Alderman, 20.8.2020.
7. Abramsky was subjected to Stalinist persecution in Belarus. He was permitted to leave the Soviet Union following an international campaign. On his arrival in London in 1931, Abramsky served initially as the rabbi of the ultra-orthodox synagogue, Machzike Hadass, in Brick Lane. It was through Abramsky's influence on the London Beth Din that the porging and sale of cattle hindquarters was increasingly controlled and eventually banned. See Geoffrey Alderman, *British Jewry Since Emancipation* (Buckingham: The University of Buckingham Press, 2014), p.359.
8. These requirements were set out in publications regularly issued by the London Beth Din, such as *The Really Religious Food Guide*.
9. Interview with Geoffrey Alderman, 20.8.2020.
10. The Federation Beth Din was established in 1966 and began issuing its own *kashrut* licences that year. The Federation Kashrus Board emerged as a separate entity in 1967.
11. *JC*, 29.7.1983 and 5.8.1983.
12. Talk given by Geoffrey Feld at Edgware United Synagogue, 6 March 2018.
13. *JC*, 25.1.1991.
14. *JC*, 24.8.1894.
15. Interview with Barbara Glyn, 1.6.2020. Under Jewish law *Cohanim* (the priestly class) must avoid corpses.
16. Interview with Joanna Benarroch, 19.6.2020.
17. Interview with Barbara Glyn, 1.6.2020.
18. Interview with Edward Hayman, 11.5.2020.
19. Ronald Hayman, *Secrets: Boyhood in a Jewish Hotel, 1932-1954* (London: Peter Owen, 1985), p.24. Although Ronald Hayman referred to him as 'Tonks', his real name was Jones.

20. Interview with Edward Hayman, 11.5.2020.
21. See Hayman, *Secrets*, p.81.
22. Notes from Edward Hayman, sent by email 24.8.2020.
23. Interview with Geoffrey Feld, 4.5.2020.
24. Interview with David Latchman, 5.11.2020. To be fully kosher, milk must be guaranteed to be free of meat derivatives (conventional rennet, gelatine, etc.). It must be produced, processed and packaged on kosher equipment.
25. *Ibid.*
26. Interview with Brian Lassman, 14.5.2020.
27. Interview with James Inverne, 10.11.2020.
28. Interview with Beverley-Jane Stewart, 29.5.2020.
29. Interview with Geoffrey Alderman, 20.8.2020.
30. Norman Lebrecht, 'I consulted Talmud: I can go to Brighton', *JC*, 5.6.2020.
31. In the large hotels there were separate kitchens for meat and milk meals, only one of which would be in operation at a time.
32. Interview with Jonathan Perlmutter, 26.8.2020.
33. Conversation with Rabbi Jonathan Romain, 19.8.2020.
34. Interview with Geoffrey Alderman, 20.8.2020. Unless they were incapacitated, observant guests would have walked up the stairs and essential lights would have been on a timer switch.
35. Roger Adworth, response to author's post on Memories of old Poole and Bournemouth Facebook Group, 21.11.2020.
36. Interview with Geoffrey Feld, 4.5.2020.
37. *Ibid.*
38. Interview with their daughter, Simone Halfin, 27.8.2020.
39. *Ibid.*
40. *Ibid.*
41. Interview with James Inverne, 10.11.2020.
42. Conversation with Brian Lassman, 1.12.2020.
43. *JC*, 11.1.1963.
44. *JC*, 21.1.1983.
45. *JC*, 17.8.1990.
46. *JC*, 18.7.1997.
47. *JC*, 13.7.1979.
48. *JC*, 18.7.1997.
49. *JC*, 8.12.1972. Today, a Fenigstein recording is a collector's item.
50. Interview with Paul Harris, 28.4.2020. Although inappropriate, it would not have been against Jewish laws to watch television on *Shabbat*. However, it would have been against Jewish laws to switch on the set.
51. Interview with Eliot Steinberg, 24.5.2020.
52. Email from Miriam Marcus, 1.12.2020.
53. Interview with David Marriott, 11.5.2020.
54. *JC*, 25.11.1983.
55. Letter to the Clerk of the London Beth Din, cited by Panikos Panayi in 'The Anglicisation of Eastern European Jewish Food in Britain', in *Immigrants & Minorities*, 30: 2, p.303.

56. *JC*, 10.2.1950.
57. Interview with Ben Grower, 22.11.2020.
58. *Bournemouth Jewish Courier*, first edition, July/August 1949. Copy kindly provided by Ben Grower.
59. Interview with Ben Grower, 22.11. 2020.
60. Interview with Judi Lyons, 4.5.2020.
61. *JC*, 13.11.1959.
62. Interview with Rita Eker (née Shapiro), 20.10.2020.
63. Interview with Norman Shapiro, 23.10.2020. Rabbi Shmuel Yosef Rabinov was originally from Lithuania, but by this time was living in Stamford Hill, London.
64. Conversation with Judi Lyons, 10.8.2020.
65. Email from Judi Lyons 22.6.2020.
66. Conversation with Judi Lyons, 10.8.2020. Lifting the heavy pot would have been regarded as work, which under Jewish law is not allowed on *Shabbat*.
67. *Ibid.* New crockery or crockery that has previously been used before it is needed for *Pesach* must be dipped in water. The immersion usually takes place in a *mikveh* (ritual bath) but, in principle, any form of running water is acceptable.
68. *JC*, 7.12.1951.
69. *JC*, 2.6.1961.
70. Covering of heads by male Jews has become more prevalent in the last fifty years or so. Previously, even many Jewish ministers would be bare-headed except during religious occasions such as services. Observant men would have worn *kippot* in a dining room to say the pre- and post-meal blessings.
71. *JC*, 18.5.1990.
72. *JC*, 4.5.1990.
73. *JC*, 30.8.1991.
74. *JC*, 28.10.2005.
75. *JC*, 3.11.2006.
76. Israel Shenker, 'On the British Seafront, Kosher Cuisine with an English Accent', *New York Times*, 6.1.1973.
77. Anonymous, out-take from, 'The Green Park', directed by Jack Fishburn and Justin Hardy, 2015. Smoking *per se* would not have been problematic, but lighting a cigarette would not be allowed. Under Jewish law it is prohibited to ignite a fire on *Shabbat*.
78. Peter Phillips, 'London's Borscht Belt – Jewish Hotels in Bournemouth', *AJR Journal*, August 2014, p.11.
79. Interview with Joan Doubtfire, 13.5.2020.
80. *JC*, 16.12.1983.
81. Manuscript, 'The Green Park 1943-1986', provided by Barbara Glyn, 22.5.2020.
82. Interview with David Latchman, 6.5.2020.
83. *Ibid.*
84. Interview with Sheila Morris, 19.8.2020.
85. Interview with Geoffrey Feld, 21.10.2020.
86. Email from Edward Hayman, 25.8.2020.
87. Email from Martin Slowe, 5.5.2020.
88. Email from Edward Hayman, 25.8.2020. Today, in Israel and elsewhere, there are 'Shabbat lifts' in Jewish hotels, which work automatically and stop on every floor.

89. David Pela, travel editor, *JC*, 16.7.1976. Sholem Aleichem was a famous Yiddish novelist who died in 1917. *Chassidic* Jews traditionally dress in garments that identify their sect.
90. Interview with Hazel Green, 25.8.2020.
91. *Ibid.*
92. Interview with Marilyn Murray, 24.8.2020.
93. Jewish religious services do not have to be held in dedicated or consecrated spaces. Frequently a space doubles as both a prayer and assembly room in a synagogue.
94. Interview with David Latchman, 6.5.2020.
95. Interview with Jon Harris, 4.5.2020.
96. Interview with David Abrahams, 25.8.2020.
97. John Colvin, post on Facebook, 24.8.2020.
98. Interview with Marilyn Murray, 24.8.2020.
99. Conversation with Beverley-Jane Stewart, 3.11.2020.
100. Interview with Frances Israel (née Richman), 19.6.2020.
101. The hotels usually used the famous Routledge *machzor* first published in 1906.
102. Conversation with Rabbi Jonathan Romain, 19.8.2020.
103. *JC*, 28.2.1969.
104. *JC*, 11.7.1969
105. Interview with Simone Halfin, 27.8.2020.
106. Interview with Hettie Marks, 28.4.2020.
107. *Ibid.*
108. See manuscript, 'The Green Park 1943-1986'.
109. See Shenker, 'On the British Seafront'.
110. Interview with Barbara Glyn, 1.6.2020.
111. Interview with Eliot Steinberg, 14.5.2020.
112. Interview with Rabbi Jonathan Romain, 30.4.2020.
113. Interview with Stuart March, 21.9.2020.
114. Interview with Jon Harris, 4.5.2020.
115. *Maftir* is the last person called up to the Torah on *Shabbat* and holiday mornings: this person also reads the *haftarah* portion from a related section of the *nevi'im* (prophetic books).
116. Interview with Paul Harris, 28.4.2020.
117. Louis Golding, *Hotel Ambassador* (Bournemouth: Ambassador, 1950), p.14.
118. Interview with Jonathan Perlmutter, 26.8.2020. At this time, it was quite usual in United Synagogue *shuls* for people to enter at the beginning of the 'Reading of the Law'.
119. *JC*, 21.6.1991.
120. Interview with Simone Halfin, 27.8.2020.
121. Interview with Sheila Morris, 19.8.2020.
122. Interview with David Abrahams, 25.8.2020.
123. *JC*, 31.10.1958.
124. *JC*, 7.12.1951.
125. Interview with Judi Lyons 4.5.2020.
126. Interview with David Marriott, 11.5.2020.
127. Interview with Barbara Glyn, 30.6.2020.
128. Email from Edward Hayman, 25.8.2020.

129. Interview with Shirley Davidson, 18.5.2020.
130. Interview with Judi Lyons, 4.5.2020.
131. *JC*, 1.3.1985. Alan Bright also ran residential homes for older people in London.
132. Interview with Jonathan Perlmutter, 26.8.2020.
133. Interview with David Latchman, 5.11.2020.
134. Anonymous interviewee, 16.6.2020.
135. Anonymous, out-take from 'The Green Park', directed by Jack Fishburn and Justin Hardy
136. Interview with Brian Lassman, 14.5.2020.
137. See Hayman, *Secrets*, p.36.
138. Interview with Shirley Davidson, 18.5.2020.
139. Interview with Simone Halfin, 27.8.2020.
140. Anonymous interviewee, 16.5.2020.
141. See manuscript, 'The Green Park 1943-1986'.
142. Interview with David Marriott, 11.5.2020.
143. Interview with David Latchman, 6.5.2020.
144. See Golding, *Hotel Ambassador*, p.14.
145. In his book, Ronald Hayman refers to Rev. Lipson as Rev. Lazarus but his brother, Edward Hayman, confirms that it is Rev. Lipson about whom he was writing. See Hayman, *Secrets*.
146. Anthony Winston, memory submitted to eastcliffcourtmemories.wordpress.com/blog/.
147. Extract from the memoirs of Edward Hayman, emailed, 20.8.2020.
148. Interview with Richard Inverne, 6.7.2020.
149. Interview with Joan Doubtfire, 13.5.2020.
150. *Ibid.*
151. It is traditional on *Yom Kippur* to raise money for a charitable cause.
152. Unnamed audience member, commenting at talk given by Geoffrey Feld.
153. Notes from Edward Hayman, sent by email, 24.8.2020.
154. *Ibid.*
155. See Hayman, *Secrets*, p.36.
156. *Ibid.*, p.36.
157. Interview with James Inverne, 10.11.2020.
158. It is customary to blow the *shofar* 100 or 101 times on each day of *Rosh Hashanah*. However, *halakha* only requires that it be blown 30 times. The various types of blast are known as *tekiah*, *shevarim*, and *teruah*. The *shofah* is also blown at the conclusion of *Yom Kippur*.
159. Interview with Barbara Glyn, 30.6.2020.
160. Interview with Simone Halfin, 27.8.2020.
161. Henry Kesselman, speaking at the talk given by Geoffrey Feld by Zoom at BHC, 17.6.2020.
162. Conversation with Brian Lassman, 1.12.2020.
163. Message from Jonathan Woolfson, Mark's son, 22.11.2020.
164. Interview with Hazel Green, 25.8.2020.
165. Conversation with his son, Mark Perl, 14.1.2021.
166. Email from Jonathan Woolfson, 17.12.2020.
167. *JC*, 29.8.1958.

168. Interview with Lennie Segal, 15.6.2020.
169. *JC*, 22.2.1991.
170. Anonymous commentator, out-take from 'The Green Park', directed by Jack Fishburn and Justin Hardy.
171. Interview with Joanna Benarroch, 19.6.2020.
172. *JC*, 16.12.1977.

8

Entertainment, Recreation and Relaxation

Even before Jews started to move away from the first areas of settlement in various parts of the country, how they spent their leisure time was beginning to shift away from the Yiddish theatre and music halls that had provided an escape from the harsh living and working conditions of immigrant Jews. Instead, the new generation of Jews born in Britain was embracing the modern forms of entertainment that were becoming popular in the non-Jewish community, particularly the cinema. Young Jews also participated in Jewish sports and social clubs, many of which were set up by the Jewish establishment as a means for hastening their integration into British society, but sometimes also because they were not welcome in non-Jewish clubs.[1] At these clubs, Jews were exposed to the panoply of British cultural and leisure pursuits, such as swimming, football and cricket.

One traditional Jewish activity that did endure was gambling. Eastern European Jews were noted for their sobriety, but gambling was endemic in the community. Despite the fact that the only legal form of betting at this time was on racecourses, by the interwar years a well-established, 'secret' network of off-course Jewish bookmakers and their runners operated in the East End. They gathered in certain alleys, such as Vine Court, that were well known to the initiated, to exchange gossip and tips and to pass over cash, wagers and purses.[2]

As Jews moved to the suburbs, they made a conscious decision not to recreate the Yiddish culture they were leaving behind and sought to emulate the leisure activities of the mainstream society of which they were becoming a part. As well as frequenting the new suburban cinemas that were opening during and after the First World War, once they were settled in their new environment, Jews joined the audiences at the new theatres that were also being established, such as the Hippodrome that opened in Golders Green in 1913, where some of the productions featured well-known Jewish actors.

The railways that had been pivotal in enabling Jews to move to the suburbs also gave them easy access to the entertainment and other leisure facilities available in the West End of London and other city centres. An important reason for leaving the first areas of settlement was to live in a more conducive environment, and many of the first Jews who moved to the suburbs spent a great deal of their leisure time simply enjoying the nearby parks, open spaces and other outdoor amenities.

As they put down firmer roots in the suburbs, Jews started to establish a range of local leisure activities that were largely modelled on those pursued by non-Jews, including cultural and literary societies, study circles and clubs that organised dances, dramatic performances, concerts and other events. In keeping with Jewish tradition, many Jews also spent their leisure time involved in charitable and welfare activities, such as orphan aid societies and committees organising visits to the sick and elderly. The myriad of Jewish card-playing circles that sprang up in the suburbs, particularly in north-west London, were a reflection of Jews arriving in mainstream society. Hettie Marks recalls: 'I grew up with cards in my hands. Our apartment was large enough to take several card tables and was always full of people playing different card games – solo, bridge or kalooki.'[3] This was a more acceptable form of the gambling that had pervaded the Jewish East End.

Many leisure activities were organised by the new synagogues that were established in suburban locations, most of which were built with attached social halls. While some of the synagogue-based societies were for adults, there was also a wide range of activities for children and young people aimed at maintaining their interest in Judaism and sustaining the embryonic congregations. Some of these activities were concerned with Jewish education, but others replicated non-Jewish bodies such as the synagogue-based Brownie and Cub packs, Scout troops and Guide companies. The first generation of suburban Jews was very ambitious for their children and during the interwar years the *Jewish Chronicle* documented the setting up of 'improving' activities for young people, such as elocution, piano and singing lessons. The interwar years also saw a growth in Zionism, which was particularly apparent amongst Jews who had moved to the suburbs. Zionist societies for both adults and children proliferated, especially during the 1930s, as a reaction to developments in mainland Europe.

During the Second World War, suburban synagogues gave a great deal of attention to organising activities for the teenagers who were not evacuated elsewhere. Adults who were not called up for war service devoted time to supporting the war effort and raising money for the victims of Nazi persecution. In the postwar years, there was a plethora of social activities for young people, initially intended as a means of reintegrating young men returning from the war, but later as a response to mounting concern about the number of young people 'marrying out'.

In the 1940s, synagogue youth clubs burgeoned, but by the 1950s young people were starting to become involved in social gatherings held outside the synagogues, and they were increasingly venturing beyond the areas where they lived. The number of suburban Zionist youth groups also increased, such as Habonim and, for more observant young people, B'nai Akiva.

With the arrival of the 'Swinging Sixties', more and more young people were lured away from organised and specifically Jewish activities by the new forms of entertainment that were opening up. Although many young Jews still spent much of their leisure time with their Jewish peers, they now wanted to associate with them more informally, such as in coffee bars or simply wandering along the suburban shopping parades. The heightened Jewish consciousness engendered by the Six-Day War led to a resurgence in membership of the synagogue youth clubs, but now this was alongside activities involving non-Jews.

The social life of Jewish adults evolved along similar lines. During the 1950s and 1960s, many Jewish families belonged to close-knit circles of friends, such as young marrieds' clubs and activities that reflected the pre-occupations of the time, including keep fit classes. While some families continued to build their social life around their synagogue, others socialised with their friends more informally in places such as teashops. Transport improvements and rising income meant they were able to look further afield for their leisure pursuits and enjoy more 'upmarket' entertainment.

The Jewish boxing and other sports clubs that had been such a strong feature of life for young people in the first areas of settlement, came to be regarded as working-class activities and upwardly mobile Jews engaged in the same types of sporting activities as their non-Jewish neighbours, such as golf and tennis. However, they were not always made welcome by the existing golf and tennis clubs. Undeterred, they established their own clubs, such as the highly successful Chandos Tennis Club in Golders Green, which attracted Jewish players from across north-west London.

The evolution of Jewish leisure pursuits is reflected in how Jews spent their time while holidaying in Bournemouth.

Early Days in Bournemouth

In Chapter 1, we saw that the first Jewish visitors in Bournemouth were mainly convalescents, concerned with improving their health rather than looking for ways of filling their leisure time. This began to change during the early years of the twentieth century when an increasing number of Jews began taking holidays in the town. The boarding houses, which evolved into guest houses and hotels, began to compete with each other in providing entertainment for their guests, and by the interwar years it was no longer sufficient to provide a comfortable bedroom and home-cooked food. Cabarets, dinner dances, fancy-dress competitions, free trips to the pier[4] and 'magnificent Christmas-time attractions' were all being offered to keep guests amused. Billiards and table tennis rooms, which had become commonplace before the First World War, were now supplemented with sun lounges, hard tennis courts and increasingly elaborate ballrooms. By the outbreak of the Second World War, the larger establishments had resident bands, including at the Avon Royal Hotel in Christchurch Road. East Cliff Court employed a professional dancer to encourage participation in the dancing that took place in the hotel several nights a week. In some of the larger Jewish hotels, dancing continued throughout the war years. However, like the food offered at the hotels, it was not until after the Second World War that entertainment became a major aspect of Jewish holidaymaking.

Being Together

In the postwar years, when Jews started holidaying in Bournemouth in large numbers, they were no longer seeking simply to get away from their normal lives; they wanted to have a good time. Their main aim was to spend time in the company of other Jews. Visiting the Ambassador in 1950, Louis Golding commented:

> They [the hotel guests] find that they have a great deal in common with their fellow-guests even before they open their mouths, supremely the two greatest emotional experiences that any race has known in human history: the unspeakable terror of the Hitler nightmare, the ineffable glory of the establishment of Israel.[5]

Understanding this impulse, the hoteliers provided ample opportunities for their guests to come together to talk informally, including in their large, comfortably furnished lounges, such as the 'Louis Quatorze' room at the Green Park. The guests also met on the hotels' verandas, and in their beautifully maintained gardens. Many lifelong friendships were struck up in the hotel dining rooms and from attending services in the hotel *shuls* (see previous chapter).

54. The 'Louis Room' at the Green Park Hotel, 95-97 Manor Road, Bournemouth, *c.* 1955.
Image courtesy of the Marriott family.

55. Part of what became the 'Lisle Lounge' at East Cliff Court Hotel, 23 (later 53) Grove
Road, Bournemouth, *c.* 1932. Image in the Flickr collection of Alwyn Ladell, https://www.
flickr.com/photos/alwyn_ladell/15668947245.

Although the hotels were soon offering a range of other diversions, the desire for guests simply to talk and enjoy each other's company remained paramount for some guests. John Colvin recalls that when his grandmother stayed in the Majestic in the late 1950s, the food on offer was very good, but his grandmother enjoyed the company much more than the food: 'Although she had only a limited command of English, this didn't seem to be a problem in the Majestic. I suspect that during the entire holiday, Grandma Baum didn't ever glimpse the sea.'[6]

Conversations in the hotels would centre around politics, football, cricket and boxing, business, Israel and, in the early days, the Holocaust. However, the favourite topic of conversation was always 'Jewish geography' – the friends and acquaintances whom the guests knew in common, and how they were related, albeit distantly, to each other. Sheila Morris recalls: 'Jews are generally very sociable people and our holidays in Bournemouth staying in the Jewish hotels were a chance to talk to people and an opportunity to meet up with people that we already knew and to get to know new people. We often stayed up until 3 or 4 in the morning just chatting.'[7] Over time, each of the hotels developed a regular clientele and were sometimes seen as being a bit 'cliquey':

> The minute an unknown hotel guest walked in, conversation became muted while the new entrants were given 'the once over' and checked for recognition: who is this newcomer, are they anyone we know, where are they from, who are their family? Then everyone went back to their *schmoozing* [socialising].[8]

The Jewish holidaymakers not only consorted with other Jews in the hotels, but also when they were out and about in Bournemouth. In Chapter 3, mention was made of the glamorous attire of guests staying in the Big Eight hotels. Between meals, but especially on *Shabbat* and during the long summer evenings, a ritual activity was for guests to walk along the promenade on the East Cliff, wearing their finest clothes. While walking, they met and conversed with people staying in the other Jewish hotels. Inevitably, the conversation turned to the respective merits and shortcomings of the hotels in which the visitors were staying. They compared food, bedroom size, furnishings and the entertainment.

According to the *Jewish Chronicle*, when out parading, the women often wore their fur coats, even when temperatures were well into the seventies, just to remind people that they owned them; it was an ostentatious display of wealth.[9] Marian Stern recalls: 'As a teenager I was mesmerised by the sight of women walking along the seafront, wearing what looked like diamond-encrusted stockings in spite of the hot weather – such a far cry from the life I knew.'[10] The aim was both to see and be seen, and the promenade became known as the 'diamond strip'. Occasionally, the smartly attired women ventured onto the beach where 'they paddled rather than swam in the sea, for fear of getting their fur stoles wet!'[11] It was the same for young people. Hannah Jacobs remembers posing on the beach wearing her white Courrèges boots.[12] Since the Jews parading in their finery were so visible, the local non-Jewish community was wont to comment, with a hint of antisemitism: 'There are so many Jews in Bournemouth, even the trees have fur coats' and 'millionaires of a feather flock together'.[13]

Illustration 7. Parading along the seafront to see and be seen. Drawing by Beverley-Jane Stewart.

This parading is captured in Gerda Charles's *The Crossing Point*:

Up and down the few hundred yards (which closely resembled as was often pointed out, the Corniche) strolled Carl Morris, ruddy-cheeked and white-haired, surprisingly athletic and gentle-looking for a tycoon, deep in conversation with the dapper Rosenthal, closely followed as they passed by the breeze of a thousand sharply turned heads and the puffing out of a thousand breaths of awe.... 'oy-oy-oy!' said the Whytecliffe visitors more to themselves than each other as outwardly, at least, a more ironic attitude (mid-twentieth century mores having made their mark) towards wealth was now the form.[14]

However, this socialising in Bournemouth was not enjoyed by everyone. Stuart March recalls that when he stayed with his family at the Langham in the 1960s, his father sometimes came for a day or two, but then headed back to London because he did not like 'all the chatting and seeing the same people all the time'.[15]

While for some the desire to be with other Jews was later replaced with a need for greater independence and space, for others it continued. During the 1980s and 1990s, the clientele at the New Ambassador, one of the two remaining Big Eight hotels, readily enjoyed being with other Jews and the '*heimische* atmosphere' of the hotel.[16]

Cards and Gambling

As mentioned above, when Jews became integrated into mainstream society, a popular pastime was playing cards. As a result, card games were one of the principal activities for those staying in the Big Eight hotels. Each of the hotels had dedicated card rooms, a specific feature of Jewish hotels. Initially, men and women played separately, but later they often played together. While women tended to play bridge and kalooki (a card game quite distinct to Jews), men tended to play poker and sometimes for startlingly high stakes. They revelled in the often heated but friendly competitions. On occasion, the card games that took place in the hotels extended over several days. Clive Gold recalls:

> While staying at the Cumberland, I once got involved in a six-day poker game. We only got up from the table to go to sleep. I played with two wealthy men: Michael Lewis, who owned most of Portobello Road and Harold Plotnik, who owned Allied Carpets. The stakes were very high, but I somehow managed to come out of it with enough money to pay for a ten-day Christmas holiday at the Cumberland.[17]

Cards games were played at different times of the day – in the afternoon as well as the evening, and often long into the night. At the Green Park, Sarah Marriott organised the women's card room. In one corner of this room there was a half-moon shaped raised dais (also used by the resident band), where Sarah Marriott sat to play cards most evenings until after 10pm. Guests would regard themselves as being highly honoured if they were invited to Sarah Marriott's card table.[18] A visiting American journalist, Isaac Shenker, commented:

> Sarah Marriott is the lady of the card chamber – it is she who introduces one guest player to another. Noted Toby Green of London, a frequent guest: 'If Sarah says, "Meet Mrs X, she's a very strong player", it means you get a good table and a strong light on it. "Nice player" means not a good player, don't make her your partner, and the lights will be poor.'[19]

For a hotel with just fifty-nine bedrooms, the dedicated card room at the Green Park where the men played was very large. The hotel organised an annual event called the 'Jeremy Tournament', which involved players bidding at auctions for the best players to compete at card games and also snooker. The winning players shared their prizes with their backers.[20]

At East Cliff Court, the guests also played cards, but the atmosphere was rather more subdued. Edward Hayman recalls: 'We provided cards and tables in the upper ground-floor lounges for visitors who liked playing bridge or solo. There was no poker or high-stakes gambling.'[21]

Such was the popularity of card playing in the Big Eight hotels that a sense of frustration sometimes built up on Saturdays during the summer months when *Shabbat* did not end until late in the evening. David Felsenstein remembers staying at the Green Park one year and seeing the card room full of people sitting at the tables, waiting for the announcement: 'Ladies and gentlemen, *Shabbos* is now out', which was followed by a furious dealing of cards.[22] One regular guest referred to this waiting period as 'the ultimate game of patience' and said: 'It was the time when the minutes were the longest in the week.'[23]

Horse racing was also an integral part of life in several of the Big Eight hotels. In those days, owning a horse, or even knowing someone who did, was seen as a status symbol. Well before it was legal to place bets off the racecourses, after lunch men often retired to their bedrooms on the pretext of having a rest to place their bets.[24] This was especially the case in those hotels at which bookmakers and horse owners were numbered among their regular guests. Louis Plotnikoff, who frequently stayed at the Green Park, is quoted as saying: 'If you're staying at Green Park, you can have as much credit as you want with the bookmaker.'[25]

A regular guest at the Green Park was a renowned bookmaker called Harry ('Chummy') Gaventa. He took bets for fellow guests, phoning them into his London office. Alan Lee explains: 'People had credit accounts in those days; money did not change hands.'[26] As well as being a bookmaker, Harry Gaventa owned several racehorses, one of which he named after the Richman sisters. Barbara Glyn recounts: 'He rang my father to check that this was acceptable. The horse was a flat racer yet it still managed to fall over on its first outing and had to be put down!' 'Chummy' also owned horses called 'Rabbi' and 'Gabbai'.[27] Another bookmaker who stayed regularly at the hotel was Cyril Stein, the founder of Ladbrokes. By the time he was seven, one young guest, who often stayed at the hotel with his parents, became known as the 'Green Park tipster'. He watched races on television with his father and his friends, tipping every race. The story goes: 'Men used to hang onto his words, sometimes betting several thousands of pounds at a time, and when his advice was successful, would leave gifts and boxes of chocolates at his dinner table.'[28]

Bookmakers also stayed at the other hotels. During the 1960s, Joe Coral, owner of Coral Bookmakers, was a regular guest at the Normandie. Paul Harris recalls: 'He used to drive up in his Rolls Royce that had personalised number plates starting with the letters JC.'[29] John, the longstanding porter at the Normandie (mentioned in Chapter 3), took bets for guests: 'He acted as the runner to the local betting shop and was well tipped for his efforts.'[30]

While most of the gambling took place in the hotels, some guests ventured out to the casino in the Royal Bath Hotel, which was located within easy walking distance of most of the hotels on the East Cliff. Apart from the gambling, the casino organised entertainment for its patrons which, recognising the make-up of its clientele, sometimes included Jewish performers, such as the Jewish impressionist, comedian, singer and band leader Johnny Franks.[31] During one end-of-year holiday in the late 1960s, the Royal Bath casino took its tables and croupiers to the Cumberland. Geoffrey Feld recalls:

> We had staying with us Mr Specterman, the father-in-law of Sir Isaac Wolfson, who was staying at the Green Park. Mr Specterman, then quite an elderly man, decided that he wanted to play Chemin de Fer [a French card game sometimes called 'Shimmy'], and by midnight he had lost around £1,000, which was a lot of money. My father, Isaac, tried to persuade him to go to bed, but he refused, saying that he wanted to win back the money he had lost. By 2am, he had lost about £2,000, so my mother Bluma intervened and eventually managed to

schmooze [cajole] him into cashing in his chips. My parents were mortified and worried that the story would soon get around, and it did! The next morning, Isaac Wolfson rang my father and asked him why it had been allowed to happen. Despite my father's protests, Isaac Wolfson still said: 'I hold you responsible for my father-in law's losses.'[32]

Card playing continued as the main recreational activity for Jews after most of the Big Eight hotels had closed, both for those staying at the remaining kosher hotels and at the non-Jewish hotels where many Jews holidayed. Suzanne Higgott recalls:

> During the 1970s, my grandparents often stayed at the Cumberland Hotel. Later, after my grandfather died, my grandmother and four of her widowed friends stayed for several years at the Heathlands Hotel, which had quite a Jewish atmosphere. The group of five played bridge together, taking it in turns for one of them to sit out to organise refreshments.[33]

However, by the 1990s, card playing was generally less popular than it had been in the decades following the Second World War. At the New Ambassador, card playing was limited to low-stake, friendly games, that mainly took place during dedicated bridge and kalooki weekends. High-stake games, such as poker, were frowned upon by the hotel's managers.[34] At the now ultra-orthodox Normandie card playing had been replaced by more religious activities (see below).

Dancing and Dance Bands

Alongside cards, dancing was a much-loved form of entertainment in all of the Big Eight hotels. Edward Hayman, grandson of the original proprietor, vividly describes the ballroom at East Cliff Court, the first of the Big Eight hotels:

> Guests would sit at tables placed on the long sides of the dance floor. You reached these by going down one of two flights of steps on either side of the ballroom. The band played from a platform on the short side opposite the entrance steps, and my mother and grandmother would sit always at the same table, on the left, near the entrance. My father would sometimes join them, but he never danced.[35]

56. The ballroom at the Green Park Hotel, Manor Road, Bournemouth, *c.* 1955. Image courtesy of the Marriott family.

Like the hotel dining rooms (see Chapter 6), over time, the ballrooms became more luxurious, even those in the smaller and less expensive hotels. At East Cliff Court, Sadie Hayman, daughter of the proprietor and later proprietor herself, took personal responsibility for organising the dancing. Having visited a hotel in another town where part of the dining room carpet was rolled back to permit dinner-dances, she arranged for a large circle to be cut out of the dining-room carpet and the floor underneath to be polished. Dinner-dances were then held in the dining room, in the hope that more people would stay on for the dancing, sitting at the tables where they had enjoyed their dinner.[36] By the mid-1950s, the Cumberland was offering 'dancing in air-conditioned comfort', and the Green Park had transformed its ballroom to create 'a piece of luxurious beauty'.[37] The ballroom at East Cliff Manor, which had blue lighting beneath its glass floor, is particularly well remembered.

After-dinner dances were held several evenings a week, increasing in frequency during peak times. The dances were a mix of traditional dances such as quicksteps, tangos, foxtrots and waltzes and more modern dances including the cha-cha and the twist, but there was not much Jewish dancing at that time. Several of the hotels also organised afternoon tea dances, usually held on Sunday afternoons.

Hotel guests danced to the music provided by resident dance bands. These bands were initially led by local musicians, such as Syd Fay, the brother of the local pharmacist, Mark Fay. He and his band, *Syd Fay and His Music*, played at the Pavilion, but also at East Cliff Manor and the Langham. He was the owner of a music shop in Old Christchurch Road. Janet Pins (née Fay) recalls: 'I remember going into the Langham one evening and my uncle Syd embarrassing my husband, who was quite reserved and didn't like dancing, by announcing that my husband was going to demonstrate the cha-cha.'[38]

The dancing (and the other events and activities) were often captured by the photographers who circulated around the large hotels. The two photographers who worked regularly in the Jewish hotels were Morris Benjamin and Harry Taylor, between whom there was fierce competition. Whereas Morris Benjamin had started his career as a street photographer, Harry Taylor was an established photographer, who in addition to being a resident photographer in the hotels, was noted for his shots of celebrities who visited Bournemouth, including *The Beatles*. He was the freelance photographer for the *Bournemouth and Christchurch Times* and for a number of London newspapers. He used a Leica camera and was known as 'Flash Harry'.[39] The photos he took at evening events were displayed later the same evening on hotel notice boards for guests to order copies.[40]

The dancing was particularly popular amongst older couples, such as Gustav and Carola Hirsch, former refugees from Franconia in Germany, where they had developed a passion for dancing and excelled at the Viennese waltz. During the 1960s and early 1970s, they stayed in several of the Big Eight hotels before settling on the Cumberland as their favourite. Even when they were quite elderly, their waltzes were often the focus of attention of other guests at the hotel, and the resident photographers mentioned above would train their cameras on them. Their daughter, Margarete Stern, recalls that when they won prizes for being the best dancers, it made her mother 'feel like the belle of the ball'.[41]

57. Harry Taylor, known as 'Flash Harry', hotel photographer in the 1950s and 1960s. Image courtesy of his son, Howard Taylor.

58. Gustav and Carola Hirsch, who won prizes for their dancing while staying at the Cumberland Hotel, East Overcliff Drive, Bournemouth, 1955. Image courtesy of Margarete and Jonathan Stern.

Over the years, some of the bandleaders and band members who played at the hotels gained a wider profile. Sonny Player, a member of Syd Fay's band, went on to appear on BBC radio programmes and to record with Parlophone Records.[42] Peter Banyard and Jean Worthy, residents of Bournemouth, who performed under the name of *Bits N' Pieces*, were the instrumental/vocal duo who appeared regularly at the Majestic in the 1970s and later at the New Ambassador on Tuesdays, Thursdays and Saturdays. Peter Banyard was a singer and guitarist and Jean Worthy was a singer who apparently 'sang just like Cleo Laine'.[43] The duo were so good that they moved to London and made it to the final of ATV's show *New Faces* in 1975.[44] Andy Summer, later a member of the popular band *The Police*, was the guitarist in the dance band that played at the Majestic Hotel. When he left for London, he was replaced by Robert Fripp, who became a founding member of *King Crimson*. Robert Fripp subsequently recalled:

> Between 1966 and 1968, when I was aged 18 to 21, I paid my way through Bournemouth College, where I was studying economics, economic history and political history by playing at the Majestic Hotel in Bournemouth...The Majestic Dance Orchestra (a quintet) played three nights a week during the winter and four nights in the summer, accompanying visiting cabaret acts on Sundays. In addition to foxtrots, quicksteps, tangos, Jolsons (fast and slow), from time to time we also played for weddings and *Bar Mitzvahs* celebrated at the hotel.[45]

For several years, Stanley Laudan[46] was the resident bandleader at the Langham, where he played nightly in the hotel's 'Crystal Room' and later, after an extension was added, in the enlarged card room. He then became the bandleader at the Cumberland, which helped to make him nationally famous. Advertisements for his later performances in London stated that he was 'formerly of the Cumberland Hotel, Bournemouth'.[47] Geoffrey Feld recalls: 'I remember he used to paint a black widow's peak (a downward-facing V-shape) in the middle of his forehead to hide the fact that he was losing his hair. Sometimes when he was performing, he got quite hot and the dye would run down his face!'[48]

┌─────────────────────────────┐
│ **THE LANGHAM** │
│ BOURNEMOUTH │
└─────────────────────────────┘

(Personal administration by Mr and Mrs. Maurice Guild)

WINTER TARIFF NOW IN OPERATION

Dancing Nightly to

Telephone: **STANLEY LAUDAN**
BOURNEMOUTH 27216   **and his orchestra**   Orthodoxy & Kashrus
(4 lines)   strictly observed

59. Stanley Laudan, resident bandmaster at the Langham, advertisement in the *Jewish Chronicle*, 30 December 1960.

For several years, the 'entertainment host' at East Cliff Manor was Johnny Franks (mentioned above) and his orchestra, then known as the *East Cliff Manor Hotel Orchestra*. He later moved to the Cumberland where he became a family friend with the Felds and Invernes. Geoffrey Feld recalls: 'He was very versatile. He played the violin, conducted the band, told jokes and did cabaret spots'.[49] By the 1970s, Johnny Franks had become very 'showbiz' and had a reputation for 'schmoozing with the stars', such as Dionne Warwick and Max Bygraves, and for wearing 'sharp suits and flashy shirts'.[50] Johnny Dumar, a Bournemouth resident, started his career working as a gym instructor on cruise ships, but decided that he preferred singing and started appearing in the large hotels in Bournemouth. He became the resident singer at the Cumberland where his potential was spotted by Stanley Laudan and he was signed by a recording company.[51]

The high-quality music entertainment at the hotels became known nationally and during the 1940s and 1950s the music being played at the hotels was either broadcast live on various radio stations, or recorded and used to provide entertainment at venues up and down the country. For example, in April 1946 Sid Grossman and his eleven-piece band, *The New Foresters*, were broadcast live at 10pm on BBC West of England,[52] and in 1956, the annual charity ball organised by the Petersfield Rotary Club featured the music of Charles Lockhart and his band from the Majestic in Bournemouth.[53]

At the tea dances held at East Cliff Court, the band was a trio of saxophone, drums and piano led by the pianist Charlie Richards (sometimes referred to as 'Captain Richards'), who had entertained at the hotel since before the Second World War.[54] According to her son Edward, Sadie Hayman made sure that afternoon tea was always served first in the ballroom at the hotel to encourage as many people as possible to take part in the dancing: 'My mother delighted in the tea dances and got annoyed with visitors who preferred to play cards.' [55]

From the outset, the Big Eight hotels employed professional or semi-professional dancers, formally known as dance hosts, but usually referred to as 'gigolos', to dance with single women. Jaqueline Toff (née Tibber), who stayed regularly at East Cliff Court both before and after the Second World War, recalls having dancing lessons with Mr Jaques, one of the hotel's dance hosts.[56] At the Green Park, there were two dance hosts, and 'people's eyes lit up when they saw that they were there'.[57] Competition to dance with the gigolos was fierce. Geoffrey Feld recalls: 'If a single woman staying at the Cumberland did not get a dance with the gigolo, there would be trouble at reception the next morning!'[58]

The role of the gigolos was paramount in the early days when families stayed at the hotels for long periods, during which the men returned to London or elsewhere to work (see Chapter 3), but the practice of employing gigolos continued well into the 1970s. For a number of years, the New Ambassador employed a gigolo, a tall, thin man who wore a black suit with highly-padded shoulders. As a result, he was referred to by young people as 'The Coathanger'. Jonathan Perlmutter recalls: 'We used to giggle when we saw him arrive and say to each other: "Oh look here comes The Coathanger!"'[59] The gigolos sometimes brought partners with them and entertained the guests with exhibition dances, or featured as part of the cabaret shows in the hotels (see below).

On Friday evenings and on Jewish festivals, when dancing and some other forms of entertainment were inappropriate for religious reasons, the hotels organised a range of permissible activities to entertain their guests, such as brains trusts, quizzes and lectures. For example, many famous rabbis, *dayanim* and top professionals were invited to speak at the brains trusts organised at the Cumberland. Guests submitted their questions for the panel before *Shabbat* or a festival commenced.[60] Panels of speakers were sometimes convened from amongst the guests staying at the hotels. These brains trusts are described with humour in Gerda Charles's *The Crossing Point*:

> The members of the improvised panel were a stockbroker, a smooth black and white man, named appropriately, Silky; a Polish woman lawyer, broad featured and shrewd; another lawyer, Bresco, a pleasant young man; and the only one listened to with a respectful interest

every time he opened his mouth was Dr Ellenberg, an American sociologist touring Europe with his mother.[61]

According to Gerda Charles, the well-fed and relaxed guests:

> ...called out from their easy chairs, interrupted the panel in the impatient, unceremonious Jewish way, got up, walked around, called across to each other, started private arguments, broke into Yiddish, exchanged dressmakers, wished each other *Mazeltov* [literally 'good constellation', but meaning 'congratulations'] shouted 'Shah!' to quieten the neighbours and disagreed with violent naivety on the political questions.[62]

Cabarets

During the summer season, and at other times during the year, dancing was followed by cabarets, which became more and more star-studded as the years progressed. Like the dance-band leaders, the cabaret performers, some of whom were local, were entertainers on the brink of becoming famous. Appearing at the hotels in Bournemouth came to be regarded as a step on the way to stardom. Many people remember seeing Dave Allen appearing at the Majestic in the early 1960s when he was relatively unknown, including Tony Klinger who recalls: 'I got to speak with him, and he told me that they were making him sleep on the snooker table. Being about eleven-years-old at the time, I believed him!'[63]

However, there were also some very established performers. Hilary Halter, who stayed at the Majestic during the 1960s, recalls that Anne Shelton, 'the famous wartime singer, who was on a par with Vera Lynn' was appearing at several of the hotels. She also recalls that a comedian named Lou Jacobi appeared at the Majestic. He was one of the artists featured on the hit comedy album *You Don't Have to Be Jewish*, released in 1965. This album was very popular with non-Jewish people, and was frequently featured on the BBC radio programme *Housewives' Choice*: 'After performing in the cabaret at the hotel, he sat chatting to the guests in the lounge until 3am, telling one gag after another.'[64]

During the 1950s, cabarets at the Ambassador included Vera Lynn and Edmundo Ros, the famous Latin American musician.[65] Peter Phillips recalls: 'Famous stars appearing in London's theatre land, like Howard Keel from *Oklahoma* and Dolores Gray from *Annie Get Your Gun*, were driven down to the Ambassador to entertain us.'[66] In 1967, the Ambassador was taken over by Nettie and Hymie Selby, who had been involved in running the Hanover banqueting suite in central London and therefore had contacts with leading entertainers of the day, which they put to good use at the hotel in Bournemouth. During the summer months, cabarets included many top acts, such as the magician David Berglass, the Clark Brothers, black gospel singers and tap dancers who had not been able to perform in America and Chan Canasta, a pioneer in metal magic, who had become a television celebrity.[67] These famous entertainers drew people from London, who met their friends staying in the hotel to enjoy the performances. Other high-profile entertainers at the hotel included Lonnie Donegan, Davy Kaye, who starred in many of the *Carry On* movies, and the Yiddish actress Anna Tzelniker. Jonathan Perlmutter recalls: 'My Dad and others of his generation who spoke Yiddish, just roared with laughter when Anna did her act.'[68]

The cabarets at East Cliff Court were lower key than at some of the other hotels. They took place in the ballroom in the middle of an evening and visitors who had been on the upper floor playing bridge or chatting would come down to watch. The hotel hired singers, musicians and comedians who were mainly local people, or those within easy reach, rather than 'big names'. However, one year, the hotel employed a group of musicians and singers, who were in Bournemouth to perform at the Palace Court Theatre. Edward Hayman recalls:

> They had a toy tandem with a man and woman rider. A cord arrangement enabled them to pull it across the ballroom floor slowly, while they sang *Daisy, Daisy*. They also had a pianist, who performed a solo, using his nose to play a couple of the notes. 'It's long enough', he quipped to the audience. I doubt whether he had considered how this joke might go down in a Jewish hotel.[69]

Another artist who performed at East Cliff Court on a few occasions was a conjurer: 'He had a cut-out lamppost as a prop. He did not use patter at all, but appeared in dishevelled evening dress, pretending to be drunk and feigning surprise at the success of each of his tricks.'[70] The performers appearing at the Jewish hotels often moved from one hotel to the next. Chris Woodward, a magician who worked at several hotels, recalls that he had to be careful where he parked to ensure that he was able to get away in time for the next performance. One season, Diana Dors appeared at the hotels. Larry and Mandy Kaye recall: 'She was a little worse the wear for drink and wasn't invited back.'[71]

The Jewish audiences developed high expectations, and were quick to leave or to engage in conversations with fellow hotel guests if they felt that a performance was not 'up to scratch'. Sheila Samuels recalls that when the comedians Baker and Willy appeared at the Cumberland, her father interrogated them before the show to check that their script would not be too risqué for her mother.[72]

By the late 1960s, when trade was beginning to decline, the hotels could no longer afford to engage so many well-known entertainers, and they started to diversify their entertainment programmes. For example, at the Cumberland, the Feld and Inverne families placed a greater emphasis on children's entertainment (see below) with the aim of attracting more families to the hotel. Even though the hotels no longer had star-studded cabarets, they continued to find ways of entertaining their adult guests. James Inverne recalls: 'On Halloween one year in the late 1970s, the Cumberland used a lot of dry ice to create a spooky atmosphere in the ballroom, and in the dining room all the staff dressed up as ghosts and the *borscht* was described as "blood soup".' Other notable events include the occasion when the hotel had an Italian evening and an Italian opera singer was brought in who sang standing on a table'[73], and the 'Pearly King and Queen' when the hotel's maintenance team built a series of market stalls: 'the long-standing waitress, Marjorie, was the pearly queen and Mr West the head waiter was the unlikely pearly king!'[74]

When the Normandie and its guests became more orthodox in the late 1980s, the entertainment was scaled down and religious activities, such as *shiurim*, were introduced instead. However, some entertainment continued, including after-dinner cabarets, albeit that they were lower key than previously. Chris Woodward, a magician, worked at the Normandie many times during the late 1980s and 1990s. He found that working with an orthodox audience presented some challenges. He explains: 'Magic is based to a great extent on audience participation, and it wasn't always easy to get a lady to saw in half. So, I sometimes resorted to asking a waitress or a receptionist to be a backup just in case I needed someone.'[75]

Guest-Produced Entertainment

Noted for its big-name cabarets, the Green Park was also famous for the entertainment provided by the guests themselves. In the late 1940s, it was decided to hold a professional boxing match at the hotel, and a makeshift boxing ring was erected in the dining room. Outrage ensued during the third and final round, when one of the boxers bled onto the dress of a flustered young woman spectator. A comic boxing match between two of the hotel's prominent male guests proved to be far more popular. The recollection is that: 'The contestants smoked cigars and splashed each other with water, wearing long shorts, robes, hats and ribbons on their gloves. The delighted audience egged the boxers on, rushing to put money on their favoured contestant.'[76]

Even more popular were the annual fashion parades and fancy-dress evenings held at the hotel. Since there was an enormous amount of competition, weeks prior to their stay in Bournemouth, guests held secret meetings to discuss what they would be wearing. Apparently, on the night of the events, children would stand by the hotel lift, their mouths agape, as the doors opened to reveal the exciting costumes. One particular fancy-dress evening became legendary: a guest dressed up as Lady Godiva and arrived in the ballroom on a horse, which promptly 'pooped all over the lovely marble floor'. Judy Richman was not impressed.[77] Barbara Glyn comments: 'The guest responsible did ask my father in advance, who said yes. I don't know what possessed him to agree, but he was a good sport. I still remember the horse clip clopping along the corridor, the lounge doors opening and the horse being led in.'[78] One Green Park guest created a sensation by being carted in to the ballroom naked with a sign around his neck saying 'The day the bottom fell out of the market'.[79] Another guest dressed up as a baby and was wheeled into the room with a sign saying 'The Wrong Pill'.[80] However, the fancy-dress turn that brought the house down was by a woman who dressed up as Bubbe Richman. She stuffed her stockings to increase the size of her legs, donned a *sheitel* and brandished a large handbag, a deck of cards and a packet of cigarettes.[81]

Guests also became part of the entertainment in the other hotels. Marilyn Murray recalls that when she stayed for several summers at the Langham, her father and uncle were 'the life and soul of the party, behaving as if they knew everyone in the hotel, whether they did or not'. On cabaret evenings, they often gave spontaneous Flanagan and Allen impersonations.[82] During the late 1950s, the Langham organised weekly 'Talent seeking contests', at which a TV and variety talent scout was present.[83] Edward Hayman has memories of people staying at East Cliff Court entertaining fellow guests in the upper lounge of the hotel, including an elderly man, who sang romantic songs 'in an unreliable tenor voice', accompanied by his son on the piano. Mrs Feldman, one of the hotel's permanent residents, sometimes performed conjuring tricks: 'She wore for these occasions a long, patterned dress and a necklace of luminous beads. She had a conjuring stick, which consisted of cylinders on a string. Held in a certain way, it was stiff, like a wand. Released, it could be collapsed into a small pack which she could secrete in some receptacle.'[84]

60. Sid and Nita Freedman in fancy dress at the Langham Hotel, Meyrick Road, Bournemouth, *c.* 1950. Image courtesy of their daughter, Marilyn Murray.

Until it became uneconomic, some of the hotels provided free teas on a Sunday afternoon, and people used to come to watch the entertainment that was also provided, often by the guests themselves. When Clive Gold stayed at the Cumberland in the early 1970s, there was a guest, a market trader, who sometimes stood up to sing with the band: 'He was terrible. When he heard that the teas had stopped, he said that he was not going to perform anymore. Everyone was quite relieved.'[85] Clive also recalls staying at the Cumberland when a fellow guest, a Polish woman, who was 'no more than four-feet tall', took the floor to perform a *Broigus* dance, a traditional Jewish wedding dance.

Gloria Stanley (née Lewis) recalls that the Majestic was a 'magnet' for younger people because of its high-class entertainment. Gloria was a singer, and on one occasion when she was staying at East Cliff Court, she went to the Majestic to meet a friend who was on holiday there. Without telling her, he had put her name down for a talent contest taking place that evening:

> Mrs Schneider stood behind the acts to gauge who got the most applause. Although I thought that I had the loudest claps, I was not given the prize. Someone in the audience spoke up for me and Mrs Schneider explained that this was because I was not a resident. However, I was eventually awarded a joint prize. Despite the fact that our relationship didn't get off to a good start, later, Mrs Schneider and I got on well and she always welcomed me at the hotel as long as I did a turn.[86]

'End-of-Year' Entertainment

The entertainment at the Big Eight hotels was particularly lavish over the Christmas and New Year period. Prior to the holidays, the hoteliers spent several months organising the 'end of year' entertainment programmes and were personally involved in ensuring that everything went to plan. Roger Vickers comments:

> Because people were around the hotel so much, we always organised a full programme of entertainment. We couldn't get away with activities such as 'guess the weight of the Christmas pudding', or listening to the Queen's speech, which was often on the programme for the non-Jewish hotels. The expectation was that there would be

varied, interesting and high-quality entertainment, and we tried very hard to meet those expectations.[87]

Geoffrey Feld recalls that one Christmas, the band at the Green Park played the carol *Silent Night* as a slow foxtrot: 'People loved it and got up and danced, but there were a number of protests, including from Dayan Swift, who rang Ruby Marriott the next day to complain about people dancing to a Christmas carol in a Jewish hotel that was licensed by the Beth Din. Ruby Marriott was warned that the hotel might lose its licence if that sort of thing continued.[88]

The cabarets staged in most of the hotels over Christmas and New Year were star spangled. To name but a few, the celebrated entertainers who appeared at the Big Eight hotels at Christmas and New Year include: Alma Cogan ('the girl with the smile in her voice'), Frankie Vaughan, Ron Moody, Marion Ryan, Ray Ellington and his Quartet (at the Green Park), Mike and Bernie Winters, Helen Shapiro, Benny Hill, Freddie Starr, Leonie Page, Norman Vaughan, Lionel Blair, Eddie Calvert ('the man with the golden trumpet') and Larry Adler (harmonica player). One regular cabaret entertainer was Ralph Slater, who was a renowned hypnotist. Geoffrey Feld recalls: 'People used to quip that when he hypnotised people, they couldn't stop eating when they came out of the trance!'[89] Other stars who appeared in the hotels over the holiday period included: Maurice Fogel (a magician and legendary mentalist – he called himself 'the world's greatest mind reader'[90]), the Nolan Sisters, Ronnie Corbett and David Kossoff. The top Jewish comedians of the day were particularly popular, including Stubby Kaye, Harold Berens, Tommy Trinder, Alfred Marks and Bernard Spear. The performers usually appeared at the different hotels on different nights, often having performed earlier in the evening at the Pavilion. The hoteliers were frequently complimented on their Christmas cabaret programmes in *The Stage*. James Inverne, who grew up around the Cumberland, recalls celebrities coming to the hotel quite regularly:

I remember being introduced to Lionel Blair in the hotel dining room. He captained one of the teams on the television programme *Give Us A Clue*, a version of charades that was one of the biggest things on TV at the time. I recollect finding it highly amusing that as he talked to us, he would illustrate what he was saying with elaborate hand gestures, almost as if he was still playing the game.[91]

'Fiesta'

at Hotel Normandie

Greet 1964

61. Menu for New Year's Eve dinner held at the Normandie Hotel, Manor Road Bournemouth, 31 December 1963. The menu is signed by Ron Moody, who appeared during the 'Fiesta' event that evening. The message reads: 'To Belle. Tres Belle! Thank you for looking after people so nice.' Image courtesy of Simon Keyne.

While the entertainment provided at East Cliff Court was generally low-key compared to some of the other Big Eight hotels, at Christmas the hotel sometimes brought in well-known acts. In his memoir of East Cliff Court, Ronald Hayman recalls that one year he watched in awe as 'The Incredible Castellani produced a fluffy little fluttering dove from a very old lady's beaded handbag.'[92] Dawn Kaffel, granddaughter of Fay Schneider, also recalls that the times that she spent at the Majestic over Christmas were 'magical'. In addition to the cabarets, there were kalooki and gin rummy tournaments, bingo sessions, table tennis competitions and film afternoons.[93] However, for Dawn, the highlight of the holidays was the New Years Eve fancy-dress competition:

Many of the guests worked in the fashion business and would send down to Bournemouth lorries filled with brilliant props and amazing costumes made in their own factories. The whole thing was taken very seriously because the guests were hoping to win some of the wonderful prizes that my grandmother had organised, including complete china tea services, sets of luggage and crocodile handbags, to name but a few.[94]

62. Yetta ('Bubbe') Richman joining in the party at the Green Park Hotel, Manor Road Bournemouth, *c.* early 1950s. Image courtesy of the Marriott family.

At the New Ambassador, the Christmas entertainment included what were called 'mystery tours'. Jonathan Perlmutter recalls: 'It wasn't much of a mystery tour at all. We always went to Corfe Castle!'[95]

Over the end of year holiday period, special activities were organised for children. Ronald Hayman later recalled that on Christmas Day, the hotel organised a children's party, which was held in the cocktail lounge where 'a red cracker and funny paper hat was waiting beside every plate'. The main treat was 'ice cream, jelly and trifle, served all on one plate'.[96]

At some of the hotels, the hoteliers entered into the spirit of things. Edward Hayman recalls that at East Cliff Court, Annie Morris gave Christmas presents, such as diaries and eau de cologne, to guests: 'They were presented after dinner by the receptionists working at the hotel.'[97] Richard Inverne, who for several years acted as the Entertainments Host at the Cumberland, recalls:

Over the Christmas/New Year period I began a tradition known as 'The Mystery Voice'. Every lunchtime, I would activate the tannoy and would spend a few minutes giving the guests the entertainments and activities programme for the next 24 hours (not unlike Gladys in the sitcom *Hi-De-Hi!*) I would get the attention of a very-noisy dining room with the introduction 'This is the Mystery Voice!' Of course, everyone knew it was me, but part of the joke was that I would strenuously deny it when asked. This went on for about ten years! One year, I decided to play a trick. I recorded that day's announcements onto tape, switched on the tannoy system and left the tape playing. Half way through the announcements, I breezed into the dining room and, standing prominently near the door, I engaged in conversation with the restaurant manager. The laughter of two hundred guests just grew and grew as I was gradually noticed and the joke spread from table to table, the 'offstage' tape still playing my voice![98]

At the Normandie, Belle and Lou Keyne fully participated in the various events held over holiday period, but especially the New Year fancy-dress competitions when they themselves dressed up. They also enjoyed the annual 'scavenger hunts'. Their niece, who regularly stayed at the hotel at this time of year, recalls: 'One year one of the tasks set was to find a blonde for Mr Keyne, so I left the hotel to locate a blonde woman, who I managed to persuade to come back to the hotel with me!'[99]

63. Belle and Louis Keyne in fancy dress at New Year Eve event, 'The Naughty Nineties', held at the Normandie Hotel, Manor Road, Bournemouth, 1961. Image courtesy of Simon Keyne.

Sports

While some Jewish holidaymakers went to Bournemouth to relax, others looked forward to more active vacations, especially those with young families. Sheila Morris recalls that for many years, each half-term holiday she and her husband 'loaded up the car with sports equipment – tennis rackets, cricket bats, footballs and swimming gear – to use during the stay in Bournemouth with our two sons. Jack played cricket with the boys and all the other children from the hotel joined in.'[100]

Many guests played tennis during their holidays. Some of the hotels had their own courts, including East Cliff Court, which were well used during the summer months.[101] Other guests preferred to use the courts at one of the many tennis clubs in Bournemouth. Keen golfers also used the nearby golf clubs. Golfing was so popular amongst the guests that some of the hotels offered dedicated golfing holidays. During the 1950s, the Green Park organised golfing weekends each autumn. A tournament was held at Broadstone Golf Club, which attracted golf players from throughout the UK.

A decade or so later, Geoffrey Feld and his brother-in-law, Howard Inverne, organised week-long golfing holidays at the Cumberland at the end of the summer season. Having arrived on a Sunday, golfers from Jewish golf clubs up and down the country played tournaments of various types on the courses in and around Bournemouth, building up to the main singles game played off individual handicaps on the Friday. On the Thursday evening prior to the final tournaments, an auction of players was held to raise money for charity: 'We used to raise about £2,000, a small proportion of which was given as a prize to the tournament winner, but most went to local and national charities. Some of the gambling fraternity staying in the hotel used to organise a book on which player was going to win!'[102] When the Feld and Inverne families purchased the Majestic in 1969, the golfing holidays were extended to include the Majestic and over one hundred golfers, their families and friends stayed at the two hotels.

Mirroring English upper-class mores, many upwardly mobile Jews had initially been interested in cricket, but they subsequently developed a liking for football. Some male hotel guests went to the local football stadium to watch weekday (not Saturday) games played by Bournemouth AFC, and became dedicated supporters of the club (see Chapter 10).[103] The Green Park Hotel held several season tickets for seats at the football ground that were handed out to favoured guests.

Young guests in particular used the table tennis rooms at the hotels and, in the summer months, the putting greens that some of the hotels offered, including the Normandie and the Green Park. Young people also played football in the grounds of the hotels, especially those with extensive gardens, such as the 'large and lush' garden at the Normandie. Jon Harris recalls: 'We used the signs saying "No Football" as goal posts!'[104] The football games were not always condoned by the hoteliers. Jon's brother, Paul Harris, recalls:

> We sometimes organised fathers versus sons and the north versus the south football matches. We put up notices all around the hotel to advertise them. Mr Lee didn't like this at all. He threatened to have our family removed from the hotel. The games continued and he gave up in the end, bowing to the inevitable. He realised that you couldn't stop boys from Manchester playing football. Everybody took the games very seriously. They were like battlegrounds.[105]

The Beach and the Swimming Pools

The seven miles of beaches with their golden sand were what drew many people to holiday in Bournemouth, especially those with children. Some families spent hours lounging on the beach, where they often met up with friends and family staying in other hotels. Jackie Kalms (née Harris) recalls: 'Every day we joined our relatives and sat with them in a great long row on the sand.'[106] In their early days, some of the big hotels had designated areas on the beach where they provided sun loungers and deck chairs. As a result, people were able easily to locate their friends and family if they knew in which of the hotels they were staying.[107]

Local professional photographers wandered along the promenade, taking shots of people walking towards them, which many former visitors have retained. One of the best-known beach photographers was Morris Benjamin ('Benjy'), who later also took photos of guests in the Jewish hotels (see above). People were handed a ticket, enabling them to collect the photographs a day or so later from the photographers' studios.[108] The beaches were fringed with numerous cafés and ice cream stalls, and occasionally families indulged in illicit, non-kosher ice creams.[109] Younger children enjoyed the donkey rides on Boscombe beach.

The beach was accessed via what is known as the 'zig-zag path', a long and winding path leading down the cliff face from East Overcliff Drive.[110] Most families preferred to make the return journey using the funicular railway, which had opened in 1908,[111] or used it in both directions when they were too frail to walk or were infant-laden and had a lot to carry. The politician Edwina Currie remembering her holidays in Bournemouth comments: 'It was considered a waste of money to use the cliff lift for the descending journey.'[112] Hannah Jacobs recalls: 'One year my brother, then aged three, went missing on the beach. My parents were frantic and all the lifeguards were out looking for him. Eventually, he was located going up and down on the lift. He was loving it and was totally oblivious of the concern that he had caused.'[113] Able-bodied citizens regarded it as a matter of honour not to use the lift in either direction. Sheila Morris recalls: 'My husband Jack was a big walker. He used to stroll around the town most days and particularly liked walking both up and down the zig-zag path.'[114] As an alternative to using the steep zig-zag path, some visitors chose to use the path that descended from the other side of the East Cliff, which had a much gentler slope. It led to the pier and passed the interesting Russell Coates Museum, which people could visit on the way to or from the beach.[115]

Not everyone enjoyed the beach. Jon Harris comments: 'I can't recall ever going into the sea, which in retrospect is a bit strange since Bournemouth is a beach resort.'[116] Outings to the beach were sometimes foreshortened by the desire not to miss meals at the hotels: 'There was a discernible exit of people from the beach late on a Saturday morning as the Jewish guests rushed back to their hotels for the *kiddushim*' (see Chapter 6).[117]

As their guests became more affluent and their expectations rose as a consequence, the hotels introduced new amenities to impress their existing clientele and attract new guests. In 1961, the Green Park installed an American-style, heated outdoor swimming pool. It was the first hotel (both Jewish and non-Jewish) in Bournemouth to do so. The hotel also erected heated alcoves to make changing more comfortable when people came out of the pool,[118] and employed swimming instructors, as a result of which many children learned to swim during their stays at the Green Park. The Normandie, the Ambassador, the Cumberland and the Majestic (which had previously had an indoor pool) followed the Green Park's lead, carried away on a tide of optimism that over time the expensive new facilities would recoup their costs. The centrepiece of the swimming pool at the Cumberland was a stone dolphin that spouted water into the pool. It became the hotel's trademark. The swimming pool that opened at the Majestic in the summer of 1967 was 'Spanish style', and included a children's paddling pool, a sun deck, billiards room and games room.[119]

64. Outdoor heated swimming pool at the Green Park Hotel, Manor Road, Bournemouth, *c.* 1962. It was the first heated outdoor pool attached to a hotel in Bournemouth. Image courtesy of the Marriott family.

When the Normandie reopened in 1988 under the supervision of Kedassia, new arrangements were introduced. Brian Lassman recollects: 'For the first year under the new licensing arrangements, there was still mixed bathing, but Kedassia stopped it after that. There had to be separate bathing for men and women, and children over a certain age also had to be segregated.'[120] Due to the laws of modesty, the most observant Jews who now frequent Bournemouth are not comfortable sharing the beach with scantily-clad sunbathers, but they are often to be seen sitting on the beach at times when there are few others there. Mark Perl comments: 'When they first started coming to Bournemouth, they created what was seen as quite an incongruous sight, sitting on the beach wearing all of their traditional clothes. The only things they removed were their shoes.'[121]

Television and Films

Soon after the Second World War, an improved form of black and white television broadcasting became available in the UK. The Jewish hotels in Bournemouth were quick to invest in the new technology as a means for entertaining their guests. Many people who stayed in the hotels during the 1950s recall watching momentous events on television during their holidays. Stuart March remembers: 'I loved watching the television in the

Langham as we didn't yet have one at home. I have a vivid memory of sitting cross-legged, glued to the TV screen along with the other children staying in the hotel, watching the coronation of Queen Elizabeth. I was aged just six at the time.'[122] During the winter months, when the weather was less reliable, the televisions in the hotel were even more popular, especially amongst the young people staying at the Green Park where there were fewer guests of their age with whom they could socialise and fewer activities for young people.[123] Rabbi Jonathan Romain recalls that at the Normandie there were often squabbles amongst the children and young people about which channel to watch.[124]

The first television provided by East Cliff Court for its guests projected a rather grainy and unreliable picture onto a silver screen and one of the porters had to be called every so often to make the necessary adjustments. It was switched off during dances to ensure that guests were not distracted from what was regarded by the proprietors as the hotel's main entertainment, the dancing. Edward Hayman recalls that the television was usually located in a lower ground floor lounge, but for the Queen's coronation, the apparatus was shifted into the ballroom so that a larger number of guests were able to watch it. Later on, the hotel purchased a more up-to-date set with its own built-in screen, but it was still switched off during dances.[125]

By the mid-1950s, most of the hotels had 'screen-size' televisions or 'mini-cinemas', and were hiring the latest films, which were usually shown on a Sunday evening and changed weekly during the summer months. At East Cliff Court, Sadie Hayman arranged for a local man with a projector to show films that she would select from a catalogue provided by the projectionist. Her son, Edward Hayman, again recollects:

> My mother was always keen to see the film, but did not want to pass through the seated visitors. She would use the rear entrance, inconveniencing the man who had set up the projector, and sit at the back. Nanny and I would follow my mother. My grandmother, Annie Morris, had no such inhibitions and, if she wanted to see the film, she would come in through the front entrance, chatting to visitors on the way to her seat.

Bournemouth's Amenities

For many guests, the Big Eight hotels provided everything they required, and some people barely left the hotels and their grounds while staying in

Bournemouth. However, the attractions of the town and the surrounding area were what brought many people to Bournemouth. Some guests made full use of the town's many gardens, cinemas, the Pavilion and other theatres at which top entertainers often appeared, galleries and also the shops, which at one point were described as being equivalent to those in Bond Street. Fitter guests enjoyed walking around Bournemouth, enjoying the scenery. There were attractions in Bournemouth and its environs for children, including the aviary, the live music at the bandstand and trying your luck at Peeks of Bournemouth teddy bear stall.[126] Jon Harris recalls going to the Tuckton Tea Gardens in Southbourne, and to the crazy golf course close to the Normandie where the family stayed.[127]

Other guests ventured further afield to enjoy the many beauty spots and tourist attractions lying within easy reach of Bournemouth. Some people chose to travel to Bournemouth by car with the intention of exploring the surrounding countryside, but some were happy to use the local buses. Guests who liked hiking and open landscapes headed for the nearby New Forest, often taking in a cream tea at one of the many thatched and 'olde-worlde' tea shops there. Those looking for history travelled the short distance to Salisbury, or to one of the nearby country houses, such as Athelhampton House and Kingston Lacey, the ruins of Corfe Castle, the motor museum at Beaulieu and Broadlands and Lord Mountbatten's home in Romsey. Favourite excursions for many were boating on the Stour at Christchurch, or visiting the gardens at Compton Acres in Poole. As time progressed, the hoteliers began to organise outings to the places within easy reach. Long trips were eschewed since guests were loath to miss a meal provided by the hotels. Brian Lassman recalls that when he was managing the New Ambassador and organising trips, he took provisions in case the guests complained of being hungry: 'We were out from 2pm until 6pm, which meant that people missed afternoon tea. Coca Cola, biscuits and crisps worked in staving off the hunger pangs.'[128]

Children

Young guests revelled in the social life available at the hotels, especially when they were reunited with children they had met on previous stays. As a result of the so-called 'baby boom', the demand for children's entertainment grew as the year progressed. Some families living in places where there were few Jews, holidayed in Bournemouth mainly as a means of enabling their children to mix with other young Jews.[129] Several of the hotels employed a children's entertainer, such as Vivienne at the Ambassador and Connie at the Majestic, who organised entertainment programmes that enabled parents to relax and enjoy their holidays. After the children were put to bed at the New Ambassador, their parents left the room telephones off the hook so that the hotel receptionist could listen in to hear if the children were crying or 'up to mischief'. They also left the bedroom doors ajar and hotel staff walked around the corridors at regular intervals, checking on the children.[130]

Morella Kayman recalls that when she was a child, staying with her parents either at the Majestic or the Normandie, the children had 'a whale of a time', organising their 'own little concerts together'.[131] James Inverne remembers the activities that took place at the Cumberland when he was a child:

> There was something called 'Children's Week' that would happen during the festivals. I remember Harry Corbett and Sooty coming several times and feeling disappointed that I couldn't be called up as Sooty's assistant because, I was told, it would look like favouritism to the guests. There was also a huge lucky dip, which was flamboyantly decorated: there was a small hole that was just big enough for you to put your hand in to get your prize. Once the lucky dip got left out by mistake and it was raided and ransacked. The children were assembled in the ballroom and given a solemn telling off by my father.[132]

The highlight of the children's entertainment programmes was the summer fancy-dress competitions, which are recalled by Ann Crook:

> We went to the Cumberland with our two small kids in 1978. It was our first year there and we didn't know about the children's fancy-dress competition. So, I had to put something together very quickly. My daughter was Batman. The second year I went prepared with green felt and a sewing kit. I cut out leaf patterns, which I sewed onto my daughter's bikini and my son's nappy, and they went as Adam and Eve. They won first prize and I really *kvelled* [felt so proud]. The interesting thing is that my uncle, Ralph Slater, who was a well-known hypnotist, had appeared several times at the Cumberland some thirty years or so earlier![133]

65. Joanna and Stephen Crook, winners of the children's fancy-dress competition at the Cumberland Hotel, 1979. Image courtesy of Ann and Michael Crook.

Children's fancy-dress parades were also held at *Purim*. David
Latchman recalls: 'I was dressed up as a cowboy. I was not a very good
subject for Mr Benjamin, the hotel photographer. I only agreed to pose for
the camera when I was allowed to hold my Matchbox car.'[134]

Like their parents, many children played cards, usually gin rummy.
There is an often-told story of Sir Isaac Wolfson sitting down one night to
play cards with a group of children staying at the Green Park, which
included the owner's son, David Marriott. The story was leaked to the local
press, which ran an article about the business tycoon playing cards with
children. It included a photograph, snapped by one of the photographers
who toured the hotels.[135]

66. Sir Isaac Wolfson playing cards with young people at the Green Park Hotel, Manor Road,
Bournemouth, *c*. 1950. The boy to the right of the image is David Marriott, son of Reuben
and Sarah Marriott, proprietors of the hotel. Image courtesy of the Marriott family.

When the Normandie became more orthodox in the 1980s, arranging
children's entertainment became more complex. Children were separated
socially when they reached a certain age and there were strict rules about
working with orthodox children. Chris Woodward, the magician previously

mentioned, who was employed by the hotel during the 1990s to organise children's parties, recalls:

> For many of the children, it was the first time that they had seen a magician first hand and up close, and so they were always fascinated with what I was doing. Magic is often very 'touchy feely', with lots of interaction between the performer and their 'assistants'. I had to find ways of maintaining my distance while retaining the children's attention. I must have got something right because I was repeatedly asked back and, even after I changed my material, I was always greeted with smiling faces from those who had seen me before.[136]

James Inverne, who worked as a porter at the Normandie in the early 1990s, recalls: 'There was not that much organised entertainment for the children, except for a magician sometimes or a film afternoon, so I used to make a point of speaking to them.'[137]

Teenagers

When they grew up, young people were able to entertain themselves. Paul Harris comments: 'Socialising at the Normandie with Jewish friends from all over the country was fun from morning until night. I don't know what our parents did all day, other than to chat to fellow guests and sunbathe. We never saw them. We just did our own thing!'[138] Another former Cumberland guest also recalls: 'Once the adults were safely ensconced in the card room, we used to get together in posses and roam the hotel. We were given a lot of freedom.'[139]

Each of the hotels had places that were attractive to young people, which varied according to the season, the weather and the time of day. In the summer months, the outdoor pools were a popular gathering place. Jon Harris recalls: 'At the Normandie, the pool was a hub of activity. It was the place to meet up with girls. The lifeguard's hut was a "hot spot". The girls liked to make eyes at the lifeguards who were "old" – about nineteen! This used to irritate us and we rolled our eyes at their antics.'[140]

In the evenings, or as a 'wet weather option', young people gathered around the juke box in the room at the Normandie that served as the hotel's *shul* (see Chapter 7), or around the fruit machines that were situated either side of the bottom of the hotel's magnificent staircase. Another popular trysting place was the Green Park's tennis courts. Young male guests were often booked into an annexe located in the hotel's grounds. It became a 'cauldron for late night rowdiness and pranks', which were apparently overlooked 'because the mayhem was confined to Jewish young people'.[141]

After dinner, young people would move in groups from one hotel to the next, referred to as 'hotel crawls', to 'see who was around and what was going on', and to enjoy the entertainment that was taking place.[142] Some of the hotels were more popular than others. The entertainment at the Green Park was largely avoided since it was regarded as a place mainly for adults and older people, and where teenagers were not made to feel welcome. The Cumberland and the Majestic were both seen as being 'livelier' and 'cool', although both hotels were particular about which and when young people would be allowed in to partake of their entertainment. Dawn Kaffel recalls:

> The Majestic Hotel was my grandmother's pride and joy. She worked extremely hard, took her job very seriously and would not let anybody get the better of her. To this day, I often hear how she used to stand in the foyer, arms folded, pointing firmly to the revolving front door and the Exit sign, as young guests staying at the nearby Green Park Hotel tried to gate crash into the Majestic for a free evening's entertainment.[143]

Sometimes the young people stayed out until late and had to sneak back into the hotel where they were staying. Jon Harris tells us: 'The Normandie had a back entrance that took you straight down to the beach. We used this entrance if we were out late when we shouldn't have been. For some reason, the window in the door used to get broken on a regular basis and John the porter would have to come along and mend it.'[144]

Romance and *Shidduchim*

The Big Eight hotels became known as places for romantic encounters between young people and, hopefully for some, for meeting a marriage partner. The late former Chief Rabbi, Lord Jonathan Sacks, once commented 'You were out of the city and feeling liberated. It was like an alternative reality.'[145] Paul Harris recalls that he was able to maintain a romance with a young woman he met on holiday in Bournemouth by writing letters to her for over two years: 'It was in 1967. I can date it from my memory that Scott Mackenzie's *San Francisco* was playing at a youth club dance we went to on our first date at Branksome Dene.'[146] His brother Jon says: 'The other day I found a file full of love letters I wrote to and received from girls I met at the Normandie. There are hundreds of them!'[147] Some young people were attracted not to their Jewish peers of the opposite sex, but to the young staff working in the hotels. Sheila Finesilver recalls that when she and her family stayed in the Cumberland, she 'fell in love with the waiters – who didn't? – particularly Tony and Bruno. Lovely Tony saw to it that I had chocolate sauce whatever dessert we had.'[148]

Amid growing fears of intermarriage, some people took their children or grandchildren to the large Bournemouth hotels with the express intention of making a *shidduch* (marriage match): 'The Bournemouth hotels were the best-ever *shidduch* hunting grounds.'[149] Some people saved up to stay at one of the Bournemouth hotels if they had marriageable sons and daughters, as described in Gerda Charles's *The Crossing Point*.[150]

The Green Park in particular was known for the number of matches that were made there: 'The hotel was *the* place for making Jews, a place for mixing and matching.'[151] Hans Eirew recalls: 'While I was still in the army, I was lured to the Green Park Hotel for a long weekend by a plotting aunt and uncle. How I escaped the machinations of a dozen determined Jewish mothers unscathed I will never know.'[152] The Richman sisters are said to have had an unerring instinct for spotting who would get along with whom and were not shy about using their talent.[153] Geoffrey Feld also recalls: 'My mother was responsible for thousands of *shidduchim* during her time running the Cumberland. If I'd had £5 for every *shidduch* she made, I would have been able to retire ten years earlier.'[154] Bluma Feld was explicit about her objectives. When interviewed by the *Jewish Chronicle*, she said: 'I want the Cumberland to be a hotel where Jewish children can meet and marry.'[155]

Even when couples did not meet in the hotels, contacts made by people who did, sometimes led to matches. Sheila Davies recalls:

> My parents went to stay in the Cumberland one weekend, and they got talking to a young man sitting at the next table in the dining room. He was staying there to recuperate after an operation. My father was very convivial and said to him that, if he was ever in London, he should come and visit them, which he did. And that's how I met my husband, Graham.[156]

During the 1940s and 1950s, many young people were happy to go along with the overt matchmaking. One young woman, heartbroken having broken up with her non-Jewish boyfriend, was taken to the Green Park for the holiday season. She later recalled:

> I had been before, but had now reached an age when all the mothers would start to buy you extra-special dresses, fur stoles and curlers for your hair. It could mean only one thing: marriage. My friends and I used to joke about it being a conspiracy. On my first evening at the Green Park, before dinner, my mother zipped me into my best satin dress and took the curlers out of my hair. I was even allowed to wear lipstick. She took my head in her hands and gave me a kiss. 'It hurts now my darling, I know. But one day you will see. To marry out is to break a link that is thousands of years old and it is a victory for all those who supported Hitler.' These words struck home to me and I will never forget them. I realised that some things are more important than personal happiness. I walked down the marble stairs to dinner that night to the tune of the band playing.[157]

As time progressed, some young people began to question the matchmaking. Hannah Jacobs recalls: 'My job on holiday was to look pretty and work towards finding a rich husband, but in my teens I decided that I wanted something more from life than simply getting married.'[158] Joy Sable describes the unsubtle matchmaking with even less relish in an unnamed Jewish hotel in Bournemouth:

> ...the weekend entertainment was obviously seeing how quickly I could be paired off with a poor chap, who was as unwilling about the whole affair as I...The chief protagonist in this dreadful charade was an aged woman who considered it her personal responsibility to see that he and I should 'make friends'...The final showdown came when we were seated in the lounge one evening. The young man's mother suddenly rose and crossed to the other side of the room, creating a silence and a very visible empty chair between him and me. My heart sank. I yawned ostentatiously, ignoring pleas to 'be an actress' and stick the evening out. Well, Glenda Jackson I am not. So, I made a quick exit, locking myself in my bathroom and cursing the hotel...I haven't been back since.[159]

Romance and matches were not confined to young people. Older men and women also met their destiny at one of the Jewish hotels in

Bournemouth, but perhaps not to such disastrous effect as depicted in Bernard Kops's 1979 radio play, *Bournemouth Nights,* which deftly captures the finer nuances of life in the Bournemouth hotels. In this play, Simon Barnett preys on the wealthy widow Sarah Abrahams, who falls in love with him dancing to the music of *Izzy Fernandez and his Gauchos* while several unattached women of a certain age size up the charming scoundrel.[160]

The Smaller Hotels and Guest Houses

At the Dolly Ross Home for the Blind (see Chapter 4), entertainment was regularly provided for the people who holidayed there. The longstanding entertainment manager at the home was a man named Raymond, who had previously been a violinist with the Hallé Orchestra. Jane Kessler, who worked with Raymond one summer recalls: 'We took the guests on various trips, usually the same each week, such as to local beaches, drives through the New Forest, and in the evening we organised various types of entertainment, including Raymond playing his violin, which he did beautifully.'[161] The regular musical entertainers at the home included the Latter family who lived in Bournemouth. Sylvia Latter, a very accomplished pianist, was accompanied by her daughter Esther, who later became a semi-professional singer. Sylvia's husband, Bill, played drums. A number of French people took holidays at the home and the Latters would sing to them in French. The family sometimes invited other entertainers to join them. Esther Schneider (née Latter) recalls: 'We developed an extensive repertoire and received several awards for our work.'[162]

At the Carlton Dene holiday home (see Chapter 4), guests also had outings and theatre trips. In the 1960s, entertainment was provided by the Bournemouth B'nai B'rith Young Adults Association (previously B'nai B'rith Youth Organisation, BBYO) and Rev. and Mrs Cohen from BHC donated a piano to the home.[163] Later on, each fortnight a music-hall style cabaret was provided by people who worked at a hairdressing salon in Westover Road.[164]

The Hartford Court Hotel run by the Latemans (see Chapter 4), located very close to the Majestic, was used to accommodate the performers appearing there. Hazel Green (née Lateman) says, 'I recall a number of famous people who stayed with us, such as the operatic soprano, Adele Leigh', and tells this story of another guest:

One day, our Spanish maid came to tell my parents that she could hear a strange rustling noise in one of the bedrooms but couldn't make out what was making it. They went to look, and eventually tracked it down. Beneath a sheet, they found a cage that housed the doves that were part of a magician's act. He was performing at the Majestic that week.[165]

People staying in the smaller hotels and guest houses had a very different experience from those staying in the Big Eight hotels. They usually left their accommodation after breakfast and did not return until shortly before their evening meal. They often spent many hours on the beach. Judi Lyons recalls: 'We often had to remind them about applying sun cream. Sometimes they came back looking like lobsters.'[166] John Colvin relates a story told to him by a friend about a trip she and her father made to Bournemouth. Her father was very orthodox and insisted on staying at the Mayfair Hotel, which was similarly orthodox (see Chapter 4):

> Father and daughter spent most of their week in Bournemouth on the beach. The father wore his formal clothing, topped with a Homburg hat. He spent the entire time in a deck chair, studying the Torah and Talmud, his standard leisure pursuit. He did have a subsidiary hobby, fashioning small items in gold, but that wouldn't have worked too well on the beach. He was happy for his sixteen-year-old daughter to sunbathe next to him. She lay on a towel, wearing a bikini, alongside him. He was seemingly unconcerned about the content of the paperback novels that she was reading. I imagine that he assumed that, being a girl, she was bound to be reading trivia. This incongruous image has stayed with me ever since I was told this story some forty-five years ago.[167]

Although the Mayfair Hotel had a billiards room and also a large ballroom, it provided very little entertainment. Norman Shapiro, nephew of its owners Esther and Elkan Shapiro, recalls:

> The clientele was mainly middle-aged and older people, and they were usually tucked up in bed just after dinner, which meant that the grand ballroom did not get used, except occasionally when my aunt Esther played the grand piano that was there. Because it was so little used, my cousin Michael set up table tennis in the middle of the ballroom and taught me how to play proper table tennis as opposed to ping pong. I became a very reasonable player as a result.[168]

The guest-house visitors usually left the beach at various points during the day to walk into the town centre, where they ate their lunch and tea and visited the gardens, often meeting up with Jewish families staying elsewhere in Bournemouth. After dinner, they talked, read or watched television. Judi Lyons comments: 'We always had to have finished dinner before *Coronation Street* started!'[169] Some also went for walks or to *daven* (see Chapter 7). Sometimes families brought with them their own games, such as charades: 'It was a different time and world – not quite as sophisticated as we would like to think we are today.'[170]

Some of larger hotels organised entertainment akin to that of the Big Eight hotels. The Hotel Florence showed the latest films in its dining room and lounge, both of which had wooden floors. On Saturday evenings, the doors between the rooms were opened to form a ballroom where dances took place led by a band.[171] The Palm Bay Hotel also had its own dance band, the *Palm Bay Trio*, to accompany dancing on its 'maple-sprung floor'.[172] During the summer months, the hotel arranged shows for the children.

67. Children's show at the Palm Bay Hotel, Sea Road, Boscombe, *c.* 1955. Image courtesy of Diana Barzilay (née Biener), the child to the right of the image.

Celebrations at the Hotels

The Big Eight hotels were often used to celebrate important events, such as engagements, birthdays and wedding anniversaries, for both guests and local people (see Chapter 9). The hoteliers went out of their way to make the celebrations special, especially for those involving their regular guests. In the summer months, the events were often held in the beautifully-tended hotel gardens.

The hoteliers sometimes celebrated their own life cycle events, or those of close family members, in their hotels. Joanna Benarroch (née Marriott) recalls that she had not one but two parties at the Green Park when she became engaged to her husband Bernard in 1985, a year before the hotel closed: 'There was one party for the family and guests and one for the staff. At the former party, people ate all the food and at the other, they drank all the alcohol.'[173] Andy Kalmus (née Forman), the niece of Fay and Maurice Guild, celebrated many of her birthdays at the Langham where the pâtissier made special cakes for her.[174]

68. Belle and Louis Keyne, at the celebration of the *Bar Mitzvah* of their son, Jonathan Keyne, held at the Normandie Hotel, Manor Road, Bournemouth, 1961. Image courtesy of Simon Keyne.

As the number of guests declined, the hotels hosted an increasing number of celebrations. In Chapter 3, mention was made of the fact that the Jewish hotels in Bournemouth were at one time the destination of choice for honeymoon couples. Later on, the New Ambassador was a major venue for wedding receptions for couples from outside the area, especially those from London, since it was more economic. After the Normandie became more orthodox, it was used for holding the *sheva berachot* (referring to the seven special blessings recited after meals when the wedding couple are present, but in this context meaning orthodox wedding celebrations) by several well-known *charedi* families, for their offspring. These included the Freshwater family, Zalman Margulies, chair of British Sugar, Dovid Menashe Rubin, descendent of the Sassover rabbi, Rabbi Meisels, a Satmar follower from Stamford Hill and Willie Stern (mentioned in Chapter 5). The weddings usually took place on a Thursday in London, and the wedding party then travelled to Bournemouth on a Friday morning for a three-day celebration. Brian Lassman comments: 'They made full use of the three acres of garden but nobody used the swimming pool in case they were seen by someone of the opposite sex.'[175]

One of the biggest events that occurred at the Normandie during this period was the wedding of its manager Brian Lassman. It took place in July 1989 and was attended by over 600 people. Brian was a Bournemouth councillor at the time, so all his fellow councillors were there as well as his and Judy's friends and relations. Brian organised the catering himself: 'People still talk about the wedding. There was a marching band from the barracks at Blandford Forum. The leader used his ceremonial sword to cut our wedding cake!'[176]

Today, during the winter months, the Normandie is mainly open for celebrations of various kinds, such as *Bar Mitzvahs*.

69. Brian and Judy Lassman's wedding at the Normandie Hotel, July 1989. Shows cutting of the cake with a ceremonial sword. Image curtesy of Brian Lassman.

The Hoteliers and Guest-House Owners

The hotel proprietors worked very long hours, and had little time for socialising outside their hotels. As a result, many socialised in the hotels with their friends, people from the local community (see Chapter 9), or with the regular guests with whom they had struck up a friendship. Some of the hotel proprietors also contributed to the entertainment. Isaac Feld had a gin rummy (his favourite card game) school, which he convened at the Cumberland three or four nights a week, to which he invited his friends. He had a book in which he recorded his winnings but not his losses. The Feld family lived in a house at the back of the hotel. Isaac used to creep into bed when he had been playing cards late into the night. Geoffrey Feld recalls that one night his mother woke up as Isaac was undressing at about 5am. He told her that he was getting ready to go to the hotel to try and catch the people who were taking things from the hotel's stores. 'That's a good idea', Bluma said, 'You should go and investigate.' So, he had no option but to go back to the hotel. It was not until several years later that Bluma admitted that she knew that Isaac had just come to bed.[177]

Bluma's mother, Alta Posner, who lived with her husband in a flat behind the Cumberland, spent a great deal of time in the hotel. She was a favourite with older guests, particularly those who were Yiddish speaking. Sheila Finesilver recalls that her grandmother, who made 'annual pilgrimages' to the Cumberland, and Alta Posner, 'a gorgeous *frum* old lady who wore an old-fashioned waved wig', were 'never far away from each other, speaking Yiddish like gudduns'.[178] Geoffrey Feld often sang with the band at the Cumberland and occasionally at other hotels as part of their cabarets. He tells the story of when he was once invited to sing at the Green Park alongside Ray Ellington, whom he already knew: 'The following day, my father had a call from Ruby Marriott to say that I was always welcome at the Green Park, but I was not to sing there again, it was not diplomatic.'[179] Richard Inverne, Bluma Feld's grandson, was at one point in charge of arranging events for children. His son, James Inverne, recalls: 'He sometimes adopted various persona to entertain the children. I think the actor in him rather enjoyed it.'[180]

Ruby Marriott was very interested in horse racing and saw no conflict between his love of Judaism and his passion for gambling on horses. He took favoured guests with him on his trips to Salisbury race course where he was a member.[181] His son David Marriott, who was an outstanding golfer (he played in the British Open), often played with Green Park guests at a local, non-Jewish golf club. David's grandmother, Bubbe Richman, revelled in the company of the Green Park guests. In her later years, she apparently spent many hours a day sitting in one of the lounge chairs arranged around the Green Park's outdoor swimming pool, chatting to the older women staying in the hotel. A former guest remembers: 'They all wore sensible shoes and stockings, and stoles. Their handbags lay on their laps. They would never have thought of actually going into the pool.'[182] Two of Bubbe's daughters, Helen and Hannah Richman, had beautiful singing voices and often sang Yiddish songs for the guests on festival evenings. They were sometimes joined by their brother, Joseph.[183] The siblings inherited their talent from their father, who had been the *chazan* at his synagogue in Stamford Hill.[184] At the Majestic, Fay Schneider relaxed by playing cards late into the night. Miriam Marcus recalls: 'I remember my mother complaining that my father, Max Colman, the head chef at the Majestic, was not present when I was born in the early hours of a Sunday morning because he was playing poker with Fay Schneider. In those days, the owners of hotels (or at least Fay Schneider) had close relationships with their staff, and even socialised with them during off-hours.'[185]

Sadie Hayman, who took over East Cliff Court from her mother Annie Morris in 1953, was generally quite shy but, despite a disability, she enjoyed the dancing that took place at the hotel, especially when she danced with the longstanding gigolos. Edward Hayman recalls: 'My grandmother seldom danced, though she was not above stepping out on to the floor with a favoured visitor. My mother always danced, most often with a host but occasionally – uncomfortably – with a visitor who had been bold enough to approach her to ask her.'[186] The dancing sometimes created tensions between Sadie and her husband John Hayman, who was wont to grumble that the hotel would be better off without the dance hosts.[187] Later on, the dance hosts at East Cliff Court were Jimmy Cooper, Norman Jaques and Mr Plant the latter of whom was a local policeman. Sadie Hayman's two sons were involved with the hotel entertainment. Edward Hayman remembers:

> Down below in the ballroom, Ronnie and I would play LP records for the younger visitors hanging around after a dance – Frank Sinatra, *The Ink Spots*. Ronnie might play the piano – I can recall him accompanying himself singing *Bewitched, Bothered and Bewildered*

at a time when we had all drunk too much to care about the quality of the rendering.[188]

Paul Harris recalls Ron ('Hymie') Fisher, one of the co-owners of the Normandie, who had been the lead vocalist in one of the top dance bands in the 1930s: 'He had a beautiful voice. He called the numbers at bingo and also sang at Saturday night dinner dances at the hotel. I still remember his beautiful rendition of *Strangers in the Night*.'[189] Similarly, at the Ambassador, the hotel director, Erwin Rubinstein, regularly sang with the resident band the song *It don't mean a thing if it ain't got that swing*, made famous by Duke Ellington. Peter Philips recalls: 'He loved being the showman and, like most good showman, he would join in the fun. Ruby was the Jewish Cameron Mackintosh of his time.'[190]

Judi Lyons recalls that her father entertained the guests staying at Villa Judi: 'Dad was always a bit of a raconteur, and often retold stories that he had heard during the day in his barber's shop.'[191] Similarly, Lennie Segal, whose parents ran Hotel Florence in Boscombe Spa Road, remembers: 'My dad was gregarious, generous and a good host. He used to entertain the guests. Dad was the MC at the weekly dances held at the hotel and was good at what I called "eccentric dancing."'[192]

Meyer Rivlin, the proprietor of Gresham Court, had a reputation for being a big gambler. As well as his regular visits to the casino at the Royal Bath Hotel, he organised frequent poker games in his hotel, which attracted men staying at other Jewish hotels and from the local Jewish community. Stuart March, whose family owned businesses in Stamford Hill, recalls that one year when he was holidaying in Bournemouth, he went to Gresham Court to play poker with Mr Rivlin: 'That night I met a young woman there who became my wife.'[193]

On occasion, encounters in the hotels led to matches for the younger members of the families who ran them. Helen Richman met her husband, Arnold Lee, when he was staying at the Green Park following an operation, and Barbara Glyn, one of Ruby Marriott's two daughters, met her husband, Howard, when he visited the Green Park. She comments: 'I have to admit that he wasn't staying at the Green Park but at the Majestic!'[194] Geoffrey Feld says that he met Susan, who became his wife, when she was 'propping up the bar drinking an orange juice' in the Cumberland: 'She was there with her parents. She was just nineteen when I met her.'[195] Simon Keyne, whose parents owned the Normandie, recalls: 'I met my future wife when she came into the hotel to meet her aunt and uncle who were staying there. I was sitting in the bar and got talking to her. I visited her in London and the rest as they say was history!'[196] The wedding in 1973 was a big event, and Belle Keyne, who was apparently very generous, hired a coach so that longstanding hotel staff could attend the reception at the Dorchester Hotel.[197]

Notes

1. This section is based on research carried out by the author in connection with her book, Pam Fox, *The Jewish Community of Golders Green: A Social History* (Stroud: The History Press, 2016).
2. Joseph Green, *A Social History of the Jewish East End in London, 1914-1939: A Study of Life, Labour, and Liturgy* (Lampeter: Edwin Mellen Press Ltd, 1991), p.308.
3. Interview with Hettie Marks, 12.11.2020.
4. At that time, it was a common sight at the pier to see coaches lined up bearing the name of the big hotels, ready to take the guests back for lunch or tea.
5. Louis Golding, *Hotel Ambassador* (Bournemouth: Ambassador, 1950), p.7.
6. John Colvin, post on Facebook, 24.8.2020.
7. Interview with Sheila Morris, 19.8.2020.
8. Email from Janet Naim, 17.9.2020.
9. *JC*, 12.4.1996.
10. Conversation with Marian Stern, 19.11.2020.
11. Interview with Barry Levinson, 7.5.2020.
12. Interview with Hannah Jacobs, 12.5.2020.
13. Interview with Clive Gold, 23.9.2020.
14. Gerda Charles, *The Crossing Point* (London: Eyre & Spottiswoode, 1961), p.188.
15. Interview with Stuart March, 21.9.2020.
16. Interview with Roger Vickers, 27.5.2020.
17. Interview with Clive Gold, 23.9.2020.
18. Interview with Hettie Marks, 28.4.2020.
19. Israel Shenker, 'On the British Seafront, Kosher Cuisine with an English Accent', *New York Times*, 6.1.1973.
20. Ilana Lee, 'Diamonds at Breakfast', *Jewish Quarterly*, Vol. 54, No. 1, p.28.
21. Email from Edward Hayman, 23.9.2020.
22. David Felsenstein, post on Facebook, Jewish Britain Group, 15 December 2018.
23. See Shenker, 'On the British Seafront'.
24. Talk given by Geoffrey Feld by Zoom, on *The Jewish Hotels of Bournemouth*, for BHC. 17.6.2020.
25. See Shenker, 'On the British Seafront'.
26. Interview with Alan Lee, 21.5.2020.
27. Interview with Barbara Glyn, 1.6.2020. A *gabbai* is an officer in a synagogue similar to a churchwarden.
28. See Lee, 'Diamonds at Breakfast', p.29.
29. Interview with Paul Harris, 28.4.2020.
30. *Ibid.*
31. Interview with Clive Gold, 23.9.2020.
32. Conversation with Geoffrey Feld, 29.11.2020.

33. Conversation with Suzanne Higgott, 12.7.2020.
34. Email from Roger Vickers, 9.1.2020.
35. Email from Edward Hayman, 23.9.2020.
36. *Ibid.*
37. *JC*, 24.12.1954.
38. Interview with Janet Pins, 27.8.2020.
39. Interview with Howard Taylor (Harry Taylor's son) 22.11.2020.
40. *Ibid.*
41. Letters in *AJR Journal*, February 2012 and October 2014.
42. *JC*, 20.11.1953.
43. Conversation with Brian Lassman, 1.12.2020.
44. Interview with Brian Lassman, 14.5.2020. They did an impression act in which they presented seven voices in three minutes.
45. See https://www.fripp.com/the-rabbi-at-the-majestic-wisdom-in-a-few-words-2/
46. Born in Cracow, Poland, he became famous as a bandleader, nightclub owner, composer and singer. When the Germans swept through his country in 1939, he was captured and imprisoned. He escaped to Russia where he continued his musical career. When Russia entered the war, he joined the Polish army which led him to Britain where he settled.
47. *JC*, 31.8.1956.
48. Interview with Geoffrey Feld, 21.10.2020.
49. Conversation with Geoffrey Feld, 29.11.2020.
50. See https://www.mylondon.news/news/local-news/stanmore-charity-crooner-johnny-franks-5966020.
51. *The Stage*, 28.9.1967.
52. *The Western Morning News*, 29.4.1946.
53. *Hampshire Telegraph and Post*, 20.4.1956.
54. Ronald Hayman, *Secrets: Boyhood in a Jewish Hotel, 1932-1954* (London: Peter Owen, 1985), p.128.
55. Email from Edward Hayman, 24.8.2020.
56. See eastcliffcourtmemories.wordpress.com/blog/.
57. See Lee, 'Diamonds at Breakfast', p.28.
58. See talk given by Geoffrey Feld by Zoom.
59. Interview with Jonathan Perlmutter, 26.8.2020.
60. Interview with Geoffrey Feld, 4.5.2020.
61. See Charles, *The Crossing Point*, p.186.
62. *Ibid.*, p.186.
63. Message from Tony Klinger, 24.8.2020.
64. Interview with Hilary Halter, 29.4.2020.
65. See Golding, *Hotel Ambassador*, p.7.
66. Peter Phillips, 'London's Borscht Belt – Jewish Hotels in Bournemouth', *AJR Journal*, August 2014.
67. Interview with Brian Lassman, 14.5.2020.
68. Interview with Jonathan Perlmutter, 26.8.2020.
69. Email from Edward Hayman, 23.9.2020.
70. *Ibid.*
71. Interview with Larry and Mandy Kaye, 11.6.2020.

72. Interview with Sheila Samuels, 11.5.2020.
73. Interview with James Inverne, 10.11.2020.
74. Recordings of interviews with Bluma Feld, carried out by her grandson, Richard Inverne, in 1996, Disc 5, kindly provided by Geoffrey Feld.
75. Email from Chris Woodward, 22.9.2020.
76. See Lee, 'Diamonds at Breakfast', p.29. The young woman whose dress was ruined was Carol Braham and the two guests involved in the mock boxing contest were Alex Findgold and David Clore. Out-take from 'The Green Park', directed by Jack Fishburn and Justin Hardy, 2015.
77. See Lee, 'Diamonds at Breakfast', p.29.
78. Interview with Barbara Glyn, 1.6.2020.
79. See Lee, 'Diamonds at Breakfast', p.29.
80. See 'The Green Park', directed by Jack Fishburn and Justin Hardy.
81. *Ibid.* Several interviewees have suggested that the woman in question was Beatrice Franks, owner of the famous lingerie shop in Golders Green Road.
82. Interview with Marilyn Murray, 24.8.2020.
83. *JC*, 22.3.1957.
84. Email from Edward Hayman, 23.92020.
85. Interview with Clive Gold, 23.9.2020.
86. Interview with Gloria Stanley (née Lewis), 28.4.2020.
87. Interview with Roger Vickers, 27.5.2020.
88. Interview with Geoffrey Feld, 4.5.2020.
89. *Ibid.*
90. See https://en.wikipedia.org/wiki/Maurice_Fogel.
91. Interview with James Inverne, 10.11.2020.
92. See Hayman, *Secrets*, p.44.
93. Talk given by Dawn Kaffel, Fay Schneider's granddaughter, at Hampstead Garden Suburb Synagogue, 'Majestic Days at the Majestic'. See https://docplayer.net/amp/138128447-These-were-the-words-of-a-shul-member-on.html.
94. *Ibid.*
95. Interview with Jonathan Perlmutter, 15.5.2020
96. See Hayman, *Secrets*, p.44.
97. Conversation with Edward Hayman, 30.9.2020.
98. Email from Richard Inverne, 19.8.2020.
99. Interview with Jenny Leigh, 27.1.2021.
100. Interview with Sheila Morris, 19.8.2020.
101. Email from Edward Hayman, 23.9.2020.
102. Conversation with Geoffrey Feld, 29.11.2020.
103. See 'The Green Park', directed by Jack Fishburn and Justin Hardy.
104. Interview with Jon Harris, 4.5.2020.
105. Interview with Paul Harris, 28.4.2020.
106. See eastcliffcourtmemories.wordpress.com/blog/.
107. Interview with Yvonne Epstein, 19.5.2020.
108. Notes from Edward Hayman, sent by email. 24.8.2020.
109. Interview with Beverley-Jane Stewart, 29.5.2020.
110. There were zig-zag paths in other parts of Bournemouth.
111. At the time of writing, the lift was not in operation due to a land slip.

112. Edwina Currie remembering her holidays in Bournemouth. See https://www. bbc.co.uk/iplayer/episode/b071fg28/holiday-of-my-lifetime-with-len-goodman-series-2-episode-14.
113. Interview with Hannah Jacobs, 12.5.2020.
114. Interview with Sheila Morris, 19.8.2020.
115. Notes from Edward Hayman, sent by email, 24.8.2020.
116. Interview with Jon Harris, 4.5.2020.
117. Interview with Geoffrey Feld, 4.5.2020.
118. Interview with Jenny Green, 19.5.2020.
119. *JC*, 22.91967.
120. Interview with Brian Lassman, 14.5.2020. Brian Lassman was dismissed by the hotel in 1994 for turning on the heating on *Shabbat*. He was awarded over £10,000 for unfair dismissal. *JC*, 2.9.1994.
121. Conversation with Mark Perl, 15.1.2021.
122. Interview with Stuart March, 21.9.2020.
123. Interview with David Abrahams, 25.8.2020.
124. Interview with Rabbi Jonathan Romain, 30.4.2020.
125. Email from Edward Hayman, 23.9.2020.
126. Francine Wolfisz, 'A Bournemouth Summer Just like the old Days', *Jewish News* 21.8.2014. See https://jewishnews.timesofisrael.com/bournemouth-summer-just-like-old-days/.
127. Interview with Jon Harris, 4.5.2020.
128. Interview with Brian Lassman, 14.5.2020.
129. Interview with Diane Langleben, 17.6.2020.
130. Interview with Jonathan Perlmutter, 26.8.2020.
131. Morella Kayman, *A Life to Remember* (London: John Blake Publishing Ltd, 2014), p.22.
132. Interview with James Inverne, 10.11.2020.
133. Ann Crook, post on Facebook, 24.8.2020.
134. Interview with David Latchman, 6.5.2020.
135. See 'The Green Park', directed by Jack Fishburn and Justin Hardy.
136. Email from Chris Woodward, 22.9.2020.
137. Interview with James Inverne, 10.11.2020.
138. Interview with Paul Harris, 1.5.2020.
139. Comment by unnamed man at talk given by the author, 20.1.2021.
140. Interview with Jon Harris, 4.5.2020.
141. See Lee, 'Diamonds at Breakfast', p.29.
142. Interview with Paul Harris, 28.4.2020.
143. See talk given by Dawn Kaffel.
144. Interview with Jon Harris, 4.5.2020.
145. Rabbi Lord Sacks, appearing in 'The Green Park', directed by Jack Fishburn and Justin Hardy.
146. Interview with Paul Harris, 1.5.2020.
147. Interview with Jon Harris, 4.5.2020.
148. Sheila Finesilver, response to author's post on Facebook, Memories of Old Poole and Bournemouth, 21.11.2020.
149. Janet Clifford, post on Facebook, Jewish Britain Group, 14.12.2018.

150. See Charles, *The Crossing Point*, p.188.
151. See 'The Green Park', directed by Jack Fishburn and Justin Hardy.
152. *AJR Journal*, October 2018.
153. See Lee, 'Diamonds at Breakfast', p.29.
154. Interview with Geoffrey Feld, 4.5.2020.
155. *JC*, 16.12.1983.
156. Interview with Sheila Davies, 29.4.2020.
157. See Lee, 'Diamonds at Breakfast', p.29.
158. Interview with Hannah Jacobs, 12,5,2020.
159. Joy Sable writing in the *JC*, 27.8.1982.
160. The play was broadcast on BBC Radio Four 2.6.1979. Warren Mitchell and Maria Charles played the two main characters.
161. Email from Jane Kessler, 19.10.2020.
162. Interview with Esther Schneider (née Latter), 3.9.2020.
163. *JC*, 12.4.1968.
164. Joss Mullinger, response to author's post on Facebook, Memories of Old Poole and Bournemouth, 21.11.2020.
165. Interview with Hazel Green, 25.8.2020.
166. Interview with Judi Lyons, 4.5.2020.
167. Email from John Colvin, 3.9.2020.
168. Interview with Norman Shapiro, 23.10.2020.
169. Email from Judi Lyons, 8.9.2020.
170. *Ibid.*
171. Interview with Lennie Segal, 15.6.2020.
172. *JC*, 29.5.1955.
173. Interview with Joanna Benarroch, 19.6.2020.
174. Interview with Andy Kalmus, 24.9.2020.
175. Interview with Brian Lassman, 14.5.2020.
176. *Ibid.*
177. Interview with Geoffrey Feld, 4.5.2020. Ray Ellington's mother was Jewish. He was brought up in the East End and spoke Yiddish.
178. Sheila Finesilver, post on Facebook, Jewish Britain Group, 12.4.2017.
179. Interview with Geoffrey Feld, 4.5.2020.
180. Interview with James Inverne, 10.11.2020.
181. Interview with Barbara Glyn, 1.6.2020.
182. Out-take from 'The Green Park', directed by Jack Fishburn and Justin Hardy.
183. Interview with Frances Israel, 2.6.2020.
184. Obituary for Helen Lee (née Richman), *JC*, 1.1.2010. As a young adult, Helen Richman sang in a renowned girls' choir that accompanied famous *chazanim*.
185. Interview with Miriam Marcus, 20.10.2020.
186. Email from Edward Hayman, 23.9.2020.
187. See Hayman, *Secrets*, p.54.
188. Email from Edward Hayman, 23.9.2020.
189. Interview with Paul Harris, 28.4.2020.
190. Email from Peter Phillips, 3.2.2021.
191. Email from Judi Lyons, 8.9.2020.

192. Interview with Lennie Segal, 15.6.2020.
193. Interview with Stuart March, 21.9.2020.
194. Interview with Barbara Glyn, 1.6.2020.
195. Talk given by Geoffrey Feld at Edgware United Synagogue, 6 March 2018.
196. Interview with Simon Keyne, 15.6.2020.
197. Interview with Adriano Brioschi, 4.1.2021.

9

The Hotels and the Town of Bournemouth

By way of context, several previous chapters (notably Chapters 1, 2, 3 and 5) have covered the development of Bournemouth as a holiday resort and the evolution of its Jewish community. The purpose of this chapter is to explore in more detail the relationship between the Jewish holiday accommodation and the town in which they were located. While some interviewees for this book suggested that the Jewish holiday accommodation operated in isolation from the town, in fact, for much of their history, there was a very close and symbiotic relationship between the hotels and guest houses and the local community, both Jewish and non-Jewish.

The Hotels and the Local Economy

One of the most obvious links between the hotels and the town is their impact on the local economy. As the Jewish hotels grew both in number and size, many businesses sprang up to meet their needs and those of their guests. As early as 1939, a *Jewish Chronicle* columnist noted: 'I am told by a friend who is holidaymaking in Bournemouth that Jewish women staying there are becoming increasingly foot-conscious. They gather, so I am told, at the Foot Clinic run by Miss Parratt in Commercial Road.'[1]

The businesses that grew up as a result of the Jewish holiday trade included those that were specifically Jewish, such as the kosher butchers, bakers and delicatessens. As already mentioned, at one point there were three kosher butchers in Bournemouth, which largely owed their existence to the presence of the hotels. One of the bakers was opened in 1949 by Lew Glaser, who had previously worked in a number of the 'leading Jewish hotels in Bournemouth'.[2] This relationship between the hotels and local businesses is illustrated by the fact that, as the number of Jewish hotels declined, so did the number of kosher shops in Bournemouth. Some kosher businesses remained, but they changed in their nature in response to the evolution of Jewish holidaymaking in Bournemouth. The shift from visitors staying in hotels to renting or buying self-catering accommodation led to an increase in the number of delicatessens and take-away businesses (see Chapter 6). When Ian Camissar took over a kosher delicatessen in 1993, he said that on Sunday mornings in August he sold over 800 bagels and in the evening his fish and chip take-away was equally busy.[3] Today, there are fewer kosher shops than there were previously, but Jewish holidaymakers continue to contribute to the local economy by the purchases they make from the kosher sections of the local supermarkets (see Chapter 6).

Over the years, the Jewish hotels and guest houses have also contributed to the viability of a range of non-specialist businesses. In his memoir, Ronald Hayman describes how his mother and grandmother spent most weekday mornings shopping for East Cliff Court in the grocers, greengrocers and the three department stores, Beale's, Bright's and Plummer Roddis, pausing to take morning coffee at the Cadena Café. Some of the goods they purchased could possibly have been ordered by telephone, but apparently the two women enjoyed the interaction with the shopkeepers and taking their advice on the best goods to buy.[4]

As well as patronising local shops, the hotels and guest houses supported a variety of other businesses, such as laundry services, builders, decorators and the several local photographers for whom a major strand of their businesses was snapping Jewish families on the beach and in the hotels. When Jewish holidaymakers started staying in self-catering accommodation, a range of businesses advertised regularly in the *Jewish Chronicle*, including cleaning, DIY and painting and decorating services, to meet their needs.

When the Jewish hotels were in their heyday and were noted for the glamour of their guests (see Chapter 3), many local businesses thrived as a result of the custom of Jewish visitors, especially the dress shops, milliners, furriers, beauty salons and hairdressers. Particularly popular with the visitors were the clothes shops run by Jewish proprietors, notably Kasmirs. Some guests rented jewellery, furs, dresses and suits from local stores for the duration of their holidays.[5] Due to the 'feel good factor' of being on holiday, the visitors were sometimes tempted to purchase luxury items in the town. The contribution that Jewish visitors made to the local economy was recognised by people in Bournemouth. When interviewed by the *Jewish Chronicle*, one resident commented: 'We are very happy to receive Jewish visitors. They spend their money here!'[6]

The other way in which the hotels and guest houses contributed to the local economy was by employing large numbers of people (mainly non-Jewish) living in Bournemouth and the surrounding area. They worked in a wide range of jobs: chefs, waiters and waitresses (different staff for different meals, such as the specialist waitresses who served the afternoon and evening teas), night and day porters, kitchen assistants, page boys, chambermaids, receptionists, cleaners, pot washers, night and day telephonists, gardeners, nurses to care for frail guests, nannies to care for children, people who looked after the laundry and the linen, accountants, office staff, maintenance staff and many more. Often, whole families and several generations worked in the hotels. Nadia Rossi comments: 'My father was the restaurant manager at the Normandie for nine years. My mother was a chambermaid and my sister, brother and I used to go in to help during school holidays.'[7] Sometimes people worked in more than one role. One former employee says: 'I worked in the Green Park when I was sixteen. I started the day doing breakfasts on the first floor, then went to the laundry for the afternoon, followed by serving afternoon teas, but the best place was working by the swimming pool serving refreshments. My last job of the day was turning back the beds.'[8] The hotels provided a valuable source of income for students and those at the start of their careers:

> My school friend, Penny, and I worked as tea waitresses in the Normandie in the summer of 1960. We wore stiletto heels and full skirts with paper taffeta petticoats underneath, and had to negotiate a rickety wooden staircase with a full tray bearing a tea pot, a hot water jug, cutlery and cheesecake. We did two two-hour shifts: afternoon tea and late evening tea and cake break. It was the best ever summer break – we had lots of fun – but at the end of it we had to go back to school to do our GCEs.[9]

They also provided valuable work experience for those studying relevant courses at the local college. Sue Goodwin says: 'I worked in a Jewish hotel for six months as part of my college course in Hotel Management. I had to work in every department. I remember being told off by the rabbi for eating food on the wrong coloured plate!'[10] People were able to enhance their careers by moving from one Jewish hotel to another, and over time there developed a network of staff working in the hotels who socialised as well as worked together. The hotels hired dance hosts, musicians, entertainers who lived locally (see Chapter 8) and also called on a wide range of external services: people who repaired the televisions and dishwashers, electricians, plumbers, delivery people, the people who maintained the swimming pools. The list was endless.

The Big Eight hotels provided over 600 bedrooms between them. Together with the additional accommodation offered by the smaller hotels and guest houses, this meant that Jewish holiday establishments made a very significant contribution to the Bournemouth hotel trade. When Maurice and Fay Guild's banqueting suite was officially opened by the Mayor of Bournemouth in 1963, it was seen not only as a boost for the Jewish community but also as a welcome contribution to Bournemouth's growing success as an important centre for national and international conferences.[11] Geoffrey Feld from the Cumberland was a director of the Bournemouth Chamber of Commerce and also sat on the board of the Dorset TEC (Training and Enterprise Council),[12] which promoted the use of technology and innovation in local businesses. In this latter capacity, he supported a number of projects in Bournemouth hotels.[13]

Relationship with the Bournemouth Jewish Community

From the time that the first Jewish hotels and guest houses were established in Bournemouth, there was a close relationship between them and the local Jewish community. Early services of what became Bournemouth Hebrew Congregation (BHC) were held at Merivale Hall, and the hotel was subsequently used as the venue for various communal events and fundraising activities. It also accommodated visiting Jewish dignitaries, including on occasion the Chief Rabbi. Mrs Klein, the wife of Rev. L. Klein, who was the first minister at BHC, let out 'lofty' rooms to 'ladies and gentlemen' visiting the town at their home in Holdenhurst Road.[14]

Following the example set by Merivale Hall, several of the other Jewish hotels that opened before the Second World War became noted for hosting communal events and for contributing to fundraising activities for local Jewish charities and organisations associated with BHC. For example, during the 1930s, Lady Sassoon, who was a regular visitor to Bournemouth and had a home in the town (Keythorpe at 25 Manor Road[15]), hosted a series of annual balls and suppers in aid of the Jewish Ladies' Guild. Space for advertising the occasions, which were billed as 'the finest Jewish social event outside London', was donated by several of the leading Jewish hotels of the time, including East Cliff Court, Berachah, East Cliff Manor, the Trouville, Hinton Court and Court Heath.[16]

The proprietors of the Big Eight hotels, which were at their busiest in the three decades after the end of the Second World War, were acutely aware of their profit margins. Nevertheless, they were very generous in respect of Jewish charities. At one point, rarely a month went by without there being a report in the *Jewish Chronicle* on a charitable activity held in one or other of the Bournemouth hotels. Their proprietors gave open-handedly to organisations, such as the Bournemouth branch of AJEX (Association of Jewish Ex-Servicemen and Women) and the various local branches of Zionist bodies, including JNF (the Jewish National Fund) and later the JIA (the Joint Israel Appeal), WIZO (Women's International Zionist Organisation) and Emunah (a charity supporting children in Israel).

Mainly in the winter months, the hotels hosted various events (bring-and-buy sales, dinners, dances, coffee mornings and fashion shows) that raised significant sums of money and they also donated prizes for fundraising activities. For example, annual dinners were held at the Cumberland to raise money for Bournemouth JIA (now UJIA), and social evenings were organised in the hotel to raise money for the Hannah Levy House care home.[17] Janet Pins tells the story of Fay Schneider once raffling a fully-loaded drinks trolley for a local charity: 'Many tickets were sold and a large amount of money was raised, but when the prize was awarded it emerged that it was only the trolley that was being raffled and not the drinks!'[18] When he died in 1993, Bertram Levitus, former owner of the Ambassador and the Embassy hotels, left over £500,000 to the Hannah Levy House care home.[19]

For many years, several of the hotels hosted the annual dinners of the Bournemouth branch of AJEX and B'nai B'rith. The annual dinner and some of the winter meetings of the Bournemouth B'nai B'rith Youth Organisation (BBYO) were held at the Majestic. Hotel Rubens (see Chapter 4) provided a venue for the 5705 Society associated with BHC (see Chapter 3). It held dances on Sunday evenings at the hotel. Members of 5705 Society also organised entertainment that was staged at the Majestic and the Normandie, such as the 1966 production of *Beyond our Ben*, which was based on the BBC radio programme, *Beyond our Ken*, starring Kenneth Horne. The Ben featured in the title of the production was its writer, Ben Grower, son of Joseph and Helena Grower, the owners of Hotel Rubens, who was a prominent member of the 5705 Society. The event was so successful that Fay Schneider presented the club with four complimentary tickets to see *Funny Girl* in London's West End during its first month. Ben Grower comments: 'This was quite something. Tickets were like gold dust!'[20] Hotel Rubens was also the venue for the very first services of the Bournemouth Reform community (see Chapter 5). Ben Grower again comments: 'BHC never forgave my father for that!'[21]

Particularly dear to the hoteliers' hearts was the Dolly Ross home that provided holidays for blind people (see Chapter 4). In 1966, Golda and Harry Gale, who ran Gale's Private Hotel, held a social evening to raise money for the home.[22] For many years, Isaac and Bluma Feld invited the residents of the Dolly Ross home to the Cumberland for lunch and tea.[23] The garden fête held at the Dolly Ross home in 1975 was opened by Bluma Feld; it raised £1,350 for the home.[24] The Guilds at the Langham held several coffee mornings in aid of the home,[25] and Fay Schneider consecrated beds at the home in memory of her husband Ben and her son Gerald.

Several of the hoteliers sat on the committees of various local bodies. Geoffrey Feld from the Cumberland was chairman of the local branch of the JIA for several years, as was his nephew Richard Inverne at a later date. Maurice Guild from the Langham was chairman of the Bournemouth branch of the Joint Palestine Appeal (JPA) and Fay Schneider was a vice-president.

Support for local causes was not confined to the hotel proprietors; their staff and associated personnel were also involved. For example, Alex Kopfstein, the catering manager at the Cumberland, 'actively assisted the many committees working for local religious and Zionist causes'.[26] Lydia Camissar, the wife of Rev. Solomon Camissar, the *shomer* at the New Ambassador (see Chapter 7), was the chairman of the Bournemouth chapter of Emunah. She organised bazaars, coffee mornings, bring-and-buys sales, tombolas and dinners to raise money for Emunah projects in Israel.[27] Many of these events were held in the New Ambassador Hotel.[28] Similarly, Rita Brazil, the wife of Rabbi Samuel Brazil, *shomer* at the Normandie, assisted with organising the communal *mikveh* and the *chevra kadisha* (burial society) at BHC.[29]

The proprietors of the Big Eight hotels also supported non-Jewish causes. Maurice Guild, who owned the Langham, was the co-founder of the Jewish masonic lodge in Bournemouth (Sojourners Lodge No.7597, consecrated on 30 June 1958), which became known as 'the Fish Lodge' because no meat was served at its dinners.[30] Over the years, the lodge supported a number of local charities including the Zetland Court residential care home that replaced Branksome Dene.[31] When he died in 1969, it was said of Isaac Feld that 'he was generous in the support of charities, and no cause within or without the community appealed to him in vain'.[32] The Richman sisters, who loved classical music, are reported as having given generously to the Bournemouth Symphony Orchestra.[33]

Daniel Rosenthall, who took over ownership of Merivale Hall in the 1930s (see Chapter 2) became the president of BHC. He was the first of many hoteliers who were appointed to leadership positions in the *shul*. Over the years, the hoteliers who took on leading roles in the synagogue included: Geoffrey Feld from the Cumberland (treasurer, trustee and life-time president); Brian Lassman, general manager of the New Ambassador and then managing director of the Normandie (president); John Hayman from East Cliff Court (he was a founding member of BHC, several times its president and then a trustee); Maurice Guild from the Langham (president); and Ruby Marriott from the Green Park (he was a longstanding member of the board of management). Hotel guests also donated to the synagogue, including Charles Wolfson, brother of Sir Isaac Wolfson, who was a regular guest at the New Ambassador, and who presented two *Sifrei Torah* to BHC in memory of his parents.[34] When the Glencairn Manor opened in 1985, there was a direct link between it and BHC in that Paula Bright, co-owner of the hotel, was the daughter of Rabbi Indech, who served the community for over thirty years.

Working in the wider Jewish community, Joseph Grower founded a Jewish newspaper, the *Bournemouth Jewish Courier*, which served the Jewish community and ran for about three years under the editorship of Lionel Kochan, who went on to become a distinguished academic historian.[35]

70. Front cover of the first edition of the *Bournemouth Jewish Courier* run by Joseph Grower, proprietor of Hotel Rubens in Bath Road, 1949. Image courtesy of Ben Grower.

During the 1950s, Elkan Shapiro from the Mayfair Hotel ran a B'nai Akiva group. This role was taken over in the 1960s by Lydia Colman, the wife of Max Colman, the head chef at the Majestic.[36] Later on, Geoffrey Feld was prominent in establishing the Bournemouth Jewish Representative Council (see Chapter 5). In 1976, his nephew, Richard Inverne, formed a drama group, the Jewish Children's Theatre, for the children from both BHC and the Reform Synagogue, which ran annually until 1988:

> I formed the theatre group in 1976 for children aged 7 to 12 years old. We would perform a large-scale play, with a cast of about 40, just before *Pesach* each year, having rehearsed every Sunday afternoon from after *Sukkot*. I wrote and directed all but one of the plays myself, on Jewish biblical or historical themes – all very epic stuff – including my own versions of *The Ten Commandments,* James Michener's *The Source, Ben Hur* and *Exodus*, based on the Leon Uris novel, not the bible chapter! It was a very good way of bringing the two synagogues together.[37]

Jonathan Woolfson, who participated in the plays, recalls that the plays were 'very ambitious and became progressively more so!'[38]

Sylvia Kay, who ran Villa Judi, cooked for the cross-communal former day centre based at Bournemouth Reform Synagogue, and after the Cumberland was sold, Bluma Feld also helped to serve meals there. For over thirty years, Bluma's daughter-in-law, Susan Feld, was a longstanding trustee of the Hannah Levy House care home.

Several of the proprietors of the Big Eight hotels worshipped regularly at the Wootton Gardens Synagogue, including those who had *shuls* in their hotels. There were no weekday *minyanim* at the Green Park, since during the week Ruby Marriott preferred to *daven* at BHC. If there were guests staying at the hotel who also wanted to *daven* on weekdays, they accompanied Ruby in the taxi he took to the synagogue. Barbara Glyn tells us: 'As a member of the board of management at the *shul*, he said that it was important to ensure that BHC could always make up a *minyan*.'[39] One former local resident recalls that when the owners of the largest hotels attended services, they stood out somewhat because of their smart clothes and because they tended to sit separately from the rest of the congregation.[40]

The religious relationship also worked in the opposite direction. Dr John Crawford, a prominent member of BHC, regularly worshipped and participated in services held in the *shul* at the Normandie. He was a committed Zionist, a gifted Hebrew scholar and a good friend of Belle and Lou Keyne. He was the doctor on call for guests staying at the Normandie. Simon Keyne, son of Belle and Lou, recalls: 'He dealt with many indulged Jewish children with great patience. I remember him once being called out in the middle of the night to tend to a young boy experiencing discomfort because he had a bit of orange peel trapped beneath one of his nails!'[41] Sam Marks, another prominent member of BHC, and who lived in a house adjacent to the Normandie, was also a regular worshipper at the hotel *shul*.

Contribution to Civic Life in Bournemouth

In addition to their involvement in Jewish affairs, several of the hoteliers were involved in the wider community. Brian Lassman was a Bournemouth councillor for eight years from 1987 until 1995. Maurice Guild, owner of the Langham, was president of the Bournemouth Hotels and Boarding Houses' Association in 1962.[42] When he was elected to this role, following the usual practice of attending the president's place of worship for a special service, some 300 members of the Association attended a service at the Wootton Gardens Synagogue to honour Maurice and Fay Guild. Among those present were the Mayor and Mayoress of Bournemouth and several aldermen and councillors. Later, Geoffrey Feld from the Cumberland was the Association's secretary. Philip and Leslie Miller from East Cliff Manor and the Richman sisters from the Green Park were also involved with the Association.

Celebrations in the Hotels

From the beginning of the twentieth century, the larger Jewish hotels and boarding houses were used by members of Bournemouth's Jewish community to celebrate birthdays and life cycle events. Shortly after it opened in 1926, East Cliff Court hosted the wedding of Phyllis Lorie, the daughter of a founding member of BHC.[43] The even more memorable wedding reception for Doris Kasmir (daughter of the Bournemouth family who owned the well-known chain of clothing shops) was held in the same hotel on 3 September 1939. In Bournemouth it was a beautiful day, but across the Channel the British ambassador had handed a final note to the German government saying that, unless by 11am it announced plans to withdraw from Poland, a state of war would exist between Britain and Germany. At 11.15am, Prime Minister Neville Chamberlain declared on the radio that this British deadline had expired, and so the country was at war. The wedding celebration was overshadowed by the announcement, but never to be forgotten.[44]

After the end of the Second World War, celebrations were held in all of the Big Eight hotels, but the hotels most extensively used by local Jewish

קוֹל שָׂשׂוֹן וְקוֹל שִׂמְחָה קוֹל חָתָן וְקוֹל כַּלָּה

Mrs. Esther Davis

request the pleasure of the company of

....

at the Marriage of her daughter

Helen

to

Mark Woolfson

Ceremony on Sunday, 1st. April 1951 at 12.30 p.m.

at the

Synagogue Wootton Gardens, Bournemouth

Reception and Dance

at the Langham Hotel, Meyrick Road, Bournemouth

3 p.m. to 6 p.m.

R.S.V.P.—Bride :
    12, Thistlebarrow Road,
    Queens Park, Bournemouth.

Bridegroom :
    36, Churchill Road,
    Boscombe, Bournemouth.

71. Invitation to the wedding celebration for Helen Davis and Mark Woolfson held at the Langham Hotel, Meyrick Road, Bournemouth, 1951. Image courtesy of Jonathan Woolfson.

families were East Cliff Manor and the Langham. The number of celebrations held at the Langham increased significantly after the banqueting hall was added in 1963.

72. Wedding celebration for Helen Davis and Mark Woolfson held at the Langham Hotel, Meyrick Road, Bournemouth, 1951. Image courtesy of Jonathan Woolfson.

The Green Park maintained that it did not provide what was referred to as 'outside catering', and prioritised serving the guests staying at the hotel. However, exceptions were made for the families whom the proprietors knew well, such as the celebration for the marriage of Larry and Mandy Kaye (née Kasmir) in 1971 since the Kayes were good friends of the Marriotts.[45] The hotel also hosted events for 'deserving causes', such as the *Bar Mitzvah* of a boy whose mother was dying and who otherwise would not have been able celebrate the event.[46] The celebration of the 100th birthday of Harry Shoerats, a well-known member of BHC, was held at the New Ambassador in 1971.[47] Rochelle Selby, the daughter of Sam and Hilda Marks, prominent BHC members and close friends of the Felds, the Marriotts and the Richman sisters, held her engagement party at the Green Park. Her wedding reception was held in the New Ambassador so that the proprietors of the Green Park were able to relax and enjoy the celebration.[48] Henry Kesselman, son of one of the kosher butchers in Bournemouth, recalls that when he had his *Bar Mitzvah* in the Cumberland, the hotel presented him with a cake in the shape of an unrolled *Sefer Torah*. He says: 'It was so large that we were eating it for weeks afterwards.'[49]

Community Entertainment

In the years following the First World War, when the number of Jewish hotels and guest houses was expanding rapidly, many of the larger establishments began welcoming the local community to use their facilities, especially their ballrooms and dining rooms. The Trouville owned by the Polakoffs was particularly noted for its hospitality, and many local people went there for dinner dances.[50] The cocktail bar at the Manor Hotel and Club run by Lew Brandon became a rendezvous for visitors and residents alike.[51]

When the Jewish hotels were in their heyday, Jewish families living in Bournemouth came to regard them as a local resource. At a time when it was comparatively rare for Jews to eat out because of the complications surrounding *kashrut*, Jews in Bournemouth had a choice of high-class hotel restaurants at which they could dine. Kenny Arfin comments: 'The hotels opened up new horizons for the Bournemouth community, which they came to take for granted.'[52] While some families were only able to afford to enjoy the hotel restaurants on special occasions, others did so on a more regular basis. Each family had their preferred restaurant, but eating at the Green Park was generally regarded as being the ultimate treat.[53] Some couples who dined at the hotels stayed on for the dancing and other entertainment, to play cards or simply to chat with the hotel guests. Like the guests, they enjoyed the experience of dressing up for dinner and the glamour of hotel life.[54]

Other Bournemouth residents used the hotels for family get-togethers. Afternoon tea at one of the hotels was a favourite for families with young children. Many of the Jewish visitors knew people, or had relatives living in Bournemouth, whom they invited to the hotels where they socialised. When some people bought holiday flats in Bournemouth as a result of their enjoyable stays in the hotels, they continued to eat and participate in the dancing and other entertainment at the hotels. However, for some less well-off local people, the Big Eight hotels were 'another world' and 'off limits' unless they were invited to have dinner or tea there with better-off family and friends.[55]

Local residents were made particularly welcome at the hotels out of season and when trade started to decline in the mid-1960s. At that point, some of the hotels began to organise special events and offer deals to attract local people, such as the dinner dances held at the Cumberland and the 'fish and chip suppers' held at the Majestic, to which Fay Schneider invited top lecturers.[56] The suppers at the Majestic were succeeded by monthly dinners held alternately at the Cumberland and the Majestic at which MPs and well-known figures from the Jewish community spoke. These dinners, which cost just 15 shillings, were organised by the men's lodge of Bournemouth B'nai B'rith, supported by the women's lodge. They drew into the hotels up to 150 people, including many local residents. For several years they were regarded as 'the social event of the month'.[57]

At one point, the Green Park was offering a special deal of 7s 6d per head for afternoon tea and use of the hotel's swimming pool.[58] As a result, many local people learned to swim at the Green Park.[59] When Jews with young families started moving to Bournemouth in the 1970s and 1980s (see Chapter 5), a Young Marrieds' Group was set up, which held many of its get-togethers in the Jewish hotels.[60] Members of the group often met for picnics by the hotel swimming pools, or to use their putting greens. Although the hoteliers carefully monitored who came in and out of their hotels, some visitors were not as they seemed. Richard Inverne recalls:

There was a local chap, a member of the BHC congregation, who would sometimes come in just for a meal with friends visiting from London or wherever. I knew him slightly and we were always polite and friendly to each other. I had been told that he had a bit of a reputation, but I wasn't particularly concerned. To me he was a customer, so he was to be treated well. One night, he was leaving and went to the cloakroom to collect his raincoat. I happened to be standing in the hall and went over to chat and to help him on with the coat. As I did so, something heavy fell out of his coat pocket. I bent to retrieve it and then stood there a bit open-mouthed: it was a knuckle-duster! 'Mine, I think', he said with a smile. I returned it – I hope with grace – and asked if he had enjoyed dinner. 'I always do!' he returned – 'See you again soon!' and left. This was my one and only brush with the 'Underworld' at the Cumberland![61]

Since the hotel proprietors worked long hours, they did most of their socialising in their hotels, including with the close friends that they had made in the local community. Janet Pins (née Fay) recalls her parents were very friendly with Maurice and Fay Guild and spent many evenings with them at the Langham: 'The Guilds travelled a lot and brought back for me autographs of interesting people they had met on their holidays.[62] Likewise, the Kasmir family were close friends of Zena and Howard Inverne, part owners of the Cumberland, where the Kasmirs spent much of their social life.[63]

Young People

There was a particularly close relationship between the hotels and young people living in Bournemouth. The hotels were both the source of free entertainment and a means for young Jews from a provincial community to meet up with those from a metropolitan environment. Martin Green has commented: 'The hotels in Bournemouth played the same role as Lake Geneva in Wisconsin, which exposed local Jewish youth to the more sophisticated young Jews from Chicago.'[64] However, some of the hotels were more welcoming of young people than others. The Majestic was very attractive to young Bournemouth residents because of the high quality of its entertainment and the 'young crowd' that it attracted, but Fay Schneider was 'quite fussy' about who she allowed into the hotel. The Green Park did not really cater for young people. Anne Filer recalls: 'My parents were friendly with the Marriotts, but they still wouldn't let me in to enjoy the entertainment. They didn't want a noisy crowd of young people in there.'[65] Geoffrey Feld comments: 'Young people used to come into the Cumberland and I used to chase them out again!'[66]

During the 1950s, the Normandie and East Cliff Manor were apparently much more welcoming of young people, especially when they needed partners to dance with their young guests on Saturday and Sunday evenings. Rhona Taylor comments: 'It made the dances more lively – better than a lot of older people sitting around. And our parents were happy for us to be there because it kept us out of so-called trouble.'[67] In its early days, the Normandie was managed by Bob and Jules Myers. They had two sons, Royston and John, who went to school locally and also attended the BHC *cheder* where they became friendly with other young people living in Bournemouth. This may account for why the hotel is remembered as being very open at that time to teenagers and young adults. Many Bournemouth residents retain fond memories of dancing in the Normandie and eating the chocolate and sponge cakes that were served at 10pm. Janet Pins says: 'And it was all for free. We didn't pay for a thing!'[68] Local teenagers also went in search of free food on Saturday mornings. They made their way into the big hotels to partake of the lavish *Shabbat kiddushim* (see Chapter 6). They went from one hotel to another until they could eat no more, mingling with the visitors, and no one knew they were not hotel guests.[69]

The young people staying in the hotels and the young residents also met outside the hotels – on the beaches, in the cafés in the town centre, such as the Kilt café, and at meetings of the various Jewish youth groups. Rochelle Selby recalls that the well-known singer Helen Shapiro once came to stay at the Majestic to recuperate from a throat illness. While she was there, she accepted an invitation to attend a meeting of the local B'nai B'rith Youth Organisation (BBYO).[70] Hazel Green, who was brought up in Bournemouth, tells the story of a young man she knew who stayed at the Green Park and decided to join a HaNoar HaTzioni *Pesach* ramble: 'Because the hotel had no experience of making packed lunches during *Pesach*, the Green Park gave him half a chicken and a box of *matzah*. We had to share our food with him!'[71] Andy Kalmus, the niece of Fay Guild, often stayed at the Langham. She recollects: 'I used to join up with a group of young people. Some were hotel guests and others lived locally. We sometimes went from hotel to hotel and got up to no good. Other times we went to a party in someone's house.'[72] Hilary Myers recalls: 'The bottom of the zig-zag path was a very good place for meeting up with the young people staying in the hotels. You were often invited back to the hotels that otherwise wouldn't have been very welcoming of non-guests. I got engaged as a result of a meeting at the bottom of the zig-zag path, but it didn't last!'[73]

As they grew up, the young people, both the residents and the hotel guests, started to look for romance. Judi Lyons (née Kay), recalls sitting on the balcony of her friend's flat that overlooked the Cumberland, awarding points to the young men whom they spotted lounging around the swimming pool and discussing which of them they might be able to 'pull' at the hotel's dances: 'They thought that they were so cool, but we sometimes said to each other that they looked pale and a bit weedy compared to the local boys, who were often tanned and quite muscular from spending time on the beach.'[74] Local resident Anne Filer recalls going to the hotels in the hope of meeting exciting young men. She says: 'I fell in love every Saturday night!', and tells this story:

> For two years I dated a young man, who turned out to be a complete scoundrel. He lived in Plymouth where there was no entertainment, so he came to Bournemouth at weekends. He said he had to go home on a Saturday evening to work in his father's shop the next day. I later found out that he wasn't returning to Plymouth at all. Instead he was going on to meet his other girlfriend, who he saw just on Sundays, telling her that he didn't come out on *Shabbos*. However, he overlooked the fact that word gets around in the tightly-knit Jewish community![75]

Illustration 8. Young hotel guests meeting young people living in Bournemouth at the bottom of the zig-zag path. Drawing by Beverley-Jane Stewart.

When they reached a certain age, some young people were positively encouraged by their parents to go into the hotels in the hope that they would find 'a good match'. Edward Hayman recalls:

When she was about seventeen, the mother of Hilary Levy (now Myers) and my mother must have got together, because she was invited to our hotel [East Cliff Court] to spend the evening with my brother Ronald. She recalls being slightly nervous and being led through dark brown corridors to the family apartment at the top of the hotel. They were both shy and found little to talk about, a lost opportunity since it later transpired that they both had a great interest in theatre.[76]

Norman Shapiro tells the story of one enterprising young man who reached an agreement with Harry Taylor, one of the local photographers (see Chapter 8) who toured the big hotels. The agreement was that Harry Taylor would alert him when he spotted eligible and attractive young women staying in the hotels. Norman Shapiro recalls:

Harry had a good eye for these things. He once spotted a very beautiful young woman and he told my friend to get to the hotel as quickly as possible. When he arrived, he found the young woman in question dancing with someone. He liked what he saw and so he interrupted the dance. He pursued her for months and she eventually agreed to marry him.[77]

As well as being a source of entertainment and possible romance, the hotels were also a source of skills and learning. Nadia Rossi, whose father was the restaurant manager at the Normandie, recalls that she used to go to the hotel to receive clarinet lessons with the resident entertainer.[78]

The Smaller Hotels and Guest Houses

The smaller establishments were generally more integrated into the local community than the larger hotels. Many of the guest houses were run by women whose husbands had full-time jobs in the town where they met both Jews and non-Jews living in Bournemouth, such as Henry Kay whose wife ran Villa Judi. Henry had a barber's shop in Boscombe, which was used by a large number of Jewish men and was a hub for gossip and information. Judi Lyons recalls: 'My father always came home full of the latest news and sometimes also risqué stories, which he refused to repeat in front of me.'[79]

Like the proprietors of the large hotels, many of the guest-house owners were also very prominent in BHC, including Jules Segal who ran Hotel Florence and Elkan Shapiro, proprietor of the Mayfair Hotel, who served terms as president and treasurer and represented the Bournemouth Jewish community at the London Board of Shechita and the United Synagogue's Education Committee.[80] In addition, Elkan Shapiro, along with John Hayman (East Cliff Court) and Wolf Siefert (Hotel Rubens) represented BHC on the Board of Deputies of British Jews.[81] Tony Ricklow, proprietor of Mount Aishel, served on the BHC Board of Management, and for fourteen years he was the *shul's* senior warden.[82] Most of the children of the hoteliers and guest-house owners attended the BHC *cheder* and had their *Bar Mitzvahs* and were married at the *shul.*

The owners of the smaller hotels and guest houses also made a contribution to local charitable activities. For several years, William Pantel was the welfare officer and then the chairman of Bournemouth AJEX. The Palm Bay Hotel that he and his wife ran was often used as a venue for BHC communal events. Mr Citron, who ran Hotel Naturium in Kerley Road, served as treasurer of AJEX. For twelve years, Tony and Rose Ricklow ran an annual *Melava Malka* event (a meal that is customarily held by Jews after the end of *Shabbat*) at the Wootton Gardens Synagogue to raise money for charity. In 1976, the event, a dinner followed by a performance of *Joseph and the Amazing Technicolor Dreamcoat*, raised over £400 for the Women's Mizrachi Centre in Netanya.[83] The Ricklows also set up the Bournemouth branch of Emunah and subsequently raised money for Emunah projects by performing in various Jewish care homes and for friendship circles in the town.[84] Both the Ricklows and the Segals organised regular social evenings at their respective hotels to raise money for charity.[85] Jules Segal, owner of Hotel Florence, was the treasurer of the Jewish Blind Aid Committee that oversaw the running of the Dolly Ross home,[86] and Rose Ricklow was the chairman of Bournemouth Women's Mizrachi.[87]

While the Big Eight hotels purchased some goods from the kosher shops in Bournemouth, the smaller hotels and guest houses bought almost all of their supplies locally and were very friendly with the Jewish shopkeepers. Their clientele used many of the local cafés for their lunch and other facilities, such as the Pier Approach Baths. The smaller hotel and guest-house owners were friendly with the proprietors of the non-kosher holiday establishments, especially when they were run by Jewish people.

The entertainment at the Big Eight hotels might have been more star-studded, but local residents also enjoyed the entertainment in the smaller establishments. Like the Normandie, the Palm Bay attracted a 'young crowd' to its ballroom and other facilities since the Pantels' twin sons, Malcolm and Colin, were friendly with young people of the same age living in the town.[88] The Grosvenor held dances on a Saturday evening and was usually the last to stop its entertainment and to serve post-entertainment snacks. Anne Flor Szewczyk recalls: 'When we were doing the rounds of the hotels, we often ended up at the Grosvenor and stayed until they threw us out!'[89] The Grosvenor also became a popular venue for celebrations for the local Jewish community.

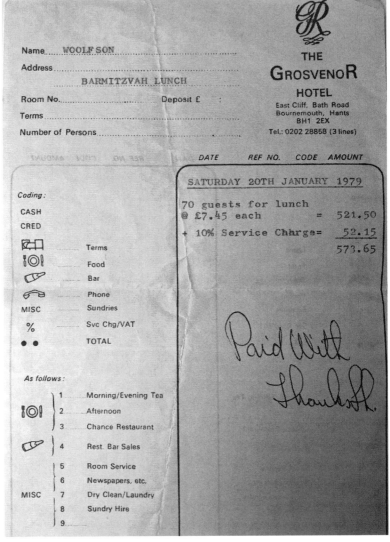

73. Local resident, Jonathan Woolfson's _Bar Mitzvah_ celebration at the Grosvenor Hotel, Bath Road, in 1979. Image courtesy of Jonathan Woolfson.

Notes

1. *JC*, 4.8.1939.
2. *Bournemouth Jewish Courier,* first edition, July/August 1949. Copy kindly provided by Ben Grower.
3. *JC*, 20.8.1993.
4. Ronald Hayman, *Secrets: Boyhood in a Jewish Hotel, 1932-1954* (London: Peter Owen, 1985), p.78 and pp.126-127.
5. Interview with Judi Lyons, 4.5.2020.
6. *JC*, 20.8.1993.
7. Nadia Rossi, response to author's post on Memories of Old Poole and Bournemouth Facebook Group, 21.11.2020.
8. Joanne Braddock, *ibid.*
9. Celia Rosamunde Wood, *ibid.*
10. Sue Goodwin, *ibid.*
11. *JC*, 25.12.1964.
12. See https://en.wikipedia.org/wiki/Training_and_enterprise_council.
13. Interview with Geoffrey Feld, 21.10.2020.
14. *JC*, 23.4.1908.
15. During the Second World War, Lady Sassoon is said to have played an active part in rescuing Jewish families from Nazi Europe, bringing them to the UK via Bournemouth.
16. *JC*, 16.12.1932.
17. For example, see, *JC*, 28.4.1967.
18. Interview with Janet Pins, 27.8.2020.
19. *JC*, 1.1.1994.
20. Interview with Ben Grower, 22.11.2020.
21. *Ibid.*
22. *JC*, 13.5.1966.
23. *JC*, 3.4.1964.
24. *JC*, 1.8.1975.
25. *JC*, 1.11.1963.
26. *JC*, 14.10.1977.
27. Email from Miriam Marcus, 2.12.2020.
28. See for example, *JC*, 15.1.1988.
29. *JC*, 24.10.1999.
30. Interview with Brian Lassman, 14.5.2020.
31. See http://www.hantsandiowprovincialhistory.co.uk/privincialhistoryPDF/Sojourners7597.
32. *JC*, 29.8.1979.
33. Interview with Judi Lyons, 4.5.2020.
34. Ivor Weintroub, David Weitzman, Stephen H. White, *Bournemouth Hebrew Congregation Centenary 1905-2005: A Celebration in Writing and Pictures of the Congregation's First 100 Wonderful Years* (Bournemouth: Zethics, 2005), p.25.
35. Interview with Ben Grower, son of Joseph Grower, 22.11.2020.
36. Email from Miriam Marcus, 2.12.2020.
37. Email from Richard Inverne, 18.11.2020.
38. Conversation with Jonathan Woolfson, 12.12.2020.

39. Interview with Barbara Glyn, 1.6.2020.
40. Anonymous interviewee, 14.5.2020.
41. Conversation with Simon Keyne, 2.2.2021.
42. Email from Josephine Jackson, 7.6.2020.
43. *Sunderland Daily Echo*, 18.11.1926.
44. Memory posted on the website eastcliffcourtmemories.wordpress.com/blog/.
45. Interview with Larry and Mandy Kaye (née Kasmir), 11.6.2020.
46. Interview with Barbara Glyn, 1.6.2020.
47. Interview with Joan Doubtfire, 13.5.2020. He was dubbed 'Britain's oldest man' when he died at the age of 111.
48. Interview with Rochelle Selby, 10.5.2020.
49. Henry Kesselman, speaking at the talk given by Geoffrey Feld by Zoom at Bournemouth Hebrew Congregation, 17.6.2020.
50. Interview with Rhona Taylor, niece of Herman Polakoff, 5.5.2020.
51. *JC*, 18.6.1937.
52. Interview with Kenny Arfin, 6.5.2020.
53. Interview with Judi Lyons, 4.5.2020.
54. Interview with Anne Filer, 30.4.2020.
55. Interview with Judi Lyons, 4.5.2020.
56. Interview with Rosamunde Bloom, 10.6.2020.
57. Conversation with Geoffrey Feld, 29.11.2020.
58. Interview with Hazel Green, 25.8.2020.
59. Interview with Esther Schneider, 3.9.2020.
60. Interview with Anne Flor Szewczyk, 26.4.2020.
61. Email from Richard Inverne, 19.8.2020.
62. Interview with Janet Pins, 27.8.2020.
63. Interview with Larry and Many Kaye (née Kasmir), 11.6.2020.
64. Email from Martin Green, 21.9.2020.
65. Interview with Anne Filer, 30.4.2020.
66. Interview with Geoffrey Feld, 4.5.2020.
67. Interview with Rhona Taylor, 6.5.2020.
68. Interview with Janet Pins, 27.8.2020.
69. Anonymous interviewee, 16.5.2020.
70. Interview with Rochelle Selby, 10.5.2020.
71. Interview with Hazel Green, 25,8.2020.
72. Interview with Andy Kalmus, 24.9.2020.
73. Conversation with Hilary Myers, 30.11.2020.
74. Interview with Judi Lyons, 4.5.2020.
75. Interview with Anne Filer, 30.4.2020.
76. See https://eastcliffcourtmemories.wordpress.com/blog/.
77. Interview with Norman Shapiro, 23.10.2020.
78. Conversation with Nadia Rossi, 5.1.2021.
79. Conversation with Judi Lyon (née Kay), 14.10.2020.
80. *JC*, 13.11.1959.
81. *Bournemouth Jewish Courier,* first edition, July/August 1949. Copy kindly provided by Ben Grower.

82. See Weintroub, Weitzman and White, *Bournemouth Hebrew Congregation Centenary*, p.29 and p.102.
83. *JC*, 23.1.1972.
84. *JC*, 24.6.1994.
85. *JC*, 8.10.1971.
86. *JC*, 8.10.1971.
87. *JC*, 14.10.1977.
88. Interview with Geoffrey Feld, 19.6.2020.
89. Email from Anne Flor Szewczyk, 17.11.2020.

10

The Jewish Hotels of Bournemouth: Their History and Legacy

A Strong Sense of Nostalgia

Over the last nine chapters we have followed the rise and decline of the Jewish hotels and guest houses of Bournemouth, set within the context of Anglo-Jewish history, the evolution of Bournemouth as a holiday resort and the development of the local Jewish community. The book has also explored different aspects of hotel life – food, religion and entertainment – and also the relationship between the hotels and guest houses (referred to generically as 'the hotels' to avoid cumbersome sentences) and the local community.

What is immediately striking about the history of the hotels is the sense of nostalgia that surrounds it. The book is largely based on oral history interviews, and it is therefore not surprising that when asked about their memories, people tended to focus on the good times and happy moments. Nevertheless, the extent of the nostalgia is still remarkable. A former Green Park guest comments: 'In the words of the song: Those were the days my friend. We thought that they would never end.'[1] Paul Harris, who stayed at the Normandie many times during the 1960s, remarks: 'I am the editor of the *Jewish Telegraph* group of newspapers and an accredited travel writer. My job takes me all over the world and none of the places I have been are as memorable as the times I spent in Bournemouth as a child and when I was a teenager.'[2] Similarly, his brother Jon Harris recalls wistfully:

> We were good boys, but not totally innocent, we pushed the boundaries a bit. We played a few pranks, such as going along the hotel corridors late at night and swapping around the shoes that had been left out for cleaning. The holidays were a bit like the Famous Five in the Enid Blyton stories. We got into scrapes and there was an air of excitement about it all. For me, the hotels represent a time of innocence and happiness.[3]

As a result of the treasured memories of past Jewish holidaymakers, Bournemouth is often referred to as 'Nostalgia-by-Sea'.[4] Many former hotel guests return to Bournemouth on a regular basis, sometimes just for a day, to revisit old haunts. Valerie Gaynor says: 'I have lunch at the Cumberland, walk along the front to the pier and get a taxi back to the station.'[5] For many years the Association of Jewish Refugees ran annual holidays to Bournemouth to recapture the holiday memories of their members.

The reasons for this level of nostalgia are not difficult to discern: the feeling of warmth that came from staying in a hotel where you were surrounded by other Jews, which created a sense of community; the family atmosphere that pervaded the hotels because they were mainly family-owned and run and because of the way in which the owners went out of their way to make their guests feel they were part of one big family; the friendly and open atmosphere of the hotels that resulted from Jews going to Bournemouth with the specific aim of enjoying themselves and being entertained; the sense of continuity that came from meeting the same people at the same time of year, having the same bedroom and sitting at the same table where you were served by the same waiter; the glamour, luxury and personal service that was such a feature of the large hotels; and staying in a hotel that was set within a beautiful environment and in a 'classy' town. Any one of these factors would have led to fond memories, but in combination they generated a legend of holidays when the sun always shone.

When interviewed for this book, perhaps inevitably, people were eager to talk particularly about the 'Golden Era' of the Bournemouth hotels and tended to be less interested in discussing how run down some of the hotels became in their declining years. In many people's minds, the history of the hotels is limited to the three decades following the Second World War, and relatively little thought is given to either their rise or their demise, the reasons for which are, to historians at least, as interesting as the explanations for their heyday.

There was also a tendency for interviewees to dwell on the glamour and the glitz of the Big Eight hotels at the expense of the smaller and less luxurious hotels and guest houses which, as we have seen, were very much part of the Jewish holiday trade in Bournemouth, and gave rise to equally warm memories amongst those who stayed in them and were run by some intriguing individuals. In fact, the diversity of the accommodation available in Bournemouth was one of the reasons why it was so successful and popular as a Jewish resort – it catered for people with a wide range of incomes and at different stages in their employment and family lifecycles.

The Historical Significance of the Hotels and Guest Houses

Neither the strong sense of nostalgia that permeates people's recollections, nor their concentration on a particular era and a limited range of the Jewish holiday establishments detract from the historical significance of the hotels. Throughout their history, the Jewish hotels of Bournemouth have played a key role in meeting the needs of the Anglo-Jewish community, which changed beyond recognition during the course of the twentieth century. The needs that the hotels met changed as the aspirations and lifestyles of the community as a whole, and those of individuals and different groups within it, evolved.

At the end of the nineteenth century, the main purpose of the Jewish boarding houses, as they were then called, was to accommodate those who were in need of respite from their daily lives, or who visited Bournemouth to convalesce. This was still their predominant role in the early years of the twentieth century, but by the outbreak of the First World War, when the number of Jewish establishments increased rapidly, they were becoming a means for Jews to escape the cramped confines of their homes and workplaces and the overcrowding of the areas in which a large proportion of Jews still lived. As mentioned in Chapter 2, advertisements for Jewish guest houses in the years before and after the First World War emphasised their spaciousness and the healthy environment in which they were set. Tuberculosis was rampant in the semi-ghetto areas, so clean air, sunshine and proximity to nature were seen as being the best prescription for tired and ailing people. The Jewish-owned and run guest houses (their name was now changing) that opened in the early part of the twentieth century allowed Jews to enjoy the benefits of Bournemouth without having to leave their religious practices behind in the city.

During the 1920s, another trend became detectable: the larger establishments started to cater for Jews who were upwardly mobile and were aspiring to take holidays rather than to escape the crowded city. While the concept of leisure did not form any part of life in the *shtetlach* in which their parents had lived, or where they themselves had spent their early years, there was now the beginnings of a Jewish leisured class, desiring to enjoy the same luxuries and comforts as the non-Jews amongst whom they were now living, including taking a holiday. Until then holidays had been decidedly reserved for *yenem* (others) – non-Jews and the Jewish elite families that had long been established in Britain.

In the interwar years, an increasing number of Jews were beginning to make their way to British coastal resorts, especially those within easy reach of the places where they lived. However, Bournemouth's growing reputation as a fashionable place to take a holiday more readily satisfied the middle-class aspirations of the new suburban residents, a proportion of whom had become quite prosperous during the war years (see Chapter 2). The American historian Phil Brown has commented that having the monetary means to take a holiday signified that 'the immigrant was no longer a greenhorn but a citizen of the world and it helped immigrants feel part of their new homeland'.[6] It was the social aspirations of upwardly mobile Jews that led to the establishment of the first Jewish hotels, which were quite distinct from the guest houses, and also to the competition amongst them to respond to the ever-rising expectations of their clientele.

Despite the depression of the early 1930s, the number of Jewish hotels in Bournemouth expanded even more rapidly than in the postwar years, and the emphasis on luxury became ever more apparent. Even for the smaller establishments, providing comfort as well as space and food was now the order of the day. Alongside an increasing desire for conspicuous consumption, a growing awareness of the rise of Nazism in Europe may have been a factor in accounting for the expansion of the entertainment offered in the Jewish hotels in Bournemouth during the 1930s (discussed in Chapter 8). There was now a mounting need for attention to be diverted from what was happening in Germany and elsewhere, and the threat of a second world war.

During the Second World War, the hotels became a refuge and a source of respite for Jews serving on the front-line and Jews remaining in the cities, who were disproportionately affected by the German bombing. However, Jewish hoteliers were already looking forward to better times. The opening of the Green Park in the midst of war was a signal of the commencement of a changed role and a new era for Jewish holiday accommodation in Bournemouth.

The Jewish community that emerged from the Second World War was not only deeply traumatised by the Holocaust, but also acutely aware of the burden of responsibility it bore as the largest and only intact Jewish community in Europe. As a result, in the immediate postwar years, the prime role of the Jewish hotels was to help Jews to forget, or at least to come to terms with the grief and horror they had escaped, but which had engulfed millions of Jews on the European continent, including their friends and relations. The hotels did this by providing a place where Jews could feel safe and obtain comfort from being in the company of other Jews while their basic needs were met, especially in ensuring, in typical Jewish tradition, that they had enough kosher food to eat. David Abrahams comments:

'Whenever the Jewish hotels were discussed at that time, people always asked: "How was the food?"'[7]

A variety of explanations have been offered for the prominence of food in the Bournemouth hotels in the postwar years (see Chapter 6 for a more detailed discussion), one of which is that eating was a source of solace from the pain of the Holocaust. Geoffrey Alderman states: 'They were celebrating their endurance and vitality after the horrors of the 1940s – eating, perhaps, to assuage the guilt of their own survival and attempting to enter into a dialogue with their Maker through the medium of food.'[8] Other explanations include suggestions that the emphasis on eating was a reaction to the limited availability of food, and sometimes even hunger, experienced during the war; that it was a means of demonstrating the success of those who were able to afford to eat to their hearts' content;[9] and that it was a symbol of how far people were now removed from the poverty of *shtetl* life. David Latchman comments: 'There was a certain elegance to being able to ask for a double portion of food, even if you only wanted to taste it, when back in Eastern Europe, people had barely been able to afford to eat.'[10] Of course, these explanations are not mutually exclusive.

The Bournemouth hotels in the years immediately following the Second World War can be compared to the spas that grew up in Western Bohemia in the latter part of the nineteenth century and endured until the late 1930s. The main resorts were Marienbad, Carlsbad and Franzensbad. They were sociable and urbane places, the setting for celebrity sightings, match-making and stylish promenading. In her book, *Next Year in Marienbad: The Lost Worlds of the Jewish Spa Culture*,[11] Mirjam Tiendl-Zadoff describes how trips to the spas in Bohemia became disproportionately popular with the Jewish middle classes, to the extent that a Jewish subculture developed. During the holiday season, shops sold Yiddish and Hebrew newspapers, kosher kitchens were opened and public readings catered for the Jewish clientele. This development took place in an era when the area of Bohemia in which the resorts were located was becoming increasingly nationalistic and antisemitic out of season. As a result, the resorts became 'destinations of temporary mass flight', which is a description that could be applied to the Jewish hotels of Bournemouth in the immediate postwar years.

Bournemouth provided a safe Jewish space not only for Jews who had mainly been born in Britain, but also for a group of more recent arrivals – the continental refugees, who had arrived in waves during the 1930s. These refugees were largely but not exclusively from Germany and Austria. A significant proportion of the newcomers were well-to-do professionals, business people and artists, who had been highly assimilated in the countries they had left. Some were able to bring with them the resources to embark on a new life. One of the types of business that was set up by the refugees was boarding houses. Their main clientele was other refugees with limited means who were newly-arrived in Britain, or who were still in the process of establishing themselves. The continental boarding houses became social centres for those who stayed in them, 'a focal point for refugee life' in a strange country and 'oases of familiar continental life and culture', as well as a source of income for those who ran them.[12]

Initially, the continental boarding houses were opened in the areas of north-west London where the refugees mainly settled, but they later opened in other areas, including in British coastal resorts. In this new setting they abounded during the 1950s, and evolved from boarding houses offering affordable accommodation to become more substantial guest houses and small private hotels.[13] Their main purpose was to provide refugees with a break from London. They offered the company of people from similar backgrounds, speaking the same language and who had faced the trauma of forced emigration. They served continental food to those who were still struggling with the British diet. Chapter 4 mentions several such establishments that opened in Bournemouth, such as Ashdale, Simar House and the Continental Hotel. They were prime examples of Jewish spaces that provided a safe, congenial, familiar and recognisable environment for refugees as they transitioned to becoming British citizens. Even after they closed, the proprietors of these guest houses continued to inject a continental aspect to the local Jewish community by founding Bournemouth Continental Circle, which met at the Cumberland.[14]

For some people, the need for safe places and a period of contemplation, reflection and adaptation lasted longer than for others. However, a desire to move on began to emerge, even though the guilt of survival was to linger for another generation. By the late 1940s and early 1950s, the main narrative amongst the Jewish hotel guests (except perhaps for the continental refugees) was: 'We arrived as penniless immigrants, we put down roots and began to prosper, we survived the war and the Holocaust. We are now bona fide British citizens, living alongside non-Jews, and we want make our mark on society, share in its rewards for hard work, and to have fun.' One commentator has suggested: 'They had nothing to lose, only to gain and they wanted to enjoy life.'[15] As a result, the social attractions of being in a hotel in Bournemouth rapidly eclipsed the hotels' healing powers. Several decades previously, Jewish visitors to Bournemouth had sought secluded vacations; now they wanted to join the throng and participate in Jewish group activities. Marian Stern recalls:

My father always looked forward to his annual holiday in Bournemouth, having worked so hard at his sewing machine from 7am to 9pm for fifty weeks a year making wedding dresses together with my mother. Their workshop was in our home, so their work was all around them. My father therefore revelled in the warmth of the welcome at the hotel, and meeting up with familiar faces again, many of them old friends from the East End of London. He became the life and soul of the party, with people surrounding him while he regaled them with jokes. He just adored being part of a crowd and I loved seeing him relaxed and happy.[16]

The hotels were quick to respond to the changing outlook of the ever-increasing numbers of Jews now visiting Bournemouth. In keeping with Jewish tradition, more Jews followed in the footsteps of those who saw Bournemouth as the destination of choice. A contemporary Jewish writer commented on this phenomenon:

Jews, I am aware, are gregarious, and they like to be where they are reasonably certain others will be, and the concentration then tends to be cumulative, more going where more go, while the less-popular resorts become less popular. The word only needs to go around that a place is full for Jews to descend upon it from every quarter.[17]

David Abrahams, who holidayed with his parents in Bournemouth in the 1950s, comments:

Wherever Jews lived, the Jewish hotels in Bournemouth became a regular topic of conversation. Bournemouth was the place to be; you weren't anyone if you hadn't stayed at a hotel in Bournemouth, particularly one of the larger ones.[18]

Having visited the hotels, an American journalist commented: 'There is hardly an Anglo-Jewish family of note that has not favoured the hotels with their custom.'[19]

The hotels became increasingly luxurious and provided more and more facilities and amenities to entertain their guests. The Big Eight hotels were the epitome of the new era with their ostentatious glamour and the opportunities they provided for their guests to display their increasing prosperity, as much to their fellow Jews as to the world in general. The rarefied atmosphere of the hotels was consciously cultivated by their owners. However, even for those who could not afford to stay in the more upmarket hotels, at least not initially, there was still a sense of upward mobility that came from taking a holiday in Bournemouth rather than in resorts such as Westcliff-on-Sea, Cliftonville, Whitley Bay, Blackpool and St Anne's. Marian Stern recalls:

> Before the Second World War, our extended family used to go on holiday to Cliftonville. The family took over a hotel for two weeks at the beginning of August. After the war, when my parents had a bit more money, they were able to afford to stay in Bournemouth, at first for a week and later, as their business grew, for two weeks. Having struggled through the war years, it was a big thing for them to go to Bournemouth rather than Cliftonville.[20]

The changes that took place in the role played by the Jewish hotels were neither straightforward nor linear, and the Bournemouth hotel experience was not the same for everyone. However, what is particularly interesting about the hotels is their egalitarianism. While they may have been largely eschewed by 'the grandees' – the small number of families that had dominated Anglo-Jewry prior to the mass immigration of Jews from Eastern Europe – they were open to anyone who could gather the means to pay for a holiday in Bournemouth. Hettie Marks tells us: 'It didn't matter how you got your money, you were just another guest, one of the clan, so to speak.'[21]

In the postwar years, there was a great variation in the wealth and social standing of the guests who gathered in the Big Eight hotels, and to a lesser extent in the smaller hotels. Some guests were either already very affluent, or were well on their way to becoming rich and famous. A generation previously, they would mainly have stayed in luxurious, non-Jewish hotels, but now they were more comfortable holidaying with other Jews, including those who were less well-off and came from more humble backgrounds. The guests were fully aware of the differences that existed between them. Clive Gold, who grew up in Portsmouth, recollects:

> A lot of the people staying in the hotels when we started going there had made money in the *schmatte* [clothing] trade. We noticed a big difference between ourselves as provincial Jews and the London crowd. The Londoners were more outgoing and up front about being Jewish, while my family took a much lower profile and were careful not to attract the attention of non-Jews. We had a Yiddish phrase

that we used, which meant 'Keep quiet, the Christians are watching us'. We also thought the Londoners were really wealthy. I remember a whip round being organised for a Jewish charity and someone giving a ten-shilling note [50p], which I thought was an absolute fortune.[22]

However, the hotels, which became the nexus of Anglo-Jewish social life, were great levellers and the guests generally mingled enthusiastically with each other whatever their backgrounds, which was encouraged by the hoteliers. Hettie Marks again comments: 'We were not wealthy, but we were comfortably off. We were aware that there were people staying in the hotel who were very rich. However, we didn't feel inferior in any way. We owned clothes shops, so we dressed quite nicely and the hotel owners treated people like kings and queens whatever their background.'[23] Similarly, Sheila Morris recalls: 'When we were staying at the Majestic one year, there was a large group of black-cab drivers from Essex on holiday there at the same time. They were a hoot and we had a great time socialising with them.'[24] This impartiality is captured in Gerda Charles's 1961 satirical novel *The Crossing Point*, which devotes a large section to describing a stay in fictitious Whytecliffe Sands (Bournemouth) at the Berkeley Hotel (possibly the Cumberland) situated on Great Rock (the East Cliff). Leo, one of the fictitious guests at the hotel, pontificates:

> Consider first of all that everyone here is bound together in a particular, homogenous mass in a way that no collection of guests in a non-Jewish hotel can ever be. In a way this is more like an ocean liner than a hotel. But a liner with only one class of cabin, that's the difference. Here, we all eat together, we are all entertained together, we all *pray* together. This morning in *shool* [sic] I had on one side of me a Mr Freiwinkel who told me – with pride mark you – (and why not?) – that he has a good, little greengrocery business in Paddington. On my other side, saying his prayers with a sort of slick dignity – but I suppose that we ought to be grateful that he says them at all – was Mr Edward Silky, stockbroker to His Majesty, Carl Morris, our happiest millionaire...[25]

In addition, the hotel guests were very diverse in their religious observance, which was tolerated and accepted provided the breaking of 'rules' was not too overt (see Chapter 7). David Latchman comments: 'In the hotels there were much bigger differences than those of social class and religious observance, such as the differences between the bridge and non-bridge players.[26]

The Big Eight hotels became ever more renowned for their indulgence, bordering on excess, but beneath the surface there were some more serious processes at play. Although a number of recent studies have helped to fill the gap, such as Panayi's *An Immigration History of Britain*[27] and Kahn-Harris's and Gidley's *Turbulent Times*[28] (although their analysis commences in 1990, therefore not covering much of the period we have been considering), it is still the case that Anglo-Jewish history tends to concentrate on the development of the community (and immigration in particular) in the years prior to the Second World War. This gives the impression that the evolution of Anglo-Jewry was complete by 1945 and that developments of the postwar era are of lesser interest and significance or somehow less worthy of study. However, the history of the Jewish hotels in Bournemouth illustrates that this was far from being the case; the Anglo-Jewish community (and individuals within it) was still in transition and acculturation was still in progress, albeit at a much faster pace than in the years before 1945, described by Todd Endelman in his seminal work on Anglo-Jewish assimilation.[29]

The Jewish hotels played a key role in accelerating the acculturation process by enabling large numbers of Jews to enjoy holidays comparable to those of the majority population, and by providing a place where the *nouveaux riches* could display and test out their recently acquired manners without exposing themselves to the possible derision of the established upper and middle classes. The extent to which they were able to relax in Bournemouth is illustrated by the way in which the hotel guests did not take themselves too seriously and were able to recognise and mock their own pretensions. For example, guests staying at the Green Park often referred to the hotel's Louis Quatorze lounge as the 'Louis Carthorse Room',[30] or 'Louis Kahn's'.[31] For many Jews, the postwar period was still about reinvention, about making yourself into something different.

However, perhaps of even greater significance was the role that the hotels played in fostering and helping to create a new Anglo-Jewish identity. In Chapter 3 it is argued that during the postwar years an Anglo-Jewish identity emerged that was not the result of a fusion of the longstanding Jewish community with that of the Eastern European immigrants, but an entirely new outlook that was fashioned by changing aspirations and circumstances. The new identity, which was liberal and unassuming, was one that was specific to Britain and quite distinct from the Jewish identity that emerged in other countries. One commentator has suggested that the generation of Jews that came of age in the decade following the Second World War 'twin tracked': they 'dressed British and thought Yiddish', they adopted British norms, whilst simultaneously retaining their Jewishness.[32]

The extent to which the Jewish hotels of Bournemouth contributed to the development of this new identity is quite remarkable. They did so by providing a non-threatening environment in which Jews felt safe to be themselves and express their culture while partaking of the British penchant for holidaying at the seaside. One man has speculated on his father's reasons for staying at the Green Park as follows: 'He spent all year pretending to be part of the English aristocracy, and once a year it was a relief to go to a place where people were just like him. He could stop trying to blend in, eat *matzah* and boiled eggs if he wanted to and revisit his roots, if just for a weekend.'[33]

In his paper, 'Des Espaces Autres', the French philosopher Michel Foucault wrote about 'other places', what he referred to as 'heterotopia' (in French *hétérotopie*), which function as a 'counter-site' to everyday life, where everything is lovely and the trips to which are suggestive of pilgrimages. Foucault puts forward several types of heterotopia, including spaces that allow for the affirmation of differences and have more layers of meaning than immediately meet the eye.[34] The hotels of Bournemouth are a prime example of such spaces. In describing the Jewish hotels, interviewees for this book frequently referred to the hotels using words such as 'a world apart', 'far removed from our normal lives' and 'a kind of Shangri-La, an ideal type of place'. Other typical comments were: 'You left the outside world behind when you were in Bournemouth', and 'The hotels were in a realm of fantasy, a place where you could go to escape the reality of your everyday life.'[35]

The environment provided by the hotels was not only safe, it was also distinctly Jewish. The hotels served their guests traditional Jewish food, organised entertainment and leisure activities that appealed specifically to Jews and the larger hotels even had their own synagogues, all of which reinforced Jewish identity (vastly aided of course by the establishment of the State of Israel), and also to build confidence in that identity. James Inverne comments: 'At the Jewish hotels in Bournemouth Jewishness was toned up rather than toned down.'[36] Contemporary commentators pointed in particular to the religious licensing of the Jewish hotels in Bournemouth and elsewhere as a major factor in maintaining Jewish identity in the postwar era by promoting a greater awareness of *kashrut*, which had been declining in the pre-war years.[37] In turn, this increased awareness of *kashrut* contributed to the boom in the kosher hotels during the 1950s and early 1960s.

Although the hotels allowed their guests to embrace, maintain and develop their Jewish identity, religious observance was not mandatory, even in the more orthodox hotels, such as the Green Park (see Chapter 7). Some guests were much more attracted by the opportunity to savour Jewish culture than to practise Jewish religion. While many families continued to holiday elsewhere in the postwar years and Jewish hotels still flourished in other resorts, it was recognised that they did not offer the same intensity of Jewish experience as the hotels in Bournemouth.

As mentioned in the Introduction to this book, to date comparatively little has been written about the Jewish hotels of Bournemouth, especially their decline. The few brief comments on their demise have commonly pointed to the rise of affordable air travel, package holidays and the opening up of Israel as a travel destination. They also mention a number of other factors that resulted in changes in holiday patterns for the population as a whole and not just Jewish holidaymakers: the increased number of women entering the employment market, geographic mobility and family dispersal, and rising prosperity. Less frequently cited are the specifically Jewish reasons for the decline of the Jewish hotels and guest houses, notably the polarisation of Anglo-Jewry, which meant that holiday accommodation that had been largely predicated on the homogeneity of Anglo-Jewry was no longer appropriate, and the increasing cost of providing kosher food and licensing the hotels, especially as the requirements of the various licensing bodies became stricter (see more detailed discussion in Chapter 5).

However, while all these factors certainly contributed to the decline of the hotels and guest houses, there is an even more important but perhaps less obvious reason for their demise, which is that they were a victim of their own success. By playing a major role in producing an integrated, self-confident and thriving Jewish community, the hotels were now no longer necessary and the formula that had worked so well for three decades, and on which the hotels had built their reputation, was no longer relevant. By the 1980s, Jews were penetrating an expanding range of middle-class occupations, small shops had been replaced by significant businesses and small-scale landlords had become successful property dealers, demonstrating that their assimilation was now nearing completion. The new generation of Jews wanted a very different type of holiday experience from their parents and grandparents, especially in terms of food, entertainment and environment. There were now many more places where single young people could meet and none of the new Jewish cookery recommended heavy kosher meals. Some Jews even came to regard the hotels as a tasteless extravagance as depicted in the satirical novels of authors such as Gerda Charles and Bernard Kops. In addition, the rise of a multicultural society meant that it was now possible for Jews to display their religious affiliations publicly rather than expressions of Jewishness being confined to specific Jewish settings, such as kosher hotels.

The argument that the success of the Jewish hotels contributed to their demise, is echoed by the American historian David Stradling. Commenting on the decline of the Catskills resorts, Stradling suggests that the collapse of the 'Borscht Belt' as a Jewish enclave was directly related to the notion that 'the Catskills had become a recognizable brand, conjuring images of a distinct hotel style, forms of entertainment, and even stereotypical guests' and that 'the very thing that had made the hotels popular, eventually contributed to their decline'.[38]

Beyond the 1980s, a small number of Jews continued to enjoy the type of holiday experience to which a large proportion of Anglo-Jewry had previously aspired, hence the continuation of the middle-of-the-road New Ambassador, but its clientele was ever reducing. That the market had changed is underlined by the short life of the two smaller hotels that opened after most of the Jewish hotels had disappeared – the Glencairn Manor and the Acacia Gardens (see Chapter 5). This decline was not peculiar to Bournemouth. By the 1980s the *Jewish Chronicle* was regretting the 'tragic' decrease in the demand for Jewish hotels in many coastal resorts, despite the fact that they still 'gave marvellous value in a truly Jewish atmosphere'.[39]

A Comparison with the Catskills

The finer nuances of the historical significance of the Bournemouth hotels are brought out by comparing the Bournemouth holiday establishments with the Catskill resorts with which they are often equated. There are many similarities in their respective histories, perhaps the most obvious of which is that the years of their rise, zenith and decline are virtually identical. Like the Jewish hotels, the Catskill resorts came to the fore during the first two decades of the twentieth century, had experienced their heyday by the mid-1960s and by the 1980s were being seen as a thing of the past, even though a small number of establishments remained open. In common with the Bournemouth hotels, the Catskill resorts commenced as a place to recuperate and escape from city life, especially the tenements of New York's Lower East Side, and later became a place to have fun and to be entertained.

Like the Bournemouth hotels, the Catskills resorts were set in an area of outstanding beauty, albeit in the mountains rather than by the sea, which added to their 'other worldly' atmosphere.

Another major similarity is that food was paramount. In both Bournemouth and the Catskills, the Jewish hoteliers prided themselves on providing a personal, high-quality dining experience, and the meals were virtually non-stop. In the Catskills, 'every night was a banquet' and people dressed for the occasion; guests were able to order what they wanted 'and send it back if it wasn't to their liking'; they were 'served with grandeur'; the diet was mainly Eastern European, Ashkenazi food and, to differing degrees, *kashrut* was observed.[40] However, the quantities of food appear to have been even larger in the Catskills than in the Bournemouth hotels. Hettie Marks, who holidayed for many years in Bournemouth and later had a holiday at the Concord (the largest of the resorts) in the Catskills, recalls being shocked by her first dining experience there: 'I was overwhelmed by the variety of food that was available. The food I was served was more than I could possibly eat and then the waiter asked me if I wanted to order a side dish!'[41] Geoffrey Feld comments: 'The hotels could have fed the developing world on the amount of food that they threw away.'[42]

Other similarities include: the fact that Catskill resorts were mainly family-owned and the women proprietors were very prominent in their running (see discussion in Chapter 3); there was a range of provision to suit all pockets; their egalitarian atmosphere (see discussion above); the tendency for guests to stay in the same resort at the same time each year; Jewish religion was an integral part of resort life and services were mainly orthodox in their manner; and the way in which the hotel staff were integral to resort life. Like the Bournemouth hotels, the Catskill resorts were full to overflowing during *Pesach* and other Jewish festivals and holy days, even when the resorts were waning, and there has been a recent revival of Jewish life in the area as a new generation has started to rediscover the beauty of the Catskills and their proximity to New York City.[43]

However, there are also some very important differences between the Bournemouth hotels and the Catskill resorts. In his book *First Resorts*, the American historian Jon Sterngass argues that the blatant exclusion of New York Jews from one hotel after another (such as the Grand Union Hotel in Saratoga Springs, the Manhattan Beach Hotel in Coney Island), propelled them to create their own 'land of leisure' in the Catskill mountains.[44] This segregation was reinforced by a number of factors, including the location of the Jewish resorts in a comparatively remote area and their clientele being drawn almost exclusively from one area – New York City and its environs.

By contrast, while pre-war visitors to Bournemouth had experienced a certain level of antisemitism (notably at the hands of Oswald Mosley's British Union of Fascists), it was not on the same scale as that experienced by American Jews and it was therefore not one of the main impetuses for the development of the Bournemouth Jewish hotels. It is this that probably accounts for the fact that, although the Bournemouth hotels had a distinct Jewish brand and non-Jewish guests were few in number, they were not nearly as insular or as all-encompassing as the Catskill resorts. Many of the Catskill resorts had their own shopping arcades, golf courses, skating rinks, ski slopes, theatres, health clubs, nightclubs, full-scale synagogues, separate children's day camps and dining rooms, and they were in a constant state of growth and development. While some guests chose not to leave the confines of the Bournemouth hotels in which they stayed, many did take advantage of the range of facilities and amenities that Bournemouth had to offer as an established town (see Chapter 8). In addition, although a large proportion of the guests came from London, they also travelled to Bournemouth from a wide range of other towns and cities and from abroad. There was also a close and symbiotic relationship between the hotels and the local community, particularly the vibrant local Jewish community, as discussed in Chapter 9.

This degree of segregation in the Catskills may account for the difference between the entertainment provided by the hoteliers in the Catskills and that offered in the Bournemouth hotels. The Catskill resorts, especially the larger ones such as Grossinger's, Kutsher's, the Concord, the New Roxy, Brown's Hotel, the Flagler, the Pines Hotel and the Nevele, became renowned for their entertainment that was specifically tailored for the Jewish guests by dedicated social directors. The Catskill resorts made the careers of many Jewish superstars, such as Eddie Cantor, Jackie Mason, Joan Rivers, Eddie Fisher and Milton Berle. Whereas in Britain, Jews had left behind most of the traditional Jewish leisure pursuits when they headed for the suburbs (see introduction to Chapter 8), in the Catskills, the entertainment programmes were dominated by Yiddish humour and theatre, despite the fact that the guests were intent on acculturation. Although the entertainment in the Bournemouth hotels featured many Jewish comedians and other Jewish celebrities of the day (see Chapter 8), many non-Jews starred at and made their careers as a result of appearing at the Bournemouth Jewish hotels. In the Catskill resorts, the entertainers were almost exclusively Jewish. As a result of these differences, British Jews visiting the Catskill resorts sometimes found their entertainment programmes 'grating', 'too obviously New York' and the stand-up comedy 'much too blue'. These comments suggest that traditional Jewish humour had perhaps been toned down in the more genteel atmosphere of the UK.

What also struck British Jewish visitors to the Catskill resorts was the sheer scale of the Jewish enclave and the gigantic size of some of the individual resorts that came to define the Catskills. Geoffrey Feld, who stayed with his family at the Nevele for *Pesach* in the early 1970s says: 'Everything was mega. The Catskill resorts made the Bournemouth hotels look like corner shops.'[45] The Jewish hotels and guest houses in Bournemouth once constituted a significant proportion of the holiday establishments in the town. However, even in their heyday, at any one time there were no more than thirty hotels and guest houses that catered almost exclusively for a Jewish clientele, and few had more than a hundred bedrooms. By comparison, it is estimated that there were well over a thousand Jewish establishments (not including the bungalow colonies) that competed with each other in the Catskills, some of which could accommodate bordering on a thousand guests.[46] American Jews holidayed in the Catskills in their hundreds of thousands, rather than the tens of thousands of Jews drawn to Bournemouth. Shirley Davidson tells this story about her mother Fay Schneider, proprietor of the Majestic:

> My mother once went to visit the Catskill hotels in America to see how they operated. The man who was giving a guided tour of one of the hotels knew who she was and kept saying to her things like, 'We have three pools, I don't suppose you do', and 'We can seat over 1,000 people in our dining room, how many do you seat?' So, when he said 'I don't suppose you have anything like this', she got fed up and said 'Oh yes we do, it's called Butlins!'[47]

When Hettie Marks stayed in the Concord, she found the dining room, which seated 2,700 people, 'beyond belief' and 'somewhat intimidating'. She also found it difficult to understand the magnitude of the nightclub that accommodated 1,500 people, and she compared the resort unfavourably to the Bournemouth hotels; it was much more impersonal: 'You never saw the same person twice and although the atmosphere was convivial and relaxed, the hotel didn't lend itself to sitting down and chatting with people, getting to know them and striking up friendships. There were no quiet and cosy spaces.'[48] It appears from this comment that the Catskill resorts lacked some basic ingredients that had been very important to British Jewish holidaymakers. Hettie's perceptions are echoed by Israel Shenker, a *New York Times* journalist, who visited Bournemouth in 1973: 'If Grossinger's is a vast jangling glory on the horizon of the American Catskills, the Green Park is a small gentle glow on the British seafront.'[49] The scale and size of the Catskill resorts (and the degree of competition between them) meant that their demise had a much more negative impact on the economy of the Catskill region than the closure of Jewish hotels in Bournemouth had on the town.

During the 1970s, former Catskill holidaymakers were 'growing more familiar with the roads around Miami, Disneyland, Las Vegas, the Hamptons and the Jersey Shore.'[50] As a result, a number of the Catskill resorts were filled with non-Jews, were increasingly given over to resident guests, or became popular with *charedi* visitors, mainly drawn from *Chassidic* sects living in and around New York.[51] However, during the 1980s, a large number of the resorts and bungalow colonies were boarded up and the whole area became very run down. Shops and other businesses in towns like Liberty and Monticello, which had been highly dependent on the hotels and had provided thousands of jobs, also closed.[52] Many holiday properties were turned into soup kitchens and welfare motels used by homeless people driven there from New York City. Some no longer exist except in the memories of their former guests. In *It Happened in the Catskills*, the legendary Catskill figure Robert Towers is quoted as saying: 'Today [the 1990s] there are times when I look around and *mer ziet keyn yidishe ponim* – there is not a Jewish face to be seen.'

This is not what happened in Bournemouth. Although the guest houses rapidly disappeared, most were put to alternative uses and many of the larger hotels, including several of the Big Eight, were taken over by new owners and continued to operate. A number were redeveloped as apartment blocks, including the Green Park. As a result, the decline of the Jewish hotels did not lead to the dilapidation and economic decay that occurred in the Catskills. Nor did the Jewish holiday trade disappear from the area, it simply changed in its nature, with visitors either transferring to the non-Jewish hotels or staying in various types of self-catering accommodation (see Chapter 5). Jewish visitors to Bournemouth remained, and still are, a significant element of the town's holiday trade.[53]

The Legacy of the Jewish Hotels

The story of the Jewish hotels of Bournemouth is a very compelling one and the hotels have left a strong legacy, particularly in respect of the contribution that they made to shaping Anglo-Jewish identity as discussed above, but also for the ways in which they enhanced the sustainability of the community. As mentioned in Chapter 8, many Jews met their future spouses while staying in a Jewish hotel in Bournemouth. This meant that not only did they not 'marry out', but also that the marriages led to future generations of Jewish offspring, a large proportion of whom remained within Judaism, thereby contributing to Jewish continuity.

Another way in which the hotels contributed to Jewish continuity stemmed from the fact that the Jewish religion was an integral aspect of hotel life. As a result of staying in the hotels and participating in religious activities, many Jews who might otherwise have left Judaism, found their faith being rekindled. This helped to reduce total assimilation. A number of young people learned to *daven* and *leyn* during their stays in the hotels. Barbara Glyn comments: 'Before *kiruv* [literally gathering in but meaning encouraging people to participate in Jewish religious activities] became a watchword, my father, Ruby Marriott, encouraged the young and not so young guests to take part in learning a *Haftarah*. I still have friends who remind me of this and are proud that thereafter they could confidently do the same at their local *shuls*.'[54] This was also the case in the guest houses. Judi Lyons, who was brought up in a guest house (see Chapter 4), has fond memories of a couple named Goldberg, who stayed at the guest house in June each year. They had fled from *pogroms* in Eastern Europe and had met on the boat to England: 'Mr Goldberg used to teach me to *daven* in the mornings. He taught me four or five readings covering basic Jewish laws, which he said would enable me to understand any Jewish text. He was a major source of my Jewish education.'[55]

The interest in Judaism generated by staying in the hotels is still evident today, demonstrated by the continuing popularity of spending time in Bournemouth during the Jewish festivals, especially *Pesach*, including by those who participate in the holidays organised initially by Stephen Wolfisz and more recently by Brian Lassman mentioned in Chapter 7. People who own flats in Bournemouth often use them during Jewish festivals. David Latchman comments: 'Time and again when we invite people to spend *Purim* with us in our home, they say, "We'd love to, but I'm going to my flat in Bournemouth for the festival".'[56] For many Jews, the taste for *Yiddishkeit* clearly lives on.

Over the years, the hotels brought together Jewish families from across the country, which generated a sense of communal solidarity. Friendships were forged that endured for several years, with the offspring of families who had met up in the hotels going on to build long-lasting relationships. This outcome was particularly beneficial for families who lived in areas where there were very few Jews. Although this legacy may have only lasted for a generation or two before Anglo-Jewry began to fragment and become more polarised (see Chapter 5), it was nevertheless an undeniable impact of the hotels.

We started this chapter with a discussion of the nostalgia that pervades discussions of the Jewish hotels of Bournemouth. There is also a strong sense of pride about the 'glory days' of the hotels and the role they played in Anglo-Jewish history. While few Jews still aspire to partake of the lifestyle of the hotels that were once so popular, they are still regarded with considerable warmth and are seen as a big Jewish success story. The long afterglow left by the hotels is particularly strong in Bournemouth itself. One commentator has said: 'The *heimishe* atmosphere of summer and *Yamim Tovim* in those hotels remains an essential part of Anglo-Jewry's folklore.'[57] David Latchman comments: 'Even if Bournemouth is not quite what it used to be, because of the Jewish hotels, the town has a reputation for being a Jewish place.'[58]

Another legacy of the hotels that is still being experienced in Bournemouth is the way in which they have contributed to sustaining the local Jewish community. From the 1960s onwards, Jews who had stayed in the hotels and had as a result fallen in love with the area, started to move to the town from all over the country, especially after they had retired. Celia Bradley, who became chairman of Bournemouth Reform Synagogue, recalls leaving Bournemouth after a holiday and saying to herself, 'I promise that I will be back.' In 1983, she was able to keep that promise.[59] Many of the retirees (like Celia Bradley) became very involved in communal affairs and made a significant contribution to creating a flourishing Bournemouth Jewish community. Although the number of Jews retiring to Bournemouth having previously stayed in a Jewish hotel is now inevitably declining, former holidaymakers are still topping up the community and adding to communal life in the town.

An important and interesting legacy of the hotels is the impact that they had on the non-Jewish community. As discussed in Chapter 9, over the years, the Jewish hotels and guest houses employed many hundreds of staff, who were mainly non-Jewish and a large proportion of whom lived in the local area. Many non-Jewish people came into contact with the hotels in other ways, such as when carrying out repairs and delivering goods. As a result, they gained first-hand experience of mixing with Jews and became acquainted with the way they lived their lives and with their customs and practices. This gave rise to an understanding and respect for Judaism that for many people was enduring. Commenting on her experience of working in the hotels, one former staff member says: 'It was a great place to work and a good way to get exposure to another world. It started my fascination for the Jewish way of life.'[60] Paul Millington, the food and beverages manager at the New Ambassador in the 1990s, recalls: 'I often sat in the office with Rev. Camissar, an absolutely fascinating man. He told me about Jewish history. It was wonderful. I could have listened all night when he started talking.'[61] Joan Doubtfire comments: 'I still light candles at *Chanukah!*'[62]

The enduring warmth for Jews and Judaism was engendered not only from contact with Jews, but also by their generosity:

> I worked at the Green Park in the late 1950s as a page boy. The uniform was grey or black trousers and a white top with green edging. I used to work alternate weekdays from 5.30pm to 8.30pm and also Saturdays and Sundays, either 7am to 1pm or 1pm to 8.30pm. I was paid the princely sum of five shillings a week for being at the beck and call of the guests and the other staff. Once, a guest asked if I could get two tickets to see Frankie Vaughan at the Pavilion. I cycled down into town and found the show was a sell-out. I went to the counter and blow me two seats in the middle of the front row had just been cancelled. I purchased the tickets for £10 (a lot of money then). When I got back and handed the guest his tickets, he gave me a tip of five shillings, the same amount as my week's wages.[63]

The families of the local people who worked in the hotels often benefitted from the largesse of the hoteliers. Joan Doubtfire tells this story of her brother George: 'When he was working as a chef in the Green Park, Miss Hannah Richman used to pack up leftover cream cakes for him to take home to our large family. My mother was very worried that he might have been taking them without permission and spoke to Miss Hannah about it. She said: "They were sent with love."'[64] Rick Clarke recalls that Maurice Guild gave him a pair of leather gloves when he was waiting for his mother to finish work in the Langham.[65] People who worked in the hotels, and also those that provided services to them, recall the generous presents they were given by the hoteliers at Christmas.

The transmission of information and understanding was not a one-way process. The Jewish hoteliers and their guests gained a great deal from contact and dialogue with non-Jews working in the hotels. Geoffrey Feld tells the story of Bill Downing, a non-Jewish barman, who worked for many years at the Cumberland. Although guests in the hotel generally drank very little alcohol (see Chapter 6), they flocked to the bar to speak with Bill, who had 'seen life' and was a 'larger than life character'. Geoffrey Feld comments: 'He had a fund of stories of the life he had lived, which was very different from ours. He was upper crust, highly educated and held forth on any number of subjects from politics and sport to wines and gourmet living. Our Jewish guests just loved him.'⁶⁶ As a result of these two-way experiences, there still exists in Bournemouth today both a remarkable understanding of Judaism and good relations between the Jewish and non-Jewish communities.

There are some less obvious and arguably less important legacies of the Jewish hotels, that are worth mentioning to illustrate the range as well as the extent of their impact. While staying in the Bournemouth hotels a number of Jewish guests attended matches of Bournemouth Association Football Club and continued to retain an allegiance to the team long after they stopped holidaying in Bournemouth. Some even handed down this allegiance to subsequent generations. David Latchman comments: 'Whenever I look at the football results to see how my favourite team Leeds United have got on, I always look at the Bournemouth score. I have passed this on to my son who was disappointed when they were relegated recently, even though he has never been to Bournemouth.'⁶⁷

In Chapters 3 and 6, reference was made to the continental waiters and kitchen staff who worked in the hotels. After the hotels closed, some of these people stayed and opened well-known restaurants in Bournemouth, including Gino, an Italian waiter at the Normandie, who opened a pizza restaurant, and Sicilian-born 'Mr Mimmo' (Mimmo Zacchia), the celebrated maître d' at the Green Park, who with his colleague Nino Benedetto opened a restaurant called 'La Botte' (known locally as 'Mr Mimmo's'), in Boscombe where Jewish residents of the town forgathered and were served kosher food. Nino and his former colleague from the Green Park, Luigi, went on to run the Amalfi restaurant in the Wessex Hotel. Others returned home where they established successful businesses or applied skills they had acquired in the Bournemouth hotels to enhance the experience of Jewish travellers. In 1987, the following notice appeared in the *Jewish Chronicle,* placed by the Grand Hotel in Rimini: 'Since we, the Arpellsa family, began offering kosher holidays 25 years ago, many of our staff have gained valuable experience in Bournemouth's kosher hotels and well understand the requirements of British tourists.'⁶⁸ The Jewish hotels also impacted on holidaying in Israel. Judi Lyons tells us: 'In the 1980s, crowds of Jews from north-west London descended on Eilat. The atmosphere at the King

Solomon Hotel there was just like it had been in one of the Bournemouth hotels a decade or so earlier.[69] Finally, mention must be made of what will perhaps prove to be the longest lasting legacy of the hotels, which is that Bournemouth continues to be a Jewish destination of choice, even if it is for very different types of holiday than before. This legacy stems both from the direct experience that Jews had of staying in the Bournemouth hotels, and also from the legend that the hotels created. There are now Jews who holiday in Bournemouth whose parents, and in some cases even their grandparents, stayed in the Jewish hotels there. The heyday of the Jewish hotels may be long gone, but their influence definitely lives on.

Notes

1. Commentator in 'The Green Park', directed by Jack Fishburn and Justin Hardy, 2015.
2. Interview with Paul Harris, 1.5.2020.
3. Interview with Jon Harris, 4.5.2020.
4. *JC*, 4.6.2010, travel section.
5. Interview with Valerie Gaynor, 21.7.2020.
6. Phil Brown, *Catskill Culture: A Mountain Rat's Memories of the Great Jewish Resort Area* (Philadelphia PA: Temple University Press, 1998), p.182.
7. Interview with David Abrahams, 25.8.2020.
8. Geoffrey Alderman, 'Abundant Southern Comforts', *JC*, 29.9.2014.
9. Sarah Marriott speaking in 'The Green Park', directed by Jack Fishburn and Justin Hardy.
10. Interview with David Latchman, 5.11.2020.
11. Mirjam Triendl-Zadoff, *Next Year in Marienbad: The Lost Worlds of the Jewish Spa Culture* (Philadelphia PA: University of Pennsylvania Press, 2012). I would like to thank Nicola Feuchtwang for bringing my attention to this book.
12. Anthony Grenville, *Jewish Refugees from Germany and Austria in Britain, 1933–1970* (London and Portland OR: Vallentine Mitchell, 2010), p.230.
13. *Ibid.*, p.232.
14. *AJR Journal*, October 1974.
15. Commentary in 'The Green Park', directed by Jack Fishburn and Justin Hardy.
16. Conversation with Marian Stern, 19.11.2020.
17. Ben Azai, writing in the *JC*, 7.8.1964.
18. Interview with David Abrahams, 25.8.2020.
19. Israel Shenker, 'On the British Seafront, Kosher Cuisine with an English Accent', *New York Times*, 6.1.1973.
20. Interview with Marian Stern, 11.5.2020.
21. Interview with Hettie Marks, 28.4.2020.
22. Interview with Clive Gold, 23.9.2020.
23. Interview with Hettie Marks, 28.4.2020.
24. Interview with Sheila Morris, 19.8.2020.

25. Gerda Charles, *The Crossing Point* (London: Eyre & Spottiswode, 1961), p.187.
26. Interview with David Latchman, 5.11.2020.
27. Panikos Panayi, *An Immigration History of Britain, Multicultural Racism Since 1800* (Harlow: Pearson, 2010).
28. Keith Kahn-Harris and Ben Gidley, *Turbulent Times: The British Jewish Community Today* (London: Continuum, 2010).
29. Todd Endelman, *Radical Assimilation in English Jewish History, 1656–1945* (Bloomington IN: Indiana University Press, 1990).
30. Ilana Lee, 'Diamonds at Breakfast', *Jewish Quarterly*, Vol. 54, No. 1, p.28.
31. See Shenker, 'On the British Seafront'.
32. Commentator appearing in 'The Green Park', directed by Jack Fishburn and Justin Hardy.
33. See Lee, 'Diamonds at Breakfast', p.28.
34. See https://foucault.info/documents/heterotopia/foucault.heteroTopia.en/.
35. Conversation with David Abrahams, 20.11.2020.
36. Interview with James Inverne, 10.11.2020.
37. See letter from L. Land, Secretary to the Kashrus Commission, *JC*, 30.5.1980.
38. David Stradling, *Making Mountains: New York City and the Catskills* (Seattle WA: University of Washington Press, 2007), p.204.
39. *JC*, 8.3.1985.
40. Myrna Katz Frommer and Harvey Frommer, *It Happened in the Catskills* (Orlando, FLA: Harcourt, Brace Jovanovich Publishers, 1991), pp.206-207.
41. Interview with Hettie Marks, 12.11.2020.
42. Conversation with Geoffrey Feld, 29.11.2020.
43. See https://www.hadassahmagazine.org/2019/09/03/young-jews-bringing-catskills-back-life/.
44. Jon Sterngass, *First Resorts* (Baltimore MD: The Johns Hopkins University Press, 2001), p.107. This topic is also dealt with in Philip Roth's *The Plot Against America*, which features an episode where a Jewish family is effectively expelled from a hotel booked months before.
45. Conversation with Geoffrey Feld, 29.11.2020.
46. Phil Brown, 'Hotels and Bungalows', www.catskills.brown.edu.
47. Interview with Shirley Davidson, 18.5.2020.
48. Interview with Hettie Marks, 12.11.2020.
49. See Shenker, 'On the British Seafront'.
50. Stefan Kanfer, *A Summer World: The Attempt to Build a Jewish Eden in the Catskills, From the Days of the Ghetto to the Rise and Decline of the Borscht Belt* (New York NYC: Farrar Strauss Giroux, 1989), p.258.
51. See Frommer and Frommer, *It Happened in the Catskills*, p.233.
52. See Brown, 'Hotels and Bungalows'.
53. See Frommer and Frommer, *It Happened in the Catskills*, p.229.
54. Manuscript, 'The Green Park 1943-1986', provided by Barbara Glyn, 22 May 2020.
55. Interview with Judi Lyons, 4.5.2020.
56. Interview with David Latchman, 5.11.2020.
57. 'All my Bourne Days', *JC*, 4.6.2010.
58. Interview with David Latchman, 5.11.2020.
59. *JC*, 12.4.1996.

60. Christine O' Grady, response to author's post on Memories of Old Poole and Bournemouth Facebook Group, 21.11.2020.
61. Conversation with Paul Millington, 27.11.2020.
62. Interview with Joan Doubtfire, 13.5.2020.
63. Jeffrey Lambert, response to author's post on Memories of Old Poole and Bournemouth Facebook Group, 21.11.2020.
64. Interview with Joan Doubtfire, 13.5.2020.
65. Rick Clarke, response to author's post on Memories of Old Poole and Bournemouth Facebook Group, 21.11.2020.
66. Conversation with Geoffrey Feld, 29.11.2020.
67. Interview with David Latchman, 5.11.2020.
68. *JC*, 23.1.1987.
69. Conversation with Judi Lyons, 14.10.2020.

Appendix 1

The Big Eight Hotels and the People Who Ran Them

The Ambassador/New Ambassador Hotel
The Cumberland Hotel
East Cliff Court
East Cliff Manor
The Green Park Hotel
The Langham Hotel
The Majestic Hotel
The Normandie Hotel

The Ambassador/New Ambassador Hotel

The Ambassador Hotel, located in Meyrick Road, was built on land that was once occupied by a private house called Leeholme. By the mid-1920s, this house had become the Westminster Hotel. In the early 1930s, it was renamed Eastry Court Hotel. In 1935, it was demolished and the Art Deco-style Ambassador (then called Hotel Ambassador) was built, set within large terraced gardens.

From its opening, the hotel was Jewish-owned and run. Its first owner was Daniel Rosenthall, who had previously run the long-established Merivale Hall, a few metres along Meyrick Road. It opened in December 1936, just in time for the 'end-of-year holidays'. It was described by its owner as 'far and away the largest, most luxurious and fully-equipped Jewish hotel in Europe'. It immediately attracted some well-known Jewish people, such as Nathan Laski. It had a hundred 'superbly-furnished bedrooms'.

The bold advertising of the hotel continued through the early months of the Second World War. The tone of the advertisements then changed to stress the comfort and safety of staying in the hotel. It had an ARP-approved air raid shelter. This attracted some long-term guests, who had left the big towns and cities. However, in July 1940, the hotel was requisitioned to become a club for American officers run by the American Red Cross.

Towards the end of the war, the hotel was sequestered to accommodate American sailors who had survived the D-Day landings. Most of the sailors, many of them former longshore-men from small American ports, were apparently surprised to see the quality of holiday accommodation to which affluent people aspired.

The hotel was derequisitioned in the early months of 1946 when it was purchased by the Levitus family from Glasgow, who had moved to Bournemouth just after the war. They stated that it was their intention to contribute to the local Jewish community in the way that they had in Glasgow. The family involved in the hotel were Emmanuel and Pearl Levitus and their brother Samuel and his son Bertram (Bertie) Levitus. The Ambassador hotel re-opened in July 1946.

By the beginning of 1948, Emmanuel and Pearl Levitus had moved to London and Bertram had opened the Embassy Hotel in East Overcliff Drive. He was later the owner of the non-kosher Melford Hall Hotel in St Peters Road. When he died in 1993, Bertram left over £500,000 to the Hannah Levy House care home in Bournemouth.

In May 1948, it was announced that the Ambassador had been purchased by a Mr A. Grossman, who would be running the hotel as an orthodox establishment. His mother, Mrs R. Grossman, also appears to have had a financial interest in the hotel, but neither mother nor son appears to have had day-to-day involvement in the running of the hotel. They employed resident directors, the most longstanding and prominent of whom was Erwin Rubinstein ('Ruby') and his wife Gertrud, who for many years were 'the face' of the Ambassador. Erwin Rubinstein, who took up his role in January 1956, was a former refugee from Konigsberg, then part of Germany. He was well known amongst the refugee community, many members of which stayed in the hotel where they enjoyed speaking to him in German. Advertisements for the hotel were placed in the journal produced by the Association of Jewish Refugees as well as the *Jewish Chronicle*.

In 1958, it was announced that a new company had acquired the Ambassador, Ambassador (Meyrick) Ltd, but Mrs R. Grossman appears to have remained involved in the hotel. In 1959, a notice was placed in the *Jewish Chronicle* to say that Mr F. W. Schwyn, who had previously been involved in the running of the non-Jewish Anglo Swiss hotel, no longer had a financial interest in the Ambassador. Throughout these changes, Mr Rubinstein continued as the resident director of the hotel.

Although the hotel marketed itself as being strictly kosher, it was not licensed by the religious authorities. Erwin Rubinstein was a skilled impresario and the hotel developed a reputation for its high-profile entertainment programme. During the summer months, it attracted stars such as Diana Dors and Maurice Chevalier.

The Ambassador was a popular hotel, but it was said that its standards of service were not quite as high as some of the other Big Eight hotels. When Louis Golding visited the hotel in 1950, he subsequently published a short account of his stay. He said that the clientele of the hotel fell into three groups – those who were already well established and quite affluent, those who were in the process of raising themselves out of poverty and foreign visitors, who were mainly people who had been on cruises that disembarked at Southampton.

The hotel underwent periodic refurbishment and modernisation programmes. Over the winter of 1955, the hotel was closed for many months to enable major renovations to be carried out. For the summer season in 1964, a new open-air heated swimming pool was opened.

Early in 1966, the Ambassador was acquired by Nathan (Nat) and Gertie Lee, who also at that time owned the Normandie (see biography for the Normandie for further details on Nat Lee). When he announced his ownership of the hotel, Nat Lee said that it was now back in 'completely Jewish ownership' after eight years, suggesting that the previous board of directors had involved non-Jews, which may have accounted for the fact that the hotel was not licensed by the religious authorities. After the change in ownership, the hotel was initially managed by David Harris, who was said to have had significant experience of operating kosher hotels. However, by November 1966, Mr Rubinstein was once again directing the hotel.

By the time that Nat Lee purchased the Ambassador, he was very frail and in the latter part of 1966 the hotel was placed on the market. It was purchased by Hyman (Hymie) Selby (originally Inselberg), who was born in Bucharest, Romania in 1901. He came to Britain at the age of twelve. His father was a travelling salesman and the family settled initially in Bethnal Green. For a short while between 1946 and 1948, Hyman Selby had been part owner of the Majestic before selling his interest in the hotel to open a restaurant and banqueting suite, the Hanover Grand in London's Oxford Circus ('Selbys of Mayfair'), which gained a reputation for outstanding kosher catering and lavish entertainment. Hyman Selby had sold the restaurant in 1966 when he was aged sixty five, but is said to have found retirement irksome, so he bought the Ambassador as a retirement project.

Before the Ambassador reopened in 1967, Hyman Selby spent £70,000 on improving and modernising the hotel. The improvements included an extended dining room equipped with air conditioning, an enlarged kitchen, modernisation of all of the bedrooms, a new dedicated synagogue, a card room, a children's room and lounges. For the first time in its twenty-year history, the hotel was licensed by the Kashrus Commission and the London Beth Din. Hyman and his (second) wife Nettie were able to use the contacts they had built up in London to secure top entertainers. The hotel was renamed the New Ambassador.

Hyman and Nettie Selby (née Leonard) ran the hotel with Hyman's stepdaughter, Joy and her husband, Sefton Eagell, who also had a financial interest in the hotel. For the first year of the Selby's ownership, Mr Rubinstein remained as the manager before he bought his own, non-kosher hotel (name unknown) in Bournemouth. He was succeeded by Mr Taverna, who was soon replaced by Brian Lassman, who managed the hotel for eighteen years.

Despite their investment in its modernisation, the Selbys did not own the New Ambassador for many years. In 1971, Alfred (Alf) and Sadie Vickers purchased the hotel with their existing business partners Max and Yvonne Green. The Vickers (who lived in Muswell Hill) already owned hotels elsewhere (the Century Group of Hotels), including a hotel in Marble Arch, London. The Eagells retained a financial interest in the hotel and were involved in its day-to-day management. Over time, the Vickers bought out both the Eagells and the Greens and the Vickers' sons became involved in the direction of the hotel. Alf Vickers' sister, Rhoda Lukover, was the co-owner of the smaller Grosvenor Hotel (see Chapter 4) and later the Grove House Hotel (see Chapter 5).

The New Ambassador became very popular with families and gained a reputation for its plentiful, unpretentious traditional Jewish food. The hotel was dubbed 'Blooms-on-Sea'. The Vickers family regularly invested in the maintenance and refurbishment of the hotel. It attracted some well-known entertainers and its longstanding resident musical duo, Joan Worthy and Peter Banyard, who both lived in Bournemouth, went on to become nationally famous (see Chapter 8). The hotel was also noted for its charitable activities. In March 1985, it organised a special weekend break, the proceeds from which were donated to Operation Moses (an initiative to evacuate the Jews of Ethiopia and take them to Israel) and in 1976, the hotel offered free holidays to pensioners from London who otherwise would not have been able to afford a holiday. The hotel diversified its clientele and became one of the foremost hotels for hosting Jewish conferences, seminars and other events. During the 1990s, it was the hotel of choice for coach tours.

Despite its diversification, by the 1990s the hotel was struggling to fill its bedrooms, the number of which had been increased from 100 to 112 as the result of converting former staff quarters. The hotel closed its doors in January 2006, almost seventy years after it opened. It was taken over by the Britannia hotel chain, which is Jewish owned, but it did not run the hotel as a kosher establishment. The hotel is now known as the Britannia Hotel Bournemouth.

The Cumberland Hotel

The Cumberland Hotel, located in East Overcliff Drive, was built during 1937 on the site of a property called Fern Cliff. Designed in the Art Deco style then at its height, it was constructed by a builder named Mr Rowley. When it appeared in the 1938 Bournemouth guidebook it was described as having over one hundred bedrooms, eighty bathrooms (many of which had *en suite* facilities), a dining room seating 200 people, a ballroom with a domed glass ceiling, a card room, lifts, central heating and air conditioning, a sun terrace, garages and much more. It had five floors. Its owner was not specified, but the *London Gazette* tells us that the first owners were Elise and Samuel Phillips, who went bankrupt in 1939. Elise Phillips had been the on-site manageress.

During the Second World War, the Cumberland was requisitioned by the government and became the wartime home of the Royal Army Pay Corps. It was derequisitioned in 1946 and run for two years as a non-Jewish hotel. Its sale was spotted by Joe Lipman, a successful property dealer, who already owned the Palace Court Hotel. Joe Lipman was related to Isaac Feld, who with his wife Bluma visited Bournemouth in 1948. They and Joe Lipman met up there and Joe Lipman asked the Felds to become his business partner in purchasing the hotel.

Coincidentally, Isaac Feld had been looking for new business opportunities. He had considered the idea of opening a restaurant in America, but this proposal had been vetoed by Bluma. They decided to buy into the Cumberland, and at *Pesach* 1949, it opened as a kosher hotel. It was the last of the Big Eight hotels to commence business, and at this time it was the largest kosher hotel in Europe.

For the first few years of the Cumberland's operation under the Felds, Joe Lipman was a sleeping partner. When he died in the early 1950s, the Felds bought his share of the business. By this time, their daughter, Zena, had married New Yorker Howard Inverne. The couple lived in America for a few years, but when they moved to England in 1952, Howard, a jeweller by profession, became the Feld's business partner. He was very active in the running of the hotel and later on his son, Richard, also became a manager.

Geoffrey, the Felds' son, joined the business in 1960, having studied accountancy in London.

Bluma and Isaac brought a great deal of experience and expertise to the running of the Cumberland. Bluma (originally Sarah Bluma) was born in 1908 in the Polish *shtetl* of Markova, the daughter of Berish Dov Pojazny and Alta Annie Grinshpan. Berish came on his own to London in 1913 and the family was not reunited until 1920 due to the outbreak of the First World War. Once reunited, the family changed their name to Posner. Isaac was the son of Alexander (Ziskin) and Annie Feld, who were also immigrants from Poland. Isaac was born in Sounskawola (now Zdunska Wola) in 1902. Having trained as a butcher, Alexander opened a butcher's shop in Christian Street in Whitechapel, which had a small seating area.

Bluma and Isaac met when Bluma was seventeen. She was then running a 'trimmings' (haberdashery) shop from her family's home in Old Montague Street, Whitechapel. They were married in Jubilee Street Great Synagogue in 1927 and for eighteen months, Bluma and Isaac worked in the shop in Christian Street. They then opened a much larger restaurant at 128 Whitechapel Road, opposite the Pavilion Theatre. This restaurant, known as 'Feld's of Whitechapel', became very famous and was frequented by many stars of the day, such as Eddie Cantor and Sophie Tucker. The Felds operated the upstairs floors as an eight-room boarding house. There was also a downstairs function room seating 150 people that was regularly used for weddings and other celebrations. When the Felds took over the Cumberland, they placed an advertisement in the Yiddish newspaper, *Di Zeit*, with the aim of attracting the clientele they had built up in the restaurant. Until the Felds were certain that the hotel was going to be a success, Bluma stayed in London for five days a week to manage the business. When Bluma moved to Bournemouth full time, she and Isaac bought a large house at 25 Grove Road where they built a tennis court that was used by the hotel guests.

Although the Cumberland was run as a family affair, Bluma Feld took on the front of house role while Isaac, who was more reserved, mainly dealt with the accounts and business matters. He enjoyed running the hotel, but was not very tolerant of children. He kept a book in which he noted the names of guests who did not behave well or who complained too much. By contrast, Bluma was considered to be 'the hostess with the mostest', making a point of becoming personally acquainted with each of her guests. An invitation to join her table to eat with her was a much sought-after privilege. Bluma was passionate about providing high quality kosher food, inspected the hotel kitchens daily and toured the dining room at both lunch and dinner to speak to her guests to ensure they were enjoying their stay.

The person with the main responsibility for the preparation and serving of the food at the hotel was Alex Kopfstein, a refugee from Austria, who had been the second chef at Feld's restaurant in London. He helped with catering for the first *Pesach* at the hotel and moved to Bournemouth to become the catering manager when Feld's restaurant was sold to Isaac's brother, Benny, in 1951.

Over the years, the hotel became increasingly self-sufficient. It established its own butchery and for a while had its own smoking house. The family purchased Freddie Ballon's bakery that operated in the town centre, which was gradually moved to the hotel grounds and extended to include a delicatessen. The bakery supplied some other hotels until they set up their own bakeries, and both the bakery and the delicatessen were used by Jewish families staying in self-catering accommodation (see Chapter 6).

During their ownership of the Cumberland, the Feld and Inverne families carried out several major modernisation and improvement programmes, the first of which was in 1959 when the hotel's ballroom and lounge were both redecorated and refurnished, a new sun room, children's playroom and card room were added and the dining room was extended. In 1964, the Cumberland's heated outdoor pool with its signature dolphin waterfall was opened and the dining room was again refurbished. In 1968, the hotel closed for several months after the autumn festivals to enable the bedrooms to be restyled and the lounges to be refurbished. The hotel employed Harry Epstein (whom Bluma knew from her East End days), owner of the world-famous bespoke reproduction furniture company, and his interior designer to oversee the improvements, which included adding bathrooms to the last of the bedrooms that were not *en suite*. In 1983, rooms were added for holding conferences and banquets.

The core of the Cumberland's clientele was middle-class families living across the United Kingdom, but the hotel also attracted some very high-profile guests, including well-known rabbis, *dayanim* and business people. The hotel was marketed as the largest kosher hotel in Europe.

From the outset, the Cumberland was run as an orthodox establishment, licensed by the Kashrus Commission and the London Beth Din. It had its own synagogue where *Shabbat* and festival services were held. In addition, for twelve years, the longstanding resident *shomer* Rev. Segal (see Chapter 7), led morning and evening *minyanim*. The hotel was also noted for its contribution to charitable and communal causes, both local and national. It hosted many large dinners to raise money for Zionist bodies and organised regular teas and social events for the residents of the Dolly Ross and Hannah Levy care homes.

During the 1950s, the hotel's entertainment programmes became increasingly star-studded, including names such as Peter Sellers, Benny Hill, Alma Cogan, Ron Moody, Bob Monkhouse, and Harry Corbett and Sooty for the children. The hotel employed dance hosts (gigolos) and a series of well-known entertainment hosts and resident bandleaders, including Stanley Laudan and Johnny Franks. The hotel's summer entertainment and 'end-of-year' cabarets were particularly popular. During the 1960s, the focus of the entertainment shifted to place a greater emphasis on entertainment and activities for children and young people.

As trade started to decline in the mid-1960s, the Cumberland began to diversify. The hotel was marketed as a venue for conferences, seminars and other events and for dedicated holidays, such as golf weeks and card weekends (see Chapter 8). Special terms were available for block bookings and 'bargain breaks' were introduced. There was a brief resurgence in business in the mid-1970s when the hotel was successful in attracting guests from Belgium, France and Holland.

In 1969, shortly before the death of Isaac Feld, the family purchased the Majestic and ran the two hotels side-by-side for four years before selling the Majestic to developers (see separate biography for the Majestic). The Cumberland continued in business for another eleven years, when it became uneconomic to continue.

The Cumberland was sold to property dealer, Rick Wright. Almost immediately, he sold it on to a young couple, who ran it as a non-kosher hotel until 1987. It was then sold to the Young family, who owned several other hotels in Bournemouth, including the Queens (formerly the Langham) and Cliffeside hotels. Despite being run as a non-kosher hotel, the Cumberland continued to attract many Jewish guests. Since the beginning of 2015, the Cumberland has been part of the Oceana hotel group (a Qatari company that owns other hotels in Bournemouth), which invested in a major renovation in keeping with its Art Deco design. It is now said to be the last free-standing Art Deco hotel in Europe.

After selling the Cumberland, the Feld and Inverne families purchased from the Lanz family, four non-kosher hotels in Bournemouth, which were run as a group for marketing and purchasing purposes under the banner of Quadrant Hotels. Geoffrey Feld directed the Heathlands and Cecil hotels and Howard Inverne directed the Anglo Swiss and Durlston Court hotels (see Chapter 5).

Bluma is said to have been devastated by the closure of the Cumberland, to which she had devoted thirty-five years of her life. In retirement, she spent her time organising card games in her apartment in the Albany apartment block and, before she became too frail, helped to serve lunches at the daycentre based at Bournemouth Reform Synagogue. When she died aged 98 in 2006, Bluma Feld was described as 'the last of the great Jewish caterers of her age' and was credited with having 'set the standard for Jewish package holidays on the south coast'.

East Cliff Court

East Cliff Court in Grove Road (originally number 23, but later 53) was the first of the luxury Jewish hotels in Bournemouth that were to become known as the 'Big Eight'. It was developed from a property named Lisle House, which had once been occupied by Joseph Sebag (later Sir Joseph Sebag-Montefiore). It was a substantial property that sat in large grounds. During 1925, it was extended to become East Cliff Court, which opened for *Pesach* in 1926 under the ownership of Annie Morris. The story is that Annie conceived the idea of opening a luxurious hotel while sitting on a bench on East Overcliff Drive looking at Lisle House and its large garden. An extension was added at right-angles to the original building, built in white stucco and in Art Deco style. The older part of the building became known as 'the cottage' and accommodated one of the hotel's main public rooms, the Lisle Lounge.

Annie Morris (née Finn) was born in the Courland (German name Kurland) region of Latvia in 1879. She married Morris (Meyer) Schlom, a tailor, who was originally from Zagare in Lithuania. The wedding took place at the Great Synagogue in London in 1897. By 1899, the couple were living in Folkestone. At the time of the 1901 Census, the Schloms were taking in a few boarders, but in 1908 Annie Schlom opened a 'strictly orthodox' boarding house in the town named The Grosvenor. A year later, the Schloms moved to a larger property, The Leas, located in a more favourable location close to the seafront. Annie and Morris had four children who were all born in Folkestone, one of whom died.

The Schlom family was naturalised in 1909 and shortly afterwards they moved to Bournemouth where they changed their surname from Schlom to Morris. Annie Morris became a boarding house proprietor, but she continued to trade under the name of Schlom. She initially ran 'superior' furnished apartments at 222 Old Christchurch Road. In 1915, she became the proprietor of Argyle House in Holdenhurst Road. Sometime after 1917,

Annie and her husband separated and she commenced trading under the name of Mrs Annie Morris. In 1920, Annie opened Maison Leontine in St Peter's Road where she lived with her daughter Sadie.

Annie Morris ran Maison Leontine until 1926 when she opened East Cliff Court. She purchased Lisle House with the help and financial support of John Hayman, one of her permanent boarders at Maison Leontine. From the outset it was clear that Annie Morris was very ambitious and was aiming to attract an upmarket clientele. Early advertisements for the hotel stated that it provided lock-up garages for twenty cars with chauffeurs, bedrooms that all had 'magnificent' sea views, central heating throughout, a lift to all floors, a 'spacious' ballroom, a croquet lawn, tennis courts and a roof garden. Annie Morris claimed that East Cliff Court was the 'most luxurious' establishment in Bournemouth.

Over the next twelve years, Annie Morris advertised East Cliff Court prominently in the *Jewish Chronicle*, never running short of superlatives to describe the hotel (see Chapter 2). It was renovated on several occasions, including in 1935 when it was 'Enlarged', 'Renewed' and 'Transformed' to make it the 'most modern and up-to-date hotel' in Bournemouth. The renovations included a new wing, which connected the 'old wing' towards East Overcliff Drive. A green-tiled roof was added over the whole hotel, which became its signature feature. After these improvements were made, the hotel was marketed for a while as the New East Cliff Court. Although she'd had little formal education and retained a strong accent, Annie Morris proved to have a great deal of business acumen.

In June 1931, Annie Morris' daughter, Sadie, married John (originally Jacob, and known informally as Jack) Hayman (born Dikoski), who was a partner in an antique shop in Bournemouth (King and Hayman). He was fifteen years her senior and lived at East Cliff Court. The marriage took place at the Wootton Gardens Synagogue in Bournemouth. The couple had two sons, Ronald and Edward. Their care was largely delegated to a nanny, who remained in the employ of the family for many years, later becoming the housekeeper. The Hayman family had a private apartment, 'the flat', within the hotel. Neither son enjoyed being brought up in the hotel and Ronald, who became a prominent author, wrote a book about his experience.

Although she had hoped to follow a career in art having studied at Bournemouth Art College, Sadie Hayman became very involved in the running of East Cliff Court. She organised the entertainment in the hotel and participated in the dancing that was the hotel's main form of entertainment. She also supervised the kitchen. Although John Hayman had a financial interest in the hotel, he did not play a major role in its operation. His input was mainly confined to contributing to business decisions and organising religious services held at the hotel.

East Cliff Court remained open during the early years of the Second World War, but in October 1942 it was requisitioned. The family moved to a house called Fremington in West Overcliff Drive with some of the staff who had worked at East Cliff Court. The hotel furniture was placed in storage and the hotel was occupied by the Royal Canadian Air Force until the end of the war. The family was reunited with the hotel in December 1945 and found it badly dilapidated. Due to the extensive repairs that were required, East Cliff Court did not reopen until September 1946. Several of the staff who had worked at the hotel before the war were re-employed, including the longstanding receptionist Miss White and the head waiter Mr Jones.

With the holiday trade in Bournemouth beginning to boom, the hotel quickly built up trade. In 1948, Annie Morris purchased the adjacent East Cliff Mansions (previously Kensington House), built at the same time and in the same style as Lisle House. By this time, it too had been extended. It was used as an annexe and for longer lettings. Guests ate in the main building where most of the bedrooms now had *en suite* facilities.

The clientele of East Cliff Court differed somewhat from the other Big Eight hotels in that it included 'the upper echelons of Anglo-Jewry', largely made up of the families who predated the mass immigration of Jews from Eastern Europe and who were more anglicised. Yiddish was rarely used in the hotel and the guests were generally less observant than those staying at the Green Park and the Cumberland.

East Cliff Court did not hold regular *Shabbat* services and guests who wished to worship on *Shabbat* and during the week generally attended services at Bournemouth Hebrew Congregation. John Hayman was a founding member of the community and had remained prominent in its activities. Festival services held in the hotel were initially led by Rev. Solomon Lipson, who had been the minister at Hammersmith Synagogue when John Hayman was growing up in the congregation. Later on, they were conducted by David Weitzman, a friend that Edward Hayman had made when they studied together at Oxford University.

The hotel was 'strictly kosher', but Annie Morris refused to have a religious supervisor in her kitchen. Food was plentiful and carefully prepared, and a great deal of thought was given to the hotel's menus, albeit that the meals were less lavish than in the other Big Eight hotels. The entertainment was also less star-studded and the entertainers were mainly local residents. According to Ronald Hayman, Annie Morris tended to be rather disdainful about what she saw as the excesses of some of the Jewish hotels in Bournemouth.

East Cliff Court, like the other Big Eight hotels, was often used as a venue for charitable events, such as the fashion show staged at the hotel by Messrs. Deanfield Fur Models and Digby Morton Ltd. in October 1954, the purpose of which was to raise money to support the Ravenswood Foundation in Berkshire for children with special needs.

In the immediate postwar years, Annie Morris remained the driving force at East Cliff Court. She was a dominant personality and maintained a high profile around the hotel, socialising with guests and closely supervising staff. However, a postwar innovation was the employment of a series of non-Jewish managers to take responsibility for the day-to-day running of the hotel, the first and longest standing of whom was George Bowman, sometimes referred to as 'Captain Bowman' due to his prior military experience.

By the early 1950s, Annie's health was deteriorating and Sadie Hayman assumed direction of the hotel. She was less extrovert than her mother and tended to remain in her office behind the reception desk rather than taking a 'front-of-house' role. Sadie continued to run the hotel with the assistance of managers following the death of Annie Morris in 1953 and the death of John Hayman in June 1954, but she found it a huge strain. Under Sadie's direction, the hotel began to encourage families with children to stay at the hotel by offering reduced rates and family suites. Previously children had not been especially welcomed. During the 1950s, four permanent residents lived in the hotel.

East Cliff Court continued to be updated and refurbished on a regular basis, including in 1951 when the dining room was remodelled and named the Morico Restaurant. In 1959, the hotel was redecorated throughout.

In January 1960, Sadie Hayman sold East Cliff Court to the adjacent Carlton Hotel that ran it as an annexe having added a number of modern features, such as a heated swimming pool. The hotel was later purchased first by the Nyman family and then by the Rosenthal family. East Cliff Mansions was demolished and replaced by the Princes Gate apartments.

After East Cliff Court was sold, Sadie Hayman moved to live in an apartment in Hove with the nanny who had looked after her sons, Clara May Lawrence, where she led a very quiet life. She died in a care home in London in 1989.

Having traded for several years as Menzies East Cliff Court, the hotel survives today as Bournemouth East Cliff Hotel and is part of the Best

Western 'Sure Collection'. The hotel was renovated in 2001 following a fire and again more recently.

East Cliff Manor

The East Cliff Manor Hotel, located in Manor Road, was built on the site of a house called 'Duncairn'. Set within pine trees and facing the sea, it opened as a kosher hotel in 1932 under the management of Ada Cohen, who had previously run the Southmoor guest house in Dean Park Road in Bournemouth.

The hotel was owned by Philip Miller. He was married to Ada's sister Susan (previously Sophia). Both Phillip Miller and the Cohen sisters moved to Bournemouth from Hackney in London, although the Cohen sisters had both been born in Whitechapel (Ada in 1898 and Susan in 1900), but later moved to Stoke Newington. Their parents, Abraham and Sarah (later Minnie), were immigrants from Kutno in Poland. Abraham was a boot and shoe manufacturer. Susan and Phillip Miller were married at Shacklewell Lane Synagogue in Stoke Newington in 1923.

East Cliff Manor was upgraded twice during the 1930s, including in 1935 when sea water baths were installed on all floors. It advertised itself as the 'most up to date hotel'. At this time, East Cliff Manor had forty bedrooms, all of which were centrally heated. Although some guests later migrated to the more luxurious hotels – the Green Park and the Cumberland – prior to the Second World War the hotel was frequented by people who were to become very prominent in the Anglo-Jewish community including Harry ('Chummy') Gaventa (a bookmaker and racehorse owner) and Israel Brodie (later Chief Rabbi Brodie).

During the first few months of the war, the hotel was further modernised and extended so that it now had seventy bedrooms and its dining room could seat 150 people. The hotel remained open throughout the war, accommodating several families who had been evacuated from London or who had lost their homes during the bombing in Bournemouth. Ada Cohen was very active in raising money for the war effort and Phillip Miller was an ARP warden in the town. To ensure the safety of its guests, the hotel installed an ARP-approved air raid shelter in its basement.

After the war, the hotel welcomed local people to use its facilities. It was a popular place for weddings, *Bar Mitzvahs* and other celebrations and a favourite place for young people to dance. East Cliff Manor was noted for its glass dance floor that turned blue with the under-floor lighting. One of the hotel's selling points was its all-weather tennis court.

During the 1950s the hotel attracted some top names to entertain its guests, such as Johnny Franks, and also some well-known local musicians such as *Syd Fay and His Music.* The hotel was updated in 1951 when more of its bedrooms became *en suite.* Although the hotel always described itself as 'strictly kosher', it was never licensed by the religious authorities or employed a *shomer.* However, Ada Cohen is said to have closely supervised the kitchen staff.

East Cliff Manor did not have a dedicated *shul,* but by 1952 services were being held in the hotel. By 1957, all of its the bedrooms had private bathrooms and in 1958 the hotel extended its premises further and installed air conditioning. The hotel prided itself on its 'friendly atmosphere'.

After the death of Philip Miller in 1956, Ada Cohen and Susan Miller continued to manage the hotel together but with support from Leslie Miller (Susan and Philip's son) and his wife Fay. Bernard Miller, Susan and Philip's other son, does not seem to have been involved in managing the hotel.

The hotel closed in 1960, not because business was failing, but because Ada and Susan were aging. By then, Susan was mainly confined to her apartment in Sterling Court in Manor Road. East Cliff Manor had been a popular hotel, offering 'value for money' holidays, and the sell-out came as a surprise to the Jewish community. The hotel was sold to a non-Jewish hotelier, who renamed the hotel as the Adelphi Hotel. It later became the Regency Hotel, which was demolished to make way for an apartment block named Adelphi Court.

After the hotel was sold Ada Cohen and Susan Miller lived together in Sterling Court. Ada died in November 1968 and Susan in 1970.

The Green Park Hotel

The Green Park, located in Manor Road, was built during 1937 in the Art Deco style that was then at its height. It was built on land formerly occupied by a property named West Chevin at the same time that Dorchester Mansions was constructed. The Green Park was initially run as a residential hotel by J. M. Saunders and Company, which accounts for the fact that each of its bedrooms had private bathrooms. It sat in almost three acres of landscaped gardens, divided into an upper and a lower garden.

The Green Park opened its doors as a Jewish hotel on 15 October 1943 when it was purchased by Reuben ('Ruby') Marriott and his family. Prior to purchasing the Green Park, Ruby Marriott (born in the East End in 1910) was running the Sandringham Hotel in Torquay. During the 1920s, Ruby's father Abraham Marriott (previously Marovitch), who had come to London from Poland in the early twentieth century, retired to Torquay after his furrier business experienced financial difficulties. He found that he was deluged with requests for family and friends to join him there. He therefore decided to convert his home into a guest house. The business was very successful and he sent for his youngest son, Ruby, then unmarried and working as a furrier, to help him run the guest house. In about 1930, the family bought the more substantial Sandringham Hotel, which Ruby managed on behalf of the family. For several years he advertised the hotel under the name of Marovitch, as this was the name by which the family was best known.

From the outset, Ruby's ambitions were evident. The fifty-bedroomed hotel was described in the *Jewish Chronicle* as 'the premier and largest Jewish hotel in Torquay' and it was claimed that its standards of luxury 'surpass the expectations of the most critical'. It had a ballroom, a billiards room and large lounges. The hotel was fully refurbished in 1936. It was 'strictly orthodox' and by the late 1930s was licensed by the Kashrus Commission and the London Beth Din. Services led by Ruby were held in the hotel on *Shabbat* and on Jewish festivals. By 1939, the hotel had become the base for the newly-established Brixham and Torquay Hebrew Congregation of which Ruby was the secretary.

In 1938, Ruby married Sarah Richman (previously Reichman), the second oldest of nine siblings (six girls and three boys). Her parents were Yetta (née Cohen) and Avroham, who were both Polish immigrants. Yetta, who was born in 1887 in Staszow, Poland arrived in England when she was aged twelve with little education. She worked in the small café that her mother opened in Hackney, which served local business people, one of whom was Avroham Richman, which is how they met. She married Avroham in Fieldgate Street Synagogue in 1903. Avroham, who had been born in 1887 in Lodz, Poland, was a button maker who established a successful button-making factory, which enabled the family to move from Whitechapel to Stamford Hill. Sarah established a dressmaking business in the family home. She was introduced to Ruby by one of her sisters who knew one of Ruby's sisters.

When Ruby and Sarah married, Sarah moved to Torquay and became involved in the running of the Sandringham Hotel. She was joined there by her sister Helen who took on the management of the catering aspects of the business. Helen proved to be a very good manager and took on more responsibilities. To begin with, the hotel's main clientele were family and friends and people looking for respite from London. Once the war commenced, several families moved to live at the hotel for safety reasons. Ruby and Sarah's first two children, David and Rebecca (later known as Rivka), were born in Torquay.

Ruby developed a liking for the hospitality trade and started looking for a larger business. He saw the Green Park advertised, which he was very attracted to because of its location in fashionable Bournemouth. It was also more accessible than Torquay and each of its bedrooms had *en suite* bathrooms, which was very unusual at the time. Although it came on the market at a comparatively low price because of the war, it was still very expensive. However, Ruby's accountant Sidney Sharpe (who lived with his family in the Sandringham at the beginning of the war) thought Ruby could make the hotel successful and helped him to raise the finance. The Sandringham Hotel was sold to Mr and Mrs Harris of Torquay. Sidney Sharpe, and later his son Donald, became the accountants for the Green Park and were regular guests at the hotel.

When the Green Park opened in the autumn of 1943, most of the first guests were mainly the people who had stayed in the Sandringham plus some families who had been evacuated to Bournemouth, some of whom stayed in the hotel for the remainder of the war. The hotel was closed for a short time during 1944 due to D-Day preparations (see Chapter 2), but the business built up very quickly when it reopened. The hotel needed a great deal of refurbishment to bring it up to the standard to which Ruby aspired. This work, such as adding a sun terrace and improving the dining room, was carried out over several years.

Initially, the hotel was run by Ruby and Sarah Marriott and Helen Richman. Three other Richman sisters became involved in the business when they left school, each developing their own niche. Helen was largely responsible for the catering aspects of the hotel. In 1956 she married Arnold Lee, whom she had met in the hotel when he was convalescing there. He was a successful property dealer. Helen moved to London after she married and her role at the hotel was taken over by Hannah Richman. Rachel (Ray) Richman became responsible for bookings and the hotel reception and Judy dealt with the hotel's finances and accounts. Sarah Marriott was largely involved in organising the entertainment.

Ruby's and Sarah's second daughter, Barbara, was born in Bournemouth in 1947 and in 1949, Yetta (Bubbe) Richman came to live in the hotel after her husband's death a year earlier. She was a larger than life character and became a driving force in the running of the hotel. She worked alongside Helen in supervising the kitchen and catering arrangements at the hotel (see Chapters 3 and 6). She was the family matriarch, always interested in her children and grandchildren. She lived in the hotel where she was cared for by hotel staff when she became frail.

Family members often came to stay in Bournemouth. They stayed in a house adjacent to the hotel in Grove Road that had been purchased by the family. The Richman sisters and the Marriotts all lived together in a large apartment in Dorchester Mansions opposite the hotel. There is said never to have been a cross word between them. Ray, Hannah, and Judy did not marry, it was said that they were married to the hotel.

The hotel flourished, and over the next two decades many improvements were made, including the addition of the *sukkah* in 1954, the erection of an annexe to provide additional sleeping accommodation in 1958 and the extension of the ballroom in 1960. However, the most notable improvement was the addition of the American-style heated outdoor pool, which opened in 1961. The Green Park was the first hotel in Bournemouth to have such a facility. Of the Big Eight hotels, the Green Park is said to have been the most orthodox and attracted many observant guests, especially during the Jewish festivals. However, non-observant guests felt equally at home in the hotel.

The hotel became noted for being the height of luxury, its strap-line being 'The greatest name in Jewish hotels', and for its high-profile clientele, the 'cream of Anglo-Jewry': Sir Isaac Wolfson, the bookmakers Joe Coral and Cyril Stein, Brian Epstein manager of *The Beatles*, Cecil Gee, Jack Cohen (founder of Tesco), three successive Chief Rabbis (the Chief Rabbis Hertz, Brodie and Jakobovits), Oscar Deutsch, president of the Odeon cinema chain, Philip Halperin, owner of the Houndsditch Warehouse, academics such as Cecil Roth and Isaiah Berlin. The hotel prided itself on its high-quality, personal service and its guest to staff ratio was 1:1. The hotel was also known for its longstanding Italian waiters, especially Domenico ('Mimmo') Zacchia ('Mr Mimmo'), who arrived at the hotel in 1961 and was quickly promoted to become the maître d'. The hotel attracted many people who had known the Richman and Marriott families in Hackney.

From the outset, the hotel aligned itself with the cause of Israel, and during its forty-three years of operation, the hotel was the venue for major fundraising dinners, for which the proprietors made no charge.

During the 1970s, when guest numbers were declining, the hotel's clientele was mainly older people, who stayed at the hotel for long periods. Ruby and Sarah travelled to New York in an attempt to attract American guests, which was only partially successful. Bubbe Richman died in 1975. During the early 1980s, Ruby's health declined and the hotel closed in

October 1986, the day after *Simchat Torah*. By that time, the hotel was in a poor state of repair. It was sold to Majestic Holidays, who ran it for a short while as a non-Jewish hotel, but in 1988 it was sold to developers Manway Homes, who demolished the hotel and built an apartment block named the Green Park. The flats were mainly purchased by Jews, some of whom were former hotel guests.

The family is now in its fifth generation, and remains very close-knit. Family members are in constant touch with each other across several continents via various WhatsApp groups. They are all *Shomer Shabbos* (orthodox). At the time of writing, Hannah and Judy are still living in the family apartment in Dorchester Mansions. Each day they send out electronic birthday and other cards to family members.

The Langham Hotel

The Langham, located in Meyrick Road, started life as a private house, which was listed under the name of 'Woodend' in 1890. By 1903, it had become a boarding house. It was renamed as the Langham Hotel in the mid-1920s when it was purchased by Walter Edward Mayger, who was an engineer by trade. At that time, it provided accommodation for around a hundred people, had a ballroom and six lounges. Mr Mayger's wife, Mabel Lucy Mayger, refurbished and continued to run the hotel after his death.

The Langham was sold in 1946 to Fay and Maurice (Morry) Guild who had been running a smaller hotel, the Spa Hotel, in Boscombe Spa Road. Trading under the name of Faymor, the Guilds opened the Langham as a kosher hotel on 2 December 1946. By this time, the hotel was offering a valet service, a children's nurse, live entertainment in the form of *Alex Haddow and his Music* and a cocktail bar. It had seventy-five bedrooms. The Guilds lived in a house in the grounds of the hotel.

Fay and Maurice were both brought up in the East End of London. Fay (previously Fanny) was one of the six daughters of Abraham (a master tailor) and Eva Danieloff. Fay and two of her sisters were born in Eastern Europe; the other three were born in the East End. The family lived in Durward Street in Whitechapel and later in Amhurst Park, Stamford Hill. After she left school, Fay became a milliner and had a shop at 157 Whitechapel Road. In August 1930, Fay married Maurice (his surname was then Goldberg) at the Great Synagogue in Dukes Place. Maurice was the son of Isaac Goldberg (a bootmaker) and Sarah Basla Zisl, immigrants from Lithuania. He was a gentleman's tailor and after their marriage he and Fay worked from the same premises in Whitechapel Road, but lived in Amhurst

Park close to their respective families. By 1935, they had changed their surname to Guild.

Fay and Maurice moved to Bournemouth in 1944 to take over the Spa Hotel. They had only been running the hotel for two years before they bought the larger Langham Hotel. The Guilds proudly announced that their new hotel had been appointed as 'the orthodox hotel in Bournemouth for international plane reservations'. The hotel was fully refurbished five years after Fay and Maurice bought it. The Langham was well known for its dining room, which was called the 'Crystal Room' because of its large chandelier. The hotel had its own *shul* that was mainly used during the peak summer season and for Jewish festivals. In the grounds of the hotel there was an additional building that was used for overflow accommodation.

The hotel was not quite as luxurious as some of the other Big Eight hotels and less than half of its bedrooms had *en suite* bathrooms. However, it was very popular with families from London, especially those from Stamford Hill because of the Guild's connections with the area. One of Fay's sisters, Hetty, married Joe Forman, owner of the well-known smoked salmon firm in London's East End, which supplied the hotel.

Although the Langham was always described as 'strictly orthodox', it was not until January 1963 that it was licensed by the Kashrus Commission and the London Beth Din and a full-time *shomer* was appointed. This coincided with the opening of the banqueting suite that was added in that year and was opened by the Lord Mayor of Bournemouth. The new suite was able to seat 700 people and was used for many conferences and outside functions. Beneath it was a spacious underground garage. A neighbouring house was demolished to make way for the banqueting suite which Maurice Guild referred to as 'The Guildhall'. In the same ambitious programme of modernisation, one of the card rooms was enlarged and a new 'American Starlight Room Bar' was installed.

Maurice was very jovial and was the 'face' of the hotel. He was very generous towards the hotel staff and their families. Fay played a very full role in the running of the Langham, supervising the kitchen and catering arrangements and taking on responsibility for the hotel's accounts. She is said to have run the hotel with 'ruthless efficiency'.

The Guilds did not have children but they warmly welcomed other people's children to the hotel, which as a result made it popular with extended family groups. The Guilds travelled widely and lived a somewhat luxurious lifestyle. Fay was always impeccably dressed. Maurice Guild drove a Rolls Royce. Fay remained close to her sisters, who often helped in the running of the hotel and frequently brought their families to stay in the hotel. Her sister Golda ran a smaller hotel in Frances Road, Boscombe, Gale's Private Hotel, with her husband Harry Gale (see Chapter 4). Harry, a former tailor, designed and made many of Fay's outfits. This hotel provided overflow accommodation when the Langham was full.

Maurice devoted a great deal of his time to raising money for charity, especially the Norwood children's home. In 1962, he was the first Jew in the town to be elected as president of the Bournemouth Hotels and Boarding Houses' Association. He was the co-founder of the Jewish masonic lodge in the town (Sojourners Lodge No.7597, consecrated on 30 June 1958). Maurice was also the president of the Bournemouth branch of the JPA (later JIA) for two years and served on the Board of Management of Bournemouth Hebrew Congregation.

Maurice died in December 1964 aged 57. Fay continued to run the Langham with the help of her sister Hetty, but struggled to maintain the hotel and business declined. The hotel was sold in 1968 for just £250,000 to a non-Jewish owner. It was renamed as the Queens Hotel. It was sold with planning permission for an additional forty-four bedrooms. After the hotel was sold, Fay moved to north-west London to be closer to her family.

In recent years the hotel, now named the Mercure Queens Spa Hotel, has been used for *Pesach* holidays organised by Brian Lassman (see Chapter 7).

The Majestic Hotel

The Majestic Hotel, located on the corner of Derby Road and Manor Road, was built on the site of the Saugeen School, which was founded in 1873. In 1932, it claimed to be the longest established preparatory school in West Hampshire. The school's alumni included John Galsworthy, the author of *The Forsyte Saga*, and Tony Hancock, the comedian and actor. In the spring of 1935, the Saugeen School moved to Colehill in Wimborne. What had been the southern part of the school site was purchased by Frank Barton Simcock, who laid the foundation stone for the Majestic Hotel (then called Hotel Majestic) and became its first owner. The hotel was very modern for the time. It had fifty-four bedrooms a large proportion of which had *en suite* facilities, an indoor swimming pool, central heating and hard tennis courts and lifts to all floors.

The hotel continued in Frank Simcock's ownership until 1946 when it was purchased by a partnership of three families from London – the Shulmans, Schneiders and the Selbys – trading under the name of Mozelle Hotels (Bournemouth) Ltd. The arrangement was that the hotel would be run by Rebecca (Becky) Selby (née Schwartz), who was born in Korovhrad, Ukraine in 1903 and Fay (previously Fanny) Schneider (née Cohen), who was born in Whitechapel in 1904. The two women took it in turns to stay at the hotel during different parts of the week while their husbands, Hyman (Hymie) Selby and Benjamin (Ben) Schneider, remained in London to run their existing businesses. The two families met up in Bournemouth at weekends. Both the Schneider and Selby families retained their homes in London, the Schneiders in Finchley and the Selbys in Willesden. Before managing the Majestic, Fay Schneider had been working with her husband in running their clothing factory, Essenel. It was located near Old Street in London and made children's clothes for C&A.

The new hoteliers encountered difficulties in securing experienced and capable staff and soon found that they had to commit more time to running the hotel than they had envisaged. The partnership did not endure. The Shulmans departed after just a few months and in 1948 the Selbys sold their share in the Majestic and opened a restaurant in London (see biography of the Ambassador). As a result, Fay and Ben Schneider, who had married in the Jubilee Street Great Synagogue in 1925, became the sole owners. They ran the hotel together for just two years before Ben's sudden death at the hotel in 1950. After Ben's death, Fay ran the hotel on her own with the help of her unmarried sister, Sally Cohen. During the years that Fay Schneider owned the Majestic, she developed a reputation for being a powerful character. She was always immaculately dressed (see Chapter 3).

There were two houses in the grounds of the hotel. Fay lived in one and the other was let out to guests when the hotel was full. The main clientele of the hotel included a high proportion of young people attracted by the hotel's reputation as 'a place to have fun'. Two older people lived at the hotel, whom Fay looked after with great care. She worked long hours, but many relatives were willing to assist to allow her to take breaks. She travelled widely to gather information on how successful hotels were run.

In addition to running the Majestic, Fay was actively and generously involved in charitable and communal activities, particularly in raising money for the Ravenswood Foundation, which cared for children with special needs at a home in Berkshire, where she dedicated a chalet in memory of Fay and Ben's son Gerald who had died in 1959. She also raised money for the women's section of the Joint Israel Appeal (JIA). The Majestic was used as a venue to support both local and national organisations. In 1953, Fay Schneider hosted a dinner for the Israeli ambassador at the hotel.

The Majestic was maintained to a very high standard. A major improvement programme in 1954 included extending the hotel's main lounge, and adding a sun lounge, card room, television room and dedicated synagogue. In 1961, continental gardens and terraces were opened that included a 'secluded' children's playground. In 1967, a 'Spanish-style' pool area was created to replace the indoor swimming pool, and the number of bedrooms was increased from fifty-four to eighty-six. By this time, only six bedrooms at the hotel did not have *en suite* facilities.

From soon after its inception as a kosher hotel, the Majestic was licensed by the Kashrus Commission and the London Beth Din. It was especially noted for its star-studded entertainment programmes, for which Fay Schneider was praised in the national press. Several nationally famous musicians commenced their careers performing at the hotel.

In 1969, Fay Schneider sold the Majestic to the Feld and Inverne families who owned the Cumberland (see separate biography). In 1973, the Majestic was sold by the Felds to Metropolitan Estates (Mr Taubman), which had hoped to demolish it and build flats on the site. However, a property slump forced Metropolitan Estates to abandon its development plans. Instead, the hotel was sold on to the Specialist Leisure Group, owners of Shearing's coach company, which carried out an extensive renovation of the hotel. Its reopening was advertised prominently in the *Jewish Chronicle* and the hotel continued to attract mainly Jewish visitors, despite the fact that it was no longer licensed by the religious authorities.

After she sold the Majestic, Fay Schneider moved to London where she opened a catering firm, working with her daughter, Shirley Davidson and her granddaughter, Dawn. The firm ran the kosher sections of the Royal Lancaster and Royal Garden Hotels. Fay planned to expand her activities to include take-away food, but at that time take-away services had to be associated with a restaurant in order to obtain a Beth Din licence. Fay died in October 1981, a month after her restaurant was opened in Swiss Cottage.

Shearing's Coaches continued to run the hotel under the name of the Bay Majestic Hotel until the firm went into administration in May 2020. The Majestic ceased trading and was placed on the market.

The Normandie Hotel

The Normandie was constructed in the grounds of a private house called Monkchester, which had been built in 1872. From 1885 until 1916 Monkchester was occupied by doctors. The house was demolished in 1936 and the hotel was built. It overlooked Bournemouth Bay and was set within nearly three acres of gardens that extended to the cliff top. It opened in 1938 under the ownership of the Walker family who were not Jewish. In 1945, it was purchased by Robert (Bob) and Julia (Jules) Myers, who had previously run the Hotel Rivoli (location unknown). They had two sons, Royston and John. The hotel was located on East Overcliff Drive, but its entrance was in Manor Road. It had an imposing lobby with a sweeping staircase beneath a domed roof.

The Normandie was initially run by the Myers as a non-orthodox hotel, but by 1949 it was being marketed as 'strictly orthodox' and had a resident *shomer*. However, it was not licensed by the religious authorities. It became a hotel that was popular with families and welcomed young people from the local community to join in its entertainment (see Chapter 8). The Myers prided themselves on their catering and often used the strap-line 'The pioneers of luxury catering at practical prices'. The Myers were also the first of the Big Eight hotel owners to introduce special winter rates. The hotel appears to have been very successful. Bob Myers owned a helicopter in which favoured guests were offered flights.

In July 1957, there was a major fire in the hotel. Its ninety guests were safely evacuated, but the damage was estimated at £40,000. The hotel was closed for many months while it was refurbished. On completion of the repair works, the hotel was put up for sale in January 1958, and reopened under new ownership on 4 April in the same year. The Myers moved to London where they had purchased Lindy's restaurant in Golders Green. They subsequently acquired a restaurant called 'Bobmyers' in London's West End.

The new owners of the Normandie were Nathan (Nat) and Gertie (Gittel) Lee, a business man who owned several cinemas, including the Savoy cinema in Boscombe. Nat Lee (previously Nathan Lipovitch) was born in 1886 in Petrikoff in Belarus, and came to Britain in 1896 when he was aged ten. Like his father, Nat initially worked as a cap and hat maker in Whitechapel. Nathan married Gertie Goldstein in 1905. The family were naturalised in 1913, by which time Nathan had a cap and hat shop at 392 Mile End Road. He and his family relocated from the East End to Bournemouth during the late 1930s.

Nathan and Gertie's daughter, Belle (born in Whitechapel in 1913) and her husband Louis (Lou) Keyne had an interest in the Normandie (the two couples traded under the name of NGLB, their initials) and were very involved with its running. Belle was a highly-educated and successful businesswoman. She studied English at Kings College, London. In 1941, she married Lou, another former East Ender. He was an artist and designer, who worked under his former name of Kiverstein, having trained first at St Martin's Art School in Soho and subsequently at the Royal College of Art in South Kensington. Belle and Lou spent the remainder of the war years running an aircraft engineering factory (KDL, Lou's initials reversed) in Cricklewood, North West London, manufacturing vital aircraft parts. The factory later moved to Hove and turned to manufacturing lighting. Belle's brothers, Julius and Sidney, became eminent doctors. Sidney captained the British bridge team.

Belle and Lou had two sons, Simon and Jonathan. The family lived in an apartment in the Normandie, along with their dog, also called Simon ('Simon Four Legs'), who roamed the hotel and the cliffs and was very popular with the guests. Although he would have preferred to have been an artist, Lou, who is said to have looked like Anton Walbrook, spent time behind the reception desk of the hotel speaking with guests. The Keyne family travelled widely, often to places which at that time were not visited by many people, and also found time to relax. Both Lou and Belle were always impeccably dressed. Lou had a boat, moored at Parkstone Yacht Club in Lillipun from which the family enjoyed fishing at weekends. The Keynes owned an apartment in Keythorpe in Manor Road, formerly the home of Lady Leontine Sassoon, where the family sometimes stayed to take a break from hotel life. Nat and Gertie Lee lived in the Penthouse of St Remo Towers in Sea Road, Boscombe. Apart from the Normandie, Nat had several business interests in the area, including a car park. He owned a Ford Thunderbird car. By comparison, Gertie ('Bubby') Lee was quite reserved and spent a lot of time sitting in the same chair in the hotel lounge with her handbag on her lap.

Under Nat and Gertie Lee's ownership, the Normandie was advertised as being 'kosher', but it was not licensed by the religious authorities. However, it did employ a *shomer*. For many years, the *shomer* at the hotel was Rev. Fenigstein, who was followed by Rev. Phillip Isaacs, previously the minister at Southampton United Synagogue (see Chapter 7).

In 1963, the hotel was the second Jewish hotel in Bournemouth to install a heated outdoor pool, and the hotel was extended in 1966 to enable each of its eighty bedrooms to be provided with an *en suite* bathroom. In the early 1970s, the reception area of the hotel was made much larger and the flooring was replaced with designer terrazzo tiles.

Following the death of Nat Lee in 1968, Belle and Lou took over the running of the Normandie with their business partners, Ron (Hymie) and Ann Fisher. The Fishers had previously owned a non-Jewish hotel, Russell Court in Bath Road, close to the pier, which they sold to buy into the Normandie. Ron Fisher, who had been the lead vocalist with several top dance bands in London, was known as 'Herman the Yodler'. He was one of eight sons, several of whom were musical. His father, Emmanuel Fisher, was the director of the London Jewish Male Voice Choir. When Lou Keyne died in 1971 at the age of fifty-eight, Belle continued in business with the Fishers, employing a manager to help run the hotel.

Although the Normandie continued to employ a *shomer* under the ownership of the Keynes and the Fishers, it was never licensed by the religious authorities. However, the hotel prided itself on the quality of its food. Advertisements in the *Jewish Chronicle* featured photographs of the hotel's team of chefs. During the 1960s, the hotel employed a number of waiters from Spain, who were later succeeded by several Italian waiters recruited by the then restaurant manager Adriano Brioschi.

The Keynes owned a smaller hotel on the West Cliff, which was used to accommodate staff. When the Normandie was full, guests were accommodated in the Mon Bijou bed and breakfast establishment at 47 Manor Road, or at the nearby Freshfields Hotel. In the grounds of the hotel there was a motel that was initially run as a separate establishment, but was eventually joined up to the hotel to provide additional bedrooms.

After it had been refurbished during the latter part of 1975, the Normandie reopened in January 1976 as a non-kosher hotel and was marketed under the new name of the Normandie International. In 1979, Belle decided to retire and went to live in a house the family had purchased in Gervis Road. She continued to travel, mainly with her bother Sidney and his wife Esther. She died in 2002.

After Belle Keyne's retirement, the Normandie was purchased by Isaac and Bertha Klug, who developed the hotel as a 'Hydro Hotel' and renamed it the New International Normandie Hotel. Although its owners were Jewish and were very involved in Bournemouth Hebrew Congregation, they did not run it as a kosher hotel. However, advertisements for the hotel welcomed Jewish guests and stated that it specialised in vegetarian food.

The Normandie changed hands several times during the 1980s. It was first bought from the Klugs by Ladbrokes, who in 1986 sold it on to Philip and Valerie Nyman, the previous owners of Cliffeside and East Cliff Court. They reverted to the name of the Normandie Hotel and ran it as a non-kosher establishment.

In 1987, the Normandie was purchased by a partnership of the Mozes brothers (owners of Goodmos Travel) and the Chomtov family, who were property dealers. This partnership owned the hotel until 2020. Under the new ownership, the hotel became very orthodox and was licensed by the Union of Orthodox Hebrew Congregation's Kedassia (see Chapter 7).

Before it was reopened for *Pesach* 1988, the hotel was renovated throughout. The improvements included a new kitchen and bakery and, in a different part of the building, a take-away and cafeteria that attracted local residents and Jews staying in non-kosher accommodation. Its main clientele was now mainly *charedi* Jews, and it was frequently the venue for conferences led by high-profile rabbis. The hotel was managed for several years by Brian Lassman. The food became more traditional and the entertainment programme was largely focussed on study and learning activities, which were mostly segregated. There was no mixed dancing or mixed bathing in the outdoor pool.

In the first decade of the twentieth century, the Normandie's owners attempted to obtain planning permission to demolish the hotel and replace it with forty-two flats. Planning permission was refused and the hotel stayed open. Over the years since then, there has been little investment in the hotel and it has become quite run down.

The hotel is open from *Pesach* until *Yamim Tovim*, but only opens for celebrations and special events during the winter months. Its clientele is almost exclusively *charedim*. During the writing of this book, the hotel changed hands and is said to be in the process of being refurbished.

Appendix 2

The Smaller Hotels and Guest Houses

Hotel/Guest House	Address	Proprietor(s)	Opened as a Jewish hotel	Closed as a Jewish hotel	Significant developments features
Alexander Hotel See Frogmore/ Alexander Hotel					
Ashdale Guest House	Beaulieu Road, Westbourne	Emil and Hilde Bruder	1946	1959	Hilde Bruder died in 1951 but Emil continued to run the guest house until 1959.
Avon Royal Hotel	Christchurch Road	Mr S. Fisher	1940	1948	Mr Fisher previously had a hotel in Margate. The Avon Royal was sold to Frederick Marshall in 1945. It was sold again in 1948 to a non-Jewish owner and later demolished to make way for a Travelodge.
Berachah	Kerley Road, West Cliff	Isaac Grossman	1922	1947	See Chapter 2 for the early development of this hotel. It later became the Kerley Hotel.
Bourne Hotel. See Hotel Rubens/ Bourne Hotel					
Braemar Royal (Dolly Ross) Home for the Blind	Grand Avenue, Southbourne	Jewish Blind Society and later Jewish Care	1957	2000	Major renovations were carried out between 1982 and 1985. It was re-consecrated in 1986.
Branksome Dene convalescent home	Alumhurst Road, Westbourne	Grand Order of Israel and the Shield of David Friendly Society	1951	1980	Purchased by the Royal Masonic Benevolent Institution.
Brenhar Private Hotel	Owls Road, Boscombe	Charles Guest	1950	1951	
Brownswood Hall Hotel	South Cliff Road, West Cliff	Mr Jacobs and Mr Newstead	1946	1947	
Carlton Dene holiday home	Stourwood Avenue, Southbourne	Jewish Association for the Physically Handicapped (JAPH)	1962	1997	It was later administered by the Jewish Blind Society and then Jewish Care.

Hotel/Guest House	Address	Proprietor(s)	Opened as a Jewish hotel	Closed as a Jewish hotel	Significant developments features
Carmel Guest House/Hotel	Lowther Road, Boscombe and subsequently Florence Road, Boscombe	Armand (Noson) and Yudit Gutstein	1967	1980	Moved to Florence Road in 1968. Under the supervision of Kedassia. During 1976, the Carmel, embarked on a major modernisation programme, making most of its bedrooms *en suite*.
Carmel Hotel	St John's Road, Boscombe	Mr and Mrs Cymerman	1946	1949	
Chine Court Hotel	West Cliff Road	Mr and Mrs Acker	1945	1953	The Ackers moved to Bournemouth from Southport. By 1947 the guest house was owned by Mr and Mrs Tanner.
Continental Hotel	Church Road, Southbourne	Mr and Mrs Schreiber	1960	1965	
Debonnaire Private Hotel	Sea Road, Boscombe	Mr and Mrs Lemel	1948	1949	
Dolly Ross (see Braemar Royal) care home					
Eaton	Madeira Road	Mr J. Myers	1945	1948	
Embassy Hotel	East Overcliff Drive	Bertram Levitus	1948	1951	In 1951 it was sold to a non-Jewish owner.
Filora Guest House	Campbell Road, Boscombe	Phil and Laura Boorman	1948	1952	
Hotel Florence	Boscombe Spa Road	Jules and Fay Segal	1955	1971	The Segals moved to Bournemouth from Cliftonville. The hotel initially had fifteen bedrooms. In 1952 there was a major modernisation programme, including extending the dining room and adding a new ballroom. In 1958, the number of bedrooms was doubled.
Frogmore/ Alexander	Christchurch Road	Mr and Mrs Cohen	1930	1947	Sold to Mr Sumroy in 1945 and renamed Alexander. Sold to non-Jewish owner in 1947.

Hotel/Guest House	Address	Proprietor(s)	Opened as a Jewish hotel	Closed as a Jewish hotel	Significant developments features
Gale's Private Hotel	Frances Road	Golda and Harry Gale	1960	1979	The Gales acquired a neighbouring property in 1960 and expanded the hotel to include a ballroom and private suites. It was upgraded and extended again in 1968. Golda died in 1975, but Harry continued to run the hotel until 1979 when it was sold and developed as flats.
Gresham Court	Grove Road	Meyer and Marjorie Rivlin and the Weimar family	1961	1978	Weimar family left the partnership soon after the hotel opened. Major modernisation programme 1968.
Grosvenor Hotel (previously the Redroofs Hotel)	Bath Road	Sydney and Rhoda Lukover and Pearl and Johnnie Michaels	1972	1980	Licensed by the Kashrus Commission.
Grosvenor Court Hotel	St Michael's Road	Mr Gradel	1945	1955 (except during years 1947-1953)	Originally licensed by Kedassia. Purchased by Betty Retter in 1945, but resold within a year to Mr and Mrs Cordis. From 1947 it operated under non-Jewish ownership until it was purchased in 1953 by Mr and Mrs Salmon who operated as a Jewish hotel for two years.
Lebonville	Frances Road	Olga and John Schutan	1946	1951	
Lewbess	York Road Sea Road,	Lew and Bess Jacobs	1945	1959	
Marin Court	Boscombe	Mrs Moisa	1930	1948	
Marlborough Hotel	Sea Road, Boscombe	Fay and William Pantel	1937	1947	The Pantels employed a manager in 1946 while they renovated and launched the larger Palm Bay Hotel opposite the Marlborough. The hotel was sold in 1947.

Hotel/Guest House	Address	Proprietor(s)	Opened as a Jewish hotel	Closed as a Jewish hotel	Significant developments features
Mayfair Guest House	Westby Road	Sam and Addie Russell	1946	1965	Extended in the early 1960s to provide 25 letting rooms.
Mayfair Hotel	Upper Terrace Road	Elkan and Esther Shapiro	1931	1960	From June 1946 the hotel was run by non-Jewish owners due to Elkan Shapiro being ill. He took on the hotel again in 1948. The hotel operated under the auspices of the Kashrus Commission. It was sold to a non-Jewish owner in 1960 following Elkan Shapiro's death the previous year.
Mountain Ash/Mount Aishel	Argyll Road, Boscombe	Mr and Mrs Jacobs	1950	1962	Sold to Tony and Rose Ricklow in 1958 when it became licensed by the Kashrus Commission as a 'dairy' establishment and was renamed Mount Aishel.
Oxford Guest House	Frances Road	Dot and Benson Stieber	1946	1971	Dot Steiber was the daughter of Isaac Grossman, owner of Berachah.
Palm Bay Hotel	Sea Road, Boscombe	Fay and William Pantel	1946	1963	Direct access to the beach.
Picardy Hotel (formerly Merivale Hall)	Meyrick Road	Mr Citron and Mrs Lewis	1948	1964	Initially opened under this name as a hydro resort and vegetarian establishment under the supervision of Dr Lewis. In 1948, Dr Lewis moved his practice to the premises in Kerley Road formerly occupied by Grossman's Berachah (see earlier entry). The Picardy continued to be run as a hydro resort under the supervision of Dr Bassam. In 1955 the hotel was acquired by Mrs Moisa who had previously run Marin Court (also cited here) and David Fieldgrass.

Hotel/Guest House	Address	Proprietor(s)	Opened as a Jewish hotel	Closed as a Jewish hotel	Significant developments features
					In 1958 the Picardy was purchased by Eric and Rose Kerpner, former refugees from Vienna who offered continental cuisine. It was sold to a non-Jewish owner in 1964.
Queen Hotel	Landsdowne Road	Mr and Mrs Cowen	1952		The Cowens were from Cardiff.
Rosemore Hotel	Consisted of two properties, one in West Cliff Road and another in St Michaels Road	Maurice (sometimes Morris) and Rose Millman	1930	1947	
Hotel Rubens/ Bourne Hotel	Bath Road	Joseph and Helena Grower Silent, non-Jewish partner Mr Nash	1946	1963	In the early 1950s, the property was marketed as the 'Bourne Holiday Flats and Apartments' and by the late 1950s it had become the Bourne Vegetarian Hotel. Joseph Grower died in 1961, aged 49, after which the property was run as a bed and breakfast establishment. It was made subject to a CPO in 1963 to make way for a roundabout.
Simar House	Herbert Road, Westbourne	Simon and Margot Smith	1956	1969	Simon Gustav Smith died in 1959 but Margot carried on running the guest house until 1969.
Hotel Splendide	Sea Road Boscombe	Lou (Lewis Alfred) and Hannah Simmons	1948	1960	Sold to non-Jewish owner in 1960.
Stevra House	Southern Road	Stephen and Golda Corren	1960	1977	
Villa Judi	Rosebery Road and then Hamilton Road	Sylvia and Henry Kay	1961	1986	The Kays had previously let two rooms in their house in Harcourt Road.

Hotel/Guest House	Address	Proprietor(s)	Opened as a Jewish hotel	Closed as a Jewish hotel	Significant developments features
					In 1968 Villa Judi moved from Rosebery Road, where it had been since 1961, to 33 Hamilton Road in Boscombe. Villa Judi was sold to non-Jewish owners in 1986.

List of Photographs

List of Illustrations

Index of Hotels and Guest Houses and People and Places